FLYING STORIES

HOW I CAME TO BE A PILOT AND ENGINEER AND WHAT HAPPENED AFTER THAT

The confessions of an aircraft engineer
and airplane pilot. The true story of one
man's pursuit of the aviation adventure.

By

Marvin Arnold

Samco Publishing   Flying Stories
www.storydomain.com   3rd Edition

First printing by 1st Books 01/07/03
 ISBN: 1-4033-9237-4 (sc)
ISBN: 1-4033-9238-2 (hc)
ISBN: 1-4033-9236-6 (eb)

Revised expanded edition printing by AuthorHouse 03/16/2007
 ISBN: 1-4033-9237-4 (sc)
 ISBN: 1-4033-9238-2 (hc)
 ISBN: 978-1-4524-8045 (eb)

Revised 3rd edition printed by CreateSpace 05/12/2011
 ISBN-10: 0615480004 (sc)
 ISBN-13: 978-0615480008 (sc)
 ASIN: B0048JQLM (Kindle)

Samco Publishing   CreateSpace   Amazon Books

Contents

*Dedicated to the preservation
of American aviation history
and those who would
rather be flying.*

FLY FOR THE LIGHT

The phrase "flying stories" as used in the title of this book is a cliché term akin to "war stories" and "fishing tales." It refers to those BS sessions pilots have waiting in the ready room or standing around the hangar when one story reminds someone of another story and so on.

The title I had originally chosen for the book was *Fly For the Light*, but I changed it to *Flying Stories* thinking my first choice might be confused with one of those New Age religious experience books. True, many who venture into the realm of flight often feel something akin to a religious experience, but that's not what *Flying Stories* is about.

To fly for the light is what a pilot does climbing out in a heavy overcast. Leaving the ground on a dreary rainy day, an airplane lifts into the air trailing small vortices of moisture behind from the wingtips and enters the clouds. As the plane climbs higher and higher, the clouds turn a lighter shade of gray. When the plane nears the top of the cloud layer, a bright silver glow engulfs everything. Then suddenly, it bursts into a beautiful sunshiny day on top. The plane is suspended, hanging as stones do not, in the air high above a white cotton blanket that stretches from horizon to horizon.

On an airline flight some years ago, I was looking out the window through misty clouds to the earth 30,000 feet below. Passengers that are pilots themselves are the ones looking out the window, listening for the gear to go down or hearing the ATC clearance to land in their heads. As my thoughts pondered the mystery of flight one more time, I hit on several good ideas for writing about my own flying experiences.

How could I express these profound thoughts without writing a whole book to go with them? I've authored engineering reports, manuals and some magazine articles, but as I pondered a collection of non-fiction stories instead of the Great American novel I always planned to write, a single sentence passed through my head like one of those moving light ads

.

on a bank sign. "Write about what you know," the standard advice given to all would-be authors. It would be a good opportunity to re-tell all those old flying stories family and friends have heard so often that we now call them out by number.

Research is the fun part of writing, so why would I want to write about something I already know about? After all, I've seen the story. I lived it. So I wrote the stories as I remembered them even if not recorded for posterity with exacting accuracy.

This book is somewhat biographical, but eclectic in its writing with a generous helping of sarcastic humor. The events are chronological within a given subject, but with gaps in the time periods. Thus, the reader is not about to read the great American novel. Most of the stories are true to the best of my recollection, but only first names have been used to protect the guilty and those who might possibly still be alive.

The title is *Stories* not Story so don't look for a beginning, a moral or an end. Life is a series of choices. Whether we choose wisely or poorly, these choices are what make up the stories of our lives. This book is simply a compilation of loosely related vignettes of my life experiences in aviation and my desire to build things, not to destroy them.

The original manuscript of these stories was thrown in a drawer in 1989 and forgotten until 2002 when it was published in a limited edition. In need of a good proofing and rewrite, the manuscript was resurrected and republished in its present form thanks to the encouragement, expert proofreading and valuable suggestions of friend and fellow aviator Commander Ken Bjork, USN (Retired). Ken flew countless hours as a Patrol Plane Commander in the P2V Neptune ASW aircraft mentioned in the military chapters of this book. He had read the original draft and volunteered his assistance in completing the final draft.

The stories begin with my boyhood recollections of what it was like growing up during World War II and the external forces which cause each of us to become what we become, in my case an engineer and pilot. Hopefully, some of these stories will give younger readers an insight into a time when the American aerospace industry was still coming of age.

Pilots were a dime-a-dozen after World War II. Who wanted pilots anyway? A hundred thousand young men had learned to fly in the military. Many did not come home, many did. The dedicated ones and the lucky ones found jobs in new aviation businesses. Some became engineers. Others test pilots and airline captains.

About this time, there were kids born in the mid 1930s who came of age in the 1950s. Born too late to be part of the era of dirigibles and barnstormers, they were also too young to fly the B-17s and P-51s or help design the early postwar birds like the P-80 jet airplane and Bell X-1 rocket plane. This in-between generation entered the work force while the baby boomers were still in grade school. They would pick up where the aviation pioneers left off and establish the United States as the unchallenged world leader in aviation.

This is the story of one of those kids who was too young to go to the last big war, but grew up in the midst of it. One of those faceless thousands of young engineers who designed and developed the million component parts that helped make air travel safer than riding a bus and put the first man on the moon. These stories, with different names and places, are the stories of the golden age of civil aviation and the forgotten pilots and engineers of that era.

As the sailor is home from the sea
and the hunter home from the hill,
the flyer is home from the sky.

Chapter One
SHOULDA BEEN A COWBOY

From my earliest childhood memories, I have no recollection of the first time I ever saw an airplane, but I do remember my grandmother telling me about the first time my dad saw an airplane. My dad, Earl Mason Arnold, was born in 1913, and raised on a farm near Tulsa, Oklahoma. Grandma told me that when dad was a small boy and saw a biplane fly over, he ran and hid under her apron saying, "That big bird is going to poop on me."

In the early 1930s, dad and his cousin Roy managed to acquire a used biplane. Roy was a year older than dad and taught himself how to fly the plane. He would land in my grandparents' pasture to pick up dad to go flying.

On one of Roy's pasture landings, he turned the tail of the biplane into some high stiff weeds that tore the fabric on the elevator and rudder. Dad and Roy used newspaper and banana oil dope to patch the tail adequately enough to get the old bird flying again. Dad joked that if they would have had color comic strips in those days they could have made their patch job a little more colorful.

My Dad

Dad's ancestry was Scot, German and English. Grandma Arnold was able to trace her ancestry to the Stewarts and to the daughter of the brother of the king of Scotland in the 1660s. Dad's grandmother was a Hinkle, a misspelling of the name Heinkel, like the German aircraft designer.

Dad's father, Jesse Earl Arnold, was a Missouri cowboy-turned-farmer when he inherited a ranch in Oklahoma from his dad who was shot by a sharecropper in an argument over a load of corn stolen by a colored sharecropper. Not surprising in view of the fact that the elder Arnold had been tried and pardoned for his involvement in a gunfight some years

1

before. Some say grandpa and some vigilantes hunted the man down and hung him. Others hold to the view that the sheriff caught the man and he went to prison. As we say in Texas, when the legend is a better story then the truth, tell the legend.

My dad knew early on that he did not want to be a farmer. He was dark haired, good-looking, not real tall, but personable sort of a fellow. During his high school years, he played football. He lettered all four years, but claimed he warmed the bench more than he played. He owned an Indian motorcycle that he ran on oil field drip-gas. He and his friends would put a bucket under the leaks from the pipeline fittings and would come back later to collect the gas when the drips had filled the bucket to put it in their old car or motorcycle, clearly one of the benefits of living near the oil fields.

After graduating from high school, dad left for Chicago where he attended Coyne Electrical Engineering School. He worked at the Harvey House Restaurant in the Chicago train station to pay for his room and board. It was a fantastic time to be in Chicago as the Century of Progress Exposition was in full swing and dad attended the Exposition several times. He was fascinated by an RCA demonstration of early television.

My Mom

My mom's ancestry was Scot, Swede and Cherokee. My grandma Swanson's father, Charles McClure, was a Deputy U.S. Marshal. His father was a Scotsman and his mother a full-blood Cherokee. He was ambushed and shot by two masked gunmen from the Star gang during the Porum Range Wars. The full story has since been written up in *True West* magazine. Oklahoma Territory was a rough place to live in those early days. McClure's wife, also half Cherokee, was born in Macon, Georgia and I believe she came to Oklahoma as a young girl with her family on the Trail of Tears.

My mother's father, Marvin Henry Swanson, for whom I was named, was an oilman and cotton ginner. His parents were first generation Swedish-Americans. His dad came to Arkansas to work on the railroads in the late 1800s.

Grandpa Swanson was a big man, well liked and respected. He owned two cotton gins and in his dealings with the farmers and sharecroppers, Granddad Swanson had the reputation of "running an honest scale." During his lifetime, he made and lost more than one fortune wildcatting for oil. He was the mayor of the town and served as county commissioner for several years. Marvin Henry had also been known to do a little bootlegging in the early Oklahoma prohibition days. I think I took after him more than a little and most of my family seem to agree on that point.

Mom, who was a year younger than dad, was one of the football team's cheerleaders and played basketball for the Beggs Demons. She was a beautiful woman and was often told she looked like the movie actress, Gloria Swanson. My mom, Lola Evelyn Swanson, had four younger brothers and one older brother. My granddad spoiled his only daughter with riding horses, cars and just about anything she wanted. She was more apt to be found wearing pants and high top riding boots than a dress, but she knew early on that she didn't want to be a small town girl the rest of her life.

When dad returned to Oklahoma from Chicago, he married his high school sweetheart, Lola. My parents moved to Stillwater where dad attended Oklahoma A&M, while working part time installing and repairing radios.

Is There a Statue There Yet

This writer was born at the Payne County hospital in Stillwater in July of 1936. The year of my birth coincided with the pinnacle of the Oklahoma dust bowl, which John Steinbeck wrote about in his novel *The Grapes of Wrath*. The Midwestern United States was in the process of drying up and blowing away. Many of the Okie farmers left for California. I was told that the summer I was born, my crib rails were draped with damp towels to keep my skin from drying out.

When I was one year old, dad opened his own radio repair shop in North Platte, Nebraska. Dad, now in his mid-twenties, was still very young looking. On one occasion, he made a house call to repair a radio and the lady of the house ran him off saying she wasn't going to let some kid fool with her radio.

While installing a car radio, not a factory option on most cars in the 1930s, battery corrosion fell in dad's eyes causing temporary blindness. With dad unable to work, we returned to Beggs to stay with family until dad recovered his eyesight.

Oklahoma Territory - It wasn't hard to get up a posse; True West Magazine story of Deputy McClure; Lola and Earl married in 1935; shouda been a cowboy, at least I carried a cap-pistol; playing on cotton bales at the Beggs gin; ONG Armory on Main Street and tanks to play on. WWII dance at the airbase; General Hap Arnold; flight instructor Lt. RJ at Enid AAC flight school; PFC Harold; Top Sergeant Roy; Corps of Engineers Sergeant Raymond a POW and highly decorated.

My Folks Called Oklahoma Home

Growing up, I spent a lot of time in that little ol' cotton town of Beggs where the steam locomotive freight trains went rolling through at high-speed twice a day. For years there was a stop light on Main Street, but it was finally taken down. If you blinked your eyes twice on old Highway 75 driving through Beggs, you'd have missed it.

My cousins and I spent a lot of summer days trying to find something interesting to do in that town where they rolled up the sidewalks at sundown. The depression-era red sandstone National Guard armory was a good place to go climb around on an old olive drab armored car and an Army tank parked there.

When my cousins and I weren't out at the Arnold farm trying to catch a horse to ride, we were down at Grandpa Swanson's cotton gin exploring the large corrugated metal gin building or jumping from cotton bale to cotton bale in the shipping yard.

On Saturday nights, the picture show down at the end of the two-block long Main Street opened up. For fifteen cents, we could see a black and white double feature, a cartoon and one of the continuing chapters of Rocketman or The Phantom.

Movies during the war years were limited in genre. They were either westerns or war movies. Somewhere in the movie the star, someone like John Wayne, would give a hundred word speech on *what America means to me*. Most of the movies that had any flying in them were war movies and managed to provide us with the latest patriotic propaganda. The movie always ended with a reminder for all of us to buy U.S. Savings Bonds and Stamps. And we did. I faithfully purchased my twenty-five cent savings stamp each week at the local post office window.

Build Up To World War II

By late 1939, the United States was on a collision course with becoming involved in World War II. "The War" would change many people's lives. Had it not been for the war, I might have grown up a cotton farmer or cowboy. Being just a punk kid at the time, I had little or no awareness of the coming war that would set my family, along with millions of others, on a different life's journey.

While still in high school, two of my mother's brothers, Raymond and Royce, along with my dad, joined the Oklahoma National Guard, which in WW II became part of the 45th Division. The National Guard in the 1930s was akin to a boy's social club. Dances were held at the local armory on Saturday nights and the two-week active duty tours were more like summer camp than war maneuvers. These Oklahoma boys were, however, fine outdoorsmen and good shots with a rifle long before they were ever called to active duty with the U.S. Army.

My dad's cousin Roy joined the Army Air Corps about a year before Pearl Harbor was attacked. Due to Roy's previous flying experience, he was made a flight instructor and stationed at Enid Airbase. About this time Central Aircraft Manufacturing Company (CAMCO) the cover company for the American Volunteer Group (AVG), was recruiting pilots for General Claire Chennault's Flying Tigers.

Roy saw a notice posted on the base bulletin board to the effect that any flight officer who wanted to enlist in the Flying Tigers could receive an honorable discharge from the U.S. Army in order to join the AVG. Roy told me that he thought about joining the Flying Tigers for the high pay and a chance to fly fighters. It was tempting, but he had just gotten married and decided not to sign up.

Defense Plants

Oddly enough, Walter Beech, Clyde Cessna, Lloyd Stearman and years later even Bill Lear, all founded their aircraft companies in Wichita, Kansas. Stearman being the predecessor to Boeing aircraft company.

In the build-up years before the war, Beech Aircraft received a contract to build BT-10 bomber trainers based on the commercial Twin Beech Model 18. The same basic design became the Army C-45 and the Navy SNB. Although originally used as a nickname for an early twin Cessna, the name Bamboo Bomber was often used for wartime twin BT's due to part of their structure being plywood. Worthy of note is that some of the fastest and best aircraft ever built in that era, like the de Havilland Mosquito, used wood in their construction.

Dad decided to head up to Wichita where he had heard the aircraft factories were hiring. Mom and I stayed with her folks until dad could find a job and come for us.

When dad arrived at Beech, he was told his skills might be of more value at the government procurement office. When he inquired there about the job, an Army Air Corps officer and procurement inspector told him that a young fellow like him wouldn't be able to do the job. The officer explained that he needed experienced men and went on to say. "I've got two dozen new airplanes out there on the ramp that I can't deliver because the radios don't work."

Dad asked if he could take a look at some of the radios that were having problems. The officer laughed and allowed as to how he should go ahead because it sure couldn't hurt anything.

Dad went to his car, got his toolbox and proceeded to the nearest airplane. By sunset that evening, every aircraft on the field had a working radio. Needless to say, he was hired on the spot. Soon after the war began, dad became chief of Air Corps electronics procurement for Beech and Boeing aircraft companies.

Some Saw Actual Combat

Raymond, mom's older brother, served in the Corps of Engineers and was captured by the Germans during the Battle of the Bulge. For several years, our family did not know if he was still alive. Years after he returned home, I asked him to tell me about the final hours before he was taken prisoner.

The Germans had surrounded his unit, but he made it to the second floor of an empty shop building in a small village. He could hear a lot of gunfire nearby. On the street below, he saw some German soldiers he thought he had shot at earlier. He still had an M1 carbine and a 45 caliber automatic, but was out of ammunition for both. He decided to hide where he was until some of his own unit showed up.

Hours had passed when he heard a man yelling in broken English, "They haff surrendered." Raymond looked out the window to see the man walking down the center of the street waving a white flag. Raymond yelled back something to the effect that it was about time those German bastards surrendered, but as it turned out, it was the other way around. His unit had surrendered and he became a prisoner of war.

Raymond always hated the Red Cross after the war. He claimed that when they arrived at the prison camp with packages sent from the states, the Red Cross people would sell them to the Nazi guards. In all fairness, even though the packages had come from the states, they were probably not being delivered by the American Red Cross.

During the winter of 1944, American prisoners were force-marched north in a blinding snowstorm. Raymond told me that many of the younger soldiers, who were stronger than he, would just lie down in the snow and die. He made up his mind to survive. He had a wife and two kids back home he intended to see again and that kept him going.

Near the end of the war in Raymond's prisoner of war (POW) camp, the prisoners began hearing the sound of heavy guns in the distance for several days. They knew by this the invasion force was moving towards them. One morning, they woke up and their German guards were gone, left in the middle of the night. At this point, the prisoners were too weak to walk out of the camp, so they waited for the allied forces to reach them. Raymond and the others were loaded onto C-47 transports and flown to England for medical care. Raymond had survived and was going home.

Raymond's brother, my uncle Royce, became a military policeman and served in Africa. The Army hired camel jockeys to take supplies to the soldiers in North Africa. Royce claimed he could smell the caravans coming a day before they got there and three days after they left. Royce also served later in Europe and was a top Sergeant in the infantry in the Korean War. Both Raymond and Royce were highly decorated soldiers, Raymond receiving the Silver Star and both receiving Bronze Stars.

Royce's twin brother, Harold enlisted in the Air Corps and you guessed it, was stationed at Enid Air Base. Private First Class Harold was assigned to the same training squadron as dad's cousin Roy, now a Captain and an instructor pilot. Harold's enlisted buddies claimed that PFC, in Harold's case, meant *Personal Friend of the Captain* because of his ability to get weekend passes to go home to see his wife in Beggs.

New Secret Weapon

In the early 1940s, somewhere in the boonies near the Boeing airfield, my mom and I would take dad's dinner to him when he worked late in the evenings. This wasn't his office where we dropped him off at work, but a remote test site. Parked near the olive drab military truck and trailer where dad and several Army guys were working was a large dish antenna. Atop another trailer were several smaller antennas going around.

The couple of times I was allowed out of the car, dad would be in one of the trailers seated in front of a large bank of electronics, monitoring several oscilloscopes. For many years, no one knew these radar installations even existed. This particular radar test sight was being used in conjunction with top-secret B-29 airborne radar navigation and bombing systems.

During the war many goods were rationed and my dad had received a draft deferment because of his secret government work. Also, because of dad's work, we were able to purchase new tires for our car and had an "A" sticker for gasoline. Mom took a lot of verbal abuse from the other wives whose husbands were overseas because of dad's apparent draft dodging status, but she never let it bother her, as she knew he was doing important work that would hopefully shorten the war. Dad always wore civilian clothes, but he carried a military ID card indicating he held the rank of an AAC Major.

The head of the Army Air Forces during WW II was General Henry "Hap" Arnold. With our last name also being Arnold, dad was often asked if he was related to General Arnold. Dad's personal private joke was to reply, "You mean ol' Uncle Hap?" and let it go at that. To my knowledge, we were no relation.

With the single exception of Jimmy Doolittle's raid on mainland Japan, there was no practical way of attacking the Japanese by air until the American forces captured Pacific islands closer to Japan.

The China-Burma-India (CBI) theater of war was the back door into China over the Himalayas. Pilots referred to the long high altitude mountain flights as *Flying the Hump*. It was the only means of attacking the Japanese occupying China and Burma by air. As I found out later, my dad had been instrumental in the development and installation of the airborne radar systems on the Boeing B-29s.

On one particular day, I recall my dad coming home from work early. He went into the kitchen with my mom and I could hear them talking quietly. For several days after that, my folks seemed very sad. It was only after the war I learned that many of my dad's friends, pilots and crewmen, had been lost during the first B-29 raid over the Hump. Dad had personally trained many of those men in the use of airborne radar. During subsequent raids, more Army Air Corps (AAC) aircraft were lost to engine trouble and bad weather in CBI than were shot down.

Taken from Beech Log, factory open house after V-J Day in fire truck; Earl in radio test lab; Beechcraft BT-10 bomber trainer; Boeing B-29 beside Stearman trainer in Wichita; Boeing XB-19; Douglas XB-15.

Playing Airplanes

Wichita, Kansas with all its defense plants became a boomtown when WW II broke out. Construction was going on everywhere. When we first arrived in Wichita, the government put us up in something akin to a tourist court and then in an old second story apartment until our new home in suburban Wichita was completed.

I had a stuffed monkey in a red and gold uniform to which I would tie a large cowboy bandanna handkerchief by strings under its arms. He was my parachute dummy. I would toss him out of my upstairs bedroom window in order to watch him parachute to the ground. After going up and down stairs to retrieve the old monk, I finally got smart and tied a long cord to him so as to pull him back up again.

Kids in 1940 didn't have lots of toys like kids today. The only childhood possessions I can recall were the monkey, a large metal Army truck with a canvas top, some lead toy solders and an English bike. That was it till I was a little older and took up building balsa wood, doped paper-skinned model airplanes.

As a kid living in Wichita during the war, I did the usual things like collecting photos of airplanes, listening to Captain Midnight on the radio and ordering a Captain Midnight secret decoder ring. By the way, the coded message at the end of the radio broadcast was "Drink Ovaltine".

The Douglas B-19 Flying Behemoth bomber aircraft was designed and built before WW II. The United States wartime propaganda promoted the B-19 along with the Boeing B-15 as the largest bombers in the world.

On a summer afternoon, while playing in the yard, I recall seeing the B-19 fly over. It is possible it was a Boeing B-15 that lumbered high above in the blue sky, but I was familiar enough with airplanes by that time to recognize it was much larger and different than other bombers I had seen fly over.

Large numbers of B-17 Flying Fortress bombers were built quickly by several aircraft companies around the country for the war in Europe. As it turned out, both B-15 and B-19 were technologically outdated prototype aircraft used as cover stories to hide the advance designed B-29 Superfortress.

At the Boeing factory ramp over on the highway, the newly assembled B-29s would taxi to an area where they would test fire the turret machine guns against a large dirt embankment. Whenever I could, I'd talk my dad into driving me over there to watch the tests.

We moved to a newly completed housing addition that was down the street from a grass strip airport, a favorite place for us kids to play. Parked in the weeds behind an old hangar was a Fairchild low wing tandem trainer that someone had crashed. I flew many a fighter mission in that old wingless Fairchild fuselage. Other kids played soldiers or cowboys, but we always played aviators.

Air Corps pilots often came to our house for dinner and I would always hang around to hear their latest flying and war stories. It was probably because of these many stories that I knew someday I wanted to learn to fly.

The War Is Over

On VJ-Day (Victory over Japan), most of Wichita turned out on Main Street to celebrate. Life in America, however, would never be the same again. Beechcraft celebrated a few weeks later by hosting a gigantic open house. People who had never seen the inside of a defense plant could now see where their friends and relatives worked.

My mom sewed some pilot wings on a military school uniform for me and I took the hatband out of the cap to make it look like one of those *Fifty-Mission* hats the Air Corps pilots wore. At the Beechcraft factory open house, a photographer took my picture in the uniform and it appeared in the commemorative edition of the *Beech Log* company magazine.

The fifty-mission crushed hat nickname originated from the number of missions a crew had to fly before being rotated home for leave. By removing the stiffening ring from the hat, it was more easily stuffed into a bag or behind the seat. With the ring removed the hat drooped on both sides.

The Eighth Air Force in Europe suffered the highest number of casualties of any unit in WW II, about twenty-seven percent. The number of missions required for rotation started out to be twenty-five. The Memphis Belle B-17 crew was first to meet the goal. As the war wore on, the number was increased to fifty.

After the war ended, Roy stayed in the new Air Force and served at Wright Field and at the Pentagon and retired as a full Colonel. My mother's twin brothers, Harold and Royce worked at Douglas Aircraft in Tulsa until they retired.

Uncle Raymond took a job mowing grass at an oil company after the war. When several wells all came in at the same time, the oil field superintendent driving flatbed truck stopped to ask Raymond, "You know anything about oil wells?"

Raymond replied, "Guess I do, I grew up in an oil field. My dad was a wildcatter," and he climbed on the truck. Years after that Raymond retired as the New Mexico superintendent for the Amerada Oil Company.

The 1940s were a time when men took their hats off when the flag passed by and folks held their right hand over their heart. Most people knew all the words to the *National Anthem* and believed in the words to the *Battle Hymn of the Republic*. There were no arguments about the fact that God was the protectorate of our great nation. Now with the passing of the *Last Great Generation,* America's age of innocence has faded.

Fairchild aircraft, Earl assigned as AF liaison after WW II; B-36 beside B-29, this picture hung in my dad's office; Earl with Vandalia flight test pilots; with WPAFB intelligence officer; Air Force Material Command staff; avionics procurement chief on milestone aircraft P-61 Black Widow; Boeing B-47 jet bombers replaces prop driven bombers; F-90 fighter airframe design so sleek, it was use in Blackhawk comic series.

Chapter Two
THE WOOD CITY KID

In 1946, we moved to Dayton, Ohio. Dad was transferred to Wright-Patterson Air Force Base and assigned to Air Research and Development (ARDC) at Wright Field. Except for my early glimpse of the radar project dad worked on during the war, I never knew exactly what it was he did at work. He never talked about his job. For example, my education consisted of bits of information like being told that RADAR was not a word like radio, but an acronym meaning Rapid Automatic Detection Alignment and Repeats.

After a brief stay in North Dayton, we moved to Fairfield. The adjoining town of Osborn was incorporated with Fairfield to become Fairborn. The main gate to Patterson Air Force Base (AFB) lay at the center of Fairborn and the backyard of our townhouse apartment backed onto a section of the airbase called Wood City.

My brother Don, who is ten years younger than myself, was born shortly after we moved to Fairborn. The day he was born, the Dayton Daily News ran a front-page story about a naval officer who had overshot his carrier and went over the side. He was fished out of the drink unharmed. My brother was named Donald Keith after that Navy flyer for no other reason than my mother thought the fellow must have had a charmed life.

Our next-door neighbor, a young Air Force officer, drove a brand new, baby blue Lincoln Continental Cabriolet with push button door openers. He must have been from a wealthy family as I am sure he didn't buy that baby on a junior officer's pay! My lifelong interest in the Lincoln marque must have began with that very automobile.

The young officer and his wife must have felt I was being neglected due to all the fuss being made over the new baby boy in the family. For Easter, they gave me a brand new Zenith radio receiver, which I prized among my favorite possessions.

DXing is a forgotten hobby that involved seeing how many distant radio stations one can pick up. Using a long wire antenna strung across my bedroom ceiling, I would sit up nights carefully tuning the radio dial and waiting for the next station identification call letters to be announced so that I could enter the station in my logbook.

Build Your Own Stuff

As indicated in the sub-title of this book, *How I came To Be An Engineer*, the next couple of chapters will dwell on what creates a sense of design. What makes an artist, an athlete or a designer is an inherent ability plus a desire to acquire that skill. The same can be said for a good designer. We learn by baby steps, not giant strides.

Before I ever heard of an official soapbox derby race, I had constructed two coaster cars. The first was built of parts from my brother's disassembled baby buggy. The body was a wooden shipping crate mounted on the buggy's springs and axle, complete with white rubber tires and spoke wheels. The soapbox buggy's steering directional control depended on which way you leaned.

For my second non-powered vehicle, the Green Hornet, I used an aircraft's drop-tank with the bottom cut out and nailed to a five-foot 2X10 plank chassis. The rear axle was nailed directly to the wood chassis. The steerable front axle used a single bolt to hold the angle iron and was steered by means of a rope fastened to each side of the front axle. The four wheels were stock wheelbarrow wheels from a hardware store.

A U-shape cockpit was cut out of the top for the driver to sit on an old chair cushion. The wheels were enclosed inside the body reflecting the bulbous auto body designs of that era. The Green Hornet was a popular radio mystery show, but the car was actually given that name after we borrowed some forest green paint from the apartment maintenance folks and painted it with a brush. It was exceptionally heavy for a coaster car, but sleek and modern in appearance.

Ohio people were big on soapbox derby races, so that summer I registered to enter the annual soapbox derby race down Wright View Heights Hill. At the race banquet, I won the door prize, a bicycle speedometer.

The day of the race, my shanghaied neighborhood pit-crew and I toiled to push the drop-tank soapbox to the starting line at the top of the hill. The car looked fast, but was probably no match for the assemblage of sleek, thin-wheeled official soapbox cars built from kits and by kids denying any assistance from their coaching parents.

Before the official trials started, I made one coaster ride down the hill. Steering wasn't that good and sitting low to the ground, I felt like I was doing about 50 mph instead of fifteen. When the derby officials arrived on the scene, I was immediately disqualified due to my non-regulation wheels.

Who said anything about regulation wheels? What rules? I didn't read any stinking rules! I went to Coach Bushmire who was one of the judges and asked if I should give back the door prize I had won? He said he didn't think so as I had won it fair and square in the drawing. Thus ended my non-powered racing career.

Oklahoma Vacations

During the nine years we lived in Ohio, my dad would always schedule his vacation for late June. When the time came for our annual vacation to Oklahoma, we'd load up the family car and departed Fairborn at the crack of dawn. Old U.S. Route 40 passed through Indianapolis and headed west. Arriving in St Louis the second day of the trip, we would change to Route 66.

Route 40 lay a little north of present I70 and ran across the flat Ohio farmland, a straight shot from the Dayton airport to Richmond and Indianapolis. Thus, the airline airways followed the highway. The old nighttime air navigation beacon light towers, which predated radio navigation were still standing in those days and could be seen from the highway.

For lunch we'd stop in Terra Haute at a grocery store, purchase a large slice of baloney, crackers and cold drinks, which we ate somewhere along the road. Dad had it figured out that if we ate breakfast at home and had a picnic lunch, then we could afford to take mom out that evening for dinner to a really nice restaurant of her choice.

It was my job to navigate during the trip. This, however, did not include making any of the decisions like which road we'd take. Dad did that. Nor when we would make the next restroom stop. Mom did that. Restroom stops were usually made after my brother and I had screamed for about fifteen minutes and, according to dad, he had just managed to pass a long line of trucks that he would now have to pass all over again.

What my navigating meant was that each hour of the trip, I was to log the miles on the odometer and determine our average speed. I would use these figures and a freebie gas company map to announce our estimated time to the next town or point of interest. A good average speed was about 50 mph on those old roads that passed through the center of every small town along the way. Each time we filled the car with gas, I logged the number of gallons and divided them into the miles driven since the last fill-up to determine our average fuel economy.

Looking forward to crossing the mighty Mississippi, the mile-wide river of legendary Tom Sawyer fame, over the Chain of Rocks Bridge was good for at least two hours of anticipation. We always stayed at the same tourist court on the bypass around St Louis, the Blue Bonnet Courts. I recall we used to pass by the Lambert Field airline terminal on the highway around St Louis.

Dad always tried to be there before dark so there'd be no chance of having car trouble on the road after dark. Before leaving the tourist court, dad would go to the office and make our reservations for the next summer because he knew exactly what day and time we would once again be stopping over. A typical postcard from my dad to his mother on our return trip read "Left St. Louis at 7 a.m., breakfast at 8:45 a.m., bacon and eggs at the diner on Hwy 40, arrived Fairborn 6 p.m., boys and Lola doing fine. Love Earl."

Dad drove the entire trip and I generally rode up front, my mom and brother in the back seat. We had a water evaporative air cooler that mounted on the passenger's window. It would cool off a little if the humidity was low, but most of the time we gave up and rolled the windows down. Route 66 to Tulsa was over a winding, narrow two-lane road through the Ozark Mountains. If we got stuck behind a truck, it'd be a while before we could pass.

Every old rickety barn for 200 miles east and west of the Ozarks was painted with an ad for Meramec Caverns, Onondaga Caves or some cave that was Jesse James' hideout. Once and only once, we actually stopped at the Onondaga Cave just long enough to take the underground tour.

Years later, my cousin Phil asked if I remembered the government men who followed dad around when we visited Oklahoma. He told me that his folks always knew dad was in town when they saw the two guys in suits and hats driving around in a black Ford. Phil remembered seeing them talking to grandpa in the feed store one time. Actually, I never thought much about it. Kids just seem to take things like that as a normal part of life.

The fact that we always had an FBI agent living next door to us also never occurred to me to be unusual. Stan, one of the agents would even pick me up after school sometimes. I remember him showing me his ID so I would know what a real FBI ID looked like. Once, I talked him into showing me his sidearm. He unloaded it first, of course. Now that I think about it, I believe the Air Corps Captain neighbor of ours might have been a G-2, intelligence officer, as I don't remember him wearing pilot's wings like most of dad's other friends.

Post War Flying Stories

The name of the Army Air Corps was changed to the Army Air Forces during WW II, but now it was a separate branch of the service known as the Air Force. We began seeing the new blue uniforms, affectionately referred to as bus driver suits. Those old style dark brown jackets, gray trousers with dark leg stripes and fifty-mission hats had always been an impressive sight to me and I was sorry to see them go.

The Air Force pilots that had flown in the war often came by the house to see dad and like back in Wichita, I would hang around in hopes of hearing some good flying stories. Stories including neat phrases like, "The flak was so thick that day you could walk on it," and "There we were at 20,000 feet."

Pilots who flew with the 8th Air Force in Europe told how, towards the end of the war, they were so short of navigators that a whole squadron would line up behind the lead aircraft who had a navigator onboard. When the lead aircraft dropped their bombs, the rest of the squadron would follow suit and release their bombs.

The bombers would often fly into bad weather and become separated from their formation. If an aircraft returned with its bomb load, it did not count as a mission not to mention how dangerous it was to land with a full load of bombs. Targets of opportunity became the order of the day. When lost over enemy territory, the pilots would find a railroad track and follow the rails to the nearest rail yard or some industrial buildings to release their bomb load.

It got so bad toward the end of the war that when the 8th Air Force crossed the English Channel, the entire German front went on alert because they never knew where in the heck the bombers would end up releasing their bombs.

One pilot told us a story of bringing back a badly shot-up B-25. Unbeknownst to him, the landing gear and indicator lights had failed. Upon flaring out for landing at his home base, a terrible racket hit the side of the airplane. Convinced that the airfield had been infiltrated with enemy snipers and they were being shot at, he pulled up and went around.

The tower advised him that his landing gear was not down. He had put the gear handle in the down position, but the landing gear had not gone down. After recycling the gear several times, it went down and locked. He had come so close to the ground on his first attempted landing that the B-25 props were picking up gravel and throwing it into the sides of the fuselage.

A C-47 pilot lamenting how bad the weather was in England said that they often returned from channel crossings low on gas and the fog would be down to the ground. With no options except to try to land, they would come in on a radio beacon. As they crossed the airfield and couldn't see anything, they would turn around and come back over again taking fifty feet of altitude off each time. They'd repeat this procedure until they either flew into something or felt the wheels touch the ground.

Vandalia Test Pilot School

Wright Field was affiliated with the test pilot school located at the Dayton Municipal Airport in Vandalia. It was here that my dad worked with some of the famous test pilots such as Chuck Yeager. The government announced two years after the fact that Yeager had broken the sound barrier on October 14, 1947. Dad had known it all the time, but was unable to tell the story until it was formally announced.

In my room, I had hung a picture of a P-80, which I mistakenly thought had been the plane used to break the sound barrier. There were reports from British Spitfire pilots who had approached or even exceeded the speed of sound in power dives, so I just assumed that was how it had been done by the P-80. Later, I discovered it was not that jet at all, but a Bell X-1 rocket plane that had broken the sound barrier.

The Bell P-59 Airacomet, the pioneer U.S. jet aircraft, first flew in October 1942 from Muroc Dry Lake later known as Edwards AFB. The P-59 was only capable of speeds up to about 350 knots and was operational only for a short time.

The postwar P-80 Shooting Star jet fighter just plain looked fast, but it and most of the jet fighters up until the century series were unable to approach the speed of sound in level flight. There had been reports of jet fighters exceeding the speed of sound in a dive that became uncontrollable. Some claimed that the only way of counteracting this out-of-control condition was to reverse the control inputs. Fact or rumor, it is doubtful anyone really knew because those few pilots who attempted it often did not live to tell about it.

Mom always liked to go for drives in the country. So when dad would ask what we'd like to do on a Sunday afternoon, I'd always vote with mom to take a ride, but my diabolical plan was to end up at the civil airport located north of Dayton near the small town of Vandalia. You were allowed to wander through the hangars as well as get to watch the airliners and private planes takeoff and land. The General Motors Aeroproducts Division that produced propellers was also near the airport at Vandalia.

Other places I remember going to were the war surplus salvage dump and to my dad's amateur radio club at the base. The HAM Radio operators at WPAFB maintained a worldwide radio net with the call letters W8AIR. Dad loved to get on the HAM radio and talk long distances. He knew the technical aspects better than most, but his Morse code speed was a little lacking.

This was the early post war era. We had just finished fighting for our very survival and there were a lot of secret projects underway. America tottered on the brink of a nuclear standoff with Russia and now gazed towards the heavens as we stood on the threshold of space.

Airplane and Rocket Playground

Our townhouse apartment backed up to a part of Patterson Field known as Wood City. Wood City was primarily a housing project with enlisted barracks, housing for married personnel, a recreation hall, theater, swimming pool, post exchange and a library. The back gate to Wood City was a stone's throw from our back door. I had friends that lived on the base and kids were largely ignored going and coming from that part of the base.

Wernher von Braun, his family and working associates had been brought to Wright Field after their escape from Peenemunde, Germany. Wolfgang von Braun, Wernher's nephew, and I were the same age. He was in my seventh grade class at school. The first day he attended our school, I recall his making fun of our math class saying he had been taught the algebra we were studying at his German school in the third grade. Wolfgang and I became good friends over the next year and he told me stories of the war.

Peenemunde was the rocket development and launch site for the V-1 and V-2 missiles that were fired on London during the Blitz. The "V" designation stood for vengeance weapon or in German, Vergeltungswaffe. The V-1 buzz bomb was a flying bomb powered by a pulsejet engine. They were designed to run out of fuel over their intended target. When the engine quit, the rudder would go full left sending the missile into a dive toward a random target. The buzz bomb had a top speed of about 220 mph. If an RAF fighter like a Spitfire or Hurricane could be vectored into the area of an incoming V-1, the fighter could easily overtake and shoot down the missile. This was not the case with the larger V-2 rockets, which entered from the stratosphere.

Wernher von Braun's personal dream was to build a rocket capable of traveling to the moon. The V-2 was a step in that direction. It was a large missile that stood about three stories high and was powered by a liquid fuel engine. The 1942 version of the V-2 could be fired to an altitude of 5.2 miles. Several V-2 rockets were test fired from the White Sands Missile Range after the war. A modified two-stage version of the V-2 set a world's altitude record when it climbed to an altitude of 244 miles above the earth in February of 1949.

As WW II was ending, the U.S. Army under General Patton were moving toward Peenemunde, but it looked as though the Russians were going to get there first. Wolfgang told me his version of what he remembered. Most of the livestock on their farm had been slaughtered to feed the retreating German army.

His father woke him in the middle of the night and instructed him to bring with him only what he could carry. He and his family walked all night to get to the American lines so as not to be captured by the Russian army and taken to Russia.

One story that Wolfgang's father liked to tell was of trying to get pencil sharpeners for their office. The German command would turn down any requests for items they considered non-essential. Their office staff was able to obtain them by ordering "honing devices for grinding conical points onto ten-millimeter wooden hand-tools."

Wolfgang left Fairborn with his family when the entire rocket development unit was moved to Huntsville, Alabama to work for the Army, but von Braun never gave up his dream of building a three-stage rocket that would someday travel to the moon.

View From My Window

After the war, captured aircraft and rockets were brought to ARDC at Wright Field and thoroughly scrutinized for any advanced technology. In the far back section of Wood City near some old training buildings, ARDC stored many of the tested aircraft. These relics of the war in Europe and Pacific were being stored there for eventual donation to an Air Force Museum, which would be established sometime in the future.

Looking out my upstairs bedroom window of the Lovington Arms townhouse apartments, I had a panoramic view of assorted captured Luftwaffe and Rising Sun airplanes. A large V-2 missile with its explosive propellants removed sat upright, held in place by four long guy-wires.

Just inside the old Wood City gate, a P-80 jet fighter had been placed on the grass lawn. The jet was probably one of the early prototypes and its engine had been removed.

Parked just beside the V-2 rocket was a twinjet engine Messerschmitt Me-262 Stormbird. The Me-262 was able to utilize tricycle landing gear due to not having a large prop like the other fighters of this era. It also seemed fairly large for a one-man aircraft. The Stormbird was powered by a JUMO-004 turbo jet engine designed by the Germans in 1937. The ME-262 had an attack speed greater than the postwar P-80.

The famous German JG-7, the Jagdgeschwaker Seven squadron, flew the Me-262s. There were approximately 1,300 of these aircraft built, although only 149 ever flew in combat. They were used towards the end of the war against our B-17 bombers over Europe. The Me-262 would have been even more effective except for its high rate of fuel consumption that limited the aircraft's time aloft. Ace WW II fighter pilot Chuck Yeager, flying a P-51, successfully shot one down when it was low on fuel and on final approach for landing at a German airfield.

A rocket plane with a short fat fuselage, the Me-163 Komet was parked nearby. It was in one of these rocket aircraft that von Braun's sister, Wolfgang's aunt, crashed and was killed during an experimental flight test at Peenemunde. There were about eighteen different versions of this rocket plane built by the Germans. This particular Komet was a Me-163B with tail number FE500. The FE prefix on the tail number was a U.S. designation, which stood for Foreign Evaluation.

Next to the Me-163 was a GO-229 one-man flying wing in which the pilot lay on his belly to fly. The cockpit of this aircraft had been sealed shut. Respecting that, us kids made no attempt to crawl inside as we did many of the others.

There was also one very unusual Japanese man-guided rocket called the Baka, meaning crazy, parked in the same area. The Baka was designed to be carried aloft and launched from a larger aircraft. Under its own rocket power, the Kamikaze pilot would guide the flying bomb into a target like an enemy ship. It contained one thousand pounds of explosives and about a half ounce of common sense.

I the far back of the Wood City area was the fuselage of a B-29 bomber with no wings or tail section. It rested in two large wooded cradles close enough to the ground for us to climb into. Next to the B-29 was the nose section of a C-54 transport.

We kids spent many hours playing pilot and crew on these two planes. We crawled through the B-29's long center tunnel and tried to figure out what we thought all the switches and controls were used for.

I came to know these two planes' cockpit layout as well as any pilot that ever flew them.

Occasionally the civilian guards, making their rounds, would run us out of our favorite playground. However, after they left, we went right back. The Air Police (AP) seldom bothered us and we got to be good friends, often going for cigarettes and coffee for them.

The B-29 fuselage is on floor display at the Air Force Museum and the last time I visited, the fuselage nose art was painted to represent *Command Decision*, the B-29 that became an Ace bomber after shooting down five Mig-15s in the Korean War. Its new nose art is a cartoon of Disney's Dopey and Doc flipping a coin, i.e. a command decision.

Additionally, many of the other aircraft I remember from Wood City have been refurbished and are presently on display at the impressive and expansive Air Force Museum on Wright Field.

I still think of the old B-29 fuselage and the other old Wood City airplanes at the AF museum as my own personal toys. I consider them to be only on loan to the museum. When I leave the museum, I will often say to one of the volunteers, "Thanks for taking care of my toys."

This is usually met with a questioning look or occasionally with a polite smile when I am mistaken for one of those old WW II hack aircrewmen that used to fly in them.

P-80 Shooting Star aircraft parked at entrance gate to Wood City; captured German aircraft, jet flying wing just out of view on right is same type that Werner von Braun sister was killed in during flight test; view from my bedroom window, German and Jap fighters flank a V-1 rocket; B-36 and B-25 at Wright Field Air Show, 1947; prototype I and II of Soap Box racers; first Whizzer motorbike built from scratch.

Chapter Three
MECHANICAL WONDERS

As a youngster, I was fascinated by the world of mechanical wonders and never missed an opportunity to take something apart to see how it worked. Being the son of an engineer and tinkerer only encouraged my oft times flawed investigations.

Dayton, Ohio was the home of Leland, Delco, and National Cash Register. It was the industrial East to me. There were small job shops everywhere that could machine or manufacture any part needed. One of my best memories was of going into the railroad repair barns down on Third Street where they overhauled the locomotives and being amazed at the sheer size and power of those old Baldwin steam engines.

Growing up around airplanes left me with little ambition other than wanting to learn to fly. I asked my mother onetime, "What will I be when I grow up?"

She replied, "You will be a jack of all trades and master of none." She was kidding, of course, but for the most part it was a self-fulfilling prophecy.

During WW II, there were no private automobiles or aircraft produced. Until the late 1940s, a person owning a '41 or '42 model car was considered to own a late model automobile. You repaired the car you owned or had it repaired. Watching my dad overhaul our '41 Nash Ambassador up on blocks in our back yard was my introduction to auto mechanics.

King Of The Back Roads

My first powered vehicle was a Schwinn bicycle with a Whizzer motorbike kit mounted on it. An Ohio driver's license was not required if the motorbike was pedal started, but was required if it had a kick-start. There the similarity between my bike and a stock Whizzer ended. What my dad did not show me, I picked up from other mechanics on how to soup-up the bike.

Dad kind of enjoyed helping me build up the bike as he had courted my mom on a 30's Indian motorcycle. The Whizzer bike's engine was bored oversize, valves ported and relieved and the compression raised. The frame was cut down for a lower center of gravity and the engine mounts redesigned.

One of my fondest memories is of riding in the early autumn on those old Ohio blacktop roads through the countryside. The trees often formed a full arch over those narrow farm roads. In late afternoon, the golden rays of the sun flickered and flashed between the tree branches as we rode at 60 mph down a seemingly endless tunnel of fallen leaves that swirled in a vortex behind the bike as it passed.

My friend Larry and I seldom encountered any traffic on those old narrow back roads. We didn't ride close together, but kept each other in distant view. We wore old leather bomber caps, more to keep our ears warm and to muffle the wind noise than for safety. Resting, by leaning forward on the bike's fuel tank, we would run our tanks nearly dry before turning once again for home.

I worked part time managing a small newspaper branch for the Dayton Daily News at Gate 12 on Patterson Field. The papers were dropped off by truck. I distributed them to the sales boxes and ran a delivery route to the base quarters on my motorbike.

The chief of the gate guards hated teenagers. At least, we were convinced he did. He had already gotten my friend Roger, General Light's son, prohibited from riding on the base. That was after a wild chase across the officer's club golf course. The chief would never have caught Roger except he hit a concrete drain and spilled his motorbike, breaking his right foot.

Sure enough, the chief got me for speeding in a residential area and confiscated my gate pass on the spot. Bureaucracies being what they are, I waited a few days, applied for another pass and got it.

Forty Ford Tudor

On one of those cold, dreary gray sky Miami Valley winter days I had gone with my dad up to Springfield to a car dealer where dad liked a certain mechanic to service his car. A light rain the night before had frozen into a wafer-thin sheet of ice, but the roads were clear for driving.

I had been saving my money to buy a car. Sitting out on the dealer's lot was a 1940 Ford Standard Tudor. About what I had been wanting and it was in my price range. The dealer offered to throw in an oil change and lube job. I paid the asking price of $125 in cash. The grease rack boy commented that he didn't think the car's grease fittings had been serviced in several years.

The ol' Ford had the slickest, shiniest black paint job. That was, until I got it home and the sheet of clear ice covering it melted. The car had been painted with a paintbrush. Oh well, that made it easy to maintain. When a little spot of rust or a scratch turned up, I just got out the ol' quart can of black enamel and touched her up. That summer, the Ford underwent a metamorphosis. Longer spring shackles were installed to lower the back. The running boards were removed and a lot of tuning was done to the flathead V-8 engine.

Auto mechanic classes were not offered at the jerkwater Bath Township High School I attended. Hot rod and custom car builders were considered hoods and disapproved of by educators and proper society. Who you dated and who you ran with was important to the local gentry, but not to me.

My mom was a pillar in the community, officer in the PTA and president of the local garden club. Thus, due to my family's standing, I'd clean up, leave my black leather jacket and jeans at home and be invited to all the best social events. I seldom missed Westminster Youth Fellowship at the First Presbyterian Church on Sunday evenings. I also earned my God and Country Scouting award at that church. On the other hand, I was equally welcome to drink 3.2-beer with the hot rod crowd that hung out downtown. It seemed natural and comfortable for me to live between the two socially separated worlds.

Auto Parts and Supply

Jaffey's Auto Supply was a local auto parts store. Jack Jaffey, a fine Jewish fellow, moved to Fairborn from back east somewhere. Most of the car dealers bought parts wholesale from him. Working part time at the Studebaker dealer, being in the business so to speak, I was one of the first to hear that Jaffey had an opening for a parts runner. I high-tailed it to Jaffey's and applied for the job, which paid big bucks, $1.75 an hour.

The company delivery truck was a red Ford Standard pickup and I put many a mile on that ol' truck. Working for Jaffey was an education in itself. He was one of those people who had a gift for gab and got along with everybody. That ol' Jew taught me more about business and human nature than I could have learned anywhere else and I liked him. Jaffey told me, "The customer is always right," and when the customer wasn't, it would be Jaffey's job to tell them. Not mine.

An Air Force officer pulled up out front of the store in a silver Buick Skylark convertible. I was working the counter and he asked for a set of radiator hoses for the Skylark. After looking them up in the parts catalog, I used a long stick to hook them from a rack high on the wall. I filled out the counter ticket and told the officer that they were $1.25 each, plus tax. The officer started in on me about how I was ripping him off.

I tried to explain that the hoses we carried were a better quality than those most other stores sold. I glanced pleadingly towards Jaffey who was waiting on another customer.

Seeing my dilemma, Jaffey came over and asked the officer, "What seems to be the problem?"

The officer complained, "Down the street at Western Auto, the hoses are only seventy-five cents each."

Jaffey asked politely, "Why then don't you just go down to Western Auto and buy them?"

"Well, they're out of them right now," the officer replied.

Without cracking a smile Jaffey said, "If we were out of them, I'd sell them for fifty cents each," and returned to waiting on his previous customer. The officer paid me, picked up his radiator hoses and left.

Rolled The New Ford

In the spring of 1953, dad bought a brand new light blue Ford Fordor. A few weeks after the car was purchased, I was asked on a Sunday morning to deliver my little brother to church school. On my way back, I decided to take the long way home, out behind the Portland Cement Plant, down through the quarry and back onto the main road.

The Lincoln automobiles of that era had been winning all the Mexican road races, so I thought I would see just what this new Ford would do. That was the first of three mistakes I made that day. My second mistake was thinking that I was an experienced competition road race driver. My third and worst mistake was getting too high in a turn on a gravel road.

That lightweight, narrow track Ford went into a four-wheel drift and off the top of the curve. As best I can recollect, it did something akin to a roll with a half gainer thrown in for good measure. Till this very day I can still see the grass in the windshield as it disintegrated before my eyes. I was thrown hard against the driver's door. The car came to rest on its two left wheels, tottered there for an instant and then fell upright on all four wheels.

The driver's door swung open and total silence replaced the deafening noises of a few seconds ago. There was a fourteen-inch triangle piece of windshield glass embedded in the seat between my legs, but except for a scrape on my left side where I had hit and broken the plastic armrest, I was unharmed. Half falling, half stumbling, I exited the car hoping maybe I hadn't done much damage. Not true. A quick walk around revealed that the roof and every corner of the car was badly mangled.

I hiked about a mile to a nearby farmhouse where I called my dad to tell him I had just wrecked his new Ford. What I was expecting to hear on the other end of the phone was my dad asking about the condition of the car or to be yelled at for wrecking it. All my dad said was, "Are you okay?"

About this time in our growing up process we learn two important lessons. Even though we have convinced ourselves we are invincible and our parents don't care anything at all about us, something happens to show us how wrong we are on both counts. When I think back on that day, I realize my folks cared and worried about me just as much as I do my own.

The insurance company totaled the car and for a few extra bucks, dad got a new 1954 Ford. Needless to say, I was seldom offered the use of the new family car again after that.

American Graffiti

Our family home was an old two-story, white-frame house that had a three-car garage. Actually it was an old carriage house. This was great place for working on old cars. Two of my friends and myself chipped in $25 each to buy a 1937 Ford coupe and modified it into a stock car. We removed all the glass from the coupe, welded in roll bars and installed a 59AB V-8 engine out of a wrecked '41 Mercury. We borrowed the needed four racing slicks from our partner's older brother who raced cars.

The eldest of the three of us was eighteen and the driver had to be eighteen to enter the stock car races at the local track, so he would be the first to race the car. The night of the race, in the first heat on the first lap, our driver was forced off a high-banked back turn and rolled the coupe. He was unharmed, but he ruined our racecar budget.

The old abandon town of Osborn was located in the Huffman Dam flood plain. Years ago, the whole town had been moved further east to higher ground. However, the paved main street of the town still remained. It was there the hot rods would assemble to drag race on the weekends. My stripped down '40 Ford Tudor was one of the best, but a lot depended on my hitting each gear shift just right without over or under-torquing the engine.

I had gone on a Sunday afternoon to answer a challenge from a '34 Ford coupe. I had specified copilots so as to decrease his weight-to-power ratio. Larry usually rode with me because his '46 Plymouth couldn't beat diddle. I beat the duce coupe off the mark and lead all the way to 60 mph where, according to our local rules, I backed off. The duce coupe kept on winding past 70 mph and claimed he had won the quarter mile, but my '40 blew his doors off and he knew it.

Someone Call An Ambulance

Near dark, after the drag races, my buddy Delbert wanted to go to some drive-in with three girls and one of the girl's brother in a '40 Buick four-door convertible. Her brother was weird. I didn't want to ride with him, but ended up in the middle of the front seat. The Ford rollover taught me a lesson about the misuse of speed this Buick guy had yet to learn.

I had just told the driver to slow his car down or stop and let me out as we approached a fork in the road where the left lane of the Y-intersection was under construction. He took a sudden left turn down the closed road. Another car had slowed up at the stop sign on the right fork of the intersection, but thinking our car would go right with the regular traffic flow, pulled out directly into our path.

We were traveling at 50 mph or better when we impacted the other car doing about 20 mph, head on. It shortened the front end of the Buick by about four feet and turned its straight eight engine sideways in its mount.

Delbert, on my right, went through the windshield. I hit the dash and cut my face on part of the broken windshield. The three girl passengers in the back seat came forward and hit the backs of our seat, but as luck would have it, the car had sedan seating, which the backs did not fold forward. Once again, I heard that sickening crunch of metal and glass, a sound I had heard once before and now had come to hate.

Somehow, I managed to get out of the car and pulled Delbert out. He was semi-conscious. Unaware I was bleeding profusely from the forehead and chin, a bystander shrieked when she looked at me. Some lady from a nearby café came and handed me a wet towel. It seemed only a short time before an ambulance arrived on the scene. They were from a local volunteer fire department and loaded one of the three people in the other car into the ambulance on a stretcher.

Putting Delbert's arm around my neck I drug him to his feet and walked towards the ambulance holding him with one hand and the towel on my bleeding face with another. Delbert collapsed into the medic's arms as we climbed aboard. Sitting between the two stretchers, I watched over the driver's shoulder as we entered the Dayton city traffic.

The co-driver in the right seat of the ambulance would radio ahead to have the traffic lights changed to red in front of us. Fascinated with this high speed run through downtown traffic, I forgot any pain from what turned out to be a broken right jaw. I was also unaware until later that the passenger from the car we hit, now laying on the stretcher beside me, died enroute to the hospital.

Upon arrival at Miami Valley Hospital, Doc Wynans, our family doctor, nearly beat us there in his Porsche. Someone we knew had called dad and he had called Doc. All I remember after that was some nurse sticking me with a needle. I woke up briefly with a bright operating light in my eyes and Doc Wynans yelling at me to, "Hold still," and then I passed out again.

Later, I counted twenty-seven stitches in my lower lip, chin and forehead. It took several months to recuperate from my injuries. With some minor cosmetic surgery and rest I was back to my old self soon enough, but there went football. However, to this day, I still get angry when I recall the incident and the reckless, irresponsible way some people operate automobiles.

Ride Like The Wind

I came across this '39 Lincoln Zephyr 3-window coupe in a rundown part of town and I thought it was about the slickest design for a car I had ever seen. It appealed to some inner sense of design that I related to, long before I knew anything about streamlining or art deco.

The guy wanted $300 for the Zephyr. It had some minor damage to the passenger side running board flange, a broke axle and the V-12 engine needed a valve job. He finally agreed to sell me the car for $200. Mom always bought me nice clothes and I don't ever remember going hungry, but her theory on money for my "machines," as she called them, was my problem. The '40 Ford was sold for the $125 I had originally paid for it and I raked up the rest.

Delbert was always a little bit crazy even before our car crash. He had this Whizzer Sportsman motorbike. The local cops chased Delbert after he ran a stop sign and he ran six more trying to get away, but they caught him. The reason he ran from the cops was because his license had already been revoked for a year. Delbert's dad gave him twenty-four hours to sell the bike. I offered him $45 and bought it.

The little Sportsman was economical and fun to ride and the Zephyr still wasn't running by winter, so I traded the Sportsman even for a maroon '41 Oldsmobile torpedo-back, two-door sedan. It had a flathead straight six engine and more importantly, a good heater. The body and drive train were good, but its engine knocked. I drove it easy cause I sure didn't want to have to fix it, too! I needed the money to get the Zephyr running.

Some of my first engineering thinking began with that car. If airplanes and racecars needed seatbelts why didn't cars? Soon the Olds was fitted with seatbelts and a makeshift sponge rubber padded instrument panel. All of this, several years before Ford introduced the padded dash. If anyone made fun of my makeshift safety devices, I'd just point to the scars on my chin and that usually closed the subject to further discussion.

When spring arrived, Sam, who worked in the shop at Jaffey's during the day and the night shift at Delco, helped me grind the valves on the flathead V-12 engine. I installed a salvaged right rear axle and the '39 Lincoln Zephyr 3-window coupe hit the ground running.

The Zephyr had a floor shift, but the long, curved shift handle was concealed by a center console extending from the dash to the floor making it appear the shift was in the dash below a large, round center speedometer and instrument cluster. The Columbia rearend was vacuum controlled giving six forward gears. You could come up beside someone doing 60 mph and still shift one more time without over-revving the engine.

The backseat of the business coupe had a narrow jump seat on which I installed hinges at the top of the seatback. This allowed the back seat to be brought up level with the back of the front seats and looked like a shelf. The trunk in the coupe had a long wooden deck. When we went to the drive-in theater, at least three people could comfortably hide in the trunk.

The Fairborn Drive-In Theater charged admission by the person, not by the car. This baffled me because so many kids would sneak in by hiding in the trunk of the cars. Most got caught when they parked and opened the trunk to let their stowaways out. The coupe's hinged back seat design permitted my stowaways to come forward in the car without opening the trunk.

Another way to sneak into the drive-in was to turn off your headlights and drive in the exit. The Zephyr had a separate set of lights called driving lamps, but your brake lights would still come on. To avoid this, I mastered the art of coasting into a parking space, but also installed a switch in the tail, brake and license plate lights wiring to turn them off.

Saturday Night Fiasco

The drive-in theater operator had apparently grown tired of kids sneaking in and hired a man to watch for trunks being opened and to also guard the exit. On a Saturday night, I hit the drive-in exit doing about 30 mph and the ol' fart jumped out in front of me waving a flashlight. I hit the brakes and slid on the gravel all the way up to him. I don't know who was scared worse, me or the watchman who looked like the proverbial deer caught in the headlights. Throwing the Zephyr in reverse, I peeled gravel all the way out the exit.

The story doesn't end here for this was a night that would live in infamy. Just down the road was the entrance to the game preserve behind Patterson Field. There were some crashed aircraft near there that were used for fire training. There was a small hill there that overlooked the lights of town and was a local make-out parking place. As we pulled in, my buddy, his girl, my girlfriend and me saw another car parked some distance away and I gave the usual four-short, two-long honks on my horn.

Turned out it wasn't anyone we knew. The car's interior dome light came on as the door flew open and the silhouette of a large man in the distance raised his arm. All I heard were two muffled cracks, but the muzzle flash of a pistol in the dark night was unmistakable. Someone was shooting at us. Crouched low in the seat, I slid and skidded into a U-turn getting the heck out of there. I also switched off the taillights thinking it would make us less of a target.

As we came back onto the highway here came a sheriff's patrol car and we flagged him down. It was one of the deputies I knew and after explaining to him what had happened, he took off into the game preserve. The deputy told me sometime later that he never found anyone that night.

In addition to being a great place to park, it occurred to me that the area also provided an excellent vantage point for viewing the B-36s when they took off and landed. I concluded it must have been Soviet spies we had come upon that night.

After dropping off my friends, a Fairborn PD car pulled me over on the way home. I knew Tiny, an overweight police sergeant, but I didn't know this guy. The patrolman said he had stopped me because I didn't have any taillights. Glancing down at the dash, I saw that I had left the tail light switch in the off position. As I opened the door to get out, I casually flipped the taillight switch on. I explained that I was sure the lights were working as the patrolman and I walked to the rear of the Zephyr where, of course, the taillights were lit.

The patrolman allowed that he may have observed me as I passed under some bright streetlights, but he was going to give me a ticket anyway for having four, forward-facing headlights, referring to my twin driving lamps. He was right. Until Ford Motor Company got the laws changed for their quad headlights in the late 1950s, dual forward-facing driving lamps were illegal in many states. I decided one traffic ticket for the *night from hell* was fair enough.

Sorry Education

At Fairborn High we had a real jerk for a principal and our math teacher couldn't calculate her way out of a wet paper bag. I asked my dad several times if I could go to Stanton Military Academy, but the extra money just wasn't there.

I stayed in trouble at school, mostly out of boredom I suppose. Except for Coach Bushmire running interference for me, I probably would never have made it through high school. Thus, without a good basic educational foundation, especially in math, I went off to college ill prepared.

Someone once wrote *I learned everything I needed to know in kindergarten.* I feel the same about learning to be an engineer or, for that matter, any trade that comes naturally to a person.

Between what my dad taught me building up electronic components as I held the parts while he soldered them in place and what I learned tinkering with all my junk, I was probably a pretty darn good design engineer by the time I was sixteen.

First car, a 1940 Ford Tudor in rework, before and after; Whizzer Sportsman; 1954 Ford Sedan I rollover not a scratch; passenger in 1941 Buick Sedan convertible head-on crash no seatbelts and nearly killed; Model A Ford I had till high school grad; 1939 Packard and 1937 Ford Stockcar in buildup; 1939 Lincoln Zephyr 3-window coupe with V-12 engine; my second car and favorite of all then and ever since.

Chapter Four
TRIMOTORS TO UFOs

During the summer of 1950, my folks decided we would take a weekend trip up to Sandusky, Ohio. The short trip, which I wasn't particularly interested in making with them and my kid brother, was to include a life-long memorable experience. I had grown up around airplanes, but had never gotten the chance to fly in one. Airliners hadn't yet become as common a means of transportation as they are today. People either traveled by car or took the train on most long distance trips.

The second day of the trip, we happened upon an airfield close to Lake Erie. As usual, I asked to stop and look at the airplanes. A local air service flew Ford Trimotors out of the field over to Put-in-Bay, a small island community off the shore of Canada. For a small fee, one could ride over and back on the Trimotor's daily mail run for a short sightseeing trip.

Some of my friends had flown before and had told me when you're flying high up in the sky everything looks like a miniature world, cars looked like models and people looked like ants. I wanted to see this for myself, so I pleaded for permission to take the ride in the Trimotor. Mom was against it, but dad said the boy's bent on flying one of these days so it might as well be now and I was off on my first flying adventure.

My First Airplane Ride

Upon boarding, I went forward to sit in the seat just behind the pilot's cabin. The copilot's seat was empty. When the pilot boarded, he was wearing mechanic's overalls, not an airline uniform. I was hoping he would ask me if I'd like to sit in the empty copilot's seat, but it didn't happen.

The ol' Ford Trimotor rolled down the grass airstrip at 80 mph and lifted effortlessly into the air. Cars, buildings and roads passed under the wings and soon we were in the realm of the birds. Before long, we were up among the clouds and out over Lake Erie like Gulliver taking giant steps. Trees and buildings were no longer obstacles as we had wings upon which to ride.

Terry and the Pirates comic strip drawn by Milton Caniff; Ford Trimotor, first airplane flight Island Air Service Sandusky, Ohio; rare formation of B-36 shortly before retired; Earl at Will Rogers Air Show, one of a kind C-99 in background.

The Trimotor landed on a small airfield on the island. We didn't deplane. The pilot went to the back, handed some stuff out to a person on the ground and we took off again for the return flight to the mainland. The noisy ol' Trimotor climbed at 80 mph, cruised at 80 mph and landed at 80 mph, at least that was the way it seemed to me. From where I was seated, I could see the instruments on the panel, but not well enough to read.

I spent most of my time pasted up against the side window. I cannot remember all the details of the flight on that day, but there is one thing, which I do clearly remember. It was on that very day I decided flying was everything I had ever expected it to be. Somehow I was going to learn to fly and that flying would become part of my life.

The Ford Trimotor came into existence as the outgrowth of Jack "Knife" Stout's all-metal aircraft designs. Edsel Ford, interested in expanding Ford's business into aviation, convinced Henry to purchased Stout's company as a means to that end.

The Ford Trimotor model 5-ATB went into service in 1929 and flew the Mexico and Central American routes for Pan American Airways until 1936. Nicknamed the Tin Goose, the Trimotors originally sold for $55,000 and were powered by three Pratt & Whitney Wasp engines. The aircraft had a top speed of 122 mph and could fly 500 miles with 13 passengers without refueling. A few of these aircraft are still flying today.

Airlines soon turned to the Douglas DC-3 and the Lockheed Vega series aircraft for passenger flights due to their higher speeds and greater payloads. For all practical purposes, Ford Motor Company's commercial aviation enterprises ended with the Tin Goose. However, during WW II, the aircraft division of Ford produced hundreds of B-24 Liberator bombers from the Willow Run plant in Michigan.

The Two UFOs I Saw

On a hot summer evening in the early 1950s, in the city park across the street from our house on Central Avenue, a ballgame was in progress on a lighted diamond at the far end of the park. A gang of us had been having a water fight at the park fountain. After awhile, everyone except my girlfriend and I wandered over to the ball field. We were lying on the grass, looking up at the stars.

In the night sky, just to the right of the Portland Cement Plant, coming toward us, were what appeared to be two aircraft flying in formation each with a single landing-light on. One was slightly ahead of the other. Being familiar with the traffic patterns in the area, I knew these aircraft were not on a normal approach to either Patterson or Wright Fields.

I was also familiar with the different sounds various types of aircraft made and could often tell the plane by the sound of its engine. I listened for the sound. There was none. This is not overly odd, as wind can delay an approaching sound. Problem was, there was only a light breeze that evening.

Helicopters, like the Sikorsky H-5, were not widely used at this time and were primitive at best. Never the less, I considered maybe that was what we were observing because they appeared to be flying much too slow for an airplane. This too is not unusual. There is a phenomenon that will make an approaching aircraft appear to stand still. This occurs when the aircraft is coming directly at the observer and descending at the same time. But, this too was not the case.

The two lights, mostly white with a bluish glow around the edges, grew from a point of light to a slightly oval shape as they came closer and we continued to watch. The people in the ballpark probably couldn't see the objects because of the bright lights on the field. My girlfriend and I were a good distance away from the ballpark, so it was pretty dark where we were.

The objects came closer. I would estimate about a quarter mile away and about 30 degrees up elevation. There was now enough ambient light from the ball field lights and the light emanating from the objects to clearly see they were not aircraft. The light emanating from the objects began to pulsate as they slowed to a full stop and appeared to be about the size of a mid-size airplane flying at 2,000 feet or a small airplane at 1,500 feet above the ground.

We were standing now, our eyes fixed on the two objects. Never will I forget the eerie feeling of thinking that something or someone was looking back at us.

The objects moved closer and paused again. They were now at about 1,000 feet, about 45 degrees up. The objects were just beyond the railroad tracks to the north of the park. I thought, surely by now I should be able to hear some kind of sound to identify the type of craft, but there was still none.

Suddenly, both objects went straight up to a point directly overhead in a fast count of ten. The objects were easily seen against the clear, black night sky. They appeared to be about the size of a bright star and were still traveling together. At their highest apex, both made a sudden 90-degree turn and disappeared eastward over the horizon in about a minute.

The next day, I described to my dad exactly what I had witnessed the night before. Knowing that he had a secret clearance, he might not tell me what it was, but at least he might tell me that I wasn't seeing things and that the technology for such an aircraft did exist.

Dad assured me that he believed what I was telling him, but nothing that he knew of could fly the way I described. Time has born this out. The truth seems to be that nothing known at that time and possibly even today could fly the way I saw those two objects fly that night.

My classmate Roger, an Air Force general's son, told me he had gotten into his dad's briefcase and read a report about three little gray men who had been brought to Wright Field for investigation. This was not too long after the purported alien space ship crash incident near Roswell, New Mexico. That rumor also ran rampant throughout the area for several years.

The UFO sightings I experienced occurred after similar objects were spotted over the capitol in Washington DC. Those were seen on radar. About the time we witnessed the UFOs in the park at Fairborn, numerous incidents of other Unidentified Flying Objects were being reported. As time progressed, these sightings were not seen on radar. Thus, either confirmation reports were suppressed or the UFOs went to radar stealthing.

Major Kehoe, a Marine Corps pilot, wrote a book on the UFO phenomenon entitled *Flying Saucers are Real*. That book best explains what I saw and fits many of the rumors I heard.

Explorer Scout Sesquicentennial Air Encampment at Clinton County AFB, second airplane ride in C-46; guard duty at Cox Municipal Dayton International Air show, 1953.

Air Scouts

The Scouting program, from Cubs to Explorers, was an important part of my life growing up. Little league baseball and other organized youth sports were not as prevalent as they are today. The only supervised activities available outside of school were at the YMCA and in the Boy Scout programs. Beginning with Cub Scouts, I worked my way through the Cub, Bear and Lion ranks. From Webelos, I joined Scout Troop 54.

There I learned about camping, canoeing, knot tying and all the things that sharpen your survival skills. We camped out at John Bryan State Park a couple times a year. The park was a glacier terminal moraine, which made it a great place to go exploring. I worked my way up merit badge by merit badge to Life Scout and also earned the God and Country Award.

However, it wasn't until I joined an Explorer Post that met at Patterson Field that I found my niche. This particular Explorer Post was one of the first Air Scout squadrons formed and was kind of an experimental program. Regular Explorer Post scouts wore the dark green khakis. Our Air Explorer uniforms were sky blue khakis with a dark blue tie and belt, a wonder to behold and we were proud of them. Air Scout merit badges were rectangle in shape with a blue background instead of round. I completed the rest of the requirements for Eagle Scout and was awarded the Explorer Silver Eagle.

Our squadron leader was an Air Force Captain by the name of Dinsmore. Captain Dinsmore's hobby was building model airplanes. On one particular control-line model, he mounted a ram jet engine that was a miniature version of the V-1 buzz bomb. Compressed air was blown into the intake in order to get the spring steel flapper valve in the engine started. It was flown by control cables and went like a bat-out-a-hell for about three times around the circle before running out of gas.

The first control wire model that I built completed one and a half turns before I over controlled and crashed it into the ground, disintegrating it into dozens of un-repairable pieces.

On a winter night, our squadron camped out on the game reservation behind Patterson Field. About midnight I got up to take a leak and it had started to snow. Before dark, we had explored a crashed aircraft parts dump near our camp. Recalling a fighter cockpit canopy laying on the ground, I

45

went to get it, dragged the canopy back to where I had bedded down and placed it over the top of my sleeping bag. When morning came, the rest of the guys woke up covered with snow. I was snug, warm and sound asleep with the sun shining in on my Plexiglas cockpit shelter.

That summer, the Semi-Centennial of Explorer Scouting encampment was held at Clinton County AFB. As part of the event we were all treated to an airplane ride. Donning our parachutes, we boarded several Air Force C-46 Commando transports. The best part was we all got to go forward and look in the cockpit while we were flying. This was my second airplane ride and now I was an old hand at this flying thing.

The Annual Dayton Air Show, a worldwide event, was also held that summer. Explorer Scouts were invited to an encampment and asked to volunteer to help with the show. The air show sponsors housed us in Army field tents on the airport grounds and provided us with AP helmets and white belts. Talk about crowd control; we parked cars, directed traffic and guarded the aircraft on display with resolute dedication.

Nobody parked where we didn't want them to park! General Eisenhower once remarked that General Patton would have made a good New York City traffic cop. After that week at the air show, the same could have been said for us Air Explorer Scouts.

Piper Tri-Pacer Demo

On a summer afternoon in 1952, my second or third girlfriend rode with me in my '40 Ford out to the Vandalia Municipal Airport were the local Piper dealer was located. I had no idea how I would pay for flying lessons, but I was intent on taking my first lesson.

Firmly, but politely, I was told by the man at the Piper office that I was too young to enroll in flying school because their insurance wouldn't cover me.

I explained, "I've been up in a large airplane a couple of times, but never flown in a small airplane. I'd sure like to."

The salesman, whom I assume was also an instructor pilot, smiled and handed me a coupon that read, "Five-dollar special introductory offer for prospective airplane buyers. A demo flight in the new Piper Tri-Pacer."

46

It took a moment for the light bulb to go off in my head before saying, "Hey, that's it, the special introductory flight offer. That's what I'm here for!"

That afternoon, I went for my third ride aloft and for my first flight at the controls of a private plane. The pilot let me take the wheel and make a few shallow turns and I watched his every move flying the plane.

When the pilot pulled the power back for landing, my girlfriend sitting in the back seat, was sure the engine had quit and she screamed out. I kept my cool though because I knew airplanes were able to glide without power.

The term "stall" applied to an airplane is the most commonly misunderstood of all aviation terms. Non-flyers think of it like stalling a car on the railroad track, but a stall in an airplane occurs when the air flowing over the wing stalls and the wing no longer generates upward lift on the airplane.

Developing sideways lift by air flowing over an airfoil is the principle used by sailing ships for thousands of years. It was only in modern times that lift was understood well enough to apply it to an aircraft for obtaining upward lift.

The Piper Tri-Pacer airplane that I first flew was the tricycle gear, post-war version of the Piper Pacer. The new plane was considerably easier to land than its tail-dragger cousin. The plane is so stable it will stall in straight and level flight and fall out of the sky at an excessive rate of descent. Pilots refer to this level flight stall phenomenon as a horizontal stall. When planes of this type stall, they do not buffet and dip the nose as is the case with most airplanes.

Piper's tandem monoplane, the Cub, had established Piper in the light aircraft business before the war. The designs for early Piper aircraft were for the most part those of Clarence G. Taylor, the founder and builder of the Taylorcraft as well as the Cub. Looking into the history of the Taylorcraft, one will discover that W.T. Piper was the secretary-treasurer of the Taylorcraft Corporation. Piper was just a much shrewder businessman and his company survived when others failed.

Packard On The Road

By 1952, new cars were readily available. The new body designs were impressive and old cars were plentiful. At one point, I owned three cars in varying stages of rebuild. However, none of them were running, so I bought a '38 Packard Sedan for $50. Today that car would be considered a high dollar classic.

The girl I had gone with for about a year moved away with her divorced mother to Ashland, Kentucky down on the Ohio River. I decided to take the Packard on a road trip to visit her. During the summer, I had been using a thick motor oil so as not to burn so much. It was a cold, fall day and the engine was probably not oiling properly. About halfway there, the Packard's old flathead straight-eight engine let out one loud clank and screeched to a stop.

The highway on which the Packard had chosen to blow itself up was the main road into Chillicothe, Ohio. As I stood looking under the hood at the hole in the side of the block where the connecting rod exited, a wrecker driver stopped to ask if he might be of assistance. The going rate for a wrecker tow was $12.50. How much I asked, negotiating with the driver, did he think the Packard would bring for junk. He thought because it was a heavy car it might scrap out for as much as $25.

The deal we finally settled on was that the wrecker driver would give me $10 cash for bus fare to Ashland and tow the Packard away. I threw in the remaining half gallon of oil in the Packard's trunk as part of the deal. With the Packard in tow, the wrecker driver delivered me, my toolbox and my suitcase to the Chillicothe bus station.

I had a small portable radio with me because the Packard's radio didn't work. I recall riding on that nearly empty bus listening to my radio. It was the first time I had ever heard the song *Earth Angel*, still one of my favorites. Even now when I hear that song, it reminds me of that trip. This story makes me think of the old joke about the guy who went to Las Vegas in a $10,000 Cadillac and came home in a $200,000 Greyhound bus.

Aero Class Canceled

Bath Township was a backwater school system ill qualified to educate the influx of the widely traveled Air Force brats. Academics at

Fairborn High School where I attended were sorry at best. Roger, the one whose dad was a general, and I got up a petition with forty names on it to start an aeronautics class.

We were promised that the class would begin in the fall and a textbook for the course was selected. When we showed up for class the first day, we were told that the class had been cancelled. No reason was given, but it is likely that the same backwards thinking that prevented auto mechanics from being taught at our school was what prevented the aero class.

The best book I ever read on how to fly an airplane was a 6x8 paperback with a silver-blue cover. The black and white, cartoon-like drawings were of two guys flying a two-seated, open cockpit pusher airplane with a twin tail boom. The guy in the ball cap was explaining to this rotund kid how an airplane flies. Wish I still had a copy of that old paperback.

Fly Royal Canadian

Remembering all those old movies where Americans joined the Royal Canadian Air Force (RCAF) to fly with the British, I thought that sounded pretty glamorous so I wrote to Canada asking how to enlist in their pilot training program.

The answer I received was that while they appreciated the Americans who had volunteered to fly with them during WW II, they were no longer accepting U.S. citizens into the RCAF.

Wright Memorial

A favorite place for us teenagers to gather on a Sunday afternoon was up at the Wright Brothers Memorial. The memorial is located atop a wooded hillside just behind Wright Field on the hill not far from where the Wrights flew their early test gliders. The hillside also overlooks Huffman Dam that was built in 1922 to protect Dayton from flood disasters like the one that nearly destroyed the city in 1913.

Huffman Prairie, where Huffman Dam is presently located, was named for the Huffman family farm originally located there. It was on this prairie in 1904 the Wright Flyer completed its first full-circle flight. The Wright Brothers' located their first flying school and hangar at the site.

Some of the dirt was taken from the floor of the old flying field hangar and placed in the foundation of the memorial.

The inscription on the Wright Brothers Memorial contains a sentence to the effect that the development of the Wright aeroplane and of the aileron brought about modern aviation. The structure of that sentence always troubled me because it implies that the Wrights invented the aileron control. They did not. They used a method known as wing warping to bank the Wright Flyer. Actually, Glen Curtis used his development of the aileron to circumvent the Wright brothers attempt to patent the airplane. Wing warping is more akin to the way a bird flies, but mechanically it is harder to replicate.

An inscription with an arrow on the wall around the memorial site points toward the Huffman Prairie flying school. It was there that some of the earliest aviators were taught to fly. Henry "Hap" Arnold, who became head of the Army Air Corps in 1938, was taught to fly by Orville Wright there. As was RAF Flying Officer Brown, who became famous for downing the Red Baron's crimson Fokker tri-wing during the First World War.

The Real Heroes

In an area between Wright and Patterson airfields, several large tracts of land were used for planting Victory Gardens. During the war years, people were encouraged to grow their own vegetables. Not everyone had enough land to make a garden so land in common was divided into plots and loaned to persons wishing to plant and tend their own gardens. The practice of planting these gardens continued for years after the war.

One weekend, a jet fighter approaching Patterson Field experienced a flameout. The pilot set up a normal glide to make a forced landing onto what he thought was an open field. As he approached the field, he saw dozens of people working in their gardens. Pulling up to miss the startled gardeners, the aircraft stalled and crashed into rougher terrain beyond the open field. The pilot saved many lives that day, but paid the ultimate sacrifice for his compassion. He was a true hero.

Patterson AFB Flight Ops

Many of the generals flying into Patterson Field parked their airplanes at the operations ramp just down from Gate One. I especially remember seeing Doolittle's B-17 parked there. It had polished chrome props and his general's stars were painted just under the pilot's cockpit window.

Yes, I know General Doolittle was famous for flying B-25s in the raid over Tokyo, but his postwar AF personal aircraft was a plushed-out B-17. Doolittle remarked many times that he felt that it was his Boy Scout training that helped him and his men survive their ordeal in China after the famous raid on Japan. This made me proud to hear a man like General Doolittle praise the Scouting program.

It was at this same operations ramp I'd pick up my dad when he'd return from a long business trip inspecting military aircraft manufacturers. The last time I remember picking him up from a flight, he climbed out of a B-25 that had been converted to a passenger carrier by sealing the bomb-bay doors and adding seats and upholstery.

As Dad unsnapped his parachute harness, he indicated that they had come through some really bad weather and that he'd had it with flying. He said this trip had worn him out and he thought he would just take the Santa Fe Chief on his next trip. He may have flown a few more times after that, but I think that was pretty much the end of his flying days.

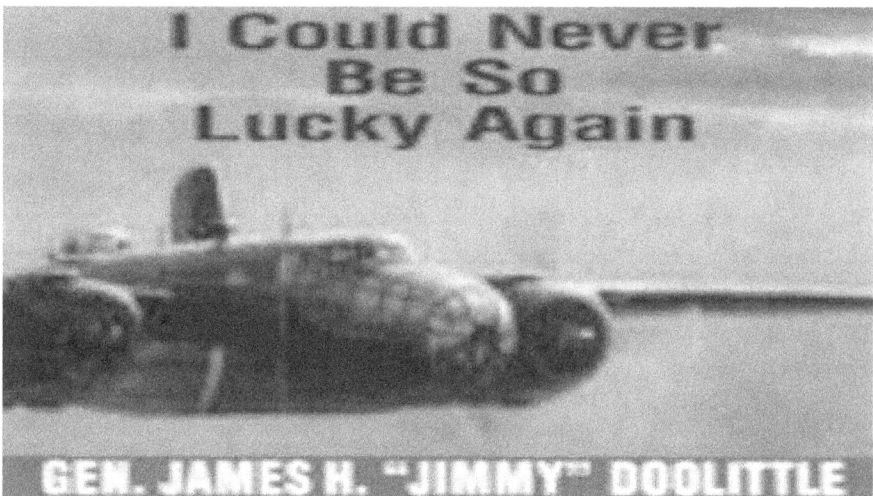

I Could Never Be So Lucky Again

GEN. JAMES H. "JIMMY" DOOLITTLE

Explorer Scout Troop and retirement as scout master; F-84 Thunderbolt on Patterson Field ramp; mock-up of Wright Pusher and recent picture of Wright Memorial; overlooking Huffman Dam from Wright Memorial, picture on right and on left were taken forty-five years apart.

Chapter Five
SOMEWHERE WEST OF EDEN

In 1954, my dad was transferred to Tinker Air Force Base in Midwest City, Oklahoma. The ol' Zephyr really wasn't in good enough shape to make the trip, so I parted with it for the same $200 I originally paid for it and boarded a train for Oklahoma.

Mom and my brother stayed in Ohio to sell the house on Central Avenue and pack to move. St. Louis was the main hub for changing trains in the Midwest. Travelers would take the Penn Central to St. Louis via an overnight Pullman and change to the Santa Fe Chief the next morning. Even in the mid '50s, almost all government-furnished transportation was still by rail.

Tinker Air Force Base was a main depot for Air Material Command and dad was taking over as Chief of Procurement for electronics. He had played a major role in bringing airborne radar to its airborne operational capability and instrumental in developing and procuring the P-61 Black Widow and P-69 Scorpion night fighters for the Air Force.

B-47s, trailing drag chutes behind them, would shoot practice approaches at Tinker. Dad commented, "If a plane can fly pulling a chute behind it, that's proof of when you apply enough power to anything, you can make it fly."

Midwest City High

The new high school was a far better school than the one I had just left and I completed my senior year there. Roger's dad had been transferred to Tinker AFB two years before and he had written to tell me how much better MCHS was than our high school in Fairborn.

There must be an unwritten rule somewhere that the new kid is going to be picked on. Earlier on, I found that if I could whip the bullies, usually by dragging my opponent to the ground, I wouldn't have to fight

53

the rest. I had been on the wrestling team for several years, but big enough now to slug it out.

While we waited on a teacher to come to class, some hood was sticking a switchblade knife into the wooden desktop. He had been trying to pick a fight with me earlier. I told him to put away the knife and if he didn't he was a coward. A lot of kids had gathered to watch, so he put the knife away and came at me. I mostly just boxed him, using long jabs to keep from getting hit in the jaw, as I didn't want that broken again.

The fight drew a bigger crowd as kids came from other classes. We knocked down every portable desk chair in the room. Actually, the kid wasn't much of a fighter. My right of passage was granted. I was no longer the new kid in town.

In order to graduate, I needed one more elective class and I enrolled in a half-year photojournalism course. From an early age, I had taken quite a collection of black and white photos with my Ansco 620 camera. I entered and won several statewide photo competitions. What I learned working in the photo lab would come in handy later getting my first aircraft company job.

Rock Around The Clock

The University of Okalahoma, down the road in Norman, had been unbeaten in football for several years. One of the players who graduated the year before me at MCHS had left his '29 Model A Ford coupe with a rumble seat at home. The car was original except for the addition of '35 Ford red spoke wheels and balloon tires. I bought it for $50. With the car he was furnished by his college sponsor, I'm sure he didn't need the old Ford. It wasn't my old Zephyr, but it was a great little car. At 60 mph, the occupants had to yell to talk over the noise.

Rumors had been going around about a new kind of music by Bill Haley and the Comets. On the night the movie *Blackboard Jungle* opened, several of us drove my ol' Model A to downtown Oklahoma City to see it. The theater was packed. Nobody was much interested in the movie, everyone had come to hear the movie's opening theme song *Rock Around the Clock*.

The class of '55 ushered in the beginning of Rock and Roll. We called it the dirty-boogie at first, a holdover from the '40s term boogie-woogie, and later the dirty-bop. That spring, we went to see some guy named Elvis who was the warm-up act for Hank Snow down at the Municipal Auditorium. The audience laughed and made fun of him when he stopped and combed his jet-black hair in the middle of a song. Some of the girls wanted to go backstage and meet this guy, so we all hung around while they visited with him. Elvis was only one year older than myself and none of us suspected he'd ever be famous.

At graduation, the senior class willed my mouth to anyone who could get my foot out of it and predicted that I would become the DJ at a bootleg honky-tonk strip joint out on 23rd Street. What happened to my classmates that coming fall sounded like the ending to *American Graffiti*. Berry went to West Point. Brewster played quarterback for OU and the pros. Ralph and Chuck became smokejumpers, but Ralph eventually return home and ended up running his dad's old furniture store. Anita Bryant, Ralph's sister's friend, became a popular singer and later owned her own music theater in Branson, Missouri.

How I Spent My Summer Vacation

The summer I graduated from MCHS, I caught a ride out of Tinker Ops on Wernher von Braun's personal C-54. I was on my way to Dayton to visit Larry and look up an old girlfriend, but von Braun's plane was headed to Washington, D.C., close enough.

When we departed that evening, von Braun had already gone to his private cabin to sleep. I wanted very much to visit with von Braun. I told his aide I was a schoolmate of von Braun's nephew and asked if I could see him, but his aide refused to disturb the most famous rocket man in the world.

We landed at Bowling Green airbase on the Potomac River and it was my first time to see the Capitol. There was a regular run between D.C. and Wright-Patterson AFB each day called the Kitty Hawk flight. I missed the flight for that day, but hopefully I'd get on tomorrow's flight. Dad's cousin, Roy, was a Lieutenant Colonel now assigned to the Pentagon. I called Roy. He picked me up and drove me around D.C. sightseeing, as it was my first time there. I spent the night at his family's house.

The next morning, Roy walked me out to the front of the Pentagon to a boat dock where the Navy ran a modified PT boat as a shuttlecraft up and down the Potomac. The C-47 used on the Kitty Hawk run that day was WW II vintage complete with canvas jump seats. It was a hot, bumpy ride all the way and there were everything from buck-privates to generals on the flight.

After knocking around Ohio for a couple of weeks, it was time to head home. At Patterson Operations, I bird-dogged up a couple of Military Air Transport Service (MATS) pilots who were waiting on some cargo to be loaded onto their C-47. They were headed for Topeka, Kansas, but said they'd be going to Tinker from Topeka the next day and I could hitch a ride with them. Look on any map, up in the corner where the little fat-faced guy is puffing wind, right there where the edge of the earth falls off is where you look to find Topeka, Kansas. I spent a week there one evening.

University BMOC

That fall, I enrolled at the University of Oklahoma. My first year at OU was not a pleasant experience. All freshman, including the frat-rat pledges, had to stay in the dorms their first year. The dorms literally became a battleground between the pledges and independent students. I was rushed by Sigma Chi and it would have been my choice, but the money would be better put to use on a new set of wheels in my opinion.

At freshman orientation, the president said, "Look to your left and to your right. If you graduate from this university, that person will not be here." What a jerk to say it, but that's the way things were. The state schools tried to flunk you out in your first year or two to reduce the enrollment.

This seemed to be my year for screw-ups because I married a girl I had dated at Midwest City high school and it lasted only a couple of weeks before we went our separate ways.

I also made the mistake of enrolling in Business Administration thinking it a fast, easy way to a Bachelor's Degree, but my natural talents lay in the technical fields. As it turned out, the bookkeeping and management courses I did take were useful in later years when *Peter's Principle* kicked in and I was promoted to management or some other level of incompetence and again when I started several of my own businesses.

Heartbreak Hotel

Across the street from the main OU campus was a popular record shop. Browsing the record racks after class one day, I came across a new 45 rpm record. "Hey, isn't this that guy Elvis Presley, the one we saw down at the Municipal Auditorium last year?" I bought the record.

My third floor dorm room faced the Quadrangle courtyard and at infrequent intervals, I'd mount my Webcor hi-fi in the window, crank the sound all the way up and put Elvis' record on playing only the one phrase, "It was down at the end of lonely street," would echo down the canyon of dorms. Before anyone could pinpoint the origin of the sound, the Webcor would be shutoff and taken out of the window. Elvis and the phantom hi-fi became a campus legend.

On a sunny spring afternoon of my second semester, three water bombs in rapid succession hit two campus cops walking down the dorm sidewalk. The two cops took off up the dorm stairs to extort revenge on the perpetrator.

A large crowd of male students gathered on the Quadrangle courtyard as the two cops went from room to room. Rumors had been going around for weeks about plans for a panty raid on the girl's dorm. Panty raids were the rage at other universities and OU didn't want to be left out.

In short time, hundreds of dorm students were milling around yelling, "Panty raid!" The crowd, lacking leadership and courage, drifted towards the girl's dorms and back again. At that point the campus cops arrived in full force.

Mobs, I learned, take on a character separate from their individual parts. The police chief's hat was taken and tossed about the crowd. Then a small group of guys started rocking one of the campus police cars to turn it over. At that point, I decided retreat was the better part of valor and I got the heck out of there.

It was my surface Navy drill night and I needed to get into my uniform to attend. Climbing the stairs to my third floor dorm room, I heard the fire alarm go off. Someone had pulled the fire call box lever. Looking out my dorm room window, I was watching this crazy crowd from above when two fire engines rounded the corner with sirens screaming.

That's when something, almost dangerous, became one of the funniest things I've ever seen. That mass of testosterone filled humanity scattered in a hundred different directions. Everyone figured the fire trucks had been called by the cops to turn the hoses on them and most didn't want any part of it. I was still laughing as I left to attend drill at the USN Reserve Center.

Texas Oil Fields

The summer between my freshman and sophomore years at OU, my Uncle Raymond got me a job working for Amerada Oil Company in Big Lake, Texas. I needed the job for money to go back to school and child support for a daughter named Vickey by the girl I had been married to briefly.

I had sold the Model A when I went off to college, so in order to get to my new job, I bought a really used '49 Hudson to make the trip south. The morning I left, I stopped at Housing Services Insurance Agency to buy liability insurance and a young lady in a cashmere sweater, high-heels and full skirt with about three petticoats under the skirt, typed up the policy for me.

In casual conversation, she mentioned she had grown up in Dayton, Ohio and I told her I had lived in Fairborn. How was I to know that the following New Year's Eve she would be my blind-date and we would be married six-weeks later?

Pulling into the oil field camp just outside of Big Lake, I spotted an old Spartan aluminum trailer. Needing a place to stay, I asked the camp manager if anyone was living in it and he told me no and I was welcome to it for the summer.

After I removed a layer of dirt from the inside of the trailer and chased all the lizards out, I was ready to call it home. I was told the hot water tank would explode if I left it lit, so I'd only light it in the evenings to take a shower and wash my cooking utensils.

It didn't take long to settle into the oil field routine. We worked six days sunup to sundown and off Sundays. On Sundays, I'd drive the '49 Hudson into town, go to church and mess around. The oil field culture rounded out my education.

The first rule on a drilling rig was that the toughest guy gets to be driller, the rig boss. Climbing on a new rig one day, I noticed a trash can with the word TRSH painted on it and I asked one of the roughnecks, "Who painted that?"

He replied, "The driller did," and I asked why he didn't tell the driller how to spell it correctly. His reply was short and concise, "You go tell him."

I worked as a roustabout, plumbing tanks. Rattlesnakes were plentiful in that part of the country and you got used to hitting the third step on a tank ladder, as they liked to nest under the first step. I also learned to shake out my boots in the morning before putting them on to get the scorpions out.

On payday, a floating crap game usually developed. It cost me a few bucks to learn that there are people who will palm the regular dice and throw a pair of loaded dice when it's their roll. Watch the shooter's buddies because if his friends drop out for a round or bet light, they know what he's doing.

When working a new well, we hauled the tanks and pipe on old flatbed tractor-trailer trucks. The speed we drove was determined by when the accelerator pedal contacted the floorboard. Routinely, we'd drive 75 plus miles to a well site. If needing to take a leak or change drivers, we'd just keep rolling, open the door, climb out, walk around the back of the cab and get back in on the other side.

Most of the time, to reach a new well site, we'd drive across the landscape. In southwest Texas, there's a lot of mesquite scrub with large thorns that'll puncture a tire. During my stay in the oil fields that summer, I changed my share of flats on those old split-ring truck tires.

One hot afternoon, we were connecting pipe using three-foot adjustable winches and this roughneck, who referred to me as the college-boy, began telling me I wasn't working fast enough to suit him. "You can kiss my backside," I told him. He took exception to my comment and knocked me off my feet with one punch. He laughed and turned to walk off.

When I got to my feet. I grabbed a long handled shovel off a flatbed truck and went after him. Expecting to bring him to his knees, he turned and looked at me. There I stood, holding a eighteen-inch piece of handle that used to be a shovel. "Oh S..."

That roughneck broke my nose, blacked both my eyes and hurt me bad, but I was still swinging when the crew broke up the fight, probably only to keep me from getting beat-up worse.

After an overnight in the small local hospital and having time to reflect on the incident, I realized that no matter how tough I thought I was, there was always going to be one more guy who was just a little meaner and tougher than I was. Thus, I resolved from that day forward, I was going to become a lover and a diplomat. My tough guy days were over.

Jack London, a young Presbyterian minister and I became good friends. Some nights, Jack would go to that part of town where the bars were and spend time talking to the forgotten men. So as not to be shunned, Jack would buy a beer, pop the top and sit on the curb holding it as he talked with them. He was a true man of God and I think of him as a mentor. I'm sure he eventually returned home back East somewhere to a congregation where he was far more appreciated.

Reverend London's small church was next door to the town's airfield. A fine lady I met years later had grown up in Big Lake and learned to fly her father's airplane. When WW II started, she volunteered to join the Women's Army Pilot Service. Florene Watson became the commanding officer of the unit based at Dallas Love Field. She and the ladies who served with her flew every type of AAC airplane delivered, but Florene always claimed her favorite was the P-51. The airport in Big Lake is named for her.

Last Air Show

The Oklahoma City airport sponsored a giant air show that fall. Dad and I went to the show and spent the whole day. It was the only time I ever saw the C-99, a cargo transport version of the B-36. During the show, a formation of six B-36s made a flyover and that was very impressive. My dad died of a sudden heart attack that November and in my mind, I will always think of that B-36 flyover as a final salute to my father.

The Girl From Ohio

Mom decided she wanted to move to a different house after dad died. We found a place she liked in the same area of Midwest City. I moved home and commuted to college. The young lady, who had written my car insurance when I had left for West Texas, now lived five doors down. Suzanne Burrows had taken a vacation from Ohio to visit her aunt. Her aunt's husband, an AF Sergeant stationed at Tinker, was leaving for Germany. Her aunt asked her if she'd like to stay with her while he was away and she did.

Suzanne, whom everyone called Tudy, graduated from Fairview High School in Dayton only a few miles from where I had gone to school in Fairborn. She was a Sigma Delta and popular with her classmates. I, of course, was the original lone eagle, hot rod and motorcycle hood.

It had been a good thing we hadn't met in high school, as she wouldn't have had anything to do with me. In fact, the first time I saw the movie *Grease*, I remarked that I wasn't aware they had made a movie about our high school years.

We went on our first date that New Year's Eve. Our second date was to the Air Force Ball at OU where Tex Beneke's band was playing and on our third date, I took her flying in a Taylorcraft BC12. I didn't even have a pilot's license yet.

When I went to make out her nametag at a church dinner, she hadn't told me that her nickname was Tudy and I wasn't sure how she spelled Suzanne. I wrote down Suzie on her nametag and she's gone by that name ever since. We were married that February.

By spring, Suzie was carrying our daughter and she wanted to return to Dayton to be with her mother and sister to have her child. Our courting car had been a '53 Studebaker sports model Champion, which I had repainted black. I traded the sports car for a '55 Ford station wagon, loaded up everything we owned and we left for Ohio.

The Dragon Lady

Dickson Talbott, Suzie's father, had a dance band in the 1930s, but had worked Aeroproducts, a division of General Motors, since the beginning of WW II. Aeroproducts made propellers for the P-39 Bell

Airacobra, Fairchild C-82 and other aircraft. Dickson became Director of the Miami Valley Civil Defense after retiring from Aeroproducts.

The Civil Defense owned a Cessna 182, but I don't think Dick ever flew in the plane. He told me one time he had enough flying, on flight-test flights at Aeroproducts in those old Fairchild C-119 Flying Boxcars, to last him a lifetime.

Milton Caniff, who drew the cartoon, *Terry and the Pirates* and Dickson had gone through school together. Both were members of a private athletic fraternity called the Ten Tigers. The Dragon Lady, one of the characters in *Terry and The Pirates* was always rumored to be based on General Claire Lee Chennault's wife who was Chinese. Possibly not true, however.

Suzie and her mother always claimed the Dragon Lady had been patterned after an oriental lady who Milton and Dickson knew growing up. The real Dragon Lady, it seems, was a Dayton local lady who had lived out her life not far from the neighborhood were Suzie had grown up.

Dad's An Entrepreneur

For a brief period of time before returning to Oklahoma, we stayed with Suzie's folks at the home where Suzie had grown up on Merrimac Avenue in the north part of Dayton. Suzie had wanted to remain in Ohio to be close to her mother and sister until her baby was born.

It was during this time that I designed a set of private pilot's wings and had them dye-cast. Advertising in *Flying* magazine, I sold hundreds of those silver wings.

The design was the standard bird wings with a center shield and a silhouette of the Wright Pusher aeroplane overlaying the shield. The wings were made of sterling silver and the few, still in existence, have become collectors' items.

When our daughter, Laura, was born in May, I wrote self-employed in the blank for employer on the hospital paperwork. This I am sure was a precursor indication of my many future careers as an entrepreneur.

It was now the post Korean War and pre Viet Nam era. The military was downsizing and the waiting list to get into Naval Cadets and flight school was at least a year. I might as well go back to college. Soon after

Laura was born, we returned to Midwest City and I enrolled in the summer session at college.

There Is A Creek

For many years we returned from time to time to visit Suzie's folks. The hill that Suzie walked up going to grade school was called Wampler's hill. When we visited, I would often take long walks down by a creek that fed into the Miami River and I wrote the following poem on the banks of that small creek.

"There is a creek that runs near a place at the foot of Wampler's hill. A creek that I have visited many times, and it runs there still. A place, in memory seems, not to be as real.

There is a rise in the street where I taught her sis to drive a stick shift Ford. The houses here are like gingerbread, the kind workingmen can afford.

I walk down by the creek at the end of Merrimac, when I am there. And think of a little girl with skinny legs and brunette hair. She climbed this hill to go to school and played along the creek right here.

I have walked this creek with wife and child, kin and friend and talked together about how life begins and how it ends. At the top of the hill, we said goodbye to the leader of the band.

There are things we ask ourselves as we walk beside this wooded stream. Things that we do not understand, perhaps the questions are not what they seem. We think of times we should have given of ourselves, and of goals we only dream.

In summer we are like the children who played here and built a fort. Now in autumn we wonder how our lives will fair in God's grand court.

In times gone by, I paid no attention to the creek that runs there still. Now I stop to look with different eyes along this creek, I guess I always will. Our lives are like this creek that runs to the foot of Wampler's hill."

Air Force Museum Wright Field in Dayton, Ohio; building two interior, started in a bone yard at Wood City in the '40s and grew into a must see airplane buff tourist attraction; main outdoor display ramp; B-50 bomber; B-1 bomber; North American XB-70 Valkyrie only surviving one of two built; P-40; Curtiss; Korean era helicopter.

Chapter Six
LEARNING TO FLY

Max Westheimer Field at Norman, Oklahoma, had been a Navy flight-training base during WW II. The large dirt mounds used for machine gun training were still at the far west end of the airfield. The land was granted to the University of Oklahoma by the government after the Navy pulled out in the late 1940s. A few private aircraft and the University of Oklahoma Flying Club were the only aircraft that used the airfield.

As an OU student, I was eligible to join the flying club and did. I didn't really have a goal of working on my private pilot's license I just wanted to learn how to fly an airplane. The flying club members were mostly a rag-tag bunch of young wanna-be aviators like myself. A few faculty members belonged, but the club was not officially sanctioned by the University.

The flying club consisted of an Aeronca Model 7AC Champion and a Taylorcraft Model BC12. In order to join the club, I had to meet with a fellow by the name of Burrell Tibbs, the club president. Everyone called him Burl. He worked as a freelance mechanic for the Fixed Base Operator (FBO). When I located him, he and another mechanic were working on a replica of an old Curtis pusher in a large hangar.

Burrell was also the official club check pilot and flight instructor. He was in his seventies and claimed to have taught Wiley Post how to fly and after listening to some of his flying stories, I'm sure he did. The membership fee was $25 and the initiation interview amounted to a single question asked by Burl, "So you want to learn to fly?" I answered in the affirmative and we proceeded to an Aeronca Champ N85066.

Lesson One

After a brief walk around preflight, we climbed into the Aeronca Champ. Burl asked me if I had ever flown an airplane before and I replied that I had not, but I had read a book about flying and was pretty sure that I could.

Burl taxied the plane out and we took off. When we reached an altitude of about 200-feet above-ground-level (AGL) Burl let go of the controls and said, "If you know how to fly, go ahead."

With great confidence, I grabbed the controls and took over. I shortly found myself all over the sky as I was seriously over controlling. When Burl finally stopped laughing, he said, "Ok, I've got it. Now let's go out to the practice area and learn how to fly."

The practice area was out over the wide sandy bottom of the South Canadian River. There were two towers that suspended an oil pipeline across the river and they made an excellent reference points for practicing coordinated figure eight pylon turns. When practicing stalls and failing to make a proper stall recovery, I learned to lean forward slightly because Burl, seated in the back seat of the tandem Champ, was notorious for thumping the student on the back of the head.

I found out after talking with other students that was his standard method of teaching. The rest of the training consisted of going ring-around at Westheimer Airfield, practicing touch and go landing, until I could do them in my sleep

Burl liked to eat lunch at a little airport cafe at the Downtown Airpark in Oklahoma City. If I scheduled instruction with him around lunchtime, we'd land there and take a lunch break. One hot afternoon, we landed, had lunch and got back into the plane to head back to Max Westheimer Field. As the saying goes, if you're looking for an airport, find a power line and there will be one nearby. Downtown Airpark was the prime example. At the north end of the field were some very large high-tension power lines.

I took off down the runway and lifted into the air, but the Champ wasn't climbing very well. We were headed straight for the power lines. That little 65 hp engine carrying two big guys on a hot afternoon and in the hands of an unskilled pilot just wasn't going to climb that steep. Determining that I had a problem, I glanced rearward at Burl grinning in the back seat.

"I got it," he said, as he took the controls and flew us under the power lines. Later, I found out that this was one of Burl's favorite tricks and I was not the first student he had initiated by flying them under the Downtown Airpark power lines.

Solo Flight

On March 11th 1957, I scheduled a dual training flight with Burl and as it happened this was his birthday. He told me I was his last training flight for the day and he intended to have some birthday cake and a few beers to celebrate as soon as we completed our flight. I doubt Burl had kept track of how many hours I had logged to date.

After a couple touch and go landings, Burl told me to taxi back to the hangar and I figured he was cutting our session short so that he could leave to celebrate. As we approached the hangar, he told me not to cut the engine and to let him out.

Burl opened the door. He turned and looked at me and asked me the same question he had asked the first day we met, "So you want to be a pilot?"

"Yes sir, I do," I replied.

"Well," Burl said sarcastically, "then why don't you let me out of here before you kill the both of us!" This was Burl's way of telling me to go shoot some landings by myself.

As I rolled down the runway solo for the first time, I remember thinking that I would pretend the instructor was still in the back seat and if I didn't turn around and look, I won't know the difference. After three touch and go landings, I taxied back to the hangar and Burl signed me off for solo practice.

Fact was I had only a total of five hours and forty-five minutes of dual when I made my first solo flight.

Aeronca Champ

Oklahoma lay in a shifting wind belt. For a day the winds would blow hard out of the south, the next day would be calm and the next day the winds would blow hard out of the north. So it went and the trick was to try to schedule the airplane on the calm day. If the plane couldn't be scheduled on a calm day, the next best thing was to fly in the early morning or in the evening just before the sunset.

The runways at Westheimer Airfield were almost as wide as some airport runways are long and were three times longer than most private airports. On a windy day, it wasn't hard to hit that big runway even in a crosswind.

I had the Aeronca scheduled to fly solo and had gone to the airport in the late afternoon as the winds had blown hard all day. It was still real windy when I arrived. Another instructor and a student had just landed and were trying to taxi the plane back to the hangar area. The dihedral on the wings of an Aeronca Champ tend to cause the plane to weathervane. Each time they attempted to turn ninety degrees to the wind, the Champ would turn back into the wind.

Several of us were watching as the instructor got out of the plane and held onto the left wing strut. The student held the left brake and jockeyed the throttle in an attempt to turn the aircraft towards the parking ramp. A gust of wind, combined with a little extra throttle, lifted the plane up and stood it on its left wing tip. The instructor took off running away from the plane.

It wasn't a laughing matter, but all of us who had gathered to watch, were splitting our sides. Now the correct thing to do at this point would have been for the student pilot to kill the mags or at least chop the power. He did neither as the Aeronca came to rest on its back. The wooden prop managed to trim a foot off both tips as it splintered itself on the concrete like a buzz saw just before the engine quit. And as I recall, it had all appeared to take place in slow motion.

The student was hanging upside down by his seatbelt as we all took off running the hundred or so yards to get to the overturned Champ. But, before we got there, the student released his seat belt falling on his head and knocking himself starry-eyed. Standing up, the stunned student pilot exited the cockpit by walking straight down the full length of the wing, punching foot holes in the fabric as he went. By the time we all got to the plane, we were falling to our knees laughing.

The little Champ was easily repaired with the worst damage having been done to the vertical stabilizer and left wing. I salvaged the chewed up prop and mounted an old chrome electric clock in the center of the hub and it hung in my shop for years.

The Taylorcraft

While the Champ was being repaired, all we had left to fly was the Taylorcraft BC12, N44061, so Burl checked me out in the Taylorcraft. Its most notable characteristic was its tendency to float or glide during flare out for a landing. In other words, best not to come in too hot or the plane would float halfway down the runway before touchdown.

Landing the BC12 in a crosswind was also a little tricky because if the plane did float, it would drift sideways off the runway. This was exactly what happened on my first dual crosswind landing in the BC12. Burl just sat there and let me float sideways a couple feet above the runway until I touched down in the grassy area adjacent to the runway.

It had rained the night before and the grass area that was normally firm enough to land on was three inches of mud. When we came to a stop, the Taylorcraft was stuck. Burl told me to get out and push on the strut as he throttled the plane out of the mud hole. I jumped out of the aircraft and both my shoes instantly stuck in the mud.

As I pushed on the wing-strut in my stocking feet the mud and water being kicked up by the propeller splattered me. Out of the corner of my eye, I could see Burl sitting in the cockpit smiling. I was sure he was thinking, that was one way to break that young pilot of drifting sideways in a crosswind landing. Once back up onto the hard surfaced runway, I went to get my shoes out of the mud.

Her First Airplane Ride

Suzie, my bride-to-be, had never flown in an airplane before in her life, let alone a light plane. Little did she know she would spend the rest of her life flying with or watching her husband fly off to somewhere? She also had no clue that most of her livelihood would be provided by something directly or indirectly related to aviation, but things like that don't seem to matter much when you're young and in love.

I coaxed her into going up with me in the Taylorcraft. Our flight took us out over Oklahoma City. Most of my flying until now had been close to the ground and so I thought I'd see what it was like higher up and climbed to 8,000 feet. As we descended enroute back to Norman, the heat thermals were already building and it turned into a pretty bumpy ride.

Suzie really didn't get a big thrill out of flying that morning. Even though she later flew many hours with me, I don't think she ever really enjoyed flying like those who are born to it. She always contended that there were only two kinds of people in the world, those who loved to fly and those who did not, and that angel feathers or something of the kind must brush those who do have a love for flying.

First Cross Country

Heading off to some boring class at OU one beautiful sunny morning, I realized it was the anniversary of Lindbergh's flight across the Atlantic. The airfield and an unscheduled aircraft beckoned me to go flying as I drove past.

Beggs, a small town south of Tulsa, was the hometown of my grandparents and was only a hundred or so miles away. What the heck, I thought to myself, I know this part of the country like the back of my hand. I'll just fly over to Beggs and buzz my grandma's house. After takeoff, I set a northeast heading and navigated straight to the little town. The town lay on a hillside, but hills don't show up very well from the air. However, the water tower read Beggs along with several senior class year postings. I had hit it on the mark.

Back in the 1920s and 30s, Beggs, like the name of many small towns, was painted on the tin roofs of the lumberyard or some other large building. The project identified the town as an air aid to navigation. The signs were helpful and appreciated by wayward pilots who were not really lost, but only temporally confused. The practice was discouraged during WW II fearing that it might aid enemy pilots in the event of an air attack.

Using my sectional chart, I was never lost. After buzzing my grandma's house, I set a course to Shawnee for my return flight to Norman. It wasn't long before I noticed the gas tank gauge, a bent wire attached to a float in the nose cowl gas tank, was almost touching the top of the fuel cap.

The tank was full when I left Norman. I had checked it during preflight. The Taylorcraft was supposed to have a four-hour range. Unfortunately and unbeknownst to me, the extra fuel for that range was carried in a wing tank and the wing tank was never filled for local flights in the interest of saving weight.

There was no way I was going to make it to the Shawnee airport, let alone back to Norman, with the fuel remaining. Eastern Oklahoma is thick with blackjack oak trees, but with an occasional cow pasture. I was faced with a monumental decision with only ten hours total flying experience. Should I make a forced landing in an acceptable cow pasture or face running out of gas over some heavily wooded area?

Circling to land in a nice size open pasture, I was way too hot on my first approach. Pulling up, I went around for another try. I was worried a little about my ability at this point, but what were my choices? Turning into the wind, I came in low over the treetops and chopped the power as soon as I saw the end of the tree line pass under the plane. The Taylorcraft settled gently onto the ground between some grazing cattle and two oil well pump jacks. The pasture was level and well grazed.

I killed the engine, set the parking brake and climbed out. I could see an oil field pump station a ways down the road, so I hiked down there. An elderly attendant was working at the station and took me into a nearby small town in his pickup to a Phillips 66 gas station.

Another major decision, do I buy premium gas or regular gas? Reasoning that premium gas might be too hard on the engine, I purchased five gallons of regular gas in a loaner gas can and returned to the Taylorcraft parked in the cow pasture. It was a hot afternoon with absolutely no wind, so I decided to sit down under a shade tree and wait for cooler air.

Late that afternoon, a nice breeze came up directly down the longest stretch of the cow pasture. When I tested the mags, I could only get about 1900 rpm, not the normal 2400 rpm. Looking around for something to throw out, I could find nothing in the Taylorcraft heavy enough to leave behind. I pushed the throttle forward. The ol' Taylorcraft bounced a couple of times on the pasture and lifted effortlessly into the air like a magic flying carpet up over the trees and I was homeward bound.

I touched down at Max Westheimer as the sun sank low on the western horizon. It was dark when I arrived home in Midwest City. My mom and my new wife wanted to know why I was so late getting in and I had to fess up to my Lindbergh's day adventure.

The next day, Burl explained to me that I had not been signed off in my logbook for flights further than a twenty-five mile radius from my home airport. Apparently there were rules about a dual, then a solo X-country and a triangle course. I continued to fly the BC12 and the 7AC to build my solo flying time. What the heck, I had successfully completed my first cross-country flight, but maybe with a little deficiency in my preflight planning.

This part of the story I now reluctantly relate. As I turned to make my first approach to the forced landing in that cow pasture, I felt the presence of someone or something in the empty cockpit seat beside me. Clearly, with as little flight experience as I had at the time, I should not have been able to execute the go around decision and subsequent successful landing. Whether it was the spirit of my late father helping me fly the plane that day or God had another plan for me, I'll not know the answer in this lifetime.

Dead Reckoning

The next fall and winter, while my wife and I were in Dayton, I wanted to finish the work on my private pilot's license. There was a small grass airstrip airport called Dahio where I went to ask an instructor to sign me off for my private pilot's license. He was not satisfied with the entries in my logbook and explained he would have to fly a dual cross-country with me before he would sign me off.

In an Aeronca Champ, I flew a triangle course which I laid out down over southern Ohio and back. Navigating by compass headings alone, I flew the course. Actually, I was lost the whole time because I was totally unfamiliar with the countryside. The instructor, in the backseat of the Champ, slept most of the trip. At any rate, I managed to hit my checkpoints and returned to Dahio Airport. The instructor signed me off to take my private pilot's exam and that's all I wanted anyway.

The Civil Aviation Authority (CAA) now known as the Federal Aviation Administration (FAA) published three rectangle paperback books on private pilot training. The books were on weather *Realm of Flight*, navigation *Path of Flight* and how an airplane flies *Facts of Flight*.

The books were simple, well written, concise and to the point. Mostly, I committed them to memory, and to this day could probably layout a navigation wind-triangle course with protractor, ruler and pencil. There was another book considered to be the private pilot's bible entitled *Civil Air Regulations and Flight Standards for Pilots* printed by Aero Publishers, which was most helpful to new pilots like myself.

The early Civil Air Regulations (CAR) covered in great detail how a non-radio equipped aircraft would be handled at a controlled airport. This included various light signals from the tower to the pilot. Lighting was also used to indicate if the airport was under Instrument Flight Rules (IFR) conditions or Visual Flight Rules (VFR) conditions. During IFR, the tower clearance lights and tetrahedron lights would flash. To my recollection, some of the tower beacon lights would flash white then red if conditions were IFR or flash white then green if under VFR conditions. However, I recently combed some old Civil Air Regulations for documentation on this and found no reference to the procedure.

In the early days of airline travel, the CAA in cooperation with the airlines, constructed beacon towers along main routes between major city airports. The concept was that an airliner could fly from beacon to beacon along an airway during nighttime or marginal visibility conditions. Nowadays, the interstate highways are so full of traffic that they are better than the old beacons ever were at night for navigation.

My First Airplane

When we returned from Ohio, I enrolled at Oklahoma City University. At OU, you were just another number, but at OCU students received individual guidance. With two years of generic college behind me, I selected a major in industrial arts, drafting and design. OCU also had an A&P school. I took advantage of this by taking elective courses in aircraft maintenance and welding.

I bought a used Morris Minor for commuting to school. Carl, a classmate of mine and I were both interested in buying an airplane. Carl owned a BMW motorcycle and was taking flying lessons at Tulakes Airport. He heard about a Luscombe that a real estate lady had taken in trade on a house and we went to take a look at the plane.

Luscombe N71931 was the slickest little plane I had ever seen. It had been custom rebuilt from an 8A short fuselage model and the all metal wings and struts from a later model 8F. The wheel-pants were the oversize streamlined kind. The plane was painted battleship gray with a yellow lightning strike down the side. Interior seats were upholstered with rolled and pleated saddle brown leather and the instrument panel was finished in black Bakelite. The asking price for the plane was $1,800. Carl had half of the money if I could raise the other half.

An instructor at OCU who taught our Tool and Jig Design course had an old Henry J, two-door sedan. These little plain vanilla cars were named after the ship building magnate, Henry J. Kaiser, one of the founders of the Kaiser-Frazer automobile company. Some of the little Henry Js were even marketed mail order by Sears & Roebuck, but America was not ready for mid-size cars. I struck a deal with my college instructor to trade him the Morris Minor for his Henry J and the $900 I needed for my part in the Luscombe and we bought the little monocoupe.

The Luscombe

The Luscombe was stored in a large hangar at Tulakes beside a Cessna 170 with a colorful guitar painted on the nose of the airplane. In script over the guitar it read Hank Thompson and indeed it did belong to the country singer. Hank would travel by Cessna to meet his band for those one-night-stand tours, but he lived in OKC. When he was in town, he and his band played down at the Trianon Ballroom, a large dance hall out by the Stockyards where the bootleggers hung out.

Carl and I couldn't afford the hangar rent at Tulakes, so we rented a relatively cheap tie-down spot. Tulakes was home base for the Aero factory where they designed and built the early twin-engine Aero Commanders. The ol' boy that started the company had been an admirer of the WW II B-25 or B-26 and wanted to design a civilian business class aircraft along the same lines, but more economical to fly.

If the wind was less than 20 mph, we had to be careful taking off or landing at the uncontrolled Tulakes airport. The Aero pilots would roll off of their ramp at the far end of the field and takeoff from that direction, regardless of wind direction. If landing according to the tetrahedron, a pilot might be looking down the barrel of an on coming Aero Commander.

Carl was a low-time student pilot and flew with an instructor in the Luscombe. I just got in it and started flying. I had never been through a spin in any type airplane, so I asked Carl's instructor to take me up and show me how to do a spin. The Luscombe was short coupled and I quickly found out the plane was not difficult to spin. The plane would spin by simply slowing it down and kicking the rudder full left or right. Turning against the engine torque was a little less of violent spin than turning with the torque.

In a spin, it always seemed to me as though the airplane was hanging nose down and not turning, but that the ground was rotating in the windshield of the cockpit. In later years, I would practice spins in a Cessna Skyhawk just for fun, but seldom ever took the plane through more than a turn and a half. The ol' 172s are so stable that the plane just kind of swings its tail around in a not very nose down rotation.

The flaps on the Luscombe, unlike the Paralift flaps on the Cessna, were not very effective except when used for a little extra lift or slowing the aircraft down. The best way to make a short field landing in the Luscombe was to cross control the rudder and aileron with the nose down. This technique is called a sideslip, but it's really more of a skid. The plane falls out of the sky like a rock so just before touchdown you had to be ready to neutralize the controls and have enough altitude to stop the descent and make a normal flair-out for landing.

The first time I tried this in a Cessna with the Paralift flaps extended, the aircraft went into a violent swinging oscillation. Turns out, that you don't side slip a Cessna with full flaps. That's one of those things that a pilot learns the hard way if someone doesn't remember to tell them about it.

There were only three main airports near Oklahoma City. They were the Downtown Airpark, the Municipal Airport, later renamed Will Rogers, and Tulakes Airport so named because it was located between two lakes and later renamed Wiley Post. All the others were grass strips or private airports. There was, however, the South Shields Airport on old Highway 77 closer to Moore than OKC. Don't look for it on a map because like most convenient airports, it is now a housing addition.

Carl made a deal with the FBO at the South Shields Airport for he and I to work alternating weekends servicing airplanes in exchange for our hangar rent. When the annual inspection came due on the Luscombe, it did not pass the compression check even though the engine always ran smoothly. Carl and I did a top overhaul on the little four-cylinder replacing the rings and grinding the valves. Aircraft partnerships and aero clubs have scheduling conflicts, but Carl and I never had a problem. He generally flew during the week and evenings. I had a night job with Hayes Aircraft at Tinker AFB and flew on weekends.

Most of our flying was at low altitudes. On Carl's first cross-country, he flew west towards the Texas Panhandle. Out there the land tends to rise up, called *Llano Estacado* in Spanish. I recall him telling about cruising at 1,500 feet as he flew west and watching the ground come up to meet him. He would climb another 1,000 feet and here would come the ground again. Carl remarked that he began to think he was soon going to be taxiing at high speed.

Private Pilot Exam

With about 60 hours of flying time under my belt or should I say, the seat of my pants, I decided I needed to go ahead and get my private pilot's license. I scheduled a test with the flight examiner's office at the Will Rogers Airport. The written exam consisted of a hundred true or false questions. After passing the written exam, the flight examiner and I proceeded to the Luscombe parked on the ramp.

Private pilot exams, up until a short time before I took my test, had included a spin entry and recovery. A few months before I took my exam, an examiner was giving a check ride to an applicant in a Piper J-3 Cub and one of them caught their shoe in the rudder pedals. Needless to say, the Cub spun all the way into the ground. Spins were no longer required on the private pilot's flight-test after that.

At first the examiner was reluctant to give me the flight exam in the Luscombe because he didn't think it had a working radio. Seems as though a new bulletin had come out which stated that pilots needed to demonstrate their ability to operate communication and navigational radio equipment. The radio in the Luscombe was a Mark One Narco, affectionately nicknamed the Coffee Grinder because of the crank knob on the receiver tuner. Finally, after convincing the examiner that the radio really did work, we proceeded with the flight exam.

The old Narco radio transmitted on a fixed frequency in the mid-kilocycle range, supposedly monitored by all control towers. They would then reply on the megacycle frequency assigned to that tower in order to give a landing clearance. The problem was finding the megacycle frequency in order to receive the tower.

Before whistle stop tuning, the receiver dial was set as close to the tower frequency as possible, hoping to hear them reply. If the reply was not received, the tower was asked to give a voice count. A short count was one to five and a long count was one to ten. After asking the tower for a count, the pilot then cranked the receiver handle back and forth until the pilot was able to hear the tower.

The navigation (NAV) receiver worked the same way except that the identifier was in Morse code. This necessitated at least being able to read some Morse code. The Fan Marker navigational beacons that pre-dated Visual Omni Range (VOR) stations had four legs that emitted a solid tone by overlapping the "A" code dot-dash and "N" code dash-dot. When between the legs, either an "A" or an "N" code signal was heard.

After executing all of the maneuvers requested by the examiner, he decided that he would have me demonstrate my newfound radio navigation ability. Newly found because I had never done it before. The examiner had me pull my ball cap down low on my forehead so that I couldn't see out the windshield. Believe me, it's a real trick trying to keep an aircraft straight and level with nothing more than an altimeter, turn-and-bank (TAB) and airspeed indicator. The TAB indicator on the Luscombe was vacuum driven by a venturi mounted on the bottom of the fuselage between the landing gear.

Tuning to the OKC radio beacon, I picked up an "A" signal and turned north hoping to cross a fan marker leg. Looking at the sectional chart in my lap, I noticed that one of the legs of the marker lay across the Canadian River. Out of the corner of my eye, I saw the red sandy riverbed go under my left wing and started a slow turn to what I guessed was the heading to the airport. Just like clockwork, the solid beacon tone came in and we were on course back to Will Rogers. After a respectable wheels landing, the examiner invited me up to the FAA field office in the terminal building and issued me my brand new Private Pilot's Certificate.

Carl and I had owned the Luscombe for about two years when we sold it. The new owner also kept it at South Shields Airport. The large curved roof, metal hangar there had been built prior to WW II. The following winter, during a heavy storm, the hangar fell-in from the weight of a heavy ice and snow storm. It crushed several airplanes including the Luscombe, which was in the middle of the hangar and damaged the worst. I don't know if it was ever restored to its original condition.

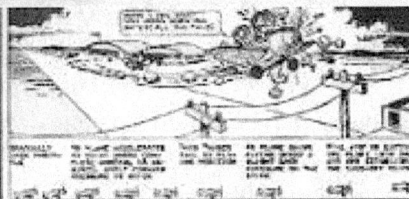

Taylorcraft BC-12 at Max Westheimer belonging to OU Flying Club; CARs and books to study for private lessons; top overhaul on Luscombe Silvair, my first airplane; Flight Deck restaurant menu, located upstairs at Southwest Airmotive on Love Field.

Chapter Seven
AERO CLUBS AND AIRPORTS

Attending OCU days and working the night shift at Hayes Aircraft meant I had to get up early on Saturday mornings, as it was the only day I could spend the whole day at the airport flying or working on the Luscombe. On one particular Saturday morning, I walked out of the house, jumped in the ol' Henry J to head for the airport. I put the car in reverse and the clutch pedal went all the way to the floor. It hung on the throttle linkage and the accelerator stuck wide open.

Picture this. I was going out the driveway and onto the street stuck in reverse gear with the engine running wide open. Odd things cross your mind at times like that. If driving down a street in reverse, do I keep to the right of the road, which was my left or the left of the road, which was my right?

Whatever, I only had a second to ponder this before I jumped the curb and was headed straight for a telephone pole backwards. The brakes, which I had already locked up, were totally ineffective at stopping the car in reverse. At the last instant, I had the presence of mind to cut off the ignition switch and came to a stop about a foot from the telephone pole.

That Henry J made me so mad that when I got out, I slammed the door so hard that I cracked the driver's side door window. For the next couple of weeks, Carl came by on his BMW motorcycle and gave me a lift to school. It was during this time that my wife's younger sister, Nancy, came for a visit. Carl asked her several times to go flying with him, but she always found an excuse not to go. He did, however, get her to go for a ride on the back of his BMW one time. For years after that, whenever Carl's name came up, Nancy would assume a slightly crouched stance like she was holding onto the handlebars of a motorcycle, make a "varoom-varoom" sound and then she'd laugh.

I traded the Henry J for a two-tone red and black '53 Buick Special convertible. One night, after I had bought the new car, I dreamed I was rolling down the runway in the Buick convertible and it lifted off and flew like an airplane. Maybe I'd been spending too much time at the airport and flying.

City Lights Of Big-D

The Hayes Aircraft contract at Tinker Field ended. I was out of college and jobs were scarce. Carl and I sold the Luscombe and Carl took off to play steel guitar in a country band. Suzie and I had visited Dallas several times and thought that we might like to live there.

In early 1960, we loaded our worldly possessions, including my two-year-old daughter and her folded-up playpen into the backseat of the Buick and we set off down Highway 77 for Big D. That evening, as the city lights of Dallas loomed on the horizon, I said to my young wife, "This is where our future and fortune lay!" Indeed it was, for we lived in the Mid-Cities area of the DFW Metroplex the next thirty years of our lives.

Flight Deck Restaurant

The Hensley Field Aero Club, which I joined, had a Cessna 170 tail-dragger that was kept at the old Army National Guard airstrip in downtown Grand Prairie. The airport had been a Navy training and auxiliary landing field during WW II. Like so many airports, after the war it had been granted to the city of Grand Prairie and the town had grown up around it.

The old Grand Prairie airport had no main runway. It was of an early design for airfields laid out in a large hexagon. The idea being, that the pre-war era Navy trainers could takeoff or land in any direction. A large portion of the pavement had weeds growing up through the cracks. The north-south center section, the prevailing direction of the winds and most used portion of the strip, was kept relatively weed-free by periodic use.

Required reading for all would-be flyers was the Ziff-Davis publication *Flying* magazine. On the cover of an old issue was the photo of a Twin Beech parked in front of the Flight Deck restaurant at Southwest Airmotive on Love Field. I had shown it to my wife back in Oklahoma and we decided someday we were going to fly into Love Field and have dinner at the Flight Deck.

After we had lived in the Dallas Metroplex for a time, we planned our evening out at the Flight Deck. My wife, our three-year-old daughter and myself piled into the Cessna 170 at Grand Prairie airport around dusk and departed for Southwest Airmotive at Love Field. My daughter liked to stand between the front seats so she could see out the window better when we would taxi.

It was a no moon night and by the time I made my approach to land at Love Field, the night was pitch-black. I made my usual short field landing on the numbers like I was accustomed to doing and that left me about a mile to taxi to the other end of the field. I should have requested to land long, but I didn't know to do that back then. The tower instructed me to turn left at the next intersection and cleared me to Southwest Airmotive.

Bouncing along down the taxiway, I came upon a stop sign. Wow, I thought, this is really a fancy airport, has stop signs on the taxiway. I stopped, looked both ways and proceeded on down the taxiway. It was then that I came upon a catering truck. The driver waved and I waved back. Then he yelled something out the window to me. I throttled back and opened my side window. "The taxiway's about 50 feet over that way," the driver hollered pointing, "You're on an airport perimeter road!"

And so there really were not stop signs on big fancy airports after all. Oh well, we eventually had a nice dinner at the Flight Deck restaurant and returned to Grand Prairie Airport later that evening. Sammy's, who actually operated their own restaurant and the Flight Deck restaurant became two of our favorite places to eat until both finally closed years later.

Hensley Aero Club

The Aero Club also had a Beech T-34 Mentor that was based at Hensley Field located just north of Mountain Creek Lake west of Chalk Hill. This T-34 still had the Korean era dark blue Navy paint job. The Air Navy and Marine Corps Reserves, Air National Guard and Chance Vought Aircraft shared the airfield.

The T-34 was my first chance at flying a retractable gear aircraft. The seats in the T-34 were aluminum buckets and the pilot and passenger had to wear a parachute or use a seat cushion in order to fly the aircraft. I believe it was a club rule to wear a parachute, because I always did and it also made the aircraft legal for aerobatics.

One of the neat features of the little Beech tandem trainer was that the canopy could be slid back and the aircraft flown open cockpit. However, the front and rear canopies could not both be open in flight at the same time. Bobby, a long time flying buddy of mine, used to like to go flying in the T-34 with me in rear the seat and we both liked to fly open cockpit, so we would split the open cockpit flight time.

The radios in the T-34 were Very High Frequency (VHF) and Navy Dallas tower operated on Ultra High Frequency (UHF). The tower was supposed to monitor a VHF frequency, but they generally kept the volume turned down because the other traffic in the area, like Chance Vought, all used the UHF frequencies. About half the time, when calling for landing instructions, they wouldn't reply. After circling the field to insure that there was no traffic in the pattern, I learned that the only way to get their attention was to fly down the active runway about tower height and then they would turn up the volume on their VHF and respond to your landing request.

The CAP Champ

The local Civil Air Patrol (CAP) squadron was also located at the old downtown Grand Prairie Airport and I volunteered to join. As a rated pilot with considerable flight experience, I was made a 1st Lt. commission and quickly promoted to Captain.

The CAP does a lot of good work with their cadet corps programs, but primarily I volunteered because of the service that the CAP provides to civil aviation in search and rescue missions for downed aircraft.

The CAP squadron kept an 85 hp Aeronca Champion in the Texas ANG hangar with some O-1 Bird Dogs. The military version of the 7AC was designated the L-16 and named the Grasshopper. However, most pilots just referred to them as a Champ.

There was always a strong wind current between the two large hangars that faced each other. The concrete pad between the two hangars was about 20X20 yards. One afternoon, by my lone self, I pulled the Champ out of the hangar, faced it into the wind and took it off in the length of the hangar pad. Because of the wind current between the two hangars, the Champ lifted off like it had been launched from an aircraft carrier.

There really wasn't any danger to the stunt because there was a large open grass area beyond the hangar pad, but I thought that Champ could do it and it did. In the two years that I was a member of the CAP squadron, we were only called out a couple of times to search for a downed aircraft. When flying a search pattern, even under the best of conditions, it is surprisingly difficult to see a crashed aircraft. I personally never located one during an actual search.

When War Birds Were Cheap

Our family physician, Doctor Almand, and I had been in the Navy together. He liked to hang out at the old Grand Prairie Airport with the rest of us airport bums. In fact, his office was just across the street. Doc made arrangements to purchase a P-51 Mustang from Nicaragua. The Nicaraguan government was selling off the remaining P-51s given them by our military.

The day the P-51 was to arrive, via ferry pilot, we were all at the airport waiting. About noon, the Mustang came in low over the field, made a tight turn to final and landed. The P-51, which had probably been shooting up the civilian population for the past ten years, still had faded Air Force insignias on the side and the tail markings identified the plane as the *Ohio Air National Guard*. No wonder the rest of the world hates us.

As the ferry pilot climbed out of the cockpit, we noticed that the radio compartment behind the pilot's seat was full of wadded up charts. Seems the pilot couldn't find any World Aeronautical Charts (WAC) for coming up from Central America through Mexico. Sectional charts being twice the scale of a WAC and cruising at close to 400 mph, he was flying through those sectionals so fast that all he could do was throw the used ones over his shoulder and grab another one.

Dr. Almand completely refurbished the Mustang, but was a little leery of the high-powered aircraft and traded it for an immaculate, bright red Beechcraft cabin-model C-17 Staggerwing.

Flying Classic

A pilot, who had restored an antique radial engine Fairchild Model-24, showed up at the annual Grand Prairie Airport fly-in. This aircraft was produced in two versions, the Ranger, with an inverted in-line engine and the Warner, with a radial engine. This particular aircraft was the radial version, my favorite of the two models. The inverted in-line engine always burned an excessive amount of oil.

The pilot/owner had a for sale sign in the window of the F24W. This aircraft was a true classic. It reflected the same workmanship as the custom coachbuilt automobiles of that era. I would have loved to have bought it, but didn't have the money at the time. The owner was gracious enough, however, to allow me to fly it around the patch a couple of times and I became even more impressed with the old bird. It had safety glass windows, not Plexiglas, and the door windows cranked down like a car window. They just don't build them like that anymore.

The Grand Prairie airport was eventually closed to all private aviation traffic and eventually the 149th Regiment of the Texas Army National Guard stopped operating fixed-wing aircraft at Grand Prairie and began the transition to helicopters out of Fort Walters at Mineral Wells.

The last time I landed at GP, I had flown over from Love Field, parked and was walking over to Doc's office to renew my flight physical when some guy ran after me to tell me the airport was closed. Of course I knew the airport was closed, but back in those days I'd land anywhere I thought I could get my plane in and back out of. "Oh, thank you for the information," I replied politely, "I'll remember that in the future," and went on over to Doc's office. What was he going to do, call a cop and have him write me a parking ticket?

Glider Flight

The Texas Soaring Association (TSA), a flying club for gliders, had a grass strip in southwest Dallas County and I had always wanted to try my hand at flying a glider. So on a Sunday afternoon when I was out for a ride with my wife and daughter, we came upon the glider airstrip maybe not altogether by coincidence. The TSA owned a tandem trainer in which they gave lessons. I parked the girls near the grass strip where they could watch the gliders takeoff and land.

Squeezing into the front seat of the tandem trainer and the instructor in behind me, the canopy was closed and we prepared to be towed aloft by a modified surplus Cessna L-19. Two guys held up the wing tips of the single-wheeled glider and with a jerk, we accelerated down the strip in tow.

The glider climbed more efficiently than our tow-plane as it struggled to pull us into the air so we appeared to be looking down on our benefactor. At about 2,000 feet AGL, the instructor told me to pull the tow cable release handle and we were on our own. The L-19 did a wingover and dove for the ground to tow the next waiting glider.

The most enjoyable part of glider flight was the absence of engine noise. However, the wind noise was louder than I had anticipated. There was nothing to flying the glider. I caught on quickly to watching my rate of descent. We chased a young hawk around a thermal to gain altitude and watched for other soaring birds so as to move from thermal to thermal. A glider is always descending. The trick is to descend in a rising current of air going up faster than the glider is going down.

After about an hour and a half, we returned to the airstrip for a landing. Coming in a little hot, the glider wanted to float down the field. The instructor pilot pulled the spoiler lever extending the spoiler panels out of the wings, which quickly destroyed the remaining lift over the airfoil.

What a great flight! I was anxious to tell the girls how much fun it had been, but they met me frowning and with half-scared looks on their faces. It seems that one of the single-seated gliders had attempted to stretch his approach glide just a little too far and out of desperation tried to land crosswind.

The glider caught the rural single-line telephone wire running parallel to the road and airstrip. The wire stretched, but never broke and just went about popping the little blue-glass insulators off of the adjoining four or five poles. The glider came to a sudden full-stop landing in about 50 feet after slamming to the ground. It was kind of like a tail hook aircraft carrier landing. The pilot was badly shaken, but uninjured.

All of this had taken place within a few dozen yards of my wife and daughter. My wife extracted a promise from me that this would be my first and last glider flight. She also added one additional request, no parachuting either. To this day, I have honored that request with the exception that one or two times while flying in the Navy, I thought I might have to break the parachute part of the promise.

The New Fast Mooney

The new Arlington Municipal Airport opened with much ceremony and the new fixed-base operator was an authorized Mooney aircraft distributor. The Mooney Master was a fixed-gear version of the sleek retractable-gear Mooney Mark 21 low-wing aircraft. One of the sales features of the Master was that it could be upgraded to a retractable at a later date. The early versions of the retractable Mooney used a torsion bar lever to extend the landing gear, but you'd better get a good grip and swing on the lever or the gear wouldn't lock. I recall the lever up was gear down and lever down was gear up, which led to some confusion. Mooney later went to an electrically operated gear like most other modern retractable-gear light aircraft.

The Mooney dealer's salesman, who checked me out in the standard Mooney, demonstrated its structural integrity by diving the aircraft at 300 mph. To my amazement, the aircraft held together. Needless to say, I was a little uncomfortable during the dive and I wondered if that was part of the standard demo. The rental rates on the Mooney were reasonable and they were based on tachometer time rather than on an hour meter, so I planned to take my next cross-country trip using the Mooney.

My wife and daughter had taken the train to Ohio to visit her folks and I was flying up to get them. Departing shortly after noon in the Mooney, I headed east on a beautiful sunshiny day. After passing Indianapolis, I began to encounter a layer of broken overcast clouds. Cruising at 6,000 feet VFR on top, the sucker holes were starting to get smaller. You are a sucker to believe you can climb out or descend through those small breaks in the clouds. It was time to descend below the cloud layer in order to complete the rest of my flight to Dayton VFR.

With several hundred hours of flying experience, I still did not have my instrument rating. Also, I was accustomed to flying aircraft more in the 140 mph range than I was to flying aircraft that cruised at 200 mph. As the next good size sucker hole went by under me, I banked the Mooney over, reduced the power and descended into the opening in the cloud layer.

Needless to say, I should have reduced the throttle even more and slowed down. The next thing I knew, I had missed the VFR hole and was in the clouds. Frantically, I scanned the full gyro panel. Every instrument was spinning, but my center-of-ass was telling me I was in straight and level flight. I was in the infamous suicide spiral that has killed so many pilots.

Luckily, I was still about a thousand feet AGL when I broke out of the bottom of the cloud layer doing 240 mph in a hard left turn and slightly nose down. I bounced on towards Cox Municipal Airport in the Mooney under the overcast, but it was at that very moment in my flying career I decided I would go to work on obtaining my instrument rating.

Can You Point To Up

The suicide spiral, as it is sometimes referred to, acts on the pilot's inner ear affecting his sense of balance. This is a phenomenon that results from centrifugal force disguising itself as gravity. It is the same effect that allows a racecar to bank high on a turn or keeps a passenger in the seat of a roller coaster when it loops. As the aircraft banks, the nose will pitch up or down depending on the direction of the turn and the pilot enters an ever-tightening turn while feeling that he is in level flight. Eventually, the aircraft stalls, drops a wing and rolls over headed nose-down for the ground at high speed.

The best procedure for descending through a cloud layer for a non-qualified or low time instrument pilot is to slow the aircraft down and trim it for level flight, pull the power off slowly to set up a 200 or 300 feet per minute, rate of descent and without touching the controls, hands off, allow the aircraft to descend through the cloud layer. Most inexperienced pilots, myself included, lack the nerve to do this. They try to drive the airplane down through the clouds as if the plane would not stay level without the pilot's grip on the controls. A blind descent works increasingly better the greater the VFR space between the bottom of the cloud layer and the ground.

Like most pilots, I have been anxious from time to time, but I can honestly say I can never recall being really afraid when flying. That is, at least not until afterwards when you realize what a dumb trick you've just pulled and then it scares the hell out of you.

To be a firsthand witness to a mighty thundercloud or view a wondrous sunset from lofty heights is a rare privilege. They say that sunrises are for copilots, but don't believe it. Even the old timers still look out the cockpit window from time to time and gaze in awe at God's creation. No matter how high or how far we fly, where we land is the place we call home.

The Ol' Lear Liar

In a high performance aircraft like a jet, this false gravity phenomenon can even make a pilot believe he is going up, so he pushes forward on the controls and flies into the ground. The only salvation from this condition is to believe the gyro instruments or fly the gauges, as they are nicknamed by pilots.

Viet Nam era carrier pilots referred to the artificial horizon attitude gyros made by Lear as the "Lear Liar" because it sometimes told the pilot what he didn't want to believe, but the ones who are still alive believed them. When you are in the clouds on a night with no moon, out over water or barren landscape, you often can't point to up with both hands. Believe your instruments no matter what your gut is telling you.

Charlie Plumb, a Nam F4 pilot, tells a story of believing your instruments. Seems a jet pilot was forced to make a night instrument landing on a carrier in bad weather and missed the first tail-hook cable, the #1 wire in carrier-pilot lingo.

The pilot applied full power to go around, but had actually caught the last arresting cable. The cable stretched and his F4 went over the bow of the carrier, hanging nose down from the cable. Charlie said, "You can understand the pilot's confusion. The ol' Lear Liar was telling him he was going straight-down at full-power with no airspeed and zero altitude."

Ground Loops

A ground loop is not a loop at all. It is to an airplane what a spinout is to a racecar. In other words, the aircraft spins around in a circle on the ground after the pilot loses forward control and it usually occurs during a landing rollout. If at a fast enough speed, a ground loop will do a lot of damage to the aircraft's landing gear or even a wing tip.

Tail-wheel or conventional landing gear airplanes, often referred to as tail-draggers, are much more prone to ground loops than tricycle gear airplanes. This is primarily due to their higher angle of attack during flare-out for landing. A nose-high attitude is required in order to make a full-stall landing and the wing momentarily blocks the airflow over the rudder. Many airplanes lack adequate directional control during this transition from flight to high speed taxiing. There are only two kinds of pilots. *Those who have ground looped a tail-dragger and those who are going to.* I knew of a DC-3 pilot that first ground-looped a Three after 6,000 hrs of flying time.

The radial engine, Cessna 190s and 195s with conventional tail-wheel gear have always fascinated me. The cockpits of these old aircraft are reminiscent of the airliners of that era. The front seat of the 190 sits very high and the visibility over the nose is poor at best, plus the pilot must assume an unusually high angle-of-attack in order to make a full-stall landing.

The alternative to a full-stall landing is to make a power on, main-gear landing known as a wheels landing, which is fine if there is plenty of runway for rollout. Some of the Cessna 190s had crosswind landing gear. The wheel axles would pop out of a ball socket to align the main-gear at a slight angle and helped to prevent ground loops, but not much.

Years ago, I had an opportunity to fly a 190 out of old Mangrum Field. On my first landing in the 190, I didn't get the tail wheel down soon enough and started losing directional control. The airline pilot, in the right seat and who also owned the plane, tapped one of the brakes snapping the 190 back straight again. Thus saving my reputation and his airplane.

Hensley Field Aero Club Beech T-34; Grand Prairie squadron CAP Aeronca 7AC Champion; Bobby, Judy and family in front of one of his favorite plane, a Swift 125; Bobby's Cessna 172 Skyhawk fully restored to beautiful condition, the 1966 Cessna G model was based at Ennis Airport for years; Bonanza I used for instrument rating and flight test; Link Blue Box trainer, WW II version of flight simulator.

Chapter Eight
PURSUIT OF RATINGS

Up until the new GI Bill was introduced, I had paid for all my flight training out of my own pocket. The Veterans Administration (VA) would now pay for ninety percent of your flight school expenses and I signed up. The commercial pilot certificate was a mere formality as I had already logged more hours than required for certification.

Attending night ground school at Goble Aviation, I quickly passed the commercial written exam and took my check ride in Cessna 150, N5648E. I thought it was kind of a laugh getting certified as a commercial pilot in a little Cessna 150, but hey, it was a common practice.

Next would come my instrument rating. There are new blind flying and landing systems being developed like R-NAV, Loran and GPS, but for the last 40 plus years, the primary system has been the Visual Omni Ranges. These VHF radio range stations tell the pilot what the bearing of the aircraft is from or to the station. A VORTAC adds Tactical UHF and Distance Measuring Equipment (DME) capability to the Omni station.

A Localizer is a fixed radial VOR with a vertical VOR, called a Glide Slope, which allows the aircraft to descend down a secondary fixed radial to a touchdown point on the runway. The Outer Marker uses an Automatic Direction Finder (ADF) to locate a fixed point on the approach. Outer and Inner Markers send a conical radio beam tone signal straight up, which sets off a Marker Light on the panel as the aircraft passes over. All of these make up an Instrument Landing System (ILS).

In the early days of radio navigation, aviation direction finders were not automatic. The pilot or navigator had to rotate the handle on the loop antenna manually until hearing a null tone. Later versions did this automatically and thus ADF.

Goble Aviation's V-Tail Bonanza

Mr. Goble was an FAA designated flight examiner and operated a flight training school out of Redbird Airport, south of Dallas. Goble was one of the world's original characters. He seldom smiled and even more seldom had anything good to say about your flying, but personally I liked ol' Goble. He was a good instructor.

Goble offered an Instrument Rating (IR) course in his Beech model 35 Bonanza, N191GA. Notice the G.A. for Goble Aviation. I had used very little of my VA eligibility obtaining my Commercial pilot's license, so I took the full forty-hour course in the Bonanza.

The Dallas Naval Air Station (NAS) had Link trainers, nicknamed Blue Boxes, to which I had access. I could have used some flight simulator time for credit on my Instrument Rating, but I did not because I enjoyed flying the Bonanza. The old Blue Box was pretty good for practicing navigation and instrument approaches, but lacked reality in simulating the feel of actual flight.

I think it may be easier to train a low time pilot to fly instruments than one who has been flying VFR for several hundred hours. It is also my belief that airline pilots depend on flight directors and autopilots far too much to be good at flying light planes with minimum instrument equipment.

After a dozen or so hours under the hood in that fishtailing Bonanza, I was still apparently holding a death grip on the flight controls while on instruments. One afternoon when I arrive for my weekly flight session, Goble had blocked out three hours of flight time for us in the Bonanza.

Goble began by explaining, "We are going to break you of putting a crease in the upholstery of the seat with that part of your body where it is most likely your brains are located."

I told you Goble was a nice guy, you just didn't believe me! It was a wonder he didn't make me taxi out under the hood. I began my takeoff roll under the hood and never saw outside the aircraft again until I flared out for a landing three hours later back at Redbird.

I navigated my way over to Love Field where we played ring-around on the ILS for a couple of hours. On one approach, while still under the hood, I actually felt the main gear touch the runway, so I guessed that I had just shot a zero-zero landing.

Next, Goble had me navigate to a couple of intersections or fixes. From time to time, he would take the controls and put me in some unusual attitude and say, "Okay it's your aircraft."

Ol' Goble was right, I could only pucker so long! After a while I began to relax my grip on the yoke and sat a little more relaxed in the seat. Most of all I had gained the confidence that I could fly the plane on instruments.

Instrument Rated

The way I prepared for my check-ride in the Bonanza was to sit in the cockpit for hours with my eyes closed pointing to an instrument or switch as I called each one out to myself. The standard Airline "T" instrument panel configuration had been adopted by private aviation with the airspeed, horizon, rate and Directional Gyro (DG) instruments forming a "T" in the center of the panel.

The best way to describe instrument flying without an autopilot is like having four pots of water on the stove ready to boil and then to keep adjusting the flame on each pot so as to just barely keep them from boiling over.

After obtaining my instrument rating, I was flying a Cessna Cardinal down to Brownwood, Texas and the weather was VFR on top with a solid cloud layer below. Brownwood was reporting 1,000 feet overcast with good visibility.

Flying VFR on top always reminded me of being suspended over a giant cotton blanket. There is no sensation of speed high above a cloud layer, but just before entering the clouds, one gets a sudden sense of speed before descending into the clouds.

It was time to try out my newfound instrument approach skills alone and under actual conditions. Brownwood only had a VOR approach and so I radioed for instrument clearance from VFR on top. Cleared for the approach, I lined up on the Brownwood VOR and began my descent. Just like magic, I broke out of the clouds, looking straight down the runway. Gosh, I remember thinking to myself this stuff really does work.

GUMP

The early model Bonanzas had a smooth row of machined aluminum toggle switches along the bottom center of the instrument panel. These switches operated lights, landing gear, et cetera. More than one pilot had placed the electric flap switch in the down position thinking that he had extended the landing gear. Beech recognized this human factors engineering error and in later model Bonanzas put a small wheel on the landing gear switch and a flat bar on the flap switch so they could be distinguished by touch alone.

In all my years of flying, I never failed to remember to extend the gear. I believe mainly because I always used the old Navy acronym GUMP spoken as, "Gas, Undercarriage, Mixture and Props." I say the words out loud before turning to final for a landing and still do this when flying a local Bonanza N346S to this very day. There is an axiom about landing gear up, which is exactly the same as the one about ground loops, *there are those who have landed gear up and there are those who are going to.*

Late one afternoon, I was sitting on the steps in the doorway of the gas shack at the new Grand Prairie Municipal Airport watching several airplanes practicing touch and go landings in the pattern. The Unicom radio was blaring away as each aircraft dutifully announced their position in the pattern.

For about a half hour, a local Comanche pilot had been in the pattern with a couple of other light planes. As the Comanche turned final for the sixth or seventh time, I noticed his landing gear had still not been extended. Running to grab the mike on the Unicom just inside the door I shouted, "Comanche landing at Grand Prairie, your gear is not down!"

The Comanche made a perfect flair out for landing and skidded down the runway on its belly. Several of us ran out to the plane as the pilot and one passenger exited. "Why didn't you go around?" I asked, "I was yelling at you on the Unicom that your wheels were not down."

Looking at me with a blank stare, the pilot explained, "I had just turned the volume on my radio down because this was going to be my final landing to a full stop and the radio had been annoying me."

A half dozen of us lifted the plane up off of the runway as someone reached through the storm window on the pilot's side, placed the gear switch in the down position and the landing gear lowered. The aircraft actually suffered very little damage. The worst damage was to the belly where an antenna had been mounted and, of course, the prop was curled on the tips.

Multi-Engine Baron

Goble had the use of a really nice Beech Baron N9543Y approved for multi-engine training for VA flight training. Now we were getting somewhere. With twin 265 hp engines, it finally felt like I was flying something. The hardest concept for a single-engine pilot making the transition to a twin is to understand that a twin doesn't always fly on one engine.

Airspeed indicators on twins have an additional mark on them. The blue line indicates the aircraft's Velocity Minimum Controllable (VMC) airspeed. Once a twin is slowed below this speed, directional control can no longer be maintained on one engine. Some twins are more forgiving than others if VMC is violated. Other factors like density altitude, how heavily loaded and pilot skills will also have an effect.

Standard procedure for practicing engine failure in a twin is for the student to identify the engine that the instructor has reduced power on and for the student to point to the corresponding prop lever. The instructor will then add back enough power to simulate the prop having been feathered.

To feather the prop means to use the propeller pitch lever to turn the blade edgewise in the air stream and thereby reduce aerodynamic drag. The easiest way to identify which engine is out is to remember this simple rule, "You are standing on your good engine." In other words, the pilot is applying rudder pressure on the good engine side of the airplane in order to keep the plane headed straight.

On my multi-engine flight-test with thirty degrees of landing flaps and gear extended, I was about to touchdown when Goble told me to execute a go-around. I applied full power, the props were already full forward and I placed the gear handle in the up position. When I was almost out of runway with the gear coming up, Goble pulled the right engine on me. I identified the engine that was out by pointing to the correct prop lever.

As I transitioned to a positive rate of climb, I had forgotten to retract the flaps. Mostly, I was intent on staying above blue line. I was holding the Baron straight, but due to a bad left crosswind that I was unable to correct for, we passed over one of the hangars clearing it by only about a hundred or so feet. A really good pilot might have milked off ten degrees of flap and maybe picked up some airspeed. Then again, maybe the Baron would have settled a little and not cleared the hangar.

Goble had more guts with a student than I would ever have, letting me fly that Baron out just a hair above VMC with a bad crosswind. After we were on the ground, Goble grumbled a bit about if we had been at full fuel and full passenger load, I might not have been able to fly that Baron out like I did, but he did allow that I had managed to carefully maintain VMC and because of this he would go ahead and sign me off for a Multi Engine Land (MEL) airplane rating. That was probably the closest thing to a compliment I ever got out of the man.

Comments On VMC

A twin-engine aircraft with an engine out will roll over on its back in an instant if you continue to maintain full power on the good engine below VMC. In order to prevent this, the power on the good engine must be retarded and the nose lowered enough to obtain an indicated airspeed at or above the VMC speed.

Pulling the power off on a good engine goes against a pilot's instinct, but a pilot has a snowball's prayer in hell of climbing out in a twin below VMC at high altitudes. With an engine out and below VMC in a twin you are a single-engine airplane with a controlled rate of descent. Pick a place to set her down or you'll drop a wing and you can kiss your ass goodbye. It's kind of like the old joke about a forced landing at night. Just before touching down, turn on the landing lights. If you don't like what you see turn them back off again.

P-factor, sometimes referred to as prop-cavitation, is not altogether distinguishable from engine torque, but it is mostly the P-factor that causes loss of centerline thrust.

There is a phenomenon similar to the engine out VMC on a twin that occurs in high-powered single-engine aircraft like the P-51 and to a lesser extent in any aircraft over 250 hp. A high-powered single-engine plane will lose directional control at slow air speeds in a high angle of attack.

Single-engine VMC occurs in a nose-high attitude when the prop blade on one side of the aircraft is taking an excessive bite of air and the opposite side is running in a cavity. Prop Cavitation combined with engine-torque will result in single-engine VMC and a high-powered single plane will crank over on its back the same as a twin.

Seaplane Rating

Brown's Flying Service in Winter Haven, Florida, offered and I guess still does, a crash course for adding a seaplane rating to your existing FAA ticket. While visiting in Winter Haven, I located Brown and his Piper J-5 Cub floatplane docked on one of the Chain of Lakes behind the Winter Haven Airport.

Over the next several days, I learned to taxi on water and how to stir up a wake on a calm surface in order to circle back on it and bounce the floatplane into the air. When there is no airport, runway or windsock, a seaplane pilot soon learns to pay attention to smoke and ripples on the water in order to determine wind direction for setting down. Notice I avoided using the term landing.

A seaplane's float or hull creates a tremendous amount of suction in the water and it takes a lot longer distance to takeoff than it does to stop on the water. The first time I flew with Brown, he suggested we land on the small lake in downtown Winter Haven and walk over to McDonald's for lunch. He headed straight for the beach and touched down a dozen or so yards from the shore. Sitting in the front seat, I was convinced we were going to end up in the McDonald's parking lot, but as soon as the floats hit the water, we came to an abrupt stop. In fact, we had to add a little power to taxi to shore and beach the plane.

Over the course of the next few weeks of flying dual in the floatplane, we explored some of the more backwater lakes, taxied past alligators sunning themselves on logs and practiced various water takeoff and landing techniques. My final flight in the seaplane was with an FAA designee examiner who signed me off for my Single-Engine Sea (SES) rating, an addition to my standard Single-Engine Land (SEL) and Multi-Engine Land (MEL) rating.

Next to the Brown's Seaplane Service dock was the winter home of the author of *Jonathan Livingston Seagull*, Richard Bach. He kept a floatplane there for a while, but I don't know if he even owns the place anymore. I recently re-visited the Brown's operation and it was still going strong. They have several more planes, a full seaplane service shop and his daughter now ramrods the flight training schedule.

Up the road north and across I4 is the Fantasy of Flight air museum where I got my first ride in an old D-25 bi-plane. I mention the museum here in the context of seaplanes because there is a four-engine Short Sunderland MK5 flying boat on display there. When I first entered the museum hangar, I mistook it for a Pan Am Flying Clipper and gasped, well I was a little disappointed. The Short flying boats were to the British Empire what the Sikorsky S-42, Martin M-130 and Boeing 314 Flying Clippers were to America for trans-oceanic flight.

Douglas ATP DC-3 Type

In the early days of American Airlines, pilot training had been conducted under contract to the American Flyers flying school at Fort Worth's Meacham Field. An elderly pilot by the name of Boardman took over the old hangar facility and operated a VA approved flight school. His former wife was also a flight instructor at Shiloh Airpark and I believe was the oldest living, currently licensed lady pilot at the time.

I was currently flying copilot on DC-3 N37F and ready to go for my Type rating. The aircraft Type rating flight-test check ride for an aircraft over 12,000 lbs is the same flight-test check-ride as the Airline Transport Pilot (ATP) rating. So if taking and passing the ATP written exam first, both ratings could be obtained with the one check ride at the same time.

Boardman's Flying School was one of the few approved for a DC-3 ATP rating. I still had some VA training funds left in my account, so I signed up to take the ATP rating course. A really sharp young pilot instructor by the name of Jim Self was my instructor for the course. Jim was a short, stocky and pleasant sort of a fellow who rode a motorcycle to work.

When we were out boring holes in the sky for practice in the DC-3, one of our favorite tricks was to head out to the chain of lakes north of Carswell Air Force Base and drop down to about 500 feet over the water. Flying low, at 120 mph close to the shoreline, we could fly-by the topless sunbathers before they heard the noise of our twin Pratt & Whitney engines coming at them. The startled young ladies would often sit straight up to see what was flying over. Dirty trick, but somebody had to do these things to uphold us pilots' reputations.

After logging about ten hours in Boardman's DC-3 N144D, I was ready to take my check ride and went to the FAA to have my logbook certified to take the ATP written exam.

Rudder Control Lock

There was about enough left in my VA flight training account for one more DC-3 flight, so I scheduled an hour of dual. Jim told me to go out and preflight the DC-3. Now keep in mind I had been flying DC-3 N37F, a commercial model. Boardman's DC-3 N144D was a converted C-47 and I had gotten used to doing the preflight on N37F. They were similar in almost all respects except for one minor, but very important difference. Boardman's DC-3 had an external rudder lock and N37F had a rudder-peddle locking bar in the cockpit.

When Jim came aboard the DC-3, I was going through the preflight checklist. After cranking the engines, I taxied out to the end of the active runway by jockeying the throttles, an easy way to turn when taxiing a large twin-engine aircraft and better than riding the brakes. Cleared for takeoff at the end of the runway, I pushed the throttles forward. The DC-3's tail came up and I was rolling down the runway on the main gear.

As I was getting close to lift off speed, a left crosswind kept pushing me to the right of the runway. Jim asked in a loud voice, "Why aren't you correcting for the crosswind, Arnold?"

"I'm standing on the left rudder already and nothing's happening!" I replied.

Jim placed his feet on the rudder pedals and exclaimed, "I know what it is!" He grabbed the throttles and pulled them both full off. "I got it," he yelled and I let go of everything. Helplessly, I watched as Jim rode the brakes, hauling the control wheel back into his lap as we went onto the south runway overrun finally coming to a stop in a cloud of dust.

Swinging the DC-3's airstair door away from the tower's view with the throttles, Jim told me to hold the brakes as he ran to the rear of the plane and went out the door. The tower called and asked if we were having a problem. I replied, "Four-four Delta, standby please," because at this point, I didn't know what the hell had happened.

Jim climbed back onboard holding the external rudder lock in his hand, a V-shaped piece of aluminum that had been slid into the rudder slot and held in place by a bungee cord to keep the rudder from swinging in the wind when parked. When I realized what I had done, leaving the rudder lock on, I broke out in a cold sweat and we both sat there looking at each other.

The reason Jim had turned the tail of the Three away from the tower was because he didn't want the tower to see him remove the rudder lock and have to file an incident report. Besides, there was no aircraft damage.

The tower called again asking if we needed assistance. Jim answered them saying, "No, we were practicing an aborted takeoff and got up a little more speed than we intended. Permission to taxi back up the active?" and the permission was granted.

We stood under the shade of the DC-3 wing drinking a coke. Jim confided in me that during the last few weeks, he had been thinking about quitting flight instruction. A few days before, a student in a Cessna 150 had stalled the plane on final approach and he had barely recovered in time. He just had a feeling his number was coming up and maybe he should move on.

I assured him that if his time were up, it sure as heck would have been today. Jim laughed in agreement and said, "Guess we better go ahead and fly because if we don't, we'll be too scared to come back and fly another day."

"Kind of like getting back on the horse that throwed you?" I said, smiling, and Jim shock his head yes. We climbed back aboard the Three and Jim radioed the tower for permission to taxi. I made a normal takeoff this time and headed out toward Eagle Mountain Lake and we cruised around the shoreline for a while before heading back to Meacham Field.

Since then, I have asked several airline pilots, like Jerry who flew the old Gooney Birds back in the mainline days, if they ever knew of a successful return to landing of a DC-3 with the rudder lock on. The question I asked was "If I had lifted off, could I have used the ailerons and differential power to bring the Three back and land?"

Most of the pilots knew of none, but Jerry told me about a DC-3 that had attempted it. The plane spun all the way into the ground killing all on board.

Only The Good Die Young

A couple of weeks after the DC-3 incident, I received a phone call from a mutual friend telling me that Jim had been killed, but not in an airplane! Jim had stopped his motorcycle on the side of the road to visit with some friends. A passing motorist, an old man, struck Jim and his motorcycle, throwing Jim into the air and fatally injuring him. He had his helmet on, but had loosened the chinstrap buckle when he had stopped.

Some of the other pilots and myself chipped in to help Jim's wife and daughter, but of course it wasn't enough. It never is. Here was a man who, in essence, had saved my life in an airplane only days before and he had just died as the result of a careless automobile driver. Go figure. I guess it was just his time and not mine.

After Jim was killed, I logged a hundred or so more hours in DC-3 N37F and became certified as a twin-engine air taxi pilot in Cessna twins, but I never returned to finish the ATP and DC-3 Type ratings. A DC-3 is a two pilot certified airplane, but only one pilot onboard is required to be rated, so what's the difference. I just flew with a type rated pilot, even though I did the flying, whenever I wanted to use the DC-3. Thus ended my pursuit of ratings.

T-6 Texan
Navy SNJ

Post WW II many small aircraft companies vied for the light plane market, but by the '60s and '70s Cessna's 152 and 172, along with Piper's 140 and 180, dominated. This primarily due to their aggressive flight training promotions; Beach, Mooney and Bellanca went after the higher end customer by promoting speed; Veterans and advanced flying enthusiasts chose to restore and fly WW II aircraft like the SNB/T-6 Texan military trainer, which made their way into civilian hands by the 1960s.

Chapter Nine
FLY OUR FRIENDLY SKY

The two most popular wing designs are the Clark-Y and the Laminar. The latter being mostly used on higher speed prop planes. However, the Laminar is susceptible to a phenomenon known as an airflow trap. Due to the uniform symmetry of the wing's design, even with adequate airspeed, at certain angles of attack the airflow over the top of the wing is approximately equal to the airflow under the wing. With little or no lift, the plane will not climb until the angle of attack is changed.

An advantage to a Laminar wing is that you can point the nose slightly down and pick up speed. This is known as getting a plane on the step. Also, enroute you can begin a slight rate of descent a hundred miles out and increase the cruise speed with very little loss of altitude.

The Laminar Flow Mooney

An aircraft dealer at Meacham Field asked me to fly a Mooney Mark 21 down to Hillsboro for a prospective buyer. Two low-time pilots, who had been hanging around the airport, asked if they could ride along. The fuel tanks were about half empty, but there was more than enough gas to make the short hop.

It was a hot summer afternoon as we touched down with the Mooney on the short grass strip. The gas boy at the FBO asked me if I needed gas. I always tried to give the local FBO a little business and told him to fill the tanks. After the prospective buyer looked over the Mooney, he wasn't interested. My two large passengers and I boarded the plane for the return flight.

An addendum to Murphy's Law might be that it is not always a good idea to have full tanks and be close to gross weight for takeoff on a short dirt strip on a hot summer afternoon.

With throttle, mixture and prop to the wall, the Mooney lifted about two feet into the air, but refused to climb and the barbwire fence at the end of the strip was coming up fast.

The thoughts racing through my mind were should I just pull the gear up and hope for the best or pull the power off and set back down taking out the barbwire fence. Then I wondered if the aircraft had any hull damage insurance coverage. Funny how fast the mind can run through things at times like that.

What really didn't cross my mind, but was pure instinct was recalling how Burl had pushed forward on the stick instead of continuing to pull back when I was trying to clear the power lines at the OKC Downtown Airpark. So an instant before arriving at the fence, I did exactly that. I pushed slightly forward on the controls and the Mooney literally leaped 30 feet into the air. By changing the attitude, I had caused the coefficient of lift over the top of the wing to break the Laminar flow trap.

Twin-engine Student Pilot

A business associate of mine, JD, was a large fellow about six foot four. He had been asking me a lot of questions about flying. He was thinking about learning to fly and asked me if I'd take him up and show him what it was like to fly in a light plane. I rented a Mooney from the dealer over at Meacham Field and I flew JD around over the Mid-Cities area. The Mooney, however, was not a good choice. JD complained about being really cramped, but he loved the flying.

JD went to the Cessna dealer and signed up for flight training. Needless to say, he could barely get in a Cessna 150, so he just bought a used Cessna 310 twin from the dealer. JD was the only guy I've known who soloed in a twin. He got his private pilot's license and multi-engine rating on the same check-ride.

JD used the twin to travel on business quite a bit, but had not yet completed his instrument rating. The weather was going to be marginal for his flight to Waterloo, Iowa the following morning and he asked me to ride along with him in the 310.

Always game for an opportunity to log multi-engine time, I agreed and we left early the next morning before sunup. It was an odd weather day with two cloud layers, one at about 6,000 feet and another at about 14,000 feet. Departure control advised us that pilots were reporting flocks of geese as high as 15,000 feet and that we should be on the lookout for them.

Flying northeast, just before the sun came up, we passed over a good size lighted city. Air traffic control reported a formation of Air Force jets refueling in our twelve o'clock position at a much higher altitude. Never before and never again have I seen such a visual anomaly. The city lights were moving under us with the lower scud layer between us and the ground. We were flying below the upper broken cloud layer and the jets, with their formation lights on, were passing overhead above that cloud layer. All of this and the dull rays of first light are impossible to describe in words what the feeling of being suspended in all that motion felt like.

With JD's business in Waterloo completed, we were ready to embark on our return flight to Fort Worth. We did the preflight in a strong bitter cold northwest wind. From the right seat, I closed and latched the door. Unbeknownst to me, I had shut the door on the coattail of my London Fog raincoat.

In a climb attitude, the airflow over the wing is different than in level flight, but when we leveled off for cruise flight, this loud thumping noise began. What was that? Suddenly, I realized that it was my coattail flapping against the outside of the fuselage.

Now, I already knew that it is nearly impossible to shut the door of most aircraft in flight once opened, but we decided to try anyway. As JD slowed the aircraft to slow flight, I popped the door into the trail position and pulled my coattail in. Forget it. Two men and a mule couldn't have shut that door. I held the door while we circled back to land. I shut the door as we touched down and we kept rolling for a takeoff.

A winter storm, which we had anticipated crossing on the way home, had suddenly become a blizzard. Enroute, we turned east in an effort to outrun the storm. Listening to air traffic control, we heard a DC-3 report they were trying to climb out of the storm and were still icing at 15,000 feet. Forget that. So we continued to move southeasterly, paralleling the front. Approaching Kentucky, we were running low on fuel and it was going to be necessary to at least make a gas stop.

The snowstorm overtook us as we approached the Paducah Airport. The odd thing about snow is that as you turn into the wind everything becomes a whiteout, but as you turn with the wind, you can see downward in the direction the snow is blowing and see the ground just like it was VFR. Therefore, on the downwind and base legs we could keep the airport in sight, but the short turn to final left us no choice but to chop the power and wait for the wheels to touch. We could see out the side windows, but could not see anything forward.

We taxied to the flight service station building, tied the Cessna 310 down and ran for the shelter of the station. One lone FAA flight service station operator was there by himself, still talking to idiots like us who had gotten overrun by the blizzard. The snow outside was getting deeper by the minute and the local motel would not even send its courtesy van to the airport to pick us up.

I have often bragged that I lived so long flying because of my back trouble, that big yellow streak that runs down the center. Many a pilot has flown into the big trashcan in the sky because of get-home-itis. JD was upset because he had this thing about not leaving his wife alone at night. I always preferred to live to fly another day and so we stayed over.

That night, I slept on the couch in the flight service station and I'm not sure where JD finally fell asleep. I was just thankful for a warm place to stay.

The fast-moving storm passed over that night and it was a bright, sunshiny morning as we lifted off and headed back to Texas. Even though the storm had moved out of the Midwest, it had not yet cleared Dallas-Fort Worth and at 200 plus mph, we were overtaking the storm. We stopped again at a small airport in northern Arkansas to take on additional fuel.

The gas boy wasn't accustomed to seeing twin-engine planes at the small airport and he inquired of JD as to how much an airplane like his cost. JD gave him an approximate price for the airplane and explained that many twins cost a lot more.

The gas boy said, "Wow, with that kind of money, I could buy half of Arkansas."

JD, who was tired and not very happy about being stuck in northern Arkansas at the time, replied, "Oh yeah, what would you do with the rest of the money?" but I don't think the boy exactly got the drift of JD's sarcasm.

Airborne on our next leg, we made it to Ardmore, Oklahoma before overtaking the storm again. Meacham Field was reporting zero-

zero conditions at the time, so we landed and parked the plane at the newly reorganized American Flyers flight school training facility there. With nothing else to do, we paid them a social visit. This was one of those old flight schools in the tradition of the early airline days.

The chief instructor wore an airline captain's uniform and ran the flight school like a college. The school could trace its beginnings to the days when they trained commercial airline pilots. The Captain was a gracious host and showed us around. It was about this time that I began thinking about the possibility of starting my own flight school and air taxi business.

That afternoon, the weather cleared and we returned to Meacham Field in Fort Worth. Thus, we concluded the return flight from Waterloo without meeting our own Waterloo.

Lenticular Clouds

Ol' Pete Falco, another business associate of mine, was a part-time real estate developer and a small time promoter. His sidekick, Gene, was a deputy sheriff. They were always roping me into flying them somewhere. Pete had one glass eye, but he loved to fly. He got his student pilot ticket and actually soloed in an Aeronca Aircoupe.

When Pete flew with me, he delighted in pointing out unimportant things. During one of our flights in a Bonanza up to Oklahoma, Pete was looking out the window and asked, "Isn't that a tornado over there?"

Without looking up I said, "I'm sure it is." Several minutes later, I actually looked in that direction. "Oh crap!" There it was, hanging out the bottom of a small Oklahoma thunderstorm about 20 miles away. I promptly changed course and gave the squall line a wide breadth.

Pete and Gene were working on this big land deal up at Medicine Park and they wanted me to fly them up to Lawton for a meeting with the landowner's attorney. Generally, we used the Bonanza, but for this trip, only a Cessna Skylane was available.

After the meeting, Pete wanted to have a look at the land from the air, so I flew them out over the area. The development lay in a valley near Mt. Scott and not too far from the Fort Sill Army Post. After circling low in the valley to view the wooded property, I began a climb out toward the mountain range that lay between our position and the most direct path of flight back to the Lawton airport.

There was a small lenticular cloud over Mt. Scott and that should have tipped me off to the down draft ahead. When we hit the down draft, the rate of descent indicator pegged out in the down position. I added full power and went to best rate of climb speed, but we were going down in a full climb. At the last minute, I turned, nearly doing a wingover back into the valley in order to keep from flying into the side of the mountain.

Flying down the valley, I circled the small mountain range and took up a heading back to Lawton. Pete was looking out the window and asked, "Are those artillery shell holes down there on the ground?"

"Yes," I replied, "I suppose they are. We are out over the Fort Sill artillery and rocket firing range, a restricted area, but right now I'd rather take my chances with an artillery shell than that mountain in these wind conditions."

Aerobatic Flight

A pilot instructor named Clark operated the small airport at Mangrum Field, north of Richland Hills in Fort Worth. At one end of the airport was an electrical high line. Landing from that direction generally required full flaps. This airport's location was the personification of the old adage, "If you need to find a private airport, look for some power lines because there is probably an airport just the other side."

Clark gave multi-engine instruction in an old Piper Apache that had a single-engine service ceiling of about two feet above sea level. Clark referred to his ol' Apache as the double-breasted humming Piper.

Clark also had a Citabra for aerobatic training and it got a real workout with students flying the plane. Clark showed me the J-bolt his A&E mechanic had taken out of the wing strut during the plane's last inspection. The bolt was nearly sheared in half. Pilots refer to these single strut bolts on high-wing airplanes as the J-bolt because if it snaps, the next thing you will be doing is explaining to Jesus what had happened. During aerobatic training, student and instructor always wear a parachute, which is good if you have time to use them.

On my own, I had already figured out how to slow roll a Cessna Skylane. It's really pretty simple. All that is required is to crank in full aileron and not chicken out by letting up on the ailerons until the horizon has turned full around in the front windshield. Letting up on the aileron halfway through, will cause the airplane to perform a split-S and come out the bottom at speeds close to Velocity Never Exceed (VNE). Not a good idea. Most aircraft will exceed VNE a little and for a short time, but it is still a dangerous thing to let happen.

I had access to a Cessna Aerobat, the factory version of an aerobatic Cessna 150 and I took several aerobatic lessons from Clark who had a reputation of being a darn good instructor. What I hadn't yet tried without an aerobatics airplane was a loop. The first time I tried it with Clark, I fell out of the top and lost all orientation. He just sat there and let me recover on my own, but we were pretty high up.

There was an older fellow who hung around Mangrum Airport a lot. He performed aerobatics in a Taylorcraft BC-12 at air shows around the Dallas and Fort Worth area and his specialty was to slow roll the Taylorcraft at 50 feet off the deck. He had also written an instruction book on aerobatics.

One day, we both happened to be at the airport at the same time and I asked him if he would give me a lesson in the Cessna Aerobat. He was interested in trying out the Aerobat and so he agreed. The first time he tried a combination loop and snap roll he lost 1,000 feet of altitude.

What if we had been at 50 feet? With all due respect, he was unfamiliar with the plane, but I decided not to take any more lessons from him as I could fly about as good as he could and I wasn't about to try it down on the deck.

Cardinal X-Country

Pilots often refer to the south central part of the U.S. as thunderstorm alley. On any given afternoon, thunderstorms will build rapidly in the heat, fed by moisture from the Gulf. Light planes were never meant to penetrate thunderstorms and generally can't climb over them.

A technique used by experienced light plane pilots is to fly up to the front of the oncoming storm and land before the high winds arrive. Then via a hangar or a good tie-down, wait for the squall line to pass. Then fly out the backside of the storm. Unless the front goes stationary, this generally only takes a couple of hours.

Starting in the late 1960s, we took our vacations in the winters to central Florida. On our first flying trip to Florida, we went in an almost new, but slow Cessna Cardinal 177. The trip down was uneventful and enjoyable. However, on our return trip, we ran smack dab into one of those mid-afternoon thunderstorms.

For a half hour or more, I tried to climb over a low section of the storm. My daughter, sitting in the right seat holding a sectional chart in her lap, seemed to be getting a little scared so I decided to give up on the climb at 10,000 feet and started a slow spiraling descent to land somewhere.

That Cardinal wouldn't climb its way out of a wet paper bag. The plane needed at least a 180 hp engine instead of a 150 hp engine. Also, why a stabulator on a Cardinal, flying elevators were engineered for speeds of 400 mph or better.

We came in over the small town of Lumberton, Alabama, located the airport, landed and parked the Cardinal. There was no one at the airport, so the three of us took a nap in the plane while we waited for the rainstorm to pass.

About dark, we made it to east Texas. After fighting the weather and a long hard day of flying, I gave up and landed at Marshall, Texas where we spent the night in a motel.

The moral of this story is when attempting to cover that many miles in a day get a higher performance airplane. As the old saying about general aviation goes, "If you have time to spare, go by air."

Christmas Lights

On Christmas Eve of 1969, some friends of ours came over to our house to visit for the evening. We had met when we bought homes in a new housing development in Grand Prairie years ago. We were sitting around reminiscing about times past. Bobby had been a heavy equipment operator, but was now a flight line mechanic at LTV. He had been with me the day I nearly ground looped the Cessna 190 and used to fly the T-34 with me.

Bobby's appearance and mannerisms were that of the large stoic ex-marine EN he was, but he was a gentle man by nature. His silhouette in a darkened barroom was somewhat imposing. In my younger more stupid years, I had a bad habit of mouthing off to the wrong kind of folks. When we used to frequent the bars out on the county line and some drunk cowboy would give me a bad time, Bobby would walk up behind me and stand there until my irritated adversary displayed the better part of wisdom and moved on.

Judy was a small lady who resembled the actress Natalie Wood. She spent most of her younger life having and raising kids. Judy always gave me a hard time. She took any opportunity to point out to my wife how I would spend any extra money I had to go log another hour of flying time, usually taking Bobby along with me. She'd add, what the two of them didn't spend flying, they'd finish off out at the county line. Only problem was, Judy kind of had the last part of that backwards.

Fort Worth had begun a tradition of outlining their downtown buildings with lights during the Christmas season. I had the business and personal use of a Piper Aztec for a while and we all decided that we'd like to go see the Christmas lights from the air. Suzie, Bobby, Judy and all our kids piled into the six-place Aztec with me.

With the kids in the far back and Judy's youngest in her lap, we took off from Garland airport. It was one of those crisp cool still-as-a-feather, no moon evenings. I circled out around Fort Worth and back over downtown Dallas cruising at about 1,500 feet AGL. With the Aztec throttled way back and in the silky smooth air, it seemed as though we were floating on a magic carpet or maybe Santa's sleigh high above the Christmas lights.

It was one of those rare and beautiful flights that you remember when all the rest are blurred and forgotten. Forty years later, the four of us still stay in touch.

Cessna Centurion

The next run we made to Florida was in a brand new Cessna 210 Centurion. This aircraft could make it with one gas stop and turn in a reasonably respectable cruising speed. A good halfway point for us on the way to Winter Haven was the Mobile, Alabama airport. When I called for landing instructions the first time I landed at Mobile I called, "Mobil tower," pronouncing it like the oil company. The tower tartly inquired if I was the aircraft calling, "mo-beal tower." Seems they had taken issue with the way this Texan had pronounced Mobile.

Cruising along the crescent of the Florida gulf coast, it was always tempting to cut a few miles off by going out over the Gulf of Mexico like the airliners do when heading for southern Florida. However, prior clearance is needed for crossing the Air Defense Identification Zone (ADIZ). In a light single-engine plane, I just never liked getting farther out over the Gulf than I could glide back to the shoreline.

Rounding the Florida Panhandle to head south, there was an old power plant on the west coast that billowed white smoke. On a clear day, you could spot the steam coming from the tall smoke stacks of the power plant a hundred miles away. I would set my heading to the north of the power plant. This heading would intersect the central Florida railroad line that went right past the Winter Haven Airport. Navigating, by flying the RR tracks was referred to by old-time pilots as flying the iron compass.

Walt Disney had just begun to build Disney World near Orlando about this time and my brother-in-law wanted me to take the kids for a sightseeing ride over the new construction rising up out of some orange groves and the middle of an alligator infested swamp. We cruised around in the Cessna 210, circling the new Disney World construction site at 500 feet AGL. My brother-in-law got airsick from the hot bumpy air, but all four of the kids loved it.

Florida In The Twin Cessna

The next trip to Florida was via Twin Cessna N6932L, a model 310k. My wife and daughter had flown to Florida earlier on a commercial airline flight for a little extra vacation.

Departing Fort Worth, I headed for Florida alone in the Cessna 310. Somewhere over Louisiana, I started wondering if I had remembered to throw my suitcase in the luggage compartment or not. The twin had a good autopilot, which took a lot of the work out of the flying. Climbing into the backseat, I peered over the back seat into an empty luggage compartment. I had left my suitcase sitting on the ramp when I was doing my preflight. Oh well, I'll buy some Bermuda shorts and a Hi-wa-yen flowery sport shirt when I get to Florida and forgot about it.

The twin was equipped with the standard fruit jar rest room, but unlike the under-powered singles I had previously made the trip in, I could almost stand up in the back seat with the autopilot on in order to, well you get the picture.

After stopping at Lakefront Airport for fueling, I was walking back across the ramp to the airplane when two hippies approached me. In those days we always called it a ramp, but now the popular term seems to be tarmac. The two young men inquired as to the possibility of them hitching a ride with me to Florida. They had heard me checking the weather in the FBO and the gas boy had probably tipped them off that they might be able to catch a ride in my plane, as I had no passengers.

They explained that they were students at some eastern college. Being a little skeptical due to recent Cuba high jacking incidents, I said, "If you are students, let me see your student ID cards."

Both quickly produced what looked like valid college ID and I agreed that they were welcome to ride along. Anyway, I could use the company. The one riding in the front seat asked if he could play his harmonica. Flying down the coastline to Gulfport, *we sung up ever song* this flyer ever knew, me and hippie Bobby McGee, a real sixties scene. Both boys were very appreciative for the ride and one of them gave my teenage daughter a handmade leather belt when she and my wife met me at the airport.

On our return, stopped for a couple of nights to visit the Vieux Carre, the old French Quarter. In those days, the new rock levy around Jackson Square had not yet been built and the JAX brewery occupied much of the riverfront.

We stayed at the just completed high-rise Marriott Hotel and that evening enjoyed a wonderful dinner at the restaurant on the top floor. The view at night overlooking the crescent bend in the Mississippi River, from which New Orleans gets its nickname the Crescent City was fantastic, almost like flying while sitting still at the dinner table.

Not To Worry It's A Twin

One of the best stories about losing an engine on a twin was in Florida. This low time twin-engine pilot had flown over to the Bahamas and was preparing to return to Miami in his Piper Twin. A young fellow approached the pilot at the airport and asked if he might hitch a ride back to the mainland with him.

The pilot agreed and as they prepared to depart, the passenger commented that he had never flown in a small aircraft before. The pilot dutifully explained that he had been having trouble with one of the engines on the Piper, but there was no need for concern because at sea level, the twin-engine plane was quite capable of making it back to the mainland on one engine.

Sure enough, halfway back to Miami Beach, the right engine sputtered and started smoking. The pilot shutdown the engine and flew the twin on to the mainland where they landed safely.

As they were getting out of the plane, the passenger told the pilot how much he appreciated telling him about the engine problem before it actually failed because he would have panicked if he had not known to expect the problem in advance. In fact, the passenger went on to say, "You seemed a lot more upset over the engine failure than I was."

The pilot gave his passenger an odd look and said, "You don't understand, it was the good engine that quit!"

Sip A Mint Julep With The CAF

The Confederate Air Force (CAF) toured the country putting on air shows. I first heard of them when they held a big air show at Greater Southwest International Airport in Fort Worth. War Birds were cheap and easy to obtain in those days and the air group had assembled a great collection of flying WW II aircraft.

The landing gear on a B-17 can be lowered manually one at a time and so as part of the air show, the B-17 pilot would fly in low over the field, trailing smoke with only one landing gear extended. Of course, the pilot didn't touchdown. The crippled bomber stunt was a real crowd pleaser.

Several T-6 Texan trainers with Japanese insignias and cockpits modified to look like Zeros would make diving runs as personnel on the ground set off explosives to simulate bombs having been dropped. This, of course, was the beginning of what is now the rather elaborate Tora Tora air show squadron.

When I joined the CAF, it was still based in Harlingen and the official motto of their mascot, Colonel Culpepper, was Sipa-mint-julep. In those days, no one gave much thought about having called it the Confederate Air Force, as it was all in good fun.

The weekend I was to officially join the CAF, Doctor Almand was going down in his red Stagger-wing Beech and an astronaut from Houston was coming in with a fully restored P-40, painted up like a Flying Tiger. I was inducted the same evening as the NASA Astronaut along with a couple other flying bums. Needless to say, not much attention was paid to any of the new members except the honored guest.

The annual homecoming fly-in and air show in those days was more for the members' entertainment than for the public. The next day, I wore my new gray khakis with silver Eagle cufflinks on the collar and gray Stetson indicating that I was now a Colonel in the CAF.

Members would line their planes up on the grass beside the runway and with doors propped open watch from the comfort of the cockpit seats, the best seats in the house. I had the good sense to stay out of the air show antics because in those days there were some combat veterans and real pros doing the flying.

I did, however, attend the pilot's briefing and recall a handout explaining Rule 23. The info sheet instructed pilots who could not identify the aircraft they were assigned, to ask any small boy who would then point the airplane out to them. The instructions for starting an unfamiliar aircraft were to re-arrange all the shiny switches in the opposite position, leave the rusty ones alone and the aircraft should start.

Exactly Where Are We

When it came time for the annual fly-in and mint julep drinking contest, my wife and I made plans to attend. I decided we would fly down in an old navy blue Cessna 310B I had recently purchased and was fixing up to resell.

It was a beautiful morning as we took off and climbed out over the clouds towards Hillsboro headed for the annual CAF fly-in at Harlingen. The weather along part of our route from Fort Worth was overcast with the tops at about 5,000 feet, but a hundred miles south it was severe-clear, an ideal day for jumping over the top VFR.

The Narco NAV/COM units worked well enough, but there was a lot of ignition noise coming through the radios. Somewhere south of Waco, the popping noise in the NAV/COM started to get on my nerves, so I reached over and turned them off. I already knew the weather was reporting severe-clear at our destination and so just flew the dead reckoning heading on my gyrocompass. Never cared much for that term, dead reckoning.

My wife was holding a WAC chart in her lap and she asked me to show her where we were at that time. Reaching over, I drew about a four-inch circle on the chart, somewhere south of Waco. She sat there for a few minutes and then said, "No, I mean exactly where are we on this chart?"

Finally, I admitted that I really didn't know, but if we came upon a large body of water, that would probably be the Gulf of Mexico and we had gone too far. We would then turn right and when we spotted some orange groves, we would be pretty close to Harlingen. Her suspicions were confirmed. "Just what I thought, you pilots don't even know where you are most of the time!"

Chapter Ten
FURTHER AND FASTER

A used car salesman and wheeler-dealer extraordinaire friend of mine by the name of Guest, was a jovial fellow about my age. He had a line of credit at the bank for importing and selling foreign cars in Dallas. The only catch was his deal with the banker required him to turn his inventory every sixty days.

Guest was a pilot and often traded cars for airplanes and visa versa. When he would get stuck with an airplane or car too long, he would bring it to me for a swap.

Our standing deal was that he would guarantee me no loss in or out of our deals. Subsequently, I let him make any profit on the deals. The result was that I didn't know from one day to the next whether I would have an almost new Mercedes at my disposal or some type of weird flying machine that he had taken in trade.

Wouldn't Fly It For It

Guest kept his planes at the Lancaster Airport, a Cessna 180 tail dragger and a Pitts Special biplane. I had gone out to the airport to pick Guest up the day he flew the Pitts in and I heard an old-timer who hung around the airport comment, "I wouldn't fly it, for it." I intended to go fly the 180 some, but Guest sold it before I had a chance.

Guest was returning from Austin in a Mooney 21 and during his descent for landing, one blade of the constant speed prop on the Mooney broke its retaining ring and flew off. The remaining half of the out of balance prop jerked the engine off of its engine mounts. As luck would have it, the engine pulled the cables attached to the throttle and mixture simultaneously, shutting down the engine.

When the incident occurred, Guest was not very high and made a wheels-up landing in an open field. Upon inspection, the engine was lying in the bottom of the engine cowl. The only thing holding the engine in the aircraft were the cowling fasteners. If this had been a Cessna on which the cowling mounts to the engine, the whole front of the aircraft would have fallen off leaving the aircraft seriously out of CG and the remaining airframe would have tumbled to the ground out of control.

The man just lived a charmed life. Guest finally sold his rather valuable antique racecar collection to a wealthy Dallas businessman. The last time I saw him, he was promoting his new company, Farm Fresh VWs, a shop out in the country near Red Oak for re-building Volkswagon Beetles to factory new condition.

Termite Free Bellanca

After a year or two of this aero and auto swapping, I ended up with an almost new Bellanca N4084B, which I was into for well worth the money, so I just kept that one.

The Bellanca had a fiberglass wing surface with a heavy wooden main spar and is one of the strongest light aircraft wings ever marketed. The A&I mechanic who did my inspections delighted in kidding me about the wood spar. He would hand me a bill for work he completed and laughingly add that there was no extra charge for spraying the Bellanca for termites.

That November, my wife and daughter had again flown via commercial to Florida to visit her sister. Thanksgiving was coming up, so as soon as I could get away from business, I was to fly down in the Bellanca to join them. The day before Thanksgiving, there were scattered broken clouds in Dallas as I departed. The Bellanca would cruise easily at 220 mph. However, a very unusual phenomenon occurred. I had a tail wind.

My ground speed was probably in excess of 250 mph as I leveled out on top of the cloud layer headed for New Orleans. Inbound to New Orleans, the overcast sky was broken enough for me to descend and proceed on to Lakefront Airport VFR rather than having to file IFR with New Orleans Approach Control.

Slowing the Bellanca down, I descended below the overcast where the ceiling was about 1,500 feet. As I leveled out at 1,000 AGL, I scanned the horizon and there was nothing except water as far as I could see in any direction. Darn it, I was too low to pickup the VOR without going back up on top. I knew I had been clipping along at a really good ground speed, but hadn't realized I had gotten myself out over the Gulf of Mexico.

Oh well, land was just to the north and so I turned to a heading of 3-6-0. In a few minutes, land appeared on the horizon and the shoreline was coming up fast. It is not possible to see very far cruising at 1,000 feet AGL or in this case AWL. Most low time pilots who get lost are flying too low. By climbing higher, they might see a landmark that would orientate them.

Nice Airport You Got Here

As I made landfall, I was looking right down the approach-end of an excellent runway. Circling to check the tetrahedron, I entered a standard airport pattern and landed. Taxiing up to the gas pump I looked around for a sign on the hangar or some sort of a name that might tell me where the heck I was. A young fellow came out to fuel the Bellanca. Not wishing to appear lost, I utter the single corniest line I have ever spoken in my flying career, "Nice airport you got here. What do you call it?"

The boy replied, "Hammond Northshore."

The name Hammond didn't register on my brain, but north shore sure did. I realize I had not been out over the Gulf at all, only over Lake Pontchartrain, a lake so big I couldn't see its shore from my altitude.

Checking the weather before takeoff, a large front to the north had started to move south. It wasn't looking good, but I decided to see how far I could get before dark. Night flying in a single-engine over the Florida swamps was not my favorite thing to do and I was certainly not going to fly into night conditions and bad weather both.

Hugging the coastline from Pass Christian on, I stayed just a little offshore of the beach to avoid any radio towers and yet close enough to shore so as not to violate any restricted areas. I radioed a guess of my position to the Air Defense Zone controller, the ADIZ. We had no transponders in most of our planes in those days. After a couple of turns for radar identification, the Air Force controller gave me my position as south of Fort Walton Beach. The weather up ahead, well lit by the setting sun behind me, looked like a black wall. It was decision time and so I asked for radar vectors to the nearest airport of any size. The controller steered me into Destin.

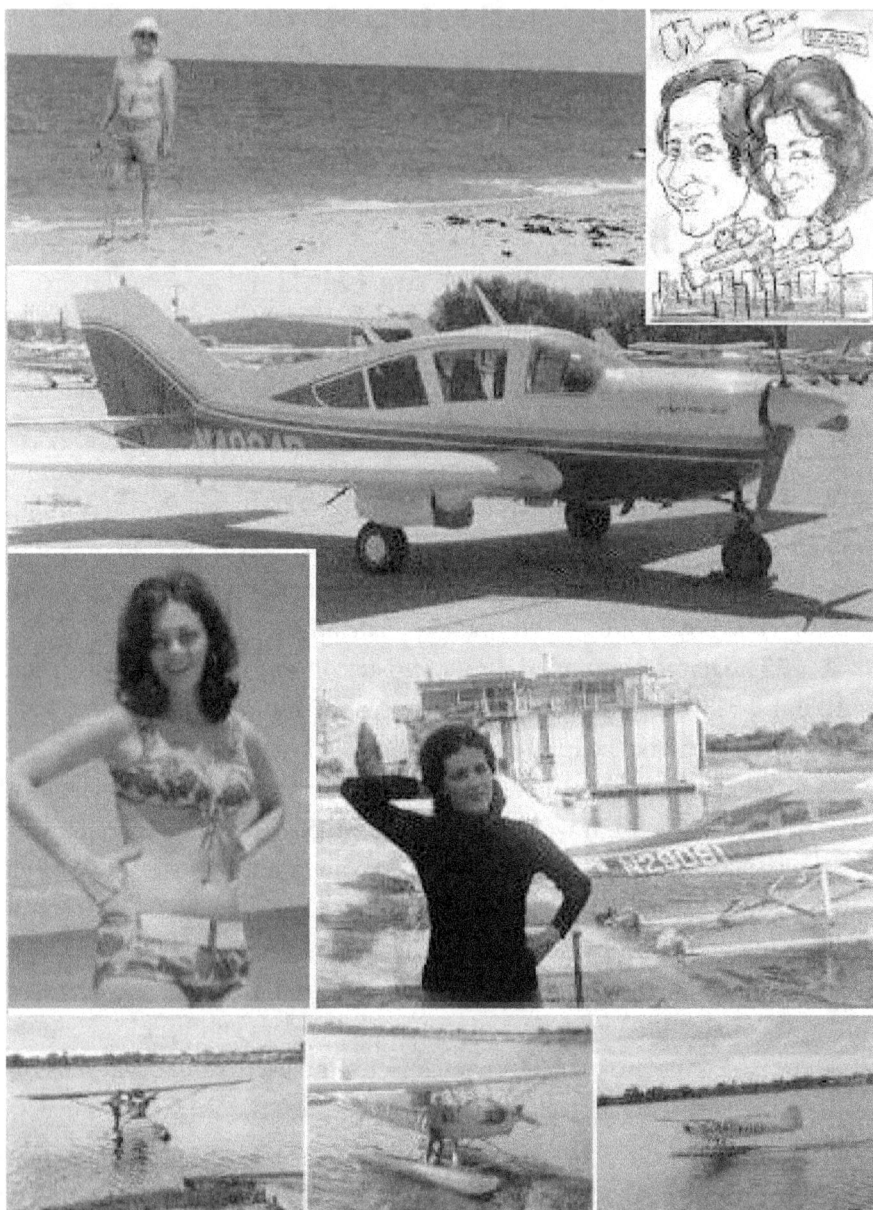

When it gets cold in Dallas, jump in trusty Bellanca and head for beaches of Florida; "I'll Follow You Anywhere" cartoon; Nancy at beach; Suzie in front of seaplane port, house in background belonged to author of Jonathan Livingston Seagull; Piper Cubs on floats at Brown Seaplane Flying Service in Winter Haven.

It was a beautifully pitch-black night, the calm before the storm. Circling the well-lit airfield to read the tetrahedron, I entered base and turned final only to find myself looking down the landing lights of a cabin class twin making a straight-in approach for landing from offshore. Verbalizing a few choice cuss words, I pulled up and circled in behind the twin. At this particular uncontrolled airfield, the locals considered the north approach from offshore to be the calm wind runway. Calm wind meaning, we don't care which way the tetrahedron is pointing. Oh well, when in Rome…

Pay Attention To Your Fuel

The next morning, after spending the night in a beach resort hotel across the street from the airport, I checked the weather again. The storm had become occluded overnight or what I call gone soft. The tops were only 4,000 feet, but it was 300 miles wide and conditions were zero-zero under the cloud layer.

The edge of the clouds ended right at the shoreline. Notice this the next time you fly near a shoreline. I believe it's due to the difference between the land and water temperatures. I watched as a Cessna 401 took off ahead, headed out over the Gulf, made a climbing turn and circled back VFR on top. Seemed like a good idea to me, so I follow him out and on top.

Climbing out, I set my VOR to Tallahassee and began monitoring approach control. It was a beautiful sunshiny day on top and the soft white clouds stretched far out over the horizon. Monitoring the radio, I listened as a Delta jet tried to shoot an approach at Tallahassee and pulled up at minimums without ever having the field in sight. The Delta pilot made one more attempt to shoot the instrument approach before departing for Atlanta, his alternate airport.

My thinking process went like this. If I loss power on this single-engine Bellanca, I would have to make a gliding descent through the cloud layer. Of course, I would attempt to shoot an instrument approach if within gliding distance of an IFR airport. This may sound a little odd, but above 6,000 feet AGL, there are usually several good airports within gliding distance. Most pilots don't even try for one.

The reality was that if I descended through the cloud layer, the next sight I would probably see in my windshield would be the tops of a lot of scrub palms. Those small palm trees being the dominant vegetation covering that part of the Florida panhandle. I scrupulously monitored my mixture, exhaust gas temperature and fuel gages for the next two hours.

An ol' timers trick is to save a little fuel in one tank, generally referred to as saving a couple of gallons for mom and the kids. Then when all the tanks are run dry except that one, you're going to have to land somewhere. It's best to have a little go-around fuel, just in case.

Northwest of Gainesville, the soft solid cloud layer started to go broken and a few miles further, I was bumping along on sunny day thermals. Relaxing in the seat, I assumed the normal mentally caged-and-locked attitude of most pilots on a long cross-country flight.

Approaching the Winter Haven Airport, I entered downwind and the Bellanca's engine quit cold. Faster than the human eye can see, I went to full forward mixture, switched tanks and turned the electric fuel pump on. The engine hardly missed a beat as it resumed its normal purring. I had run the selected fuel tank dry a few thousand yards from my destination. Sure makes a difference when you pay attention.

In Case Of Fire Don't Say Hah

After a week or so I headed back to Texas in the Bellanca with my wife and daughter. We usually made this flight in a twin instead of a single. As we flew high above the thick foliage of the Florida Panhandle, I decided that some instructions on the subject of forced landing procedures might be appropriate.

I explained that if we had to make an engine-out landing in the bush covered swampy terrain we were presently flying over, that just before touchdown, the single door on the right side of the cockpit was to be popped open. Not to worry, it would not fly all the way open, as the air stream would keep it in the trail position. This was to prevent the door from becoming jammed and unable to be opened as a result of a crash landing.

"If I say, get out! Don't ask why, just get out." In particular, if there was any smoke or fire, get out quickly. As the old joke goes, *don't say huh, cause you're gonna to be talkin' to yourself.* A short time later, we landed for fuel and a cold drink at Fort Walton Beach.

Fuel-injected engines tend to flood when the engine is hot and will quite often throw a flame out the exhaust stack. In the event of an exhaust stack fire, the best procedure is to go ahead and let the engine start so as to blow the flames out of the exhaust. However, if the fuel explosion in the stack is too great, it can sometimes bust the exhaust stack brackets.

We boarded the Bellanca and as I started the hot engine, this was exactly what happened. The engine sputtered, smoke and flames came out the exhaust for just an instant. After the engine was running, I decided it would be a good idea to shut it back down in order to go inspect the exhaust.

Turning to my two passengers I said, "I need to get out for a minute and check the…" I stopped mid-sentence when I realized I was talking to myself.

Standing on the tarmac twenty feet away were my wife and daughter with their arms folded watching me. I climbed out of the Bellanca laughing. It appeared that they had been paying attention during my forced landing lecture. "You told us if we saw smoke or fire to get out, so that's what we did!"

Eunice For The Night

As we passed New Orleans enroute back to Dallas, weather advisories were reporting the autumn storm over east Texas and northern Louisiana was building rapidly. I was aware of the storm from an earlier briefing, but planned on circling it to the south via Lake Charles and Houston. We were overtaking the storm and as objects began floating around in the cockpit, I realized we weren't going to make Lake Charles before the storm hit. The nearest airport on our sectional chart was located right in the middle of the rice-growing belt of Louisiana.

As I lowered the gear for a straight-in approch to landing, we went by the town's water tower. My daughter read the name, "We're in Eunice," she said. Two distinct sounds followed, the screech of the tires on the blacktop runway as we touched down and the second sound was an erp, muffled by a brown paper bag. The later sound had emanated from my wife in the back seat who had been taking the worst of our fishtailing in the rough air.

123

The airport's resident mechanic was just closing up and checking the tie downs on the parked aircraft in preparation for the impending storm. There was no additional room in the hangar and so he helped me secure the Bellanca on one of the tie downs.

The mechanic gave us a lift into Eunice and dropped us at the only motel in town. The rain had started and the wind was kicking up as we ventured across the motel parking lot to the restaurant, both incidentally owned by the same Cajun gentleman.

A small group of locals were laughing and visiting as we entered. All were speaking Cajun French. To their credit, when they realized we spoke no French, all immediately converted to American English. Courtesy still existed in that small town and we appreciated their making us feel welcome.

Ten Years Before Oliver Stone

Understanding that our stopover in Eunice was not by choice, the cafe owner, a large rotund man, introduced himself and joined us at the table. He insisted we try his mother's Cajun cooking and it just happened that she was in the kitchen cooking a specialty called crawfish bisque. He asked if we would like to try a bowl on the house. My small slender wife, who has always been a real culinary experimenter, accepted and finished off all three bowls by herself. For the next several hours, the storm outside raged on as we were treated to a variety of Cajun home cooking and interesting conversation.

In the movie *JFK*, by director Oliver Stone, the opening scene is of the assistant district attorney standing in the doorway to Garrison's office. He says something like, "Hey boss, they just shot the President." That Assistant DA, retired now, was the owner of the motel and restaurant and the gentleman we were presently having dinner and visiting with.

I guess because we had mentioned we were from Dallas, our host began to tell us about his experiences working as an assistant to Garrison during the JFK investigation. He pointed out the window to a small clinic across the street from where we were sitting and said, "That is where the woman from Dallas was taken," and he went on to explain she had been thrown out of a car and left for dead. He had personally interviewed the woman, a prostitute and former stripper that had worked at Jack Ruby's bar. "They are going to kill the President, she told us, but she wouldn't or couldn't tell us who they were."

We heard the story from beginning to end and it was exactly the same as the story told in the movie, with one exception. We were being told the story ten years before the movie was made.

When the café closed, we went to our motel room and checked the weather. It appeared the storm was now going to rage for some time. The next morning, we rented a car and drove back to Dallas. Driving out of the storm, we saw trees uprooted and pieces of buildings everywhere. The decision to land and not attempt to cross the mother of all storms had been a good one.

An instructor pilot, who had wanted to log some time in the Bellanca, caught a ride with a student pilot down to Eunice that weekend and returned the Bellanca back to Love Field for me.

The T-6 Texan

One of the other airplanes I bought from Guest was a T-6 Texan military trainer. Actually, it was a Navy SNJ version. The FAA did not have provisions for certifying an SNJ for civilian use, so the aircraft had to first have all of the service bulletins incorporated for it to become a T-6 and then it could be licensed as a private aircraft.

Needing to meet the requirements for checkout in type for the higher performance aircraft, I had Guest bring the T-6 over to Amon Carter Field. Guest explained that he wouldn't fly the T-6 from the back seat, so he climbed in the front and said he would go around the pattern a couple of times with me while I tried to land the T-6 from the backseat.

In a normal taxi or flare-out, it is hard to see over the nose of the T-6 from the backseat. In the early days of WW II, I had been told that the young Air Corps and Navy cadet fighter pilots had to be able to takeoff and land these trainers from the backseat before they flew the single-seat fighters. Anyone who has ever sat in a WW II tail-wheel fighter aircraft like the P-40 or Corsair can understand why.

On my takeoff in the T-6, using the long concrete runway, I quickly raised the tail and made my takeoff roll on the main wheels. The T-6 flew exactly like a small DC-3.

Flying the pattern, I turned final, lined up with the runway and established a slow rate of descent. As I assumed a nose-high attitude for touchdown, I watched out the right side of the cockpit for the large blue Butler Aviation hangar to go by. As I passed the hangar, I eased the power off and made a perfect three-point landing the first time.

Guest allowed as how he couldn't make a landing any better than that from the front seat. "Beginners luck," I replied modestly and it mostly was. We flew back to Lancaster Airport to drop Guest off and he made the landing in the T-6 from the front seat. The old Lancaster airport only had a short north-south landing strip in those days.

Climbing in the front seat for the first time, I taxied out to the end of the runway and began my takeoff roll. There was a strong right crosswind and before I could get the tail wheel up, the P-factor kicked in and I drifted to the far left side of the airstrip. The yellow cones protecting the landing strip runway lights were starting to move under my left wing and I figured that in about a second or two, my left main landing gear was going to start knocking out lights.

Keeping the plane straight with the rudder, I laid the stick over to the right and had enough aileron control to lift the T-6 onto its right main gear until it got enough air speed to lift off, now known as the ol' one wheel takeoff technique.

The factory installed military tube-type radios had long since been pulled out of the T-6 and trashed. Someone had installed a Narco transceiver that worked fairly well except that the aircraft had no ignition or fuel pump noise suppression filters. The trainer's radio had a lot of static. At cruise power, I could barely hear over my headset and had to throttle back in order to call the tower.

Thus, standard procedure for entering the radio-controlled pattern at Amon Carter Field was to approach the control zone at cruise speed, retard the throttle and glide momentarily while contacting the tower. Coming back up on the power and entering downwind in a glide lessened the static enough to hear clearance for landing. Wind noise from flying open cockpit made it worse.

Albuquerque

My brother graduated from college in Albuquerque and decided to stay. The Cessna 310 was now being used for going west to Albuquerque as well as southeast to Florida. VFR enroute from Dallas to Albuquerque, I was trying to beat a weather front, but it didn't work out and we had to land at a small airport in Santa Rosa, New Mexico.

The airport's ramp was full of socked-in cross-country light aircraft. Pilots going west had landed to wait for the front to pass. Most were not instrument rated, but I was. After calling Albuquerque and discovering that there were no imbedded thunderstorms and that the front had become stationery, I filed an IFR flight plan and we loaded up to depart.

I recall a half dozen VFR light airplane pilots watching wishfully as we taxied out. Immediately after takeoff, we went full IFR and maintained a full-power climb. No matter how many times I had made this particular flight, when I knew there were rocks on both sides of me, I didn't relax until I knew we were well clear of the highest mountain peak in any direction. At about 14,000 feet, we punched out of the top of the clouds and could see Mt. Taylor off in the distance. It was clear as far as the eye could see from Sandia Mountain west.

East of Albuquerque is the Tijeras Pass that lies between Sandia and the Montoya range to the south. It's a good idea not to fly through the Pass, but go over one of the mountain peaks, which are only about 10,000 feet because the air currents in the pass are bad most of the time.

One thing I learned the hard way is not to forget that the airspeed indicator reads a little slow when landing at a high altitude airport. The first time I landed at Coronado Airport north of Albuquerque in the Cessna 310 twin, I approached the runway at my usual indicated landing speed. I used up the entire runway and was pumping the brakes so as not to run off the north end of the runway and onto the dirt overrun. Put there, I assume, for sea level pilots like myself.

There are certain terrains around the country where an airplane seems to always go into what pilots call automatic-rough. One such place is the arid valley between Santa Rosa and Moriarity. Coming off the backside of Sandia Mountain on a hot afternoon headed east, an airplane will not stay level.

Even at 14,000 feet, it's a rough ride. The wings rock all the time. First you're up 300 feet and then down 200 feet. That's the ride until you get back down off the high plains on a hot day. An autopilot helps take some of the work out, if you have one. Otherwise, it's like riding in a jeep on a rough road, just relax and roll with the bumps!

Hot Air Balloon Races

The first time I heard the phrase "balloon races," I laughed out loud. How do you race in a hot air balloon? The balloon competitions held in Albuquerque were originally called the World Hot Air Balloon Championships, but is now generally referred to as the Balloon Festival.

Twenty plus years ago, Cutter Aviation, the local Beechcraft dealer, sponsored the first balloon event at the main Albuquerque airport. Cutter's son had become interested in hot air ballooning. He and some of his cronies dreamed the whole thing up. When they decided to hold it a second year in an open field down by the Rio Grande, we attended. We were thrilled at the 85 or so hot air balloons that showed up. Now the event annually attracts over 1,000 balloons of every shape and size from all over the world the first full weekend of October.

While balloon racing sounds like an oxymoron, it turns out that it's not. Balloons move with the wind currents. In the unique valley where Albuquerque lies, the wind currents move in different directions at different altitudes. Thus, by changing the balloon's altitude, it can be navigated directionally.

Two very successful businessmen, Max and Ben, were local Albuquerque balloonists who became famous by setting world hot air balloon records. One afternoon, my brother called me from Albuquerque to say, "I just went up with Max."

"Didn't even know you were interested in ballooning," I replied. He laughed and went on to explain that he wasn't, but while at his bank, he had ridden up in the elevator with Max.

Max was killed in a suspicious balloon crash near the Soviet border. Ben crashed sometime later in his personal cabin class twin. Taking off from Albuquerque International Airport on a ski trip, the nose luggage compartment came open and something flew into the prop. Attempting to turn back onto the airport runway, the aircraft spun into the ground killing all on board.

West to Vegas

Las Vegas, Nevada was an easy flight from Albuquerque in the Cessna 310 and we started flying out there more often. The weekend of my brother's college graduation, we left Albuquerque in heavy overcast conditions and flew down the valley towards Acoma until I was able to climb out through the broken clouds.

As we climbed to VFR on top, I inched up to 14,500 feet in order to get over the top of a small ridge of thunderstorms. I was rattling away, talking when I realized I was carrying on a conversation with myself. My four passengers were sound asleep. Waking everyone up, I told them that they couldn't sleep at this altitude due to the danger of hypoxia and that in just a few more minutes I could descend back down to 10,000 feet.

We were over the desert and from my own experience I've found that you can fly higher over mountains without the same loss of oxygen. I know of no studies on this, but my personal theory is that the vegetation that produces the oxygen is higher up in the atmosphere and thus, the mountain air is a little richer in oxygen than the air over sea and desert.

Flying back from Vegas on a summer day in the Cessna 310, I decided to drop down and have a look at the meteor crater near Winslow, Arizona. After buzzing the crater, I landed at the Winslow airport to give my passengers a break and treat everyone to a cold drink.

Winslow was one of those small one-airline airports that an air carrier out of California flew an old Convair into once a day. The Eagles song, *Take It Easy* seemed to have taken on a surreal meaning that afternoon.

Lifting off from Winslow on the hot, bumpy afternoon, the ol' 310 went into automatic-rough as we climbed out. As I lowered the nose, it looked as though 160 mph was all she was going to do. At that point, my brother who was riding in the right seat looked down at the red indicator light on the gear handle and suggested that we might make better time if I'd retract the landing gear. I guess that's better than forgetting to put the gear down.

Lake flying around Chain of Lakes in Central Florida; Beech Twin Baron used to get multi-engine rating at Goble Aviation; Las Vegas, Nevada when the town wasn't that big yet; our Cessna 310k Twin; trips to Albuquerque Balloon Festival that just got bigger every year.

McCarran Field

The airport at Las Vegas, an AAC base during WW II has about as strange a history as the casino town itself. When I first started flying into McCarran, Howard Hughes' Summa Corporation operated the FBO. At one time, Hughes had offered to buy McCarran Field and build Las Vegas a new international airport farther out of town. They should have taken him up on it because the Las Vegas Strip has now overtaken the airport.

The old burned-down Rancho Las Vegas was still standing when I first started going to Vegas. One could still feel the ghosts of the old '30s and '40s Hollywood crowd haunting the place. The early Las Vegas Strip, known by old timers as the County Line, included large parcels of barren land covered with sand and limestone gravel. Hughes bought up much of this land with funds from the sale of TWA.

On the corner of McCarran Airport, nearest the Strip, was a small startup aircraft manufacturing company. The land was part of the airport, thus preventing developers from grabbing it up. The property was isolated from the taxiways by a large drainage ditch, effectively preventing access to the airport and owed its existence to some politically motivated reason.

The owner, president and promoter of the aircraft company lived on the property not far from the combination showroom, hangar and factory. He was an interesting, but rather eccentric older gentleman whose dream was to build a small private jet aircraft called the Starship.

On one of my frequent flights into McCarran, I decided to pay a visit to the Starship's promoter. Actually, I just knocked on his door and introduced myself. He was gracious enough to give me a private tour of his then financially defunct enterprise. In the middle of a hangar-showroom, stood a full-scale mock-up of the Starship. The most unique feature I can recall of the aircraft's design was that it had an unusually wide and stubby fuselage.

The interior was reminiscent of an old, large airliner's cockpit with no center aisle. Passengers sat three abreast with a panoramic view of the cockpit overlooking a roomy flight deck. Of course, the design was not practical from an aerodynamic standpoint, but it was one of the most unique designs for a small corporate jet that I had ever seen.

Don't know what ever happened to the promoter and his Starship project, but obviously someone in cahoots with the county was trying to force him out of business. I was interested at the time because it would have made a great FBO and indeed, it became and still is just that. They were flying Grand Canyon sightseeing tours out of the place last time I noticed.

First Airplane To Land On DFW

When work on the new Dallas/Fort Worth (DFW) regional Airport began, the crews worked seven days a week. One Sunday afternoon, while I was out flying the T-6, I noticed all the construction equipment was parked and no one was on site. I approached from the north, lowered my landing gear and made a long straight-in approach to the new main runway. The wheels touched, I applied throttle and was airborne again.

No one saw me or at least I never heard anything about it if they did. Thus, I had been the first plane to land at the new airport. Several weeks later, a North American Jet Star landed at DFW with official permission. A photo of the jet along with the headline, "First plane to land on the new airport," were on the front pages of the Dallas Morning News and Fort Worth Star Telegram, but I knew better.

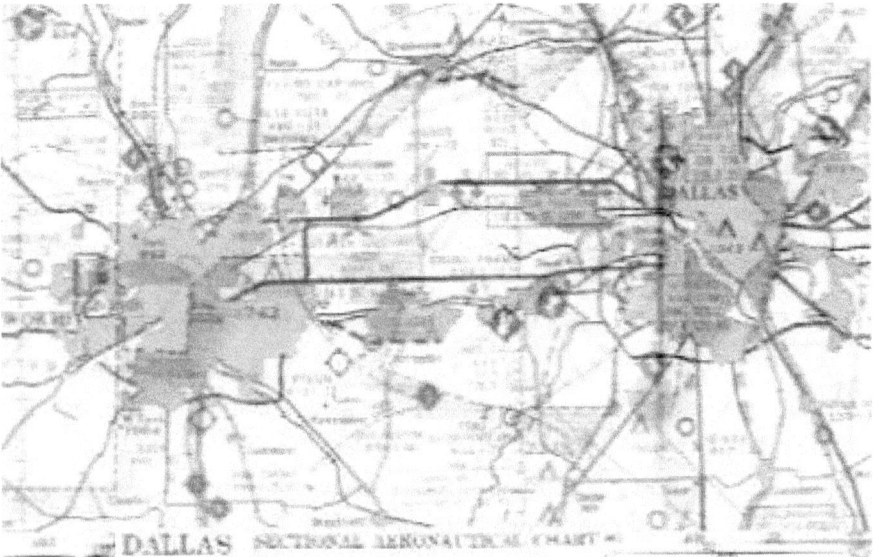

Chapter Eleven
NAVAL AVIATION AN OXYMORON

By age sixteen, I was sick of school, always bored and hated the high school I attended. Like many young men seeking adventure, I decided it might be time for me to join the Navy and see the world. On a Saturday morning, I drove my old car to the downtown post office in Dayton, Ohio where the Naval Recruiting office was located on the second floor. I told the recruiter on duty that I was thinking about joining the Navy.

The recruiter politely informed me that at age sixteen, I could not join his Navy and even at seventeen not without written consent from a parent. He then proceeded to give me the standard and still best advice for a young man, which was to stay in school and get a good education before taking on the Navy and the world.

With my ego somewhat deflated, I thanked the recruiter for his time and told him that I would be back someday to sign up as this was what I wanted to do. From time to time, I would peruse the brochure the recruiter had given me describing the different enlisted ratings in the Navy. The one that most appealed to me was the description of an Airborne Radio Operator.

Port Columbus

The following year, I found out about Naval Air Station Port Columbus and an Air Reserve unit there that I wanted to join. My mom said no, but my dad said that he would sign the papers for me to join the reserves if I would promise to finish high school and go to college. I agreed and signed up.

Recruits were required to take a physical examination when enlisting. I passed everything until I took the eye exam. I had better than 20/20 vision, but the medic who gave me the exam said I was colorblind. "I am not!" I told him. "I've never had any problem seeing colors. "Point to a color and I'll name it."

"Yes you are," the medic replied, "if you can't read the numbers in these flip cards, you're colorblind."

As it turned out I am what is called pastel blind. Some greens and some blues apparently appear to me as differing shades of gray, but I have no trouble with other colors. Without knowing it, over the years, I had trained myself to identify one shade of gray as green and the other shade of gray as blue.

That, however, was of no help in picking the numbers hidden within the bubbles on those flip cards. I could join, but the test for an aircrewman was stricter. Fortunately, the final test for color blindness in the Navy was the Farnsworth Lantern test, which I did pass and was still able to become an aircrewman.

Now a Navy airman striker, I would drive my old '39 Lincoln Zephyr 3-window coupe up to NAS Port Columbus one weekend every month to attend reserve drills. With the rest of the non-rated folks I slept through the usual tech-training classes. My first year in the Naval Air Reserve (USNR-Air), I only pulled Kitchen Police (KP) duty once, peeled potatoes for a half day.

For chemical warfare training, we entered a small building, put on gasmasks and were told that a tear gas capsule would be exploded and one by one, we were to step to the door, remove the gasmask and recite our name, rank and service number. Each airman took his turn at the door. From that day forward, I assure you, no trainee ever forgot his service number.

After exiting the chamber and facing into the wind, it felt like someone had thrown a handful of chili pepper juice in your face. Told to keep our hands off your eyes, we all lay on the grass waiting for the tears to clear from our eyes. The drill was intended to show us how well a gasmask worked and we decided they worked darn well. In this was period just after the Korean War and the heightening Cold War. Nuclear weapons and biological warfare had become the main threats to our generation.

By the time I was eighteen, I had met all the requirements to become a full-fledged, three-green-stripe Air Naval Reserve airman. The surface Navy wore white stripes. Red stripes designated engineering. Construction sailors or Seabees were identified with blue stripes. The green stripes had been used for an orderly until after WW II and were considered less than prestigious ratings among surface Navy sailors. The green stripes were now being used by the Navy to designate non-Petty Officer airman. Old salts would mistake us for an orderly.

Gedunk, pronounced gee-dunk, is the Navy's nickname for a snack bar. The walls of the gedunk at NAS Port Columbus were decorated with original artwork of the characters in the comic strip *Terry and the Pirates* drawn by Milton Caniff. Impressive for me as Caniff's comic strip was one of my favorites.

F4U Corsair Squadron

The patrol squadrons during this time period were flying the PV2 Harpoon, a plane similar to the PV1 Lockheed Ventura and the civilian Lodestar. Some of the coastal squadrons still operated Martin Flying Boats. However, I never had a chance to fly in one. Only Petty Officers flew aircrew in the patrol squadrons (VP). There were a couple of fighter squadrons (VF) based at Port Columbus that flew Chance Vought F4U-4 Corsairs.

On a drill weekend the summer between my junior and senior years in high school, The personnel office called me in and told that I hadn't met the requirement for an annual two-week training cruise. One of the VF squadrons was leaving the following day for their cruise and had an open billet for an ordnanceman striker. I'll just go with them I told the yeoman and he cut my orders. Actually, I believe I was supposed to go to Great Lakes Training Center for boot camp, but it would turn out, I never had the pleasure.

As it turned out, a Consolidated Vultee PB4Y-2 Privateer was assigned to the VF squadron as a support aircraft. Most of the support personnel flew in an R5D, but I laid claim to being the ordinance aircrewmen on the Privateer. No one seemed to care so I acted like I knew what I was doing, helped load the plane and climbed aboard. Those in their right mind don't normally volunteer for ordinance duty. It's a hot, sweaty and sometimes dangerous job involving long hours.

The old Privateers were the Navy's version of the Air Force's B-24 Liberator. The obvious difference in appearance between the two planes being that the P4Y had a single large vertical stabilizer and the B-24 had the twin-tail empennage.

My VF squadron was headed for Masters Field Marine Corps Air Station just outside Miami, Florida. Don't bother to look for it on a map, as it has long since become a housing addition. Most of the Petty Officer rated men in the squadron were veterans of the Korean War and even some from World War II. The ordinance crew usually worked twelve-hour shifts and I was gung-ho. I'd sit and listen to all the war stories as we linked .50 caliber shells to load them into the Corsairs.

Non-rated airmen like myself were assigned to KP duty for at least one day of a two-week cruise. It was still dark when I reported as ordered for my day on kitchen police and was put to work in the scullery washing pots and pans.

About an hour had passed when the Flight Line Chief came storming through the chow hall door dragging some chubby, young one-striper behind him. The Chief yelled out, "Cookie, here's your replacement. Arnold you come with me!"

Seems the Chief had a couple of senior ordinancemen ragging him about what happened to their helper. I believe that was the last KP I ever pulled. I always think of the engineman sailor in the *Sand Pebbles* who claimed that if you were good at what you did, they'd take care of you.

After my first few days on the line, I was fully checked out in ground servicing the Corsairs. This meant I was to be on the ramp at sunup every morning to help preflight the Corsairs. Actually, I think some of the older Petty Officers just didn't want to get out of their bunks that early.

After checking the oil and fuel tanks, each aircraft engine had to be run-up and a Yellow Sheet filled out. Suited me fine because I learned how to start and preflight those big radial engine fighters. A Yellow Sheet was a detailed checklist of the aircraft's mechanical, electrical and instrument systems. This checklist determined whether the aircraft would be up or down for flight status on that particular day.

The pilot assigned to one of my Corsairs had an aircraft catch fire and burn out from under him during the Korean War. Needless to say, he was a little spooky about engine fires. Standing by the fire bottle as he cranked the engine for a morning flight, he flooded the exhaust stack and it flamed excessively. Using a hand signal, I tried to get the pilot to rev up the engine in order to blow the flame out, but he didn't respond. By the time I got the fire bottle safety pin pulled and the nozzle up to the exhaust stack, he had shutdown the engine, was out of the cockpit and looking over my shoulder.

Each aircraft's machineguns were loaded with its own color rounds. We coated the tips of the bullets with a sticky, non-drying paint. The purpose of this was that when the bullet passed through the airborne target, it would leave that unique color mark on the cloth. This way, we could grade the pilots on their gunnery practice hits.

The biggest problem with this practice was that the sticky paint gummed up the machine guns to the point where they would sometimes even stop firing. Because of this, each night we had to remove every gun from the aircraft's wings, disassemble and wash them with 130 octane avgas. Then reassemble the guns and reinstall them prior to the next day's flight. For two flights a day, we sent the planes out and waited on them to come back. Surprisingly, you can learn to sleep comfortably in the shade of an aircraft wing on a concrete ramp during the heat of the day, if you're tired enough.

Prior to group takeoff, we prepared a long cheesecloth tow target and took it out to the end of the runway for the sacrificial Corsair to tow aloft. Even though the towline was three hundred feet long, it wasn't pleasant for the aircraft tow pilot to sit there while .50 caliber shells whizzed past his tail. I think the pilots drew straws for the job each day.

We'd spread the target out and S-turned the towline on the runway. The tow aircraft would get a good running start and jerk the target into the air when the line ran out. On return, the pilot would make a low pass over the field and drop the target. We'd pick it up and score the number of different colored marks. We knew the colors of the particular pilot firing and if he was one of the good ol' boys, he'd get graded a little better than some of the crap-heads that complained about everything.

Miami Beach Liberty

Over the weekend the Corsairs flew over to Gitmo, sailor's slang for Guantanamo Bay, Cuba. This was pre-Castro Cuba and the place was wide open to the Yankee dollar. The pilots took lists of who wanted any duty-free items brought back and I ordered a bottle of Channel No.5 to take home to my mom. The fighters departed for Gitmo and we got a couple of welcome days off. We were not allowed to go on liberty except in class-A blues and winter wools were a little hot in Miami that time of year.

On my first night off base, I went to a nearby bar with some of the old hands. In Ohio, at age eighteen, it was legal to drink 3.2 beer, but in Miami anyone in uniform could order from the bar, no questions asked. One of the local Ohio beers was Burger beer, so I ordered my usual, "I'll have a Burger please."

The bar hop looked at me a little funny and told me that they didn't serve sandwiches at that bar. So much for ordering a beer, so I decided I would try one each of all the different kinds of mixed drinks I had ever heard of.

After three mixed drinks, the distance from the bar stool to the floor looked to be about 40 feet. I climbed down into the distant canyon below and made my way out of the bar. There was a four-lane highway between the bar and the Navy base. I stood for some time, looking in both directions for oncoming traffic. It went through my mind that my mom would kill me if I got myself run-over and somehow that made sense at the time.

When the highway looked clear for about a quarter mile in both directions, I crossed as fast as I could and ran into the chain link fence that surrounded the base. Finding my way, hand over hand along the eight-foot chain link fence I eventually came to the guard shack. After taking one look at me, the Marine MPs on duty had a good laugh and helped me find my ID card.

Back at the barracks, they had been having a water fight with the pump handle fire extinguishers and someone was asleep on my top bunk. He refused to get out because he said that his mattress was wet. I knew in my clouded mind that I was going to have to lay down real soon or I was going to fall down and most likely would not be able to get back up again. Lifting up the mattress, I rolled him out of the top bunk and he hit the floor with a loud thud. What have I done to this poor guy, I thought. But he got up, stumbled over to another bunk and lay back down.

The following evening, several of us took the bus to Miami Beach. At a bandshell on the beach, there was a Latin orchestra playing and couples were dancing in the park. The two guys I came with, picked up a couple Latin chicks and wanted to stay. So I left to wander in and out of several different hotel parties along the beach allowing them to assume I was one of their alumni or frat-rats. No one asked me to leave. Several, who didn't have a clue who I was, shook my hand and explained how sorry they were when they heard I had gotten drafted.

Sometime after midnight, I was walking along the beach behind the cabana at the Fontainebleau Hotel on my way back to find a bus stop. A couple of young schoolteachers from back east were sitting in the pool area near the beach visiting with the one girl's boyfriend and I stopped to visit with them.

One of them ordered me a fancy rum drink with a little umbrella in it and we talked until the wee hours of the morning watching the stars and staring out over the dark Atlantic. I had nothing else to drink that night, having learned my lesson the hard way from the hangover I had earned the night before. Thus, ended my first Navy liberty.

Four Engines Outrun Hurricane

Two days before we were scheduled to return to Port Columbus, the weather bureau began reporting a hurricane headed our way. We had no weather satellites and thus no long lead-time advance warning in those days. Hours before the hurricane hit, the squadron Commanding Officer (CO) made the decision to fly all our aircraft out of the area as the storm was going to come ashore near our location. Worse yet, the storm was forecast to cause widespread heavy rain for most of the east coast.

The Skipper, the Patrol Plane Commander (PPC) and copilot (PP2C) went to make one last check on the weather. The Plane Captain (PC), an enlisted flight engineer, preflighted the plane. I loaded the rest of the tools and equipment into the PB4Y and we took off just ahead of the storm. The weather overtook us about halfway back to Port Columbus. We could have outrun it if we had been flying away from the storm, but we were paralleling its course at a right angle.

When I saw a forty-pound toolbox floating around in the back of the plane, I realized we were in some really rough air. After strapping down everything with ropes and tie-down cables, I went to watch the instruments over the PC's shoulder. The rate of climb indicator was pegging out up, then down. The altimeter looked like a high-speed time clock doing the same thing. The PC said I better get strapped in, so I went forward and buckled myself into the nose gun turret. I couldn't even see the wing tips and the rain was so heavy it was coming in the cracks around the turret.

Late that afternoon, approaching Port Columbus, the landing conditions were zero-zero. There were no VOR, DME or ILS approaches in those days. Our pilot was an old experienced pilot and set up a long final approach. The Ground Controlled Approach (GCA) guys were keeping us on course, but staying on glide path was another thing entirely. When you're losing 500 hundred feet and gaining 500 hundred feet every other minute, it's hard to nail the glide slope.

Hearing the wheels hit, I said to myself, thank God we're finally on the ground, but I could still couldn't see anything. The power came up and we were airborne again. A second later, we were on the ground again and this time I could see the runway lights passing by the windows.

It was still raining hard as we parked the aircraft and all climbed out. We were standing under the wing to stay out of the rain when the copilot went over to the landing gear and picked a limb out of the strut. "See I told you we hit something," he said, holding up the small branch for proof. Obviously, we had taken the top out of a tree just before touchdown.

"That ain't all," the PC added. "We hit the ground!"

"Nah," the pilot rebutted. "No way we were on the ground."

An old brick factory in line with the runway just outside the boundary fence had been torn down years before, but the cracked and partly mud covered brickyard foundation remained.

The next morning, our PC got a pickup and drove out to where he thought we had hit the top of a tree. What he discovered was that about 50-feet the other side of the small tree were two short, but very distinct main-gear wheel tread marks on the brickyard ground. He came back and took us out to see for ourselves. Any landing you walk away from is a good one, they say, but evidence indicated we had made more than one.

The fighters couldn't stay in the air like we did in the old Privateer. When the squadron pilots started reporting in, we found out the Corsairs were scattered all over the southern U.S. at any National Guard air base or airport they could find.

THE USS Ross DD-563

After my dad was transferred from Wright-Patterson AFB in Ohio to Tinker AFB in Oklahoma, I left my weekend air reserve unit at Port Columbus taking with me fond memories of some good times. Thinking I had no other options, I joined a reserve surface unit in Oklahoma City. The worst part was giving up my green airman stripes, which I had worn proudly. So, for a short time, I was an ordinary seaman.

I graduated in 1955 from Midwest City High School and planned to enter undergraduate school at the University of Oklahoma in the fall. There is probably no good reason for this story in a group of flying stories except that summer, I was offered a front row seat in which to view how the surface Navy coordinated anti-submarine warfare in the era prior to the proliferation of U.S. and Russian nuclear submarines.

I needed to take another two-week Navy training cruise. In those days you did what you were supposed to do because if you didn't, you'd get a letter in the mail that began with the word "Greetings" from your local draft board.

Posted on the Reserve Center bulletin board was information about several two-week cruises to Puerto Rico and I thought to myself that sounds like fun, so I signed up for one. Unbeknownst to us landlubbers, this was a long-standing joke among the yeomen. There were no reserve ship cruises to Puerto Rico. All of the cruises were temporary duty (TDY) with the regular Navy fleet and you took the luck of the draw.

When my orders arrived, I had been assigned to two-weeks duty on the USS Ross out of Norfolk, Virginia. A round trip airline ticket was enclosed. Maybe this wasn't all bad. One of the airline legs was on an airline that was flying the new British Comet, the first jet passenger aircraft to be placed in commercial service.

However, the Comet had recently experienced some structural failure and had been grounded. Another seaman from my surface unit also drew the same assignment. We were traveling together and flew on a Vickers Viscount, a new turbo-prop airliner.

My shipmate and I arrived at the Norfolk Naval Base and as we entered the dock gate, the Marine MP on duty asked me for my ID card. I took it out of my wallet and handed it to him. He broke it in half and handed it back to me snarling, "Never let your ID card out of your possession, sailor."

I began to suspect this might not be my kind of Navy and the next two-weeks would bear that out. We boarded U.S. Navy destroyer DD-563 the USS Ross, reported for duty and were off on our two-week shanghaied adventure. The Ross was a Fletcher class destroyer. Whatever that meant? So I looked it up. Basically, it's bigger than a destroyer escort, smaller than a cruiser and a lot smaller than a battleship. The largest watercraft I'd ever been on was a six-passenger speedboat and that was on a lake.

The next morning, I was sound asleep in my bunk located in the bow of the ship when I heard this terrible crashing noise. Trying to get out of an unfamiliar bunk quickly, I hit my head on the bunk above me. What had awakened me was the anchor chain falling into the anchor locker just forward of my bunk. No one else was around. When I went topside, the chief on duty acted surprised to see me because he had reported me absent at muster and assumed that I had missed the ship's sailing. I guess the regulars thought it was funny not to bother waking up the reserve kid.

After a chewing out from the chief, he sent me to the executive officer who chewed me out again and assigned me to the highly technical job of chipping paint off the first gun turret deck. I was also told that it was against Navy regulations to get sunburned. With my fair skin, it was going to be difficult not to get burned from the sun's reflection off the water, but some how that regulation seemed to make sense to the officer explaining it.

Obviously, what they did on these old destroyers was start at one end, chipping off the old paint and repainting it until they got to the other end. Then, start all over again. It was, however, peaceful cruising out there on the ocean waters.

At sea, I learned to tell how far away we were from the coast by the green or blue shades of the water and watched the dolphins run along the sides and chase the bow as though they were racing with the ship. On occasion, I would see flying fish come out of the water and travel long distances through the air. I guessed they were feeding on insects just above the water.

On one sunny afternoon, while executing my prerogative to chip as much paint as I cared to, a large submarine surfaced about a quarter mile off our side. The ocean was very calm at the time and the boat just seemed to materialize right out of thin air. It is really a very eerie feeling to watch a sub surface close up for the first time.

Our ship was scheduled to take part in submarine chasing exercises for the next couple of days and I was ready for a change in duty. Standing port or starboard watch above the bridge was a whole lot more interesting than chipping paint. Well, everything is relative isn't it?

Every 24 hours, I had to stand a four-hour day watch and a two-hour night lookout watch. For some reason, I always seemed to catch the mid or first watch. When I asked why I always caught the middle of the night watches, the boatswain mate laughed as he explained that he set the watches alphabetically starting with the mid-watch. My last name began with "A" and of course, he started with me. I got the message.

Blimp Attack

When the sub's antenna is out of the water, they can communicate with the surface ships via radio. Late that afternoon, we joined up with several other destroyers and a cruiser. An Anti-Submarine Warfare (ASW) blimp was also in the area. After dark, the fleet exercises with the submarine commenced and to make matters more interesting, a heavy overcast had rolled in.

At night, the sea glowed like it was lit with a florescent light down the sides of the ship as it cut through the water. I knew it was only the phosphorous in the salt water that caused this, but it gave the ship a ghostly glow in the nighttime darkness and even more pronounced from atop the lookout deck.

In the wheelhouse below, I could hear a lot of chatter over the radio, so I assumed we were chasing the sub I had seen the day before on this particular night. The blimp was also somewhere above us in the clouds. Suddenly, out of nowhere, I heard the roar of two radial engines as the blimp descended out of the clouds just over my head. A large splash in the water a few feet off our port side and a muffled boom in the water followed the sound of the blimp's engines.

We had been mistaken for the submarine by the blimp and what had hit the water was a Practice Depth Charge (PDC). Needless to say, our Mustang Captain exchanged a few choice words over the radio with the blimp pilot. The term mustang denotes an officer who had come up through the ranks. I've often wondered what would have happened if that PDC landed on the deck where I was standing lookout and exploded.

Tin Can

The weather cleared the next day and when I reported to stand port watch that afternoon, visibility was unrestricted and clear from horizon to horizon.

A few months earlier, the Ross had hit a waterlogged tree floating just below the surface and did some major damage to the bow. Because of this, the Captain had emphatically ordered the lookouts to report any and every object sighted.

The sailor standing watch next to me on the starboard side was looking through his binoculars and sounded off, "Tin can at zero three zero, sir."

Tin Can is the nickname for a destroyer escort. The Officer of the Day (OD) or bridge officer on duty grabbed his binoculars and commenced scanning the horizon to the right of the bow. After a minute or so, the Captain came out on the bridge deck and also started looking.

By now I'm looking over to the starboard even though I was on port watch. Finally, the OD looked up to the starboard watch and asked, "What kind is it again, sailor?"

The sailor took another look through his binoculars and replied, "Looks like peaches to me, sir." Even the old, seldom smiling Captain got a laugh out of that as we watched an empty one-gallon can float past the right side of the ship.

Man Overboard

Steaming along, actually the ship burned diesel, on a rather quiet afternoon, I watched the boatswain mate walk down the side of the ship with an old ragged, taped up, life preserver in his hand. He flung it as far off into the water as he could and someone yelled, "Man overboard!"

Instantly, an alarm bell went off, men stopped their work and took up assigned positions on the ship. There were a lot of commands being issued from the bridge as the Ross slowed and made a hard turn to the right.

In the midst of this commotion, I tried several times to get the attention of someone down on the bridge deck to explain that it was only an old life preserver and not a man and we shouldn't worry about it. I continued to be ignored. Finally, I yelled down, "It's not a man overboard, it's a piece of junk!"

The OD looked up at me and sarcastically said, "It's a drill." Well, who said a kid from Oklahoma that grew up in Ohio was supposed to know anything about the sea-going Navy anyway.

In dock, we had to cross a moored aircraft carrier going and coming ashore and I got a chance to look around. Firmly, I resolved that the closest I would ever get to the big pond again would be flying over it in an airplane too large to land aboard an ocean going vessel. Until many years later when I went aboard a large vacation cruise ship in the Caribbean, I kept my vow.

The second week of the cruise, we steamed into the North Atlantic. One night while standing lookout, the waves started breaking over the bow and splashing against the lower forward gun turret, approximately the height of a third-story window. The sailor standing watch with me explained that he had seen the waves break over the second gun turret before, so not to worry.

Want To Fly Join The Air Force

After my infamous cruise on the USS Ross, I drilled at the Reserve Center in OKC a few more times. I would go into the room where they gave the physicals and practice on the color blindness flip cards. There were twenty-four cards with different shades with numbers hidden in the colored bubbles. By getting someone to name the six or eight cards I always missed, I tried to memorize the patterns on the cards and sometimes I could.

If all I wanted to be was a jet jockey, why not just go join the Air Force. The AF took high school graduates for pilot training, so I walked into the AF recruiting office and told the Sergeant, "I want to be a pilot. Where do I sign up?"

The ol' Sergeant, who's stack of ribbons went up over his left shoulder, explained that he would have to send me to the Air Force training base at Wichita Falls. He handed me a voucher for a bus ticket, shook my hand and I was off.

The next morning, after spending the night at a hotel in beautiful downtown Wichita Falls, I reported to the base. I was sent to a building where I took a written exam. The airman giving the exam told me that with scores like I had made, I was as good as in. I started feeling pretty good about my chances.

Next, I was sent to take the physical exam and I busted the color test. Once again I insisted, "Point to any color and I will name it for you, I am not color blind."

The flight surgeon allowed that maybe I wasn't exactly color blind in the truest sense of the word, but if I couldn't pass the card test, he wasn't going to pass me for a flight physical. The AF allowed for no other test like the Navy's Farnsworth lantern test or the Army's yarn test.

It was a long bus ride back home that night. What was I going to do? Ever since grade school, I had planned on becoming a jet pilot and had never even considered any other option.

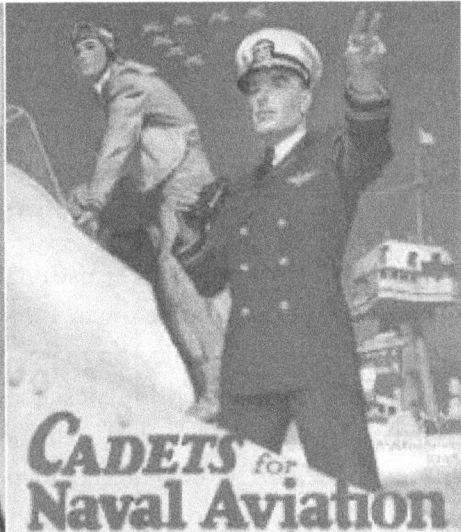

Chapter Twelve
THEY FLY ON SUNDAYS

In the fall, I enrolled at the University of Oklahoma and transferred to the Naval Reserve surface unit at Norman for drill. I had only one goal in mind, get two years of college and apply as a Naval Aviation Officer Cadet (AOC).

OU was a land grant university and these were mandatory military draft times for all males over the age of eighteen. This meant that every able bodied non-veteran male under the age of thirty five that wanted to stay in college signed up for one of the Reserve Officer Training Corps (ROTC) programs during their freshman and sophomore years.

The primary requirement for joining the ROTC was to have a pulse and to be able to stand up slightly more erect than an orangutan. Guys that wanted to go to advanced cadets and could not pass the AF eye exam went in the Army ROTC program.

My first inclination was to sign up for Naval ROTC, but that required a four-year commitment. You were, however, paid a small salary like in the reserves. The Air Force and the Army ROTC only required two years of attendance and only paid its cadets if they continued on in the advanced two-year program.

Signing up for Naval ROTC would probably have been the best move for me. Being in the reserves like some of the other ROTC students, I could have drawn both ROTC pay and Naval Reserve drill pay. However, if I could not get into aviation cadets after graduation, I would have been obligated to spend four-years in the surface Navy and that was not going to happen.

Air Farce ROTC

To meet the college requirement, I signed up for Air Force ROTC, but after trying to enlist as a pilot once already, I had no plans of going in the Air Force. I could enter the Naval AOC program with sixty college credit hours, if not married. That seemed like the shortest path to my goal. Thus, my plan was to finish my sophomore year and apply for AOC as I had already passed the Navy's flight physical exam.

The AFROTC program classes on air power were reasonably interesting, but Tuesday afternoon drills were a real bitch. Oklahoma's unpredictable weather had us marching in winter Class-A wool uniforms on 90-degree days. That was less than conducive to enhancing one's espirit de corps.

Having no plans to go on to advanced AFROTC, my second year was pretty much of a coast. There were some real geeks in the senior officer cadet corps that delighted in intimidating the underclassmen. One hot afternoon, returning to my dorm from the drill field with my cap cocked on the back of my head, my jacket unbuttoned and my tie loosened, a late model sports car screeched to a halt and backed up towards me.

I saw it was one of those rich-kid cadet officers on me like a traffic cop. Demerits could affect your grade point and I didn't need any. My grade average was bad enough as it was.

Thinking fast, I removed my nametag and stuck it in my pocket. The cadet officer approached and asked my name. I said, "Robert Anderson, sir," as I proceeded to put my uniform in order. He wrote me up for being out of uniform and not having a nametag. I hoped there wasn't a real cadet by that name because if there was, he sure as heck got a demerit that day.

Return to Naval Air

Someone told me about a Naval Air Reserve VP squadron at NAS Dallas in Grand Prairie, Texas. It was the largest Naval reserve base not located on a coast. The Navy mainly kept it open for the convenience of refueling cross-country aircraft and because the Chance Vought aircraft factory, which manufactured the F4U Crusaders, shared the runway.

NAS Dallas sent an R5D to the Will Rogers Municipal Airport once a month to pickup USNR airmen in the area. We were picked up on Friday evening and returned us home late Sunday evening. This beat the heck out of going to drills one night a week with a surface unit. I was assigned to VP-702, a patrol squadron, just what I had been wanting.

The Neptune and ASW Patrol

My new reserve squadron was flying the older P2V-4 Neptune. The letter "P" being Navy designation for patrol aircraft, the number "2" being the second patrol bomber purchased from that manufacturer, the "V" standing for Lockheed. The dash numbers following the aircraft indicated its modification. Newer versions being flown by the fleet were the P2V-5F. The fifth version along with many other improvements added the tail-boom stinger for the Magnetic Anomaly Detection (MAD) equipment. The F-modification, in this case added the outboard jet engines.

The range for a fully loaded P2V was about 4,000 statute miles. However, an early model set a world's non-stop, non-midair refueling record. The Truculent Turtle flew from Pearce Aerodrome in Australia to Port Columbus in September of 1946.

The original Lockheed P2V weighed in at about 39,000 pounds, but by the time they got through hanging all of the ASW gear on them the P2V-5 weighed in at about 40,000 pounds. The P2V-5F and later versions had a gross takeoff weight of over 70,000 pounds with a full fuel load. No wonder they added a pair of J34W jet engines to the long-winded ol' Neptune to help her takeoff. Top speed with two-a-turning and two-a-burning was about 330 mph at low altitude. At 14,000 feet maybe 400 mph, but she would really be burning up the fuel to get that speed.

Lockheed was famous for building aircraft with strong main spar structures and with the exception of the Boeing B-50, several Lockheed models were the only aircraft certified to fly into the eye of a hurricane at the time.

Many uncertified aircraft have been flown into hurricanes. My cousin Phil flew aircrew on an Air Force C-54 in the Pacific. He recalled how in the mid-fifties, they were often ordered to divert towards possible developing typhoons and hurricanes to report back on the storm's condition and position.

Ocean-going sailors DD653 escorting light cruiser off Norfolk; ROTC drill at OU; AF ROTC cadet uniform; Corsair squadron from NAS on flight training; PY-2 four-engine support aircraft; loading wing machine guns on Corsair Naval Reserve flight line where SNB and SNJ aircraft were made available for Korean era pilots to stay current on flight time.

NAS Alameda

On my first cruise with VP-702, we went to NAS Alameda across the bay from San Francisco. For a young aviator like myself, the area reeked of aviation history. This was where the legendary Pan American Flying Clippers first originated their trans-Pacific flights. Circling the Bay area was the first time I had ever seen a large shipyard from the air and a giant aircraft carrier looked like a postage stamp. Yes indeed, I had made the correct decision by joining a land-based air unit.

The Navy was still operating blimps and several were assigned to a reserve unit at Alameda. This, however, was the last time I recall seeing blimps in actual ASW service.

During the two-weeks we were there, I never saw the entire Golden Gate Bridge. In the mornings, the bridge would be completely covered by fog and by noon the fog would roll back just enough to reveal about half of the bridge. I still recall flying over Sausalito and how the mountains were always a deep dark blue, almost purple, as we came in over the bay. I took a great photo with our ship-rigging camera once. It was high quality, but of course was in black and white.

Over the weekend, I ventured over to the then small artist's colony at Sausalito. After looking across the bay to San Francisco, I went to find a pay phone and called my wife. A year or two before, she had bought a large framed print of a painting of the San Francisco Bay. Not that she liked the painting so much, but because the colors matched her new furniture. Over the phone I asked her, "Guess what, I'm looking at?" It was the exact picture we had on the living room wall and obviously the spot where the original had been painted.

During this cruise, a regular Navy P2V had to ditch in the drink several hundred miles out. Our squadron participated in the night search with no success. The aircraft's crew were located early the next morning and picked up by a surface ship. Of the twelve aircrewmen, all had survived the water ditching, but two died of hypothermia during the night. It is noteworthy that the survivors were the heavier crewmen and that the two lighter-weight men, those with less body fat, did not survive.

Our P2V-4s had a 70,000-candlepower searchlight built into the forward part of the right wing tip tank. This light could be manually directed with a pistol grip from the cockpit. It was a lot of fun to come in low over a ship at night and light it up with the searchlight. The crew on board the ship could probably read a newspaper in the dark as we passed over.

During the second week, at crew briefing, the CO read us a memo from the area Merchant Marine organization. The gist of the memo was that we were eliminating the helmsman's night vision with our searchlights. They claimed that the helmsman had to be replaced and his replacement paid overtime. The memo went on to say that if we didn't stop doing it, they were going to bill the Navy for the overtime. Not exactly sure how you bill the Navy for anything, but the CO asked us to stop and so we did.

One of our P4Vs took a seagull through the front windshield during takeoff. Both pilots and the PC in the jump seat ducked and no one was injured, but what a mess. It took two days to clean all the bird feathers and stuff out of that cockpit.

Our P2V-4 aircraft were used for ASW patrol and training, even flying some of the regular Navy's coastal fan patrols. Pilots needing instrument currency training were relegated to the Beech SNB twin-engine trainers. A light twin trainer does not rate an aircrew position, but regulations required an observer, a lookout, to be on board during simulated under the hood instrument flight conditions. I took a half dozen of these sightseeing flights around the Bay area as an observer.

The Navy aircrewmen in the 1950s and early 1960s wore the silver combat aircrew wings as aircrew designations. The Marine Corps still uses that style of wings badge. There were three small holes in the scroll above the wings for inserting small gold stars. Each star had a meaning, air-to-air combat, air-to-ground combat and air-to-sea combat. Wearing the wings without the stars designated a non-combat trained aircrewman.

In the late 1950s, the Navy authorized a new style of aircrew wings. The new wings were the larger gold observer's wings worn by airborne weather observers and back seat jet jockeys, except they now had the letters AC of the anchor.

I had acquired a pair when I was at Port Columbus and when I showed up back at NAS Dallas wearing the new wings, I was challenged several times as to the authenticity of the wings. Our post-exchange (PX) eventually ordered the wings and within a year, every aircrewman on base was wearing the new gold wings with their Class-A uniforms. Personally, I still preferred the old style silver wings design and I still have mine.

An Air Naval Reserve Squadron is an odd lot of men who for one reason or another are attracted to the adventure of flying. Some were veterans who enjoyed continuing their duty part-time. Others were there only to fulfill a military obligation. We had some Navajo Indians that came over from Albuquerque. Their only employment other than the reserve was fighting forest fires for the government. Their standard greeting was "Yaa-ta-hay," meaning hello and we all used it when they were around.

A slang word that caught on was *tool'in*. There was this movie actor kid from California. I had seen him in a TV commercial once. A group of us were standing around and he was explaining about an incident that had happened while they were airborne. "You see," he said, "We were tool'in around the pattern…" and one of the pilots asked what tool'in was. He replied, "You know, like in tool'in around," breaking everyone up. I'll remember them all as a great bunch of aviators.

Return to Port Columbus

When my wife and I returned briefly to Dayton, Ohio where my daughter Laura was born in Xenia. I transferred back to NAS Port Columbus. They would soon be getting the Lockheed P2V-5F Neptunes being rotated down to the reserves as the new P2V–7 versions were delivered to the fleet squadrons.

In order to meet my annual two-week training requirement, I signed up for a P2V electrical systems training class at NAS Brunswick, Maine. When we landed at the base, there was eight feet of snow beside the runway. The tails of the planes on the taxiways looked like shark dorsal fins moving across the snow.

The base had the first helicopter squadron I had ever been around. They were flying the early Sikorsky twin-rotor jobs and I was able to bum my first ride in a chopper. In an airplane, I never experienced a sense of height. However, coming into hover for touchdown in a helicopter gave me a sudden sensation of height and messed with my Altiphobia.

With the tech school under my belt, I was promoted to Aviation Electrician Petty Officer 3rd Class. That spring, we returned to Oklahoma and I enrolled at Oklahoma City University taking mostly design classes and an Airframe and Engine (A&E) class as an elective. To stay active in the reserve, I requested a transfer and was re-assigned to NAS Dallas and to the newly formed VP-704, which now coincided with the OKC Will Rogers airport pickup.

NAS Los Alamitos

On my second VP squadron cruise, we were still flying the P2V-4 with only the two recips, no jets outboard yet. The squadron departed as each aircraft was made ready for NAS Los Alamitos located south of Los Angeles. Not to be confused with NAS Alameda across the bay from San Francisco. Patrol planes were lone eagles and seldom flew in groups.

Due to fuel allocations, there was some kind of bookkeeping advantage to our getting fuel in transit from the Air Force with gas chits. The AF had lots of money, but the Naval Air Reserve was always short on funds.

We landed at Amarillo Air Force Base near the site of old English Field. It was a B-52 base for a while and after the Viet Nam war as an Army Air Depot. The bases are closed now and the 13,500 ft runway is being used as the main Amarillo airport.

A freshly painted shiny white fuel truck came out and topped off our P2V with 115/145-octane Avgas. After takeoff and reaching cruise altitude, Commander Moore, our squadron CO, dozed off with an enroute chart in his lap. Our copilot, a young Lieutenant, was flying. I was riding the jump seat and we were BS'ing about something or another.

The rest of the crew had all settled in for the six-hour flight to the west coast when the right engine started to pop. This woke up Commander Moore. The copilot came forward with the mixture on that engine about the same time I was thinking that would be a good idea. The right engine calmed down for a minute, only to be followed by the left engine starting to pop.

We had just crossed Sandia Mountain and were about 14,000 feet above Kirkland Air Force Base, which at that time was a Strategic Air Command (SAC) base and also where atomic bombs were stored. The Commander radioed for an expedited landing at Albuquerque and we began a slow spiral to the runway with full rich mixture and both engines cutting out all the way in. The Commander hadn't wanted to call a Mayday, declare an emergency, as there was always a lot of paperwork to filled out afterwards. We just wanted to get the plane on the ground and check it out.

General Curtis LeMay was head of SAC at the time and he was notorious for faking emergency landings at his bases in order to check their security. We touched down and two jeeps with APs holding burp guns stopped us on the runway at the end of our rollout. The Commander told everyone to wait in the plane and he went to identify himself so they would let us park.

After checking a couple of plugs that were fouled, we drained some fuel from the two main tanks and sent it over to the lab. Turned out the avgas was contaminated with jet fuel (JP), basically a high-grade kerosene. Some phone calls back to Amarillo AFB revealed that the gas truck that fueled us had recently been repainted for use as a 130-octane fuel truck, but that it had previously been used for JP. Obviously, they had failed to drain all the old fuel out of the truck's tank.

The AF de-fueled our plane and re-fueled it with fresh avgas. Needless to say, we did an extensive ground run up prior to takeoff. And so a change of fuel and a change of underwear later, we departed for the coast.

Rocket and Bomb Target Practice

Our P2Vs carried eight rockets under each wing. To qualify as combat ready, each pilot had to fire a given number of practice rockets and drop some practice bombs. I don't think anyone ever failed this test. They just tried their best. The rocket firing range was located in the desert outside the small town of Fallon, Nevada. Several large bulls-eye targets the size of half a football field were painted in the sand.

There was a place on the pilot and copilot's windshield frame to mount an optical cross-hair gun sight. For firing rockets, we would start at 6,000 feet and push over into about a 30-degree dive. At 3,000 feet, the pilot would fire one rocket from each wing. I was standing up bracing myself against the bulkhead between the two pilots in order to score hits on the target. After a few routine dives, I got my 35mm color camera and was taking photographs. I took some great shots through the cockpit windshield. That was until one of the pilots was a little late on his pullout and hauled back a bit too hard on the yoke. I was looking through the camera's viewfinder and busted my ass on the deck.

We were flying in one of two orbital patterns around the rocket range with other P2Vs from our squadron. The plane diving on the target to our right was still in its dive when the eight-man life raft mounted on the left side of the rear fuselage, exploded out the side. It inflated immediately and tumbled harmlessly over the horizontal stabilizer and floated to the ground. We saw the whole thing. They returned to NAS Fallon and landed. When we completed our runs, we landed to have a look. Other than the loss of the raft and side panel, no harm was done. Maybe it was the G-forces that had popped the raft, maybe improper installation or maybe just one of those freaky things.

The practice bombs were ten inches long and weighed a couple of pounds. They had a charge in them that looked like a shotgun shell. My ordinanceman was a young, three-stripe airman. As we made passes over the bomb target, the pilot would radio him over the intercom system (ICS) when to drop a practice bomb out of the rear hatch. It wasn't long before I caught on he was only dropping one bomb at a time. We had cases of those practice bombs on board and this was going to take all afternoon.

Making my way to the aft section, I put my parachute on and laid down on my belly looking out the open hatch beside the ordinanceman. Each of us took two bombs in each hand and released them on a 1-2-3-4 count when the pilot called. This put an adequate spread across the target and guaranteed at least a couple good hits. After the eighth pass, I looked back and there was still one more full case. On the next pass I dumped the whole box. On that last pass, the target spread must have looked like it was hit with a giant shotgun blast. I called forward to say we were out of practice bombs. No questions were asked.

Back in L.A. that weekend, the crews divided into two groups. Those that needed a long, over-water navigation training flight and those that just wanted to go somewhere different. The first group was off to Hawaii and the other group voted to go to the Seattle World's Fair.

One of our reserve pilots, a civilian lawyer, needed to attend an emergency meeting back home in OKC. He wanted to take an SNB and do a 2-day turnaround. Of course, no one wanted to go with him. I was working on building time for my FAA Commercial license and told him I'd go as observer, if he'd let me fly.

I went over to Seal Beach to Turk's Bar that Saturday evening and we departed Sunday morning. Some SMBs may have had autopilots, but this one did not. In the heat thermals over the Rockies, that Twin Beech beat me to a pulp. After a few hours, I looked pleadingly at the Lieutenant, "You want to fly for a while?" I asked.

"Nope," he replied with a grin. "You wanted to fly, have at it!" He made the landing at Will Rogers and my young wife was there to pick me up. Monday afternoon we returned to NAS Los Alamitos and I've never liked a Twin Beech since.

NAS Dallas

By the end of my fourth fall semester in college, I was still a couple-dozen credit hours away from an engineering degree. Remember the rules, you could go to Naval AOC with 60-credit hours if you were single, but if you were married you had to have a full degree.

It was the second presidential term of Eisenhower and the economy had gone down the tube. I had a family to support and I had four years of college plus the equivalent of an Associates Degree in Drafting and Design. However, I still lacked a semester and a half to complete my Bachelor's Degree. Unable to find a decent job in Oklahoma, on my next drill weekend, I drove to Dallas so that I could also look around for a job.

Chance Vought Aircraft, now called LTV for Ling-Tempco-Vought, was located on the other side of the runway from Navy Dallas. I walked into the employment office to apply for work as a junior engineer. When the laughter in the office died down, I was told that LTV had just laid-off 6,000 employees due to the F8U Crusader contract having been cancelled by the government.

In order to draw two-week's pay and stay in the barracks while I job-hunted, I signed up for a two-week technical training class. Navy Dallas had a Marine VF fighter squadron flying North American Saber jets and a couple of VR transport squadrons flying the Douglas R5D. More to the point, the VP squadrons would soon be getting the P2V-5F and the Navy had recently decided to train the reserve patrol squadrons in ASW.

Apparently, the training officer had seen my personnel file when I reported for tech school and he explained that NAS Dallas had been selected as one of the three reserve ASW training centers. How would I like to come on board as an aircrew-training instructor? The Temporary Active Reserve (TAR) program allowed a Petty Officer to pick his station assignment.

I explained that I wanted to apply for aviation cadets, but wasn't quite eligible yet. Actually, I had one other pressing problem. If I stayed out of school to work very long, I was going to get a draft notice and I'd have to go on two years active duty wherever they sent me. Here I would have to sign up for three years, but what he offered sounded appealing.

The training officer pointed out that I was almost ready to go up for 2nd Class Petty Officer and when I made 1st I could apply direct for AOC at that time. Also, if I wanted to I could attend college locally in the evenings. I said okay and he sent me to interview with Commander Kovak, the officer in charge of the new ASW Training project. If he liked me, I was hired. Kovak was my kind of officer and I signed up.

The first order of business was to go through an instructor's training school. The class was made up of mostly senior Petty Officers who taught in-service and tech training classes. Instructors had to give a short lecture on some aspect of training for their final exam.

Most students in the class were nervous and gave otherwise dry and boring lessons. Being well aware that I was the new kid on the block and even worse, a college kid, I needed an icebreaker. The subject I chose was "If all else fails, read the manual," and I told an off color joke to make my point. I was the only one in the class with the nerve to do this and it worked. I was accepted into the ol' boys club, so to speak.

The new ASW training unit would consist of the Commander, a Chief Petty Officer (CPO) and three rated Petty Officers. We were given an empty wing in the building that housed the Link trainers to set up our equipment. Trucks began arriving with giant crates of equipment, which we unpacked like a bunch of kids on Christmas morning. We had no idea what we were getting.

The crates contained an elaborate sonobuoy sound simulator console, an ultra sound water tank which was used to simulate radar signals and about every conceivable piece of out dated ASW training equipment that the regular Navy wanted to get rid of.

At this time, the Russians had about four hundred conventional submarines. Conventional meaning diesel electrical powered subs. The U.S. submarine fleet had gone nuclear and thanks to the foresight of Admiral Rickover, we had a bunch of them. Our nuclear submarine capacity was pretty scary in that many of those subs could carry sixteen Intercontinental Ballistic Missiles (ICBM).

With all due credit to SAC, the U.S. submarine fleet may have been the single greatest deterrent throughout the Cold War. Our Naval ASW air units were quite capable of countering a conventional submarine threat, but as would soon be proved to me later during exercises in the Caribbean, these tactics were relatively useless against a high-speed nuclear powered sub.

Not long after going on active duty, I was promoted to Aviation Electrician (AE) Petty Officer 2nd Class. That, plus flight pay, off base married rations pay and proficiency pay 1&2 for being in a critical rate now I was making more that if I had hired on as a junior engineer on the outside. Not to mention an allotment check that went to my first daughter.

For the next two and a half years, I would divide my time equally between instructing aircrewmen in the classroom and flying with the various reserve squadrons. Each year, a couple of us aircrew instructors would go along with each of the squadron's two-week training cruises. Occasionally, we would form up a special team to compete with an Atlantic or Pacific Fleet joint maneuver.

A lot of our training cruises were off the West Coast in that our sister training facility was NAS Los Alamitos. Thus, we logged a lot of flight time between Dallas and the West Coast. In all my time as a Navy aircrewman, I don't recall any fatalities or serious injuries in our reserve squadrons. Their flight safety records were excellent, but then again, we did have a lot of experienced pilots and aircrewmen in those days.

Transit Blimp

An amusing incident occurred at NAS Dallas when a transit blimp the Navy used for public relations landed for an overnight stay. All of the ASW blimps had been decommissioned by this time. The base still had one of the old mooring-masts, which was rolled out to secure the blimp. The crew of the blimp had stopped over to attend the annual Texas-OU football game and street party. The crew was in a hurry to go on liberty and apparently spent the night in Dallas.

NAS Brunswick P-2Vs in snow; first helicopter ride; view from P-2V nose bubble and right wing with searchlight in wingtip tank. From pilot's seat coming in on surface target; P-2V instrument panel; looking aft out observation bubble to rear of old model P2V-4 gun turret still installed; view through cockpit windshield diving on rocket target in Falon, Nevada, note circle target in upper right-hand of photo

That morning when I reported in, everyone was asking if I had seen the blimp. I hadn't and went to take a look. The blimp was still attached to the mooring mast, but was standing nearly straight up on its nose with its tail fins up in the air.

During the night, a low-pressure front had moved through the area. Needless to say, no one on our base knew anything about blimps, but apparently there was a chain attached to a valve that allowed the pressure in the blimp to be released in order to keep the blimp level.

When the blimp crew arrived, they were somewhat upset to find that no one had taken care to release the pressure valve. One of the flight line crew told them that they ought to feel lucky that the darn thing was still there! After the crew leveled their airship and calmed down, the base Ops Officer suggested that the next time they came to Dallas, they might want to take time to give us some instruction on the care and feeding of their large floating object. That was if they expected us to baby-sit the blimp for them.

Wing And A Prayer

We flew on Sundays and I guess that's why they called us Weekend Warriors. On a routine weekend training flight out over the Gulf of Mexico in a P2V-5F, a couple hundred miles south of New Orleans, the right engine started smoking. We had likely busted a jug, a cylinder head, on the radial engine and it was pumping oil from the case onto the hot exhaust stack. The ventilation system was picking up the smoke and within seconds, the entire aircraft cabin filled with smoke. I wasn't PC that day. I was sitting at the Nav table training a couple of radar operators. The smoke was so thick that you couldn't see your hand in front of your face, but there was no fire.

Finally, the pilots realized that if they'd shut off the air vents, the smoke would stop coming into the cabin. As soon as they did, the cockpit cleared and the pilots proceeded to feather and shut down the right engine. We were plenty high and so they took their time cranking up the two outboard jets. We obtained a clearance to NAS New Orleans and without declaring an emergency, made a routine landing.

After a phone call back to Dallas, the decision was made to leave our plane there until our own mechanics could go down and repair it. NAS Dallas sent an R5D from the VR squadron to pick us up. Needless to say, we took a pretty good razzing from the Douglas pilots for them having to come and get us. A popular magazine advertising slogan for Lockheed Aircraft at the time was "Look to Lockheed for Leadership." The VR aircrew improved on the slogan by saying, "Look to Lockheed for Leadership and Douglas for Transportation."

On the return flight, riding in the back of the R5D, we waited for the pilot to get up to cruise altitude and trim the aircraft up. Then six or eight of us got a cup of coffee and strolled to the rear of the plane. We waited a few minutes for the pilot to re-trim and then we walked back to the front again and waited for the pilot to re-trim.

It took one more time before the pilot caught on and yelled back, "Would you guys just find a seat and sit down." Everyone had a good laugh because payback is always heck.

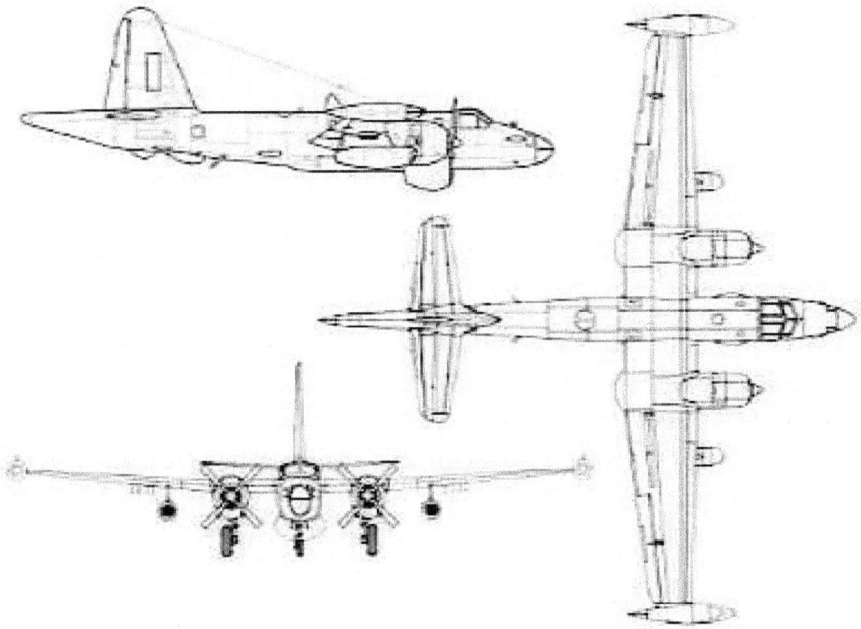

Chapter Thirteen
ASW PATROL SQUADRON

On the P2V, behind the pilot to the left of the PC's fold-down jump seat, was the infamous *186 Panel.* Pronounced one-eighty-six panel, this bulkhead consol contained most of the aircraft system's circuit breakers and some electrical components. The panel was so named because it was located at aircraft station line 186.

An aircraft is dimensioned from nose to tail by station numbers equal to inches. Thus, the 186 panel was located at 186-inches behind the nose or station zero of the aircraft. Like a ship, the up and down measurements on an aircraft are measured by inches above and below an arbitrary water line.

Aircraft lofting evolved from shipbuilding and thus were dimensioned the same. The draftsmen and designers were called *Lofters* because they worked in the lofts above where the ships were being built.

The P2V Neptune

The Lockheed P2V could be boarded from the nose wheel-well into the cockpit area or through the larger hatch in the rear belly. If an aircrewman ever had to bailout, the rear hatch would be the first choice. The wing-spar on a P2V ran through the center of the fuselage and was referred to as the wing beam.

Directly above the wing beam was a plastic observation dome for sightings with a sextant. The dome/hatch could be removed and laid on the deck. On hot days, the hatch was always opened when boarding to let the heat vent out and often left open in flight. It was noisy, but cooler.

During taxi, a crewman would sit on top of the aircraft with his legs dangling through the hatch and talked to the pilots over the ICS. I often performed this task, as it was fun sitting up on top of the big bird as we taxied out. On a hot day, it beat the heck out of the high temperatures inside the flight deck, but most of all it probably saved many a wing tip collision, especially during night time taxi.

The radio operator's station was located just aft of the wing beam. Down a short stairway into the rear fuselage was the galley and ordinanceman's station. In this section, you could stand full up, unlike the forward flight deck where you had to stoop to walk. There were drift flares and sonobuoy launch tubes located in this rear area. In addition to an electric stove and cooler, there was a canvas bunk for taking a nap.

In the nose wheel-well crawl space, there was a small window to look through in order to see if the hook-like latch had locked over a roller bearing on the nose gear strut. Standard procedure on an approach to landing was for the PC to drop down into the crawl space and verify that the gear was in the down and locked position.

Sometimes, when the gear was lowered at too high an airspeed, the gear would not latch into the locked position. If this were the case, the nose gear would fold up when the full weight of the aircraft settled onto it. Over the years, more than one P2V had skidded in on its belly radar dome (Radome). The gear could be kicked into the locked position if it failed, but the best procedure was to slow down and recycle the gear.

Upon checking, the PC would call out "The gear is down and locked, sir."

However, on one routine flight, the following incident occurred. On final approach to a landing, the pilot was intent on his approach and the PC hollered out "The gear is NOT down and locked, sir."

The pilot was only listening for the key phrase down-and-locked and replied, "Roger" as he continued the approach.

The anxious PC repeated, "NOT down and locked. I said, NOT locked, sir!"

The startled pilot pulled up and executed a missed approach. When the gear was recycled, it locked. Subsequent to that incident, the procedure was changed for the PC to report, "The gear is UNSAFE," if indeed it was.

As for a nose wheel failure, although a potentially dangerous problem, it was not normally a serious condition on a P2V. Even the early P2V series were equipped with a large Radome on the belly. If the nose wheel failed, the aircraft would skid along on the runway, tearing up the

Radome, but with very little damage to the rest of the aircraft. Fortunately, I was never on one that failed. Although on several occasions, we had to recycle the gear in order to get the nose wheel to lock.

When the nose gear failed to lock after many attempts, the procedure was to circle the base in order to burn off any excess fuel before attempting to land. Thus, while the plane circled, the crash crews were alerted and almost everyone on the base had time to hear about it and find a good place in the shade to sit and wait to watch the landing technique the pilot would use. In the only incident I ever witnessed, the hydraulics held the aircraft up long enough to get a jack under the nose.

Regulations dictated that we had to wear our crash helmets for takeoffs and landings. I usually put my helmet on for takeoff, but with a full fuel load onboard, it wasn't likely anyone would survive a crash on takeoff. Our standard issue flight jumpsuits were coated with a flame retardant, which nearly made them insufferable to wear in hot weather. After one or two washings, they lost the coating and were as comfortable to wear as cotton khakis.

We were to wear our parachute harness at all times. Over water, to also wear our inflatable rubber life vest nicknamed a Mae West for the buxom film star. At altitude, you had time to put on your harness and low over the water, there wasn't time to jump anyway. So, of course, no one did.

Over the South Pacific, you might survive in the water long enough to get the life raft out, but up north or in the Atlantic, you'd freeze to death in a matter of minutes without an all-weather water suit. With a suit you might survive an hour or two hoping to be picked up.

Sometimes out over the water, especially in the Pacific, we might hit a wind shear. The plane would gain 500-feet and before you could grab hold of something, lose 500-feet. It was a good idea to keep your seat belt on, at least loosely. During a wind shear, one of our crewmen received a broken arm when he floated into the air and tried to break his fall hitting the deck.

The ol' P2V could easily stay out for ten to twelve hours, even fourteen if need be, but most of the time our patrols were only eight hours. Except for rigging the occasional ship, we mostly bored holes in the sky. The far back bunk was always cold at higher altitudes, so my sleeping place of choice was on the floor beside the navigation table. For one thing, I could get to my crew station quickly, if needed. The crew had to climb over the wing beam to the cold back-end from time to time, as that was where the pee-tot tube, slang for relief-tube, was located.

In the Naval Air Reserve Training command (CNARESTRA), an aircrewman had to either be an aircrew instructor or qualified in a needed aircrew position to draw flight pay. There were some politics involved among the AD's who had to rotate the flight pay, but ASW types like myself, stayed on regular flight pay.

Our regular ordinanceman on Cmdr Novak's crew wasn't a real gung-ho aircrewman, but needed the flight pay for his young family and was also a very good cook. He would draw ham, eggs, bread and coffee from the mess hall instead of our other option, which was to draw box lunches. We ate pretty well on long flights. When he wasn't cooking, he kept the coffee pot going. The flight deck could call for a hot cup of java to be passed up over the wing beam anytime.

On a routine weekend drill flight, I was onboard as an instructor, and the reserve PPC decided his crew needed to do a bailout drill. He announced the drill over the ICS and rang the standby-to-bailout bell. The first or short bell ring meant standby for ditching or bailout. The crew was to put on their Mae West life vests and crash helmets. If bailing out, assuming you had your harness on, you had to also snap on your parachute. In this case, we were at altitude and so it was a bailout drill. The reserve ordnanceman on this flight wore his chute-harness all the time. That should have told me something.

The second or long bell meant bail out. After the first bell, I felt a sudden rush of air through the cabin and realized the rear belly hatch had been opened. Diving over the wing beam and down the aft stair, I was barely able to grab the reserve ordinanceman who was fixing to jump. He had been asleep in the bunk and hadn't heard over the ICS that it was a drill.

Radio Crew Position

Aft of the wing beam was a small compartment where the long-range radio operator crew position was located. We rotated crew positions because in the reserves we never had enough men to fly with a full crew compliment. I was a qualified PC and as a radar operator, but often had to go back and set up the high frequency (HF) radios. Unintentionally, I had fulfilled my once upon a time boyhood ambition to be an airborne radio operator. Not a lot of our crewmen could tune those old HF radios. My dad, having been an amateur radio operator, had taught me a lot about radios even before entering the Navy.

Those forty-pound ARC-14s radios located in the radio operators crew station, would tune into almost any frequency, but the transmitter had to be setup with a separate crystal-controlled tuning unit. Thus, the required frequency had to be manually tuned from the radio compartment so that the pilots could switch to it from their communication (COM) switchbox in the cockpit. These guard channels were mainly to maintain contact with Air Traffic Control (ATC) center when we were too far out and too low to talk to them on UHF. We used them more in the Caribbean.

On a long night patrol out over the Pacific, I was sitting in the radio compartment tuning around on the shortwave band receiver for some music when I came across an English language news broadcast. As I listened, I was thinking how drastically the world situation had changed since I had last heard the evening news. When the station identification came on, the announcer said, "You are listening to Radio Moscow."

There was a trailing wire cable antenna for the HF radio that could be reeled out of the rear of the plane. The end of the cable had a lead ball weight, sometimes referred to as a fish, to help hold the antenna vertical in flight. The antenna could be reeled out 60-feet or more below the belly. This long wire antenna had to be reeled in when flying between cloud layers because if the antenna touched a cloud layer with a different static charge than the one we were currently flying through, it would melt the fusible link connecting the antenna in the rear bay and/or fry the antenna, cut it off like it had been cut with a cutting torch.

Russian Trawlers

Rigging a ship means to come in low and fly alongside the ship, taking photos of it with a hand-held camera that produced a large negative to show the ship in great detail. Off the west coast the ships we rigged were a wide assortment of tramp steamers and merchant ships. Russian trawlers were not often seen, but a prize catch when found.

Russian trawlers, used during the Cold War, were spy ships made to look like commercial fishing vessels, but were equipped with elaborate electronic listening devices. They had a large array of antennas that could be taken down when approached by Navy surface vessel or patrol aircraft.

We were required to fill out a brief form identifying the characteristics of each ship we rigged. This method was used to track almost all ships going in and out of our coastal areas during the Cold War. Comparing the many different sighting reports provided very accurate tracking of all shipping. With today's AWAC aircraft, the faster P3V Lockheed Orion and modern satellite surveillance, these low level patrols are no longer as essential as they used to be.

Normally, when rigging a ship the aircraft would fly a parallel course to the ship, but if we intended to buzz them for effect we'd came in straight across their mid-section. When we buzzed a merchant ship of suspicious origin and rattled their portholes, we could tell it was a European crew because they would give us the ol' center-arm-up. If, however, it happened to be an American crew, we usually got the middle-digit as we flew by. I don't recall any sailors ever jumping overboard when we buzzed them like in the movies. They had enough sense to know we wouldn't hit the ship, only rattled their portholes a little.

A trawler's crew was capable of taking down and covering up its antenna array in a matter of minutes. On the rare occasion when we did come across a legitimate Russian trawler, we tried to get on top of it before they could take down their antennas. The procedure we followed was to pick up a suspect on long-range radar, quickly try to get a bearing and range on the target and then switch the radar to standby so as not to be picked up by the trawler's Electronic Counter Measures (ECM), basically a radar receiver.

More than likely they had us on their radar, so we'd turn like we were flying away, but descending so as to disappear under the radar horizon. At a couple hundred feet over the water, with engines at military power, we'd turn to the heading to intercept the trawler. The pilots would use the radar altimeter to judge the height over the water.

Creative ingenuity being what it was, the trailing wire antenna or at least the threat of them became the reserve air Navy's weapon of choice in our thin line of defense against the Russian trawler fleet. We had heard of it being used and on this one occasion, I was relatively sure we were onto a hot bogey. Our crew and some others had rigged the same ship a few days before. I think that trawler's crew may have been getting a little tired of taking down and putting up their array.

From the APS-20 station, I called the flight deck, "Permission to lower the trailing wire antenna," fully expecting a negative reply.

Instead, "What the hell, let's give it a try," was the answer. I scrambled over the wing beam and lowered the trailing wire antenna all the way out as we approached the trawler amid-ship. The object being to bring the cable and lead ball across the trawler's antennas, popping insulators and busting poles as we went over. Other crews had done it before. This procedure wasn't in the book, but if executed properly, would knock a trawler out of commission for two or three-days minimum. Who were they going to complain to?

I didn't even feel a jerk when the cable hit. Either I had let out too much cable or the pilot was too low and I think the ball hit the side of the ship and bounced into the air. If we did any damage to their long wire antennas, it was pure luck. It stripped the lead ball weight off of the end of our trailing wire and I was afraid it had bent the cable reel, but it hadn't.

The fun part was when the pilot executed a pullout, did a tight turn and came back parallel to the trawler for a second pass. We could see the crew standing on deck shaking their fists at us. This meant that if we hadn't done some damage, at least they darn well knew we had tried.

Runaway Varicam

The P2V was a fantastically durable airplane. It had a thick wing spar like a B-29 and would take extreme turbulence without structural failure. However, it did have two design faults. The first, as aforementioned, was about the nose gear failing to lock in the down position at high air speeds. The other was a variable camber (Varicam) trim design on the horizontal stabilizer. This trim system used electro/hydraulic motors linked mechanically to the stabilizer to vary or warp the aerodynamic curvature for providing nose-up and nose-down trim.

One of the procedures that we trained for on the earlier models was known as run-away Varicam. If the nose-up trim failed in the nose-up position, adding power to the aircraft would cause the P2V to fly into a power on stall. Until the P2V-7 series, where the pilot had control, the pilot had to fly the plane while a circuit breaker or relief valve taken off line.

The prevailing theory on how to fly out of condition was to reduce power and enter a left bank, the normal attitude that an aircraft tends to nose-down, until the failure was resolved. We heard rumors of it occurring in the fleet, but it must have been a rather rare because I can't recall any such incidents with our planes. I understand that the P2V-6 and P2V-7 had a different override procedure for the runaway Varicam, but I was out of the service before the –7s entered the reserves squadrons.

Argentia Newfoundland

Leftover from the latter part of World War II, those old APS-20 radar sets were very effective for searching an area 100 miles ahead. At night, it was really good for navigating along a coast. Water absorbed the radar waves and the earth reflected them displaying a map-like silhouette of the coastline.

On a night flight up the East Coast to Newfoundland, we soon ran out of VOR stations and had to navigate on the old LF radio ranges. We were headed to NAS Argentia, some Canuck airfield where the U.S. had a joint Naval operation agreement. Sitting at the radar station and comparing the coastline to a sectional chart in my lap, I was able to give the pilot headings to steer over the ICS, which he cross checked with the LF until he decided my heading were better. In fact, when we got closer, I told him where to look and he had the airbase lights in sight

Our PPC on this trip was the base Executive Officer. He was also our pilot training officer. He and Commander Kovak were our two best pilots. The first time I flew with the Exec, he boarded the aircraft and threw his parachute harness behind the seat. I remember thinking this pilot has no intentions of bailing out of this plane. He intended to bring the bird home and that was my kind of pilot.

The next morning when we were ready to depart Newfoundland, there was a driving rain and visibility was zero-zero. I could not see the tip tanks as we taxied out to the runway for takeoff. Kovak was in the pilot's seat and the Exec was flying copilot. Kovak ask me to go forward to the nose, get on the ICS and see if I could see the runway centerline.

The nose observer's seat on a P2V is entered through a crawl space beside the nose wheel landing gear. I climbed in the nose station seat and called back that I could see the centerline of the runway just fine. The nose crew position was normally not occupied during takeoff, but I buckled-in. I was to call out if we were left or right of the runway centerline.

Commander Kovak put the nose wheel on the centerline and pushed the throttles forward. The white-line was barely visible through the rain streaked nose canopy and I doubt the pilots could see it at all from the cockpit. At rotation speed (V1) we were lined up fine, lifted off safely and climbed out at (V2) through the driving rain. We broke out into a sunny sky a few thousand feet later or as I mentioned in the preface, we flew for the light.

Anytime we flew up north to New England, orders were placed to pick up fresh live lobsters for the base CO and others. On this particular flight to Newfoundland, a couple of old 1st Class AD Petty Officers had come along. I assumed they just wanted to get away for a few days, but unbeknownst to me, during the night they had unbolted the searchlight housing on the front of the right wingtip tank, collapsed the fuel bladder and stacked 24 cases of Canadian whiskey into the tip-tank.

On the return flight, we stopped at Providence, Rhode Island for a routine customs check. When the inspector came aboard the aircraft, he immediately found a case of Canadian whiskey not very well hidden in the radio compartment, which had been intentionally placed there for the inspector to find. Someone paid the duty on the decoy stash and we were off. As an unwilling participant in their little rum-running scheme, I was glad I hadn't known anything about it until after we got back.

Inch As Good As A Mile

Behind the radar operator's station was the navigator's table where charts could be spread out. We had no navigators like in the old flying boat days. The pilots and crewmen like myself were all trained in dead reckoning and we could drop wind drift smoke flares.

The radarman's seat could be rotated to face the navigation table and the reason I avoided learning, or at least denied knowing how, to play 42 or pinochle. Commander Kovak liked to play pinochle with two other crewmen and they generally played at the NAV table. Whenever the pilot climbed out of the pilot's seat I'd bust my tail for the front seat. Most of the rest of the crew didn't want the seat anyway. I'd turn off the autopilot and practice flying the gages.

Commander Kovak had flown in Korea and returned to civilian life after the war. The best job he could get was as a crop duster and he soon decided that he had a better deal in the Navy. At any rate, he was one heck of a good pilot and I logged several hundred hours of front seat time flying with him or maybe I should say, with whatever reserve copilot (PP2C) was with us at the time.

Approaching the Dallas Metroplex from the east we had to crossover Love Field traffic to get to Navy Dallas. I had been in the pilot's seat for an hour or so when Commander Kovak had grown tired of playing cards and relieved the copilot. The copilot promptly stretched out on the flight deck to take a nap.

We were not yet in the DFW control zone and I was straight and level at about 8,000 feet inbound on the Dallas VORTAC. Commander Kovak, of all things, was reading a *Flight Safety* magazine, a monthly Navy publication.

A dark shadow came over the cockpit and as instantly as it had come it was gone. A half second later, we were looking down the exhausts of a Boeing 707 Delta airliner, descending into Love Field. Expecting to be rocked or even rolled by the airline's vortex, I got a death grip on the yoke. But not even a ripple. Vortex only occurs when the wings are loaded and the airliner was descending rapidly.

It was a classic case of us being below him and the airliner being above and behind us. It was doubtful that they ever saw us or received an ATC radar advisory.

Turning to look at Kovak, I fully expected to be ordered out of the pilot's seat and allowed never to take the controls again. He just looked up from his magazine and remarked, "They sure get big when you get that close to them, don't they," and went back to reading his magazine. As the old cliché goes, an inch is as good as a mile.

Aviation Aircrew Candidates

With the draft still in effect, the Air Navy was getting more volunteers than it could train so the regular Air Navy initiated an Aviation aircrew Candidate (AvCad) program and sent them to the reserves. The Army and Air Force Reserve and Guard had initiated similar programs. These programs allowed an individual to serve only six months on active duty and then remain in a reserve unit for the next seven and a half years.

Avcads were sent to A-School in Memphis, Tennessee for a rating, but some of these schools only took four or five months to complete. After that, they were sent to us to finish their active tour of duty. I guess we were supposed to make aircrewmen out of them in that time. The classes I used to teach to six or eight students mushroomed to twenty or more students.

We put them through basic sonobuoy, ECM and radar operation courses, but it's really difficult to keep students in class eight hours a day, plus our actual airborne training capability was limited, except when reserve pilots were there on weekends. Between classes I had AvCads scrub decks, polish floors and paint bulkheads to occupy their time. Now I had become as bad as those regular Navy swabbies back on the USS Rose.

If a trainee fell asleep in my class, I had a mop bucket just around the corner from the sonobuoy trainer. During my lectures, if someone nodded off to sleep, without missing a beat, I would pick up the mop bucket and as the rest of the class watched, drop it right beside them. The sleeping trainee would be startled awake and the rest of the class would get a good laugh out of it. Needless to say, most then stayed awake in my classes not knowing when the next shoe might drop.

Properly Trained Officer

We got a new assistant ASW training officer assigned to our unit, a Lieutenant Commander who had been a single-engine jet pilot in a VF squadron. He had flown Panthers and Cougars in Korea, but knew little and cared less about ASW. He was only there to finish his twenty for retirement. On Sunday mornings, he'd sit in the training office with his feet up on the desk and read the funny papers. If anyone asked him what he was doing, he'd reply, "Studying for Commander."

A year or so earlier, I had designed some file cards for tracking each aircrewman's training progress. This goes back to the thing about who was authorized to wear the gold aircrew wings. Each class attended during the training regiment of flight and ground school was marked on the cards indicating qualified for a specific aircrew position. In order to send them to the printing office, I assigned some made-up official looking form number to the file cards. With the addition of some new aircrew classes, it was time to update the file cards.

The new officer and I first became acquainted when I was redoing one of the file card layouts and the he saw me marking up the cards to be reprinted. He commenced to chew me out. Something to the effect of who did I think I was, modifying an official Navy document without authorization.

Looking up from my work, I saw Commander Kovak and the Chief standing in the doorway behind him. They were laughing at my getting chewed out and my trying to explain the made-up form number. I'm sure Kovak explained it to him later because after that the new LtCmdr and I pretty much became friends. He liked to tell flying stories and I was always willing to listen to a good flying story. During one of our many bull sessions, I asked him if he had ever bailed out of a jet fighter, as I knew the old Panther and Cougar jets were notorious for flameouts.

"Well almost," he said and went on to tell me that while flying off a carrier, his Cougar's engine started to surge and appeared to have flamed out. Climbing out on the wing, he looked down at the water 6000 feet below. "While hanging onto the side, I reached back into the cockpit and jockeyed the throttle back and forth until the engine started again and I climbed back in. So you see, I almost bailed out one time."

On another occasion, we got off on the subject of UFOs and he told me about an experience he had, "One night over Los Angeles, I was flying a North American F4J Fury and I spotted several UFOs flying at a higher altitude and I attempted to climb up to their altitude. Each time I would get close to them, they would move rapidly away. I never got near them, but I'm convinced to this day, that UFOs do exist!"

I've talked with other pilots who had similar encounters. This did me a considerable amount of good finding out that others, who had no reason to lie about it, had seen them too.

A-Bomb Tests

During the Cold War era after WW II between our Allies and the Iron Curtain, the United States planned a round of nuclear tests in the

Bikini Islands. In order not to tie up a regular Navy unit, NAS Dallas was asked to activate one of its patrol squadrons. VP-703 was designated to be that unit. In order not to work hardships on married families and career professionals, a call went out for volunteers from all the VP squadrons.

I was one of the station keepers transferred to VP-703 to help train and re-qualify the aircrewmen for the new composite squadron. On the day the squadron mustered to depart for the West Coast and their final leg over the Pacific, to my disappointment, one of the volunteers named Bruce did not make muster at the assembly hall. He was an electronics technician (AT) and a real asset to the squadron.

The P2Vs were lined up, engines running and ready to taxi when I saw Bruce wheel into the Flight Ops parking lot. I took off running to meet him, grabbed one of his bags and we both ran for his waiting P2V. The lookout sitting in the open top hatch, I'm sure had called the pilots over the ICS and he was yelling for us to come on and pointing to the rear belly hatch. We threw his stuff on and I gave Bruce, who was a little short, a boost in through the hatch. I was still laughing as they taxied out.

The primary duty of the VP squadron assigned to the atomic testing was to patrol the waters surrounding the test area in an effort to clear it of ships. By far, the largest violators of these restricted waters were fishing vessels from China and Japan. Having been assigned to VP-703 to train them made me eligible for the joint AF and Navy Commendation to this unit.

The Bikini atomic bomb tests would make interesting stories for those who participated to tell for years to come. They were witness to the last of the atomic explosions to be detonated in the earth's atmosphere. Bruce told me years later that he got so accustomed to the testing that when he was off duty, he could actually sleep through a distant atomic explosion.

In the early days of the Viet Nam conflict, several of the other crew I help train qualified me for the RVN Armed Forces medal and the RVN Training medal. I earned the usual NDS and NR medals, plus Expert and Marksman with 45, 38 and 50 calibers. I also qualified for the Expeditionary medal via a clandestine Cuban operation out of Rosy Roads, but it was never entered in my service record and I never received a Good Conduct medal for reasons, which I will attempt to explain in the next chapter.

My flight crew on P-2V flight deck, Cmdr Kovak far right, note crash helmets on Nav table; main hangar at NAS Dallas; my crew on ground in Newfoundland; VP-702 squadron, old models P2Vs prior to -5F; 1959 NAS Alameda; one of last Navy blimp squadrons; crew on ground in Albuquerque awaiting de-fueling; teaching survival training May West and in flight gear; blimp cross-country; Cougar soon to be retired.

Chapter Fourteen
NINETY MILES OFF THE COAST

As the Indo-China and Cold War tensions continued, our training flights became more and more restricted in the Pacific. Most of our flights were now conducted in the Caribbean. NAS Dallas based squadrons regularly flew to Panama, Gitmo and Puerto Rico for training.

If the subject of Russians or the USSR being in Cuba came up, our standard reply was, "Don't worry, they're still ninety miles off the coast."

On training flights into Panama, we landed at an Air Force base, home of a C-130 squadron. The based was surrounded by lush jungle vegetation and the barracks were large screened in buildings, somewhat akin to camping out with a roof overhead.

The main military force for Panama was referred to as the Guard. It was patterned after our own National Guard, a remnant of years of U.S. occupation. Panama City was a thriving metropolis with everything from luxury hotels to massive slums. The two things I remember most about Panama City are the constant honking of car horns and vendors selling fried *platanos* (plantain similar to a bananas) on the street.

Cuba Libra

Guantanamo Bay, our base in Cuba nicknamed Gitmo, was and still is a permanent U.S. Naval base with a history dating back to the Marine Corps landing in the Spanish American War. During Fidel's revolution against Batista, we sometimes saw cannon fire in the mountains while flying off of Cuba's southern coast.

Americans mostly had a free run of Cuba until the U.S. government decided that Castro's banditos, who were trying to conquer the Batista regime, were a bunch of Commies and restricted military liberty into the mainland.

There was, however, a small Cuban settlement just outside the main entrance to Gitmo. Up until the full Cuban embargo, liberty was permitted in this village.

On a hot sultry summer afternoon in one of the village bars full of U.S. sailors, Marines and a few reserve airmen, a rag-tag bunch of banditos wandered in for a beer. They explained that they were *los insurgencies* fighting for *la revolucion*. Between drinks a tall slender, unshaven member of their group would walk out the front door and fire a couple of rounds into the air with his old Springfield O3A3 rifle and yell, "*Viva la revolucion.*" And guess what, at this writing ol' Fidel is still *el presidente de* Cuba.

Rosie Roads

In Puerto Rico, there was an old airbase at Roosevelt Roads nicknamed Rosie Roads. The British had used the base during World War II, but now the Navy was using it as a base for ASW operations throughout the Gulf of Mexico and the Southern Caribbean. Flying weather conditions were excellent most of the year, except during hurricane season.

The best job a weatherman could hope for would be as a weatherman in Puerto Rico. All he'd have to do is get up every morning and forecast, "It will be 85 degrees today, sunshine and light rain showers expected this afternoon," and go back to bed. He would be right ninety percent of the time, a better average than most weathermen back in the states.

During a weekend off, some of my crew and I bummed a ride into San Juan with one of the regular Navy guys who had a car. San Juan was really two cities in one. The uptown was crowded with fancy beach hotels and restaurants. The old town squares down by the Spanish fort were where the average Puerto Rican came to hang out and socialize. In each of the town squares, there was a public TV that usually had several dozen people standing around watching.

Most of the Puerto Rican people were bilingual and I seldom met an unfriendly local. In the small towns on Saturday night, you could always find a steel band playing with people sitting around listening, dancing and drinking. The one thing that struck me as being very unique about the Puerto Rican people was that when they went out for a Saturday night, they took along grandma, grandpa and all the kids.

When one of our crews was not flying, I'd take the men over to the large Olympic size swimming pool on the base and spend the afternoon training them to inflate a Mae West and board an eight-man life raft in wet flight gear. In addition to having a lot of fun, the aircrewmen quickly found out how hard it was to survive in the water with their flight gear on and how difficult it was to climb aboard a life raft.

On the far side of the base along the ocean shore there was a white sandy beach, which was excellent for snorkeling. The water was so clear that even at a depth of six feet or more, the bottom appeared to be only a few inches deep until you stepped in. Swimming or snorkeling inside the reef was unlike swimming in the murky shores off the Continental coast. We were cautioned not to swim outside the reef because there were schools of barracuda, which I was told were more dangerous than sharks.

Down the beach a ways, there was a long pier that extended out past the shallow water. Cargo ships used the pier to drop off supplies for the base. These types of piers were referred to as boondocks, I guess because it was out in the boonies and I'm sure where our high-top lace boots got the nickname boon-dockers. We wore the black boon-dockers with our dungarees and the brown rough-out boon-dockers with our flight suits.

Standard issue with our flight gear was a really durable hunting knife intended for cutting your way free of parachute lines. In the evenings, when we'd climb the stairs in the old wooden barracks, I unsheathed my knife and throw it up the large open stairwell to stick it in the old wooden plank wall.

This developed into a regular nightly contest to determine who was the best knife thrower. To make mine a little lighter and better balanced for throwing, I cut the top knob off the handle with a hacksaw. As the contest grew, we ruled only one throw per crewman, per evening. I got to where I could stick it in the wall consistently from 15-feet away or let's just say I seldom had to buy the beer.

ASW War Games

Being able to fly out of Rosie Roads was our squadron's first opportunity to practice with a nuclear submarine. It didn't matter which submarine we were assigned to for an exercise, if it was a nuke, they always identified their boat as the USS George Washington.

Small vessels like PT boats and launches are correctly called boats, but a submarine regardless of size, is the only ship in the Navy that is correctly called a boat. During these exercises, it became apparent to us that the conventional tactics we were using to locate and track diesel electric submarines were fairly useless against the Nautilus Class submarines. The speed of USN nuclear subs has always been classified. However, considering that the USS George Washington could take off in any one of 360 degrees at speeds of 40 knots or better underwater made them very hard to catch.

The methods used to detect a submarine by patrol aircraft were surface scan radar to detect a conning tower or a fully surfaced boat, ECM to pickup their radar, dropping sonobuoys in a cloverleaf pattern and using MAD gear. That was all we had. That stuff was classified information thirty years ago, but you can see it all on the cable TV channels now. It's kind of like that copy of an *Aviation Week* magazine article that was found at the Pentagon stamped SECRET.

A sonobuoy, dropped by a small parachute, deployed a sonar microphone and transmitter antenna upon hitting the water. By tuning to different buoys on different frequencies, the sub's propeller noise could be tracked and the sub's underwater course *guesstimated*.

Our MAD equipment would indicate a fluctuation in the earth's magnetic field when a large metal object like a sub disturbed the field. The readout on a MAD was similar to the needle graph on a seismograph. Modern subs have coils of wire wrapped around their hull for inducing a counter Electro Magnetic Field (EMF). This makes them almost impossible to detect with MAD equipment.

On an assigned morning patrol, flying off the coast of Rosie Roads, we rendezvoused with a Washington class submarine. The sub came up on our UHF frequency and transmitted that they were ready to play games. They gave us a bearing and distance to them. By the time we got there, the sub had submerged and we began a standard search pattern dropping sonobuoys, but were unable to locate the sub.

Ever so often, the sub would stick its UHF antenna out of the water and taunt us by radioing their new bearing and approximate distance. After several hours of this, the sub came to conning tower depth. We picked it up on ECM and radar and headed for the contact. The sea swells were high that day and the sub's dark color blended into the water. We didn't even make visual contact until we were nearly on top of the sub.

We probably passed directly over the top of the submerged sub several times, but our MAD gear never indicated a contact, thus leading me to believe the sub must have been equipped with some kind of reverse magnetic polarity device.

The day after our practice submarine chase, my squadron was due to rotate back to NAS Dallas and another squadron was due in to replace us. That evening, our squadron threw a big party. Bacardi rum was ninety-five cents a bottle in Puerto Rico where it was produced and was actually cheaper than beer to drink. The CO hired some entertainers who played steel drums, complete with dancing girls.

At any rate, the party degenerated into hauling the large tub full of iced down Bacardi and pineapple juice back to the barracks in a flight line pickup. The steel bunks were pushed back to the wall and everyone fell asleep on their mattresses thrown on the floor in a big circle around the tub.

Sometime around sunup, I woke up with someone shaking me. When I pried my eyes open, I was looking up into the face of our training chief from Dallas. I couldn't figure out where I was and I asked the chief, "How did I get back here?"

The chief and his crew were all laughing at us camped out in the center of the barracks. When I finally got myself awake, I realized the other squadron had flown in overnight and had just arrived.

Bay Of Pigs

In April of 1961, the CIA backed the infamous invasion of Cuba known as The Bay of Pigs. It was obvious to us at NAS Dallas that something was afoot because they had activated one of our VF squadrons and assigned it to the fleet. Our detachment of Marines was also sent aboard a carrier. A gunny corporal friend of mine told me later that when they woke up the morning of the invasion, all the insignias and markings on the Navy aircraft onboard had been painted over.

Another interesting story told to me was about a Marine Corps Captain who was circling overhead in a Fury waiting for orders to support the Cuban freedom fighters. When the order came to return to the carrier, he could see what was happening and he went in to make a strafing run across the beachhead where Castro's tanks were moving into position to attack the landing forces. He did this supposedly to warn the invaders that they were walking into a trap. No court martial or hearing was ever held to the best of anyone's knowledge because our official propaganda line stated that the U.S. was not involved.

During the third year of my tour of duty at NAS Dallas, my wife took a job in the Technical Publications Department at Chance Vought Aircraft. We always called it the Bomber Plant. My wife worked Monday through Friday and I worked every weekend, except when there was a fifth weekend in the month. Remember, we fly on Sundays. With the extra income from my wife's job we purchased a new Morris Minor, which was the first new car we had ever bought. It was kind of like a British made water-cooled, front engine Volkswagen.

When I met my wife for lunch, I had to change out of my dungarees and into civvies and then back again after returning from lunch. Four changes of clothes a day really got to be a pain, but it was Navy regulations. The base had the duty nights arranged so that Petty Officers only caught the overnight duty every eighth night. To get out of duty night, you could pay another Petty Officer, usually one of the single guys who lived on base, to stand your duty for a few bucks and I often did.

Missiles Of October

All ASW aircrew training instructors were required to have a secret clearance. The main reason for this was that we had access to the codebooks that were required to be onboard certain flights. During World War II, both the German and Japanese codes had been broken and with the advent of computers almost any code could be broken in no time at all. The U.S. method of coding changed to a different key every few hours based on Greenwich Mean Time and thus, the codebooks were only good for 24 hours. We kept them in a safe in Cmdr Novak's office and only a few officers knew the combination.

In October of 1962, we began noticing a lot more coded traffic over the airways. The ASW training building had a full HF radio station. When I reported to the base on the morning of the Cuban Missile Crisis, we were told that all leave had been cancelled and those of us living off base were now confined to the base. We went to Defense Condition (DEFCON) Two, as the news broke about the Russian ships carrying missiles that were headed for Cuba. The question was, were they going to try to run our U.S. Naval blockade.

Married personnel were given a couple of hours to go home and prepare their families for what could possibly be the beginning of World War III. Needless to say, anyone who knew what was going on, was scared once the reality of the situation began to set in. When I got to the house, I told my wife to stay home from work and not to take our daughter to nursery school. We loaded the Morris Minor with canned goods, bottled water, blankets and first aid stuff. When she dropped me back at the base, I told her to fill the car with gas and keep it full.

My instructions to my wife were probably similar to those given to many other wives at the time. We lived in Grand Prairie and there was open country to the south, the Texas hill country. I told her if war broke out, to head south as far away from the Metroplex as she could get because I didn't know where I would be and didn't think I'd be able to get home to go with them. At least, I would know the general territory they were heading to and could find them later.

The DFW Metroplex was an excellent candidate to be an ICBM target. General Dynamics and Carswell Air Force Base were located in Fort Worth. Carswell was a SAC base at that time with a squadron of B-52s and General Dynamics was building the B-58 Hustler bomber. The area was a prime target. Dallas was the home of TI, LTV and NAS Dallas.

When I reported back to the base, we started assigning the crews we had available to aircraft. There wasn't time to activate a reserve squadron. The crews could be made up mostly of base personnel, but we soon realized we were seriously short of pilots. One squadron was due in that weekend for drill and a few reserve pilots, most of whom were bachelors, showed up on their own and volunteered to fly if they were needed.

Our national defense plan included the shutting down of all navigation aids and rotating broadcast stations. This was called going to Controlled Electronic Radiation (CONELRAD) emissions condition. This precaution was taken so that enemy aircraft could not use our radio stations to home in on, as the Japs had done at Pearl Harbor. Thus, any aircraft we put in the air would have to resort to basic navigation techniques.

At ASW, I prepared as many standard operational flight cases with codebooks and charts as I had materials for, including chronometers and sextants.

A group of us went to the ordinance storage area to see what types of bombs and missiles were in storage. The only weapon we found was one sidewinder missile that had been left by some transit aircraft and it didn't fit our wing mounts, so we were left with nothing but some PDC, target rockets and a couple cases of practice bombs. We were not prepared to help with any defensive effort.

That night when I reported for guard duty as roving patrol and picked up my equipment belt, I noticed the usually clip-less .45 automatic was heavier than normal. The Chief Petty Officer (CPO) of the watch said, "Yes, it's loaded."

Although aircrewmen rated side arms, I had never been issued one to carry with live rounds in the clip, even though I had qualified as marksman on the firing range. Up until now, we had always joked that the .45 automatics we carried were to beat someone over the head with or to throw at them. To this day, I get kidded when I tell this story about defending NAS Dallas in an atomic war with my trusty .45 automatic.

We posted as many guards at as many critical places on the base we could think of like the water supply, the fuel depot and the base perimeter. The only real plan that we had was to get the aircraft airborne and out of the area if those idiots did push the button. Beyond that, we had no workable plan.

Conventional Armed Nuclear Age

Like most Americans, we sat by the radio and TV and listened while two world leaders, who had been given far too much power, played a horrible game of bluff poker. Carl Sagan wrote about the nuclear arms race saying, "It was like two men in a room, ankle deep in gasoline, arguing over which one had the largest hand-full of matches."

If all out war had broken out, there would not have been time to activate the reserve units. In an age of fifteen-minute incoming missiles and nuclear weapons our military was forced to rethink the entire reserve program. Traditionally, since the Revolutionary War, the Spanish American War and as late as World War II, the regulars would be getting their ass kicked until the militia, in later years what became the State Guards, National Guard and Reserves arrived to reinforce them.

The last conventional war this country would fight was in Viet Nam. Once again, it was proven that people fighting for their own country could not be defeated. A former Air Force Captain, who flew an F-86D in Korea, told me that his squadron had two Korean Air Force pilots. He said that he would come in low over the treetops on ground strafing runs with a death grip on the stick. When he didn't think he could get any lower, he'd look down. Fifty feet below him would be the two Korean pilots who were kicking the rudders in order to get a better spray of bullets on their strafing runs. The difference was that the Korean pilots were fighting for their own homeland, he wasn't.

View From The Fleet

My brother-in-law was the intelligence officer on the carrier USS Enterprise during the Cuban Missile Crisis. He later told me that accidentally or intentionally, their ship had ended up being the only large U.S. Navy ship between the Russian cargo ships loaded with missiles and their intended Cuban port. He talked several times via radio to the Secretary of Defense, Robert McNamara giving him first hand updates.

Like it or not, they were going to be the ship that had to turn the inbound Russian ships around stopping them by whatever force necessary. Their orders were firm and not negotiable.

The world will never know what was going through President Kennedy's mind, but as it turned out Khrushchev blinked first. Russia agreed to remove all of the nuclear missiles from Cuban soil and a couple of weeks after the Crisis, reconnaissance photos were published in the press. The photos showed what appeared to be missiles shrouded under canvas on the decks of the Russian cargo ships departing Cuba. Kennedy had agreed to remove our missiles from Turkey so Khrushchev could save face.

SNAFU

Situation normal all fouled up. Our daily routine eventually returned to normal at NAS Dallas, as normal as things can get around a bunch of idiots who fly airplanes. The weekend of the annual Texas OU football game celebration arrived. I was late getting home that night after celebrating in the streets of downtown Dallas on to discover that my daughter had come down with the measles. Subsequently, my wife and I were up all night tending to her. What I am going to do now is try to explain why I never received a Navy good conduct medal.

The next morning, I went through the main gate late and I had a civvies shirt over the top of my dungarees. The gate guard on duty was a fellow that I had never met before and he stopped me insisting that I go in and talk to the Junior Officer Of the Day (JOOD). The JOOD, a Chief Petty Officer, was new and had just transferred to the base. I didn't know him either. Needless to say, an argument ensued.

The CPO was pounding on my chest with his finger to make his point when I pushed his arm away. As I did, he stepped backwards putting his foot into a wastebasket, stumbled backwards and broke a windowpane. It might have been funny, but just then the OD walked in and it was the base Admin Officer, who had also been up most of the night handling some problem with some locker stealing over at the barracks. He said I was going to Captain's Mast and that was it.

At the time it seemed rather serious, but looking back, it was kind of comical. Calling over to ASW, I told my Chief what had happened and to call my wife and ask her to bring me a clean set of dress whites. After lunch, I reported to the Captain's office. The Yeoman who worked for the Admin Officer stopped me in the hall and said, "I have been told to tell you to just keep your mouth shut and everything will be okay," and I agreed. As I entered the Captain's office, there stood Cmdr Kovak, my Chief and the JOOD.

This was embarrassing. My wife and I had recently sat at the same table with the Captain and his wife at a banquet a few weeks earlier. Plus, Cmdr Kovak was not a happy camper over one of his men being called on the carpet. The Captain, who obviously hadn't had a very good night either, began to chew me out. Something along the lines of disobedience and damage to government property were listed among my many sins. Then he said, "What do you have to say for yourself?"

Desperately I struggled for an answer. I had agreed to keep my mouth shut. I replied, "I'll pay for the window, sir."

The Captain looked away to keep from letting anyone see him smile. After, the snickering in the room died down, he asked Cmdr Kovak to speak on my behalf. I'll always regard his reply as one of the finest compliments I have ever received. He said, "Arnold isn't real sharp when it comes to wearing the uniform and isn't real good at military protocol, but when I want a job done right, I send Arnold to do it."

"Enough said," the Captain concluded, but he had to do something along the lines of discipline. Without giving much thought to it, he simply informed the Admin Officer not to recommend me for advancement to 1st Class Petty Officer for six months. In other words, temporarily frozen in rank.

To be fair, the Captain probably thought the punishment was only a slap on the wrist. There was only one problem with his order, I was eligible to take the rating exam the next month and my enlistment was up in three months. This meant I would have to re-enlist for two years if I wanted to take the next exam. The reason I wanted to make the next rating exam was so I would be eligible to apply for Aviation Cadets and go to flight school at Pensacola. Also, I was bumping the age limit at the time.

For the next several weeks, I mulled over the pros and cons of my continuing in a Naval career and discussed it with my wife over and over. Seven more years of service meant that we would likely stay till retirement and could expect long separations.

I had received an offer from Chance Vought Aircraft for an engineering job in cockpit design. The offer was the career path I had originally intended to pursue and I decided not to re-enlist in the Navy. It was probably the hardest career decision I ever made.

When I do reflect back on it, I recall the character that William Holden played in the movie *The Bridges at Toko Ri,* a civilian lawyer recalled to Korea as a reserve Navy jet pilot and like that character, I would have probably ended up dead in some rice paddy in Southeast Asia. Who knows what choices we really have in life and what choices we only think we have. Had I continued to pursue becoming a jet fighter pilot, I might have missed many of the life adventures that my wife and I have enjoyed together.

Civilian Airman

I received an honorable discharge from the Navy after eight years of active and reserve service and this made me eligible for VA flight training on the GI bill and I took advantage of it. Additionally, I enrolled in some advanced engineering courses at the University of Texas in Arlington.

Even though I wasn't career military, there was reluctance on my part to leave the service. The reserves would now get the P2V-6 series

Neptune as the fleet began receiving their new Lockheed P3V Orion, Navy version of the Electra airliner.

Braniff Airlines, based out of Dallas, was one of the first airlines to use the Electra on their routes. Early on, an Electra came apart in a thunderstorm north of Dallas. Scores of volunteers helped walk the fields looking for pieces of the aircraft that had literally disintegrated in mid-air.

This was uncharacteristic of a Lockheed built aircraft in that they had always been known for building strong airframes. As it turned out, the angle that the engines were mounted on the wings produced a harmonic vibration that eventually led to wing spar failure. The whole thing was strangely reminiscent of the plot in a movie starring Jimmy Stewart and Marlene Dietrich, *No Highways in the Sky*. In the fictional story, Stewart plays a bookish engineer that predicts the failure of the empennage on a new British airliner. Subsequent modifications by Lockheed soon made the Electra very durable. The Navy version of the Electra, the P3V Orion, all had the stronger wing.

Military Career Continued

After leaving active duty service, I remained in a reserve squadron for a time, but it wasn't the same as being in the middle of all the action. In retrospect, I should have completed the balance of the eleven years I needed for a reserve retirement, but I did not.

While working as a design engineer at Chance Vought, I joined the Texas Army National Guard (TNG) as a member of the 149th Aviation Regiment, an observation unit assigned to the 49th Armored. These eye-in-the-sky light planes became Forward Air Controllers during Viet Nam and a unit known as the Ravens preformed valiantly in the jungles of Southeast Asia.

Entering the guard as a warrant officer candidate, I was able to take advantage of a fast track aviation wings program for commercial pilots. I completed flight check qualification in the L-19 Bird Dog, (re-designated later as an O-1). Some of the pilots were able to also qualify in the twin T-42 Cochise, a Beech model 55. However, our small unit based at the old Grand Prairie airport only had the six Cessna L-19s assigned. Drill weekends were usually spent dealing with maintenance problems and some kind or another qualification.

Annually, the TNG aviation regiments flew their L-19s down to Fort Hood for summer camp to operate out of Gary Field. The tank corps guardsmen were a motley but dedicated bunch that loved their work. They literally lived in their tanks and on a hot, dusty Texas afternoon, they got to be a little smelly. Likewise, they probably thought guys like us were crazy to fly around in those underpowered aluminum kites. It's the ol' Catch 22; you got to be crazy to want to fly, but if you know you're crazy then you can't be crazy. As Yossarian said, "That's a pretty good catch, that Catch 22."

Word came down that the 149th and others were going to be transitioned to helicopter units and pilots not helicopter rated would be cycled through Mineral Wells for rotary wing training. The L-19s were to be phased out and the light airplane, flying club days were over for the guard.

The French had pulled out of Viet Nam leaving us holding the bag and things were heating up. I put my name on the list for helicopter school, but soon all dates were cancelled except for those who would agree to go on active duty for two years.

In all honesty I've never liked helicopters. Ironic, as years later I ended up working for Aerospatiale Helicopter and flew many shakedown flights in choppers. Veterans had the option of declining active duty, but it met leaving the guard. With the offer of a good engineering job waiting at Lockheed, I opted out. Chief Warrants WO-2 and above were permanent ranks, but a Warrant Officer 1st pilot was not and I was honorably discharged from the TAG.

Some years later, I joined the New Mexico guard as a Lieutenant. As a Captain I served as Commanding Officer of the Clovis unit. The New Mexico State Defense Force under the Department of Military Affairs was integrated into the State Guard. I was promoted to Major and assigned as Chief Information Officer (CIO) G-6 to Headquarters in Albuquerque. During that time, I was awarded the NMNG Outstanding Meritorious Service medal presented to me by Major General Laurence Morrell and signed by Governor Bill Richardson.

My collection of service ribbons, badges and citations from the Naval Reserve and the Army Guards were starting to make me look like a South American general and maybe it was time to hang up the ol' military service cap, but continued for a while longer serving on staff of the U. S. Volunteers America where I held the brevet rank of full Colonel before officially retiring.

Flight line at NAS Dallas with North American FJ Fury fighters used by Marine reserve squadron; Chief AP (Airplane Pilot) last Chief AP retired in early 70s; Navy AD Sky Raider with long-range fuel tank and searchlight installed, it would run out of oil before it ran out of fuel; TNG L-19 Bird Dog like those assigned by the 149th Aviation Regiment post-Korean era; Warrant Officer flight school class; NMSG and USV commissioning; Suzie and me on AFB flight line with C-47 like ones I used to fly; my brother Don, myself and others were invited guests of honor at a Cannon AFB ceremony.

Chapter Fifteen
DALLAS LOVE FIELD

Come back with me now to those thrilling days when I was still trying to make a living as a pilot. With a hearty, "You are cleared for takeoff and an immediate left turn out." The lone pilot flies again. Back to those days of yesteryear when aviation was still growing up, to the glory days of General Aviation that would never be again.

The first time I landed at Love Field, the terminal building was still on the Lemmon Avenue side and there were some old WW II B-17s parked nearby. The old terminal was torn down when the new terminal was built with an entrance off of Mockingbird Lane on the other side of the airfield.

True or not, I always heard the story that in old Dallas, years before my time, there was a dirt road off of Mockingbird Lane nicknamed Lovers Lane. A new airfield was located near there and thus, the origin of the name. When WW II broke out, Love Field became an aviation staging area. Florene Watson, whom I mentioned in an earlier chapter, was based there as an Army ferry pilot and CO of the Women Army Service Pilots (WASP) unit at Love Field.

Dallas Love Field became a major airport in the 1950s due to the geometric growth of the city of Dallas. The new Love Field terminal was completed in the early 60s and was a modern architectural wonder with marble floors, a five-story rotunda and a three-story balcony overlooking the airline parking ramps.

In the center of the terminal stood a large bronze statue of a Texas Ranger that was moved there from the old Amon Carter Airport terminal in Fort Worth. The inscription on the base read *one riot, one ranger.* Were it not for Southwest Airline flights, the present terminal would have been abandoned or turned into a civil aviation terminal long ago.

Meacham Field, Fort Worth's main airport, located north of town, was a thriving General Aviation airport, but had been unable to support airline service over the years. Fort Worth folks had to drive to Dallas Love Field to catch an airliner.

Back in the 1930s, Dallas and Fort Worth began a long running feud, which started over who would get an Exposition, which was finally held at what is now Dallas Fair Park.

The wealthy newspaper publisher of the Fort Worth Star Telegram, Amon Carter, Jr., donated a large tract of land between Dallas and Fort Worth for the purpose of building a regional airport on the Dallas/Tarrant County line. After much negotiation, a deal was cut with Dallas to close Love Field and make Amon Carter the main airport when it was completed.

The fatal blow to the project was dealt when it came time to place the location of the terminal building. Dallas wanted it on the Dallas County side and Fort Worth wanted in on the Tarrant County side of the runways. Amon Carter, Jr. insisted that because he had donated the land, he would be the one to say where the terminal was built.

The terminal was built on the Tarrant County side and the social war from the 1930s once again reared its ugly head. The Dallas airline clientele refused to drive to the new Amon Carter Airport and Love Field continued to grow.

To complicate the problem, most carriers had already signed gate lease agreements with Amon Carter. The large prop airliners like the Douglas DC-6 and the Lockheed Constellation would land at Amon Carter Airport to pickup and deplane the Fort Worth passengers. They would takeoff, cruising at 1,000 feet AGL for an immediate landing at Love Field where they would deplane and pickup the Dallas passengers. We lived in the Mid-Cities at the time, so the airliners went right over our house.

If you have ever wondered or questioned why the new DFW Regional Airport terminal buildings all face inward to the center of the airport, well that's the county line. *And now you know the rest of the story.*

Central Airline

Braniff Airlines was based at Love Field. American Airlines had started in Fort Worth years earlier, but had moved away. There were two other carriers who served the region, Trans Texas Airways (TTA) affectionately referred to by the local gentry as Tree Top Airways and Central Airlines.

Shortly after I got out of the military, Central Airlines was hiring copilots for their DC-3 runs. Their offices were located at the entrance to Amon Carter Airport. I interviewed with the Chief Pilot and was tentatively hired for the next class for copilot training.

Ozark Airlines was Central Airline's main competitor and was fairing better financially than Central. Before the next pilot class started, Ozark bought out Central and took over all of Central's routes. Ozark was flying mostly twin-engine Convair equipment and had a surplus of DC-3 pilots. Needless to say, the DC-3 copilot's class never convened.

After all of the airline carriers moved their operations to Dallas Love Field, Amon Carter airfield was renamed Greater Southwest Airport.

Mustang Aviation

Mustang Aviation was the FBO in the large blue hangar at the far-east end of Love Field beside the Delta Airline hangar, across the street from the Coke plant. With no flying job on the horizon, I went to work as a design draftsman for a small research company on Mockingbird Lane down the street from Mustang Aviation and would stop by on my lunch hour.

A fellow by the name of Hoover partnered with Toots Womack in the Mustang operation. Toots was an old time pilot and one of the original Quiet Birdmen. The Quiet Birdmen was formed by early aviation to aid the widows and orphans of downed flyers. Toots had this mischievous pet parrot that had free rein of the hangar offices and would chase you like a dog down the hall.

Hoover claimed to be the heir to the vacuum cleaner fortune. Whether true or not, the best quote I can attribute to Hoover was, "I know there's a lot of money in the aviation business because I put a bunch of it there".

Hoover talked Bob Smith, of Aerosmith Aviation, into letting him have the Piper dealership on Love field. Hoover's main operation was running an air taxi service and he flew a lot of the twin-engine flights himself. All the brand new Piper single-engine models sat around mostly unused. So I talked Hoover into letting me fly some air taxi runs in the singles on the weekend. Most of the runs were delivering oil well parts to some Podunk airport out in the West Texas oilfields.

Air Taxi Arrow

The other air taxi pilot that flew for Hoover flew copilot in the twins because many exec's insurance required two pilots. He was assigned to check me out in the new retractable Piper Arrow. I don't think he had flown the Arrow very much because it was brand new. After a short checkout, we returned to Love Field to land. He placed the gear lever in the down position, I assume to show me how it was done, but the three green lights on the instrument sub-panel did not come on.

He panicked and said we were going to have to make a wheels-up landing. Trying not to be too bold, I suggested that we hold off doing that for a while and let's climb on out and fly around a little bit. We had plenty of fuel. In fact, our tanks were nearly full and we didn't need to do a wheels-up landing with all that fuel onboard.

I reached in the glove box to get the aircraft manual and began to thumb through the pages. Actually, I was looking for the circuit breaker locations. It was then that I noticed the instrument panel lights were on. I turned the panel lights to off and suggested we slow down and lower the gear again. Sure enough, all three lights came on. They had been on all the time, but not bright enough to see in the sunlight.

Airplane Rental

Student pilots were not allowed to depart or make landings at Love Field. This was probably some type of city ordinance and not an FAA regulation. Private pilots could, however, fly out of Love Field and there sat all those new Piper single-engine aircraft that were not being used.

I asked Hoover if he'd put insurance coverage on the aircraft for rentals, which didn't cost much as they were already insured for air taxi use. I began checking people out in the various Cherokee models and the weekend rental business exploded. Why wouldn't it, with brand new airplanes to fly?

Hoover eventually got out of the Piper dealership business and turned it back over to Aerosmith. I preferred not to sit around and write gas tickets so I left when the planes did. This experience stuck in my mind and influenced my thinking on what type of aircraft to rent, if I were to operate an FBO.

Capital Aviation

The old Cessna distributorships, like the original Ford automobile distributorships, were independently owned before Cessna Aircraft Corporation began to buy them all up. The independent Cessna distributorships were operated a little like a squadron, complete with CO and Exec.

Capital Aviation, owned by Ragsdale Aviation in Austin, based its Cessna distributorship at Dallas Love Field. The late 1960s and early 70s were the heyday of general aviation. The Capital Aviation Cessna distributorship was moving six hundred plus new Cessna aircraft a year. A large number of the pre-owned light planes on the market today were built during this era.

Several young pilots, like myself, volunteered regularly to ferry aircraft from the Cessna factory to Dallas. It was a good way to log free flight time and get to fly new models. Cessna introduced a new learn-to-fly program called Discover Flying and Capital Aviation hired me full time to promote the new program.

Robert, the senior sales rep for Capital, was assigned to show me the ropes and taught me what everyday light airplane flying was all about. The first day I showed up at Love Field to go to work for Capital, Robert said we were going to fly down to San Angelo and told me to get a new Cessna 150 out of the nearby hangar. We were walking to the airplane before I had a chance to have a second cup of coffee.

In rapid succession, I asked, "Where are the charts? Do we want to file a VFR flight plan? What's the weather enroute?"

He answered, "The weather's fine, look at the sky."

I taxied out and took off. "Where are we going again?"

"Head up to the east side of Lake Belton and then turn southwest." That was the closest thing I got to any flight instructions. Kick the tires, crank the engine and look out the window. That was Robert's way of flying. His instructions were simple, but concise in that they avoided the restricted airspace over Fort Hood. I had been introduced to driving a light plane to work like most people drive their cars to work everyday.

The Discover Flying Cessna was nothing more than one of the new slant-tail Cessna 150s with a wild orange and turquoise paint job and a bursting sun logo on the tail.

For the next year or so, I flew around Texas in a small Cessna Skyhawk when I could get one and a 150 when I couldn't. Bob always took the Skylane demo. Ebor, our ol' ex-Navy WW II pilot boss, wouldn't let us fly the twins. I landed at every local airport on the chart and tried to sign the operator up to buy a Cessna 150 and a Skyhawk, which qualified them as a Discover Flying Center. I also made every air show and fly-in in the region with the brightly painted Discover Flying 150.

Cessna Wichita

Cessna Aircraft Corporation in Wichita, Kansas, held a big sales meeting for all the Cessna distributors to introduce the new Discover Flying program. The guest speaker for the event was Paul Harvey. Being a Paul Harvey fan, I positioned myself to sit at his table in order to visit with him during the banquet.

Most of the conversation was about whether or not Nixon would resign the presidency. I asked Mr. Harvey what he thought the outcome would be.

He replied, "He will resign, the press will get him."

Those words were spoken a year before Nixon did resign. I did not think he would resign and suspected Mr. Harvey was not anti-Nixon, but amazed at his ability to predict the outcome.

The conversation took a lull, as it sometimes does, just as I made a comment about the prime rib that had been served. It was a little too rare for my liking and I said, "Back in Texas I saw a dead cow on the highway hurt worse than this steak."

Unbeknownst to me, the tall gentleman seated at our table was the president of Cessna. When he got up to introduce Mr. Harvey, he began by saying, "I think that everyone enjoyed their dinner this evening," and then looking straight at me, he added, "except maybe a few from Texas," and everyone had a good laugh.

Garland Airport

Returning from Wichita in Ragsdale's Cessna 401, he offered to drop me off at Garland Airport. We had a Discover Flying Center at Garland and it was closer to where I lived than Love Field. I was in the right seat and Ragsdale was talking to me the whole time. Ragsdale commented that he hadn't landed at Garland in years and so when we got closer, I pointed the runway out to him.

The old Garland Airport used to sit out in the open surrounded by pastures. LBJ Freeway was under construction and was cutting off the north end of the runway and apartments were encroaching on the airport.

Ragsdale, now in his late middle age, was a man who flew an airplane almost everyday of his adult life. He never moved forward in his seat. He sat there, leaned back comfortably and put that 401 on the numbers.

About that time I realized what being a pilot was all about. A pilot really never gets good until he flies everyday. Ragsdale taught me a lot about the aviation business. His philosophy was to sell something everyday and it didn't matter if it was a cylinder head gasket or an airplane. Sell something.

Garland Airport was where a fellow by the name of Brussard, a self-ordained minister, used to land his P-51 and P-38. He owned his own church on an airport up near Paris, Texas and his hobby was restoring old WW II aircraft. Brussard had quite a personal collection of flyable war birds. The first summer of the Discover Flying program, I put together an air show and fly-in at the Garland Airport with all the new Cessna models on display. Brussard flew in with his own small air force and put on a one-man air show, flying one aircraft after another.

We also ferried and stored some of the new Cessna planes at Garland Airport. This was convenient for me as I only lived a couple of miles from the airport. By calling the Universal Airport Communications (UNICOM) at Garland, they would give my wife a ring on the landline to come and pick me up.

If the airport was closed, I had a UNICOM receiver at the house, which she'd keep on when she knew I was flying in late. I would call Flying A Ranch inbound, a made-up place, for landing advisory. She would be out to pick me up in her VW Beetle by the time I had my Cessna pushed into the T-hangar.

An old AF pilot, the bookkeeper at Capital Aviation, was bringing in a new Skylane from Wichita and I was waiting for him at the Garland Airport to take him back to Love Field. When the factory new Skylane taxied up, I saw that the lower windshield and instrument panel were badly smoked up. The plane had a full electrical failure about 50 miles out.

Wanting to know the details of what happened I asked, "What was the first thing you did when the electrical fire started?"

He said he turned the autopilot off to fly the plane manually and then began to shut everything else down. Suspicions confirmed, all pilots mistrust autopilots. During the first moon landing by Neil Armstrong, he did the same and manually flew the Lunar Lander in for the touchdown.

Night Thunderstorm Flying

Capital Aviation planned a big weekend dealer meeting at Lakeway Inn near Austin to introduce the new Cessna model year. Ebor and I were flying down in the Cessna 310. He was finishing making some phone calls and I was trying to get him going, as I knew there was a storm front moving-in.

Most of the crew had left earlier that afternoon in other aircraft. Ebor was great to work for, but a chain smoker, lived on coffee and antacid tablets having spent way too many years onboard a Navy carrier.

We finally took off from Love Field about dark in the company Cessna 310 twin. I had never flown with him before, but knew him to be an expert pilot. The lightning and black clouds rolled in and it-was-a-dark-and-stormy-night.

"Maybe we ought to file IFR," I suggested.

"Hell no," he replied, "They'll just vector us right into one of those damn thunder bumpers." and he told me to watch for the lightning strikes. As each lightning bolt lit up the clouds ahead, Ebor would turn the plane's heading twenty degrees to the left or right, an old trick he had learned from many years of over water flying. "You see," he said, "the most turbulent air is where the static electricity is and the lightning indicates it. Always stay ahead of the squalls."

The correct term for a thundercloud is cumulonimbus, but a pilot I knew used to call them cumulonymphi because, he said, "They'd screw you every chance they got."

We landed VFR that night at the resort's private airstrip. Several of the Cessna pilots from Wichita, enroute to the dealer meeting, spent the night in Oklahoma. The only other pilot that came through was a Cessna rep in a model 206 who had filed IFR. He had been a MATS pilot in WW II.

Ragsdale wanted the flashy little Cessna 150 on display at the lodge for the meeting. So early the next morning, Robert taxied the Cessna 150 down the resort's two-lane main road with me in a golf cart ahead of him waving the cars to the shoulder. We parked the plane on the front lawn of the clubhouse.

Slow Rolls & Negative Gs

Ebor didn't like Robert and I flying together because he thought we ought to be headed different directions and thereby getting more work done. On one occasion, when we did fly together, Robert taught me to slow roll a Cessna 182 Skylane. The only trick to a smooth slow roll I found out was simply not to chicken out on the ailerons.

If the pilot didn't hold the yoke all the way over to the stop in the Skylane, the plane was going to split-S out the bottom of the roll. Not good for the airplane at all and might cause your passengers to have to change their jockey shorts.

A roll was not a good idea in the slower, lighter Cessna 150 and Skyhawk. The vertical stabilizer had been known to collapse in a snap roll on the 150. The Skylane had enough power to easily perform a roll and the following maneuver as well.

The ol' float-the-ballpoint-pen in the cockpit magic trick was the other little stunt that Robert taught me. The trick was to lay a ballpoint pen, the heavier the better, on the top of the instrument panel and float the pen through the air.

This was accomplished by placing the aircraft in a shallow dive, pulling up into a smooth climb and pushing over in a slow ark to obtain a zero gravity (G) condition. In a Skylane, the best speed was about 180 mph. As the airspeed started to playoff, you'd push forward on the control yoke with a steady but smooth motion and the ballpoint pen would float through the cockpit. It was a good idea to make sure your flight case was tied down so it didn't hit you in the back of the head and your coffee cup was empty.

After a little practice, it was possible to maneuver the pen into the palm of your hand by the amount of forward control pressure. It's an eerie sight, but impressive when executed properly. You had gotten good when you could put the pen into the palm of your hand without moving your arm to catch the pen.

Boring Holes In The Sky

Coming back into Dallas, the city could be seen long before getting there. At an elevation of only 600 feet, Dallas lay across a wide sprawling plain. Approaching the large city from a distance, it seemed to rise up out of the haze and materialize on the horizon. The glow of Big D's city lights could be seen a hundred miles out on a clear night.

Up high, the world looked like a rolling roadmap. After hours and hours of boring holes in the sky, I learned that another way to break the monotony was to drop down on the deck and fly low over the countryside.

An interesting, but worthless piece of information I discovered flying over cattle country was that sheep would look up when a plane passed low overhead, cows did not. The only thing I figured out was that lambs were in danger from large birds of prey and the larger calves were not.

On a couple of occasions flying across cattle country, I'd land in a cow pasture for a restroom break. Continuously grazed grasslands were usually fairly smooth for landings and takeoffs, but best to hold the nose wheel off a bit till seeing how rough.

Near Quanah, Texas, there were two large mesa mounds that rose up out of the prairie. The Indians held powwows there and this was how the mesas got the name Medicine Mound. Going in or out of Quanah, I'd drop down and fly between them.

The town of Quanah was named for the half-breed Comanche Indian bandit, Quanah Parker. In his later years, he'd come down from Oklahoma to ride in the 4th of July parade.

We had a single-engine Cessna dealer at the Quanah Airport who sold a couple of new single-engine planes a year to the farmers and ranchers around the area. Based on his annual sales and on the population of his area, a Dallas Cessna dealer would have been selling a couple of thousand aircraft a year to match the same sales percentages.

The small growing community of Runaway Bay, north of Fort Worth, had finished building a new airport and I was always checking out new FBOs for a possible Cessna dealership. Shortly after I landed, the mayor of Bridgeport with a local newspaper photographer arrived to take a picture. My photo standing beside my demo Cessna Skyhawk appeared on the front page of that week's local newspaper. Turned out that I had the dubious honor of being the first pilot to land on the new airport.

Dallas Love To San Anton

Our executive secretary was an attractive, middle-aged divorced lady who dated a Cessna salesman in San Antonio. On weekends, she'd hitch a ride going south Friday evening. She was a gutsy gal and would fly with most anyone. Robert and I tried to keep on her good side by connecting her up with rides because she approved our expense account reports.

On a Friday evening, she flew with me to Garland Airport where I had a hop lined up for her with one of our young volunteer ferry pilots to San Antonio. Like many of the aircraft stored for a while, the battery on the new Skylane was down. A Cessna 150 was easy to prop, but a six cylinder Skylane was not.

A 150 wouldn't recharge unless there was some juice left in the battery to activate the charging unit. A Skylane did not have the same electrical system and would charge while flying.

Making sure the young pilot had the brakes set good, I gave the prop one heck of a good swing and it started the first time. Good because there wasn't much chance of starting one by hand after it had been flooded. Pulling the wheel chalk, I stepped aside and waved bye as they taxied out.

Management handled our large multi-engine dealerships at Addison, San Antonio and Houston, not Robert and I. However, Ragsdale was a stockholder in GenAero at San Antonio and we got free remain overnight (RON) service there.

We seldom ever put a hundred hours on a new plane and more than once I sold my demo with an hour's discount on the spot and caught a ride home. Needing warranty service was a good excuse to RON at GenAero. So when I knew I was going to be in San Antonio, particularly over a weekend, my wife and daughter would ride along with me. Suzie liked to stay at the LaPosada down on the Riverwalk and we'd have dinner in the rotating dining room atop the Hemisphere Space Needle.

I had stopped a GenAero returning to Dallas one afternoon and met up with one of the reps out of the Houston office. Didn't know him very well, our paths had only crossed on a couple of occasions. He was a young fellow and struck me as a little eccentric. I noticed that he didn't wear a watch.

To my way of thinking, real pilots wore fancy watches and they were an essential accessory to a pilot's wardrobe. The young pilot argued that if a person was tuned to their metabolic clock, they always knew what time it was within a few minutes. Besides, he added, there was usually a clock on the instrument panel for timed-turns in a holding pattern.

The next day, I took my watch off and have never worn one since. He was right. Once I got used to not wearing a timepiece, I found that I was able to tell the time within a few minutes and always within plus or minus a reasonable tolerance. I tend to mess up a little crossing multiple time zones and when Daylight Savings Time starts or ends. Try it and don't be afraid to guess, you'll usually be right.

Departing Dallas Love

The biggest single hazard for light planes at Love Field, particularly after the introduction of heavy jets like the Boeing 747, was getting caught in a wing-tip vortex.

Many private pilots, by dumb luck alone, have never encounter the problem. A pilot had to burn it into his head that it was there and touchdown beyond the heavy's touchdown point and to rotate and climb out prior to where the heavy lifted off.

Sometimes the airliners were lined up ten deep for takeoff at Love Field and the tower would only release them at the rate of one every three minutes back then. The local small aircraft jockeys, like myself, learned to ask for an intersection takeoff with immediate right turn out. This would allow for a departure between the heavy's takeoff and landing Vortex. Otherwise, you could be waiting in the departure lineup for half an hour.

Love Field enjoyed an amazing safety record through the years. Throughout its entire history, a large aircraft had never crashed into downtown Dallas. Remarkable in that many of the departing flights climb out right over the main downtown area. The Coca Cola bottling plant, located at the northeast edge of Love Field, did experience the occasional close call.

Jerry, a TTA copilot at the time and now a retired captain for Continental Airlines, told me of one such incident. After passing V1 on takeoff and out of runway on a hot summer afternoon, their right engine on his Convair 440 blew a jug.

With Mockingbird Lane and the Coca Cola bottling plant coming up fast, Jerry said, "There was nothing left to do except pull the gear lever up and hope for the best." Jerry didn't think they cleared the Coke sign on top of the building by more than a foot or two.

As they turned out over affluent, swimming pool infested, north Dallas part of the engine cowl fell off. They returned to Love Field executing a safe single-engine landing. Jerry said that he read the papers for weeks after that, expecting someone to report finding that engine cowl in the backyard, but he never heard or read a word about the incident.

Before banks had electronic check clearing centers, a person could write a check and it would take three days to get to the bank and clear. There was good money in short haul airmail contracts and flying cancelled checks for the banks. A pilot we all knew, flew the Dallas to Texarkana canceled check run every weeknight in a Cessna 320 based at Love Field.

One morning he didn't return. Searchers found the wreckage in the Piney Woods of East Texas. It appeared as though the plane had been flown into the ground in straight and level flight at cruise speed. The pilot had likely fallen asleep.

A rather odd crash occurred on approch to Dallas Love just to the east of the field when a company Aero Commander, which flew a regular shuttle run between Love Field and their factory at Greenville, fell into a grade school playground in the Highland Park area. Witnesses said that one wing folded upward on the Aero Commander and it dropped straight down.

Normally, the school yard would have been filled with children during that time of the afternoon, except the principal had called a teacher's meeting and school had been let out an hour early that afternoon.

The crash investigation revealed a very significant statistic. Even though the aircraft had only about ten thousand hours of flying time, it had over sixty thousand landing gear cycles because of its short hops. This routine had literally fatigued the wing's main spar until it snapped, kind of like bending a paperclip back and forth until it breaks.

Your Plane Is Waiting

The Love Field terminal had a gate for air taxi and private aircraft, but the terminal gates still used the old air stairs, not the all weather second story gates like they have now. My wife's sister, Nancy, and her first husband, were due in on an airliner at Love Field for a visit.

I called ground control and advised them that I needed to pickup an air taxi passenger that was arriving at the American gate and gave them the parties' name. I taxied my single-engine Cessna Cardinal up beside their flight as it shut down and waited for the passengers to deplane. Nancy's husband was suitably impressed when they announced over the airliner PA system that Mr. Phillips' private aircraft was waiting.

Nancy never cared much for flying, let alone flying in little airplanes like my Cessna, but it was just a short hop from Love Field over to Garland Airport. I sat Nancy in the right seat so she could see out better and when I cut the power to turn final at Garland Airport, she put a permanent scar in my right arm with her fingernails, convinced the engine had quit and the plane was about to fall out of the sky.

Ciudad De Acuna

We had a Cessna dealer in Del Rio, which was at the end of my trip south and due to the distance it was always an RON. It was one the best airports down along the Mexican border and a good place to slip off to and hide out for a couple of days.

We'd go across the border to eat at a Mexican steakhouse that had live entertainment and served large cuts of the best steaks. I enjoyed the music, but my TexMex wasn't good enough to get the standup comedian's jokes. He seemed upset when I didn't laugh so I just pretended to laugh when everyone else did.

Sitting on the porch of the Del Rio airport office one hot afternoon, I leaned back in an old wooden chair and struck up a conversation with a man in bib overhauls sitting beside me. "What do you do?" I asked.

"I'm a sheep rancher," he replied.

When I inquired as to how many sheep he had, he told me that he owned about nine thousand head and went on to explain how they put a notch in the sheep's ear every year and then sell off the ones with three notches. Making conversation, I asked casually, "What does a sheep sell for these days?"

"They go for $60 to $80 a head, depending on the market."

Doing some quick math in my head, I realized the gentleman leaning back on the porch chair visiting with me had an annual income of a couple hundred thousand dollars a year. Not to mention that this was in days when we were selling new Skyhawk for $7,950. The lesson for that day was don't judge a person by their appearance.

In the wintertime, when the ceiling was low, the best route from Del Rio to San Angelo was straight up the highway. It was helpful to know that there was an oil company radio tower at Eldorado and one more just north of it alongside the highway. In low visibility, the best thing to do was to stay right over the highway because the towers were, of course, off to one side.

On this one particular trip, my brother Don had flown down to Del Rio with me the day before and we were returning via the low ceiling highway route when Don remarked, "It's only 60 miles to San Angelo."

A little bit amazed at his accuracy, I said, "Yes, that's about right. How'd you know that?"

"Oh, I read a highway sign back there when we went by."

Have The Field In Sight

Statistically the weather in and around Dallas produces sunshine during the day 360 of the 365 days a year. Probably true, but morning ground fog was not an unusual occurrence around Love Field.

One early morning, approaching Love Field from the Bachman Lake side, which I had done dozens of times before, I turned to line up with the runway lights and advised the tower, "I have the runway in sight."

At about 400 feet, my eyes finally focused on the car traffic running up and down what I had mistaken for the active runway. In the fog, the streetlights on Lemmon Avenue gave the illusion of being the runway lights.

Without further hesitation, I executed a quick right and left turn and landed on the main runway. No one was the wiser. Well, except maybe the tower operator who probably saw my landing lights on final and who had asked if I was sure I had the runway in sight.

Braniff Pilot Class

Still thinking about hiring on with the airlines, I continued to build my flight time and in particular, retractable gear time. A captain for American Airlines owned a Bonanza he rented out at the old downtown Grand Prairie Airport. He required anyone who flew the Bonanza to be checked out by him personally before he would let them rent it.

After a brief checkout in the Bonanza, we were visiting about my interest in going to work for one of the major air carriers. He asked how many hours I had and I told him about twelve hundred. He said that I flew as good or better than half the copilots that he flew with everyday so why didn't I just put some P-51 time in my logbook.

Only ever having sat in the cockpit of a P-51, I told him I didn't know where I'd get the bucks to fly a Mustang.

"You don't understand," the Captain explained laughing, "I'm referring to a Parker 51 ink pen."

When hiring time for the next pilot's class at Braniff Airlines came around, I was number twenty-one for an interview in the chief pilot's office. As I sat in the waiting room, I struck up a conversation with a young Air Force Lieutenant who had just gotten off active duty as a jet instructor pilot.

They had hired nineteen for a class of twenty and his interview was next before mine. Needless to say, the chief pilot came out after talking to the young Lieutenant and politely told me he had filled the class. So to heck with it, I'd just have to find another way to fulfill this flyers quest for the sky.

As it turned out, looking back on my misplaced ambitions, I probably would have hated the job anyway. Getting up in the middle of the night to meet some oddball flight schedule and sleeping in some strange hotel room wasn't my idea of a pleasant and glamorous life style. Just maybe being an airline captain wasn't what it was cracked up to be. An airline captain, who was close to retirement, once told me that if it hadn't been for the high pay, he'd have quit flying the main line long ago.

Old skyline of Dallas; Love Field when it used to be serviced by prop driven aircraft in the 50s and 60s; aircraft on Mustang Aviation ramp on Love Field; Capital Aviation offices at Love Field; Cessna 172 demonstrator; Discover Flying 150 being taxied up on grass at Runaway Bay Lodge; Colorful paint job of Discover Flying Cessna 150 Aerobat.

Chapter Sixteen
FLIGHT DYNAMICS

When Cessna Aircraft Corporation bought out Capital Aviation's Dallas based distributor and the Houston based distributor, they combined the two and moved the headquarters to Houston. Not wishing to relocate to Houston, I left the company.

Bob Smith, the owner and founder of Aerosmith, the Piper distributor, was Cessna's biggest competitor in the Texas market. He hired me the next week to continue doing for Piper what I had been doing for Cessna.

The one condition I placed on my employment was that I would also be able to fly the twin-engine planes, which I had not been able to do with Capital with the exception of the Cessna 337 Push-Pull, which I had flown a couple of times.

Ol' Bubba, one of the pilots who had worked for Smith for a long time, was assigned to check me out in a Twin Aztec for insurance purposes. It was apparent to me from the beginning that Bubba wasn't a real sharp pilot, but I went along cheerfully with the charade. We climbed up to 6,000 feet and he asked me to establish a steep climb at full power.

One didn't have to be a mind reader to know that he was going to pull one of the engines off on me in a full power on climb attitude, so I was prepared.

The object of this maneuver was to see if I could be lulled into losing directional control of the aircraft. If I rolled it over on its side, I'd have failed the flight test. The expected correct procedure was to lower the nose and pull enough power off the good engine to stop the rotation before VMC.

Needless to say, I was way ahead of the aircraft and we returned to Love Field without any additional checkout. As it turned out, one day in the not too distant future, I would save Bubba and myself when he came close to killing the both of us during an instrument approach in a Turbo Navajo.

Navajo Approach

Maurice, a local businessman and self-appointed aviation expert, had made some money in another business and was now an investor in Aerosmith. He was on the board of directors and fancied himself a high-powered efficiency manager. He was always on my ass about one thing or another, but I generally managed to ignore him. His second marriage was to a lady pilot, who was always borrowing one of the company airplanes.

The area northeast of Dallas was often referred to as Thunderstorm Alley during the summer. On a typical summer afternoon, we got a call from Maurice's wife somewhere in Arkansas that she was weathered-in at some small airport in Aerosmith's Cherokee 235 demo. The weather was VFR in Dallas, but not across the state line in Arkansas.

Bubba and I left in the company Turbo Navajo to pick her up. Somewhere around Texarkana, we went VFR on top and filed for an ADF approach to the Podunk Arkansas airport. Assuming an absence of towers and mountains, the best way to make this type of approach is on a long and slow descent. Close in on the approach, however, never chase the needle on an ADF indicators.

Bubba went after that approach like a kamikaze pilot. Before I knew what was happening, he had us in a hard left bank with every indicator on the panel spinning. He hadn't slowed the Navajo down enough and was chasing the needle.

"Whoa," I exclaimed and grabbed the yoke to level the wings and eased the nose up. "Let's don't get in such a big hurry about this," I said as we passed over the airport. "How about we circle back and try this again."

With Bubba calmed down and the Navajo slowed down, we circled back and got established on the outbound heading to the ADF. With and nailed the approach heading this time, we broke out of the clouds looking down the runway at about 400 feet AGL. We never discussed the incident afterwards.

Cherokee 235

It was still drizzling rain, but the visibility was good and I knew it was VFR to the west. I checked the gas and preflighted the plane. There seemed to be enough gas to make Dallas, so I suggested that Bubba and the lady passenger go on back to Dallas in the Navajo. There was an FBO with fuel at the airport, but they had already closed up and gone home. I took off as the sun was setting. It would be dark before I got back to Dallas and once again I was going to miss my dinner.

Impatient to get home, I set the 235 to maximum cruise power and was cutting down the miles. Hadn't been a good idea because the engine had been drinking gas at the rate of about twenty-five gallons an hour. As the city lights of Dallas appeared on the horizon, it was a pitch-black night with no moon. I went to economy cruise and ran the right tank dry so as to use it all and the left tank was indicating almost empty.

I decided not to try to make Love Field because if I was going to run out of gas, the best place to do it wasn't over downtown Dallas. Calling Dallas approach, I asked for radar vectors to the nearest airport, which turned out to be White Rock Airport in far east Dallas. The dim lights of the airport were swallowed in the city lights and evening traffic. Dallas Approach was kind enough to give me headings and distance to the airport as I descended. As the distance grew shorter, I never saw the airport until I was looking down the runway lights.

The next day I filled only the wing tank I had run dry the night before. Enroute to the Denton Airport, I timed how long it took for the tank to run dry. It took twenty minutes. I could have made Love Field, but it would have been close. If I had reduced power to economy cruise much earlier, I would have had fuel to spare. Sometimes slow is better.

Greater Southwest Aero Club

Several years after I had been a member of the Hensley Field Aero Club, the club hired a civilian flight instructor to manage the club. Steve, the club's new manager wanted to update all the club's aircraft to new Skyhawks. I was the rep for Capital Aviation and Cessna at the time. I thought they were crazy for giving up the T-34, but I fixed them up with all new planes at dealer cost.

Steve was a Delta airline copilot expecting to make captain soon. This chance acquaintance of my meeting Steve would begin a relationship that eventually culminated in our starting our own Cessna dealership at Greater Southwest International Airport (GSW), the old Amon Carter Field.

There were a few flight schools in the area that were using the Piper Cherokee, but certainly not in the numbers that were using the Cessna. Pipers were desirable rental aircraft. I had proved that at Mustang Aviation and so I hit on the idea of starting an aero club using Piper Cherokees.

GSW Airport seemed a likely place to start an aero club, so I contacted my ol' buddy Steve, the Delta pilot, and outlined a plan. Cessna was offering attractive aircraft financing and to compete, Piper also began offering finance and lease plans. Steve co-signed the leases on a new Piper Cherokee 140 and a Cherokee 180. One of the incentives I used to talk Steve into my proposition was that as the chief pilot for the club, he could personally use the club planes anytime he wanted.

There was a very successful VA approved flight school at GSW, Flight Dynamics, Inc. (FDI), which was a Cessna dealer even before I worked for Capital Aviation. FDI did very little airplane rental business. Nevertheless, they were not happy to see an aero club in competition with them on an airport where they had previously enjoyed exclusivity.

The aero club started out as a not-for-profit operation and had been intended only to get a couple of new Cherokees in service. In order to use the ramp for tie-down, you had to be an airport tenant, so I leased the smallest office available in the old airline check-in counter area down the hall from FDI.

The owner of FDI knew me as his old Cessna rep. The airport manager knew me as the new aero club manager. Piper didn't know Steve and I were silent partners and only Steve knew I was trying to figure out how to start my own FBO. After a couple of years of boring holes in the sky to sell planes on every Podunk airport within 200 miles, I was ready for a new challenge.

The new Southwest Aero Club took off. Pardon the pun. It worked because private pilots enjoyed flying new aircraft at reasonable prices, i.e., retro Mustang Aviation. That was, it worked until the large Piper dealer over at Meacham Field got wind of it and he complained to Aerosmith.

Maurice told me to shut the club down and he would assume the leases on the two planes. It was a matter of pride on my part. I wasn't willing to do that and Maurice fired me on the spot. Bob Smith, Aerosmith's founder, told me later he would have overruled Maurice if I had come to him, but I hadn't.

In addition to his full time job as a Delta Airline pilot, Steve owned a karate school in Irving. Steve wasn't around much and now, out of a fulltime job, I hung around the airport a lot.

Amon Carter Field

The Amon Carter Terminal building was a very unique structure dating back to the time when architects actually took their time to build a thing of beauty. The main hall of the terminal building was several stories high. Large art deco figurines decorated the walls and the marble floor was inlaid with a giant brass outlined Texas Lone Star. The restaurant in the terminal overlooked a panoramic view of the airport ramp and was now only kept open for the convenience of airport employees and the occasional wandering flight crew or lone pilot.

At the entrance to the long circle drive leading up to the terminal building sat the only remaining B-36. The Convair B-36 had been donated to the city of Fort Worth after the Air Force decommissioned them. The General Dynamics Employees Club had been given the responsibility of keeping the old Bird up, but vandals and souvenir hunters had long since taken its toll on the orphaned ten-engine Peacemaker.

After Amon Carter, Jr., departed for the great newspaper pressroom in the sky, the airport management vacated the facility upstairs that had been Carter's personal office suite. The office had been a place where Carter would entertain and impress dignitaries and politicians passing through town.

Carter's giant mahogany desk and matching furniture was stacked in the hall and I inquired as to what was going to happen to the stuff. The airport manager, a stereotypical and lifelong bureaucrat, but likable old fellow, indicated it had to be disposed of and would I like to make an offer. "You see," he explained, "none of us can use the furniture as it belongs to an estate and that would be considered a conflict of interest."

What the heck, I bid $100 for the lot and my offer was accepted. Now I had two aircraft, a hole in the wall operations office, a bunch of really impressive furniture and no job. There may have been a message in there somewhere, but it escaped me.

Flight Dynamics Incorporated

As it turned out, the owner of Flight Dynamics, Inc., was a flash-in-the-pan, would-be millionaire who had made some good money traveling around the country giving motivational seminars. The name of his original company was Speech Dynamics. He had bought the flight school shortly after the government approved flight training under the new Viet Nam Veteran's Administration Education Act, also known as the second GI Bill.

A flight school had to have been in existence for two years prior to obtaining certification by the VA and the Texas Education Agency (TEA) and so he had bought a struggling FAA approved flight school from some old flight instructor and promoted it into a first class flight training school.

Technically, FDI was still an authorized Cessna dealer, but were really end-users. They bought a half dozen new Cessna 150s and a Skyhawk every year, but never sold anything except their used aircraft when they were ready to buy new ones.

Robert had educated me to the fact that an aircraft can be sold outright or it can be sold one hour at a time, it makes no difference which. He even developed an X-Y graph chart that showed the efficiency of this concept. The graph illustrated how the operator can purchase new aircraft equipment and use the first forty percent of the life of the aircraft nearly for free. We sold a lot of aircraft to flight schools, using this concept. It also probably accounts for why there is still a good supply of older Cessna aircraft on the market today.

Flight Dynamics Corporation

The owner of Flight Dynamics, Inc., had been playing stock options. The stock market was moving steadily downward and many of his margins were being called. Their chief pilot told me that he thought FDI might be picked up for a little of nothing because flight hours had fallen off and several of the new aircraft on the ramp were behind on payments.

Seemed worth a shot, so I put Steve up to approaching the owner with a proposal. The FDI owner didn't know Steve, but Steve was a personable sort a fellow and I felt like he could close the deal. The offer we made was to assume all of the FDI liabilities if the owner would transfer the VA and FAA approved flight school to us. The certifications were the only real asset FDI had. The owner agreed. Overnight we owned a flight school and fourteen aircraft owned us!

The south wing of the Amon Carter Terminal was the old check-in counter and flight departure area in the airline days. Behind these counters were offices, formerly occupied by the various junior airline executives. All along the east wall of these offices were windows that looked out over the airline concourse towards the Dallas skyline.

The largest of these rooms was used as a ground school classroom and another for a pilot's ready room where an instructor and student could have a cup of coffee and discuss a flight lesson. The plushest of the three offices, the carpeted one, I took for my office and furnished it with my recently acquired prestigious Amon Carter furniture.

We used the old airline passenger counter for checking the school and rental aircraft in and out. The lobby surrounding the counter was never used, so I decorated it with all kinds of Cessna and Piper banners to keep it from looking so barren. I also scrounged up some old couches, easy chairs and a coffee table for the empty lobby. I told the airport manager it was for the use of the general public, but he was well aware that no one wandered down to that area except our customers.

The large concrete aircraft-parking ramp that had been used to accommodate DC-3, DC-6 and Constellation airliners was now filled with Cessna & Piper light airplanes. There were a couple of larger aircraft, a DC-3 and a Convair 240, parked over on the grass. The airport did not allow individual parking, so we fell heir to these aircraft who sublet the space from us. The office across the rear stairwell to the ramp belonged to Web Thomas Aircraft Sales and they parked a few planes on the ramp, but mostly they just brokered planes. Web was a true gentleman.

The trade style FDI and their red logo had wide local public recognition. The problem was the previous owner wanted to keep the old corporation for tax write-off purposes and we had to let him retain the Inc. I kept the name Flight Dynamics as a trade style for certification and advertising and I incorporated under the name Flight Dynamics Corporation (FDC), only a minor nuance from an I to a C, but technically not the same company.

The FDI chief pilot was leaving to fly for a commuter airline and so Steve put his name on the FAA Approved Flight School certification as chief pilot. All the transfers and approvals were accomplished with relative ease. Besides, if you run everyone out of business on minor technicalities, who is going to be left to regulate?

We started flying day and night to produce revenue. Even canvassing students on the phone to get them on the schedule. A new Cessna 150 sold for $4,900 and would bring $3,500 with about 500 hours total time (TT). The trick was to turn the aircraft while they still looked new and had good time before overhaul (TBO) left on the engines. Private owners, unlike flight schools, didn't put a lot of hours on the aircraft.

Slowly, I brought the aircraft payments up to date and began selling off the higher time 150s for about what we owed on them. Cessna Finance Corporation (CFC) offered full floor plan financing, so why not.

Most of the Cessna aircraft were financed with CFC and were all two to three months past due on payments. CFC had not yet wised up to the fact that FDI and FDC were not the same folks. As soon as possible, I started making up some of the back payments on the aircraft. There was no way anyone would have loaned us the money to buy all those airplanes starting out.

During the first few months, any profit we made went into the aircraft. I would tear out a coupon for the furthest behind aircraft payment and mail it off with a check. Sometimes, even a little before I had the money because before the advent of computer banking, I could get 3-4 days float while my out-of-state check cleared our bank. CFC never sent any of them back, so it worked.

The problem was that about eighty percent of our flight time hours were billed to the VA and we were not paid on them for a least a month or so. This left us with very little cash flow and not enough money to pay the instructors, let alone buy gas for the planes. Fortunately, Suzie was full time on staff at the University of Dallas and that was how we were paying the household bills. We made it through the first month on my Enco gas charge card and Steve's MasterCard.

Drowning In Paperwork

The bookkeeper for Aerosmith, Alma Jean, was a slender blonde, thirtyish and professional in appearance. She was raising three kids, but had always wanted to learn to fly. Maurice had promised her flying lessons when she hired on, but he never followed through on the commitment.

I flew her over to the Piper dealership at Meacham Field once to deliver some aircraft titles and on the return flight she asked about aerobatics. I put the Cherokee 180 into an easy aileron roll, which I might add it does very sloppily. As we rolled out, I looked back over at her with her hands in her lap to hold her skirt down. "Oh," she said. I stopped at GSW Aero Club to check on things and I showed her around the operation.

I didn't know Alma Jean very well, but the day I left the Love Field office, I was telling her about the backlog of paperwork awaiting me at FDC. She said, if Steve would give her flying lessons, she'd come over and help out. I told her that Steve sure would and I'd provide a Cessna 150 at no charge.

That Saturday, Steve took her out for her first flying lesson and after lunch she began sorting through the backlog of VA billings forms. Late the following Monday morning she showed up and announced she'd had it with Maurice. She quit that morning and would work for us for whatever we could pay her.

If we could get some of that VA billing money coming in, I told her, maybe we could all get paid. With that, she tore into the stacks of hour meter readings, pending eligibility certificates and billing forms with a vengeance.

Everyone called her AJ because I did. I had made her corporate secretary of record so she could sign forms as an officer of the corporation and told her to sign her name using only her initials and last name.

AJ stayed. I had a head for aviation and she had a head for business. The checkbooks were always in balance, the P&L was up to date and the accounts receivable were collected. I never had to question her work. Over time, I came to think of AJ as more of a partner, than an employee. On slow months, she'd draw half a paycheck just like I did. However, when FDC finally started making a little money, I had the corporation buy both of us company cars and paid her health insurance.

I knew AJ hadn't gone to college and I asked her one time how she came to understand business and bookkeeping as well as she did. She told me that, at age eighteen, she went to work for an old man in Dallas who owned a bunch of bars. He instructed her to dress up like a lady in high heels and to carry a purse in which she was to bring him the collected bar receipts, as much as $50,000 at a time. He taught her how to check inventory, how to tell when someone was skimming and how to keep books.

Aztec Trainer

We needed a twin-engine aircraft to meet the requirements for multi-engine flight training. The previous owner had a Piper Aztec, which he owned personally and agreed to leave it while he tried to sell the plane. We could lease the plane for $65 per hour dry. That, plus fuel, didn't leave much room for profit, but at least we could continue to offer a multi-engine rating.

Each time an aircraft was checked out, a clipboard containing the last hour meter reading with the keys attached went with it. The meter was read prior to departure and again at the end of each flight. One evening, I routinely locked up the flight school and all of the keys to the aircraft, which was standard procedure. The next morning, the first flight out in the Aztec, indicated that there were three hours of missing time on the hour meter between the time we closed the night before and the first flight of the following day.

The tower closed at 10:00 pm each night, but I questioned the operator anyway. There was no record of the Aztec having flown. Drug runners would steal an aircraft in the middle of the night, make a run to the border sometimes returning the aircraft before it was missed. Other times, leaving the planes parked almost anywhere. However, the missing three hours of flight time did not quite correspond to a Dallas to Mexican border round robin? How the Aztec was unlocked and started could also not be explained unless someone had a duplicate key.

On Cessna aircraft, not sure about Pipers, there were only about twenty different keys. During my tour of duty with Cessna, I accumulated one of each of these keys on a master key ring, which came in handy when we lost the keys to a plane. After questioning everyone remotely involved,

I finally concluded the missing time on the Aztec would always remain a mystery.

Twin Comanche

An airline pilot buddy of Steve's had a Piper Twin Comanche that he agreed to lease to us for $35 per hour dry. This was a better deal because we could bill it at the same approved rate as the Aztec. The problem was that this Comanche was plumb squirrelly. Not good for a training aircraft.

For weeks, I had heard stories that at cruise speed the Twin Comanche would suddenly nose over, but I remained skeptical of the reports. There was an air show and fly-in at Weatherford over the weekend and I flew the Twin Comanche over with Suzie and Laura. I recall, the FAA had set up a mobile tower and there was a traffic jam for takeoff that hot dusty afternoon.

Passing over Carswell Air Force Base at cruise speed on our return to GSW, I nosed the Twin Comanche over slightly for an enroute descent. Without any warning, the plane pitched forward as though someone had pushed on the control wheel. I estimated we pulled at least a half a negative-G.

Immediately, I reduced the power and as I did, the forward pressure on the control wheel released. What was discovered later was if the horizontal stabilizer on a Piper Twin Comanche was even a fraction of an inch out of adjustment it would cause this to occur. A service bulletin repair was installed on the Comanche that solved the problem, but the plane had already gained a reputation of being squirrelly.

Complimentary Ground School

My daughter, Laura, was in her early teens and some of the crowd she hung out with were all interested in learning to fly. Laura probably wasn't that interested herself, but she pretended to be in order to get me to sponsor a free ground school for her friends. One of the boys was the Delta chief pilot's son, so it was also good politics for Steve. A couple of the boys in the class went on to fly for commuter airlines and then on to fly for major carriers after they graduated from college, so I guess it came to some good after all.

The first time I let Laura takeoff a Cessna 150, as she reached takeoff speed, she kept pushing forward on the control wheel thinking that she did not have enough airspeed to lift-off. Guess what, you can fly a Cessna 150 with only the nose wheel on the ground and the main gear up in the air.

After a couple of hours of practice, she got where she could land and takeoff adequately. She should have, she had been flying in the right seat since she was five years old. However, she soon lost interest in pursuing even a student pilot certificate. Been there, done that, I guess. Laura had the potential to be a good pilot and was already an excellent navigator, but the desire wasn't there.

Aero Shell

We were now operating six Cessna 150s, two Cessna Skyhawks as instrument trainers and a newly acquired Cessna 310K for twin-engine training. Flight time on the Cessna 150s was so heavy that we were performing hundred hour inspections on the aircraft on the average of every three weeks.

Parts were always a problem and at least one aircraft was down all the time. We would cannibalize the downed aircraft for parts to fix the others and keep them flying. The standing joke was that the little trainers were a pack of wolves, if one fell to its knees, the others would eat it alive.

A mechanic by the name of Howard offered to maintain our planes on a contract basis, but our business soon became so demanding that he ended up working full time on our birds. The previous owners had been using the Humble or Enco, which later became Exxon, engine oil in the 150s and were having to do top overhauls on the engines as early as 600 hours on some of them.

Howard insisted we change to Aero Shell engine oil. So we stopped letting the airport's Enco dealer, Butler Aviation, check and add the oil in our aircraft. Sure enough, after switching oils, we found we could get 1100 to 1200 hours out of the older used Cessna 150 engine before overhaul.

Rule 23

We had no hangar facility, but the old south passenger wing of the terminal building extended out onto our ramp. Howard used an old baggage handling office to store parts and supplies. In the heat of the afternoon, he would pull the aircraft up into the shade of the passenger wing in order to work on them.

The only thing preventing an aircraft from going full-up under one of the old luggage bay sections was a four-inch steel post centered on an overhead steel and concrete beam. I looked it over and decided the post was not structural and we could use the bay as a maintenance hangar if the post was removed.

Knowing that I would have to deal with bureaucrats in order to obtain permission, I applied Rule 23 to the problem. Rule 23 states, "It is easier to obtain forgiveness than to obtain permission." Taking a cutting torch to the steel support, I cut a half-inch gap out of the support post and waited for several days to see if the structure settled onto the gap.

If the gap had closed, I would have welded it back together and forgotten about it. The structure would likely be torn down in the not too distant future anyway, so what was the harm. The gap didn't close indicating that the structure hadn't budged. I went to the airport manager and asked to rent the space under the passenger wing. After obtaining the lease, Howard removed the center post completely with a cutting torch.

Bureaucrats

Government bureaucrats are not one of my favorite things, but of course one could not even slightly detect that by what I have written so far. At one point, it seemed to me that the government would have been better off to just install a desk and telephone with one bureaucrat at our facility and thus save lots of money over the numerous briefcase carrying flunkies who constantly intruded on our daily routine.

A young gentleman showed up in my office. His gray business suit was wrinkled from one too many nights of staying in cheap motels. He asked to see the manager. As a general rule, a guest without a briefcase with a tie and a bulge in his jacket was FBI, without the tie probably DEA.

With a briefcase and in a three-piece suit, probably a T-Man or IRS. Who was this guy?

He informed me that he was with OCEA. I wondered what the heck that was. Seemed as how the small prefab building we owned had a restroom and he advised me that upon inspecting our restroom facilities, he was going to have to write a violation report because the dimensions on the restroom pots were not to specifications. What to do? I didn't know whether to laugh or cuss. I just asked the gentleman to write up whatever he felt like he needed to and please leave.

The TEA Nazis

The Texas Education Agency required each VA approved flight school to send in a schedule of their ground school and curriculum. The curriculum was no problem because we simply used the standard FAA ground school curricula enhanced considerably by our own training aids. Plus, most of our flight instructors and myself held FAA Ground Instructor ratings.

We had so many students working odd hours that it necessitated our holding ground school any time they might show up. Often the same instructor who gave the student personalized ground training also flew with him, so we just scheduled ground school from 7:00am until 10:00pm everyday.

The TEA examiner couldn't handle that concept and the day that he and his assistant arrived to examine the school, he indicated that he was going to make us publish regular scheduled hours for our classes.

After the discussion became somewhat heated, due to our not being able to convince them that the students actually received more personalized training the way we did it, the examiner asked everyone except myself to leave the room. He then proceeded to explain to me that unless we changed our catalogue to his satisfaction, he would close down the flight school.

Rising to my feet, I walked over and got in the examiner's face and stared him right in the eye. After a long pause, I said, "Look, you Nazi SOB," which was followed by another period of silence as we stared at each other. It was questionable at that point as to whether we were going to start swinging or laugh. Then I said, "You know what I'm going to do?"

"No what?" he replied.

"I'm going to change that damn catalogue exactly the way you want it."

My instructors kept giving their students ground school at the student's convenience, except I had them write out two counter receipts instead of one. I ran into the examiner a few times after that and he'd start laughing when he saw me coming.

The Karate Kid

Steve was still a copilot for Delta and there were no openings for captain at the Dallas hub. Steve, however, found out that there were openings for captains out of the New Orleans hub, so in order to get promoted to captain, he started deadheading his flights out of Dallas into New Orleans.

Steve's karate school was also taking a lot of his time. The group out of California that had franchised his karate school was affiliated with Elvis and Priscilla Presley. This was how Steve had originally met Elvis and he would fly to various karate meets in order to hang out with the Presley crowd.

The following spring, I asked Steve to lunch and told him that I needed to talk to him about something. The week before, Steve had presented Elvis with a matched set of engraved karate swords on stage at the Las Vegas Hilton. Between his duties with Delta Airline and managing his karate school, Steve had become less and less involved at Flight Dynamics.

At lunch, I explained to Steve that Flight Dynamics had become my main focus. Where as with him, it was just a passing fancy. I would like to buy him out if he was agreeable.

Steve asked, "Why do you need to buy me out? You run the place like you want anyway. I'm not involved all that much."

"When we started," I explained, "this was just a passing interest for me like it is with you now, but without intending for it to become so, it looks like FDC is going to be my primary livelihood for the next few years."

Steve was a Mormon and an elder in his church and he had always been more than fair with me in all our dealings. In fact, he jokingly called me a Jack Mormon to which there was some underlying meaning that I never really quite understood. I'm not sure, but I think it was a compliment.

"Well, how does $5,000 sound to you?" Steve asked.

Actually, it was less than I had expected. "Sounds great to me and you can come and use an airplane anytime you want," I replied and we shook hands on the deal.

New Chief Instructor Pilot

Normally I kept six or seven full-time flight instructors on staff and paid them on commission so the more they flew, the more they made.

A lot of veteran pilots were now cycling back from tours of duty in Viet Nam as the war ended. Most were looking for ways to build their civilian flight time enroute to a better paying airline or company pilot job. Many were excellent pilots, but it lead to a lot of turnover in instructors.

Needing to take Steve's name off of our FAA Flight School certification as chief pilot, I hired a young pilot by the name of Ted. He had been flying a plane for a construction company and was not ex-military.

Ted met the requirements for chief pilot and although several of the other pilots had more experience than Ted, I needed someone dependable who would stay with me and not move on at the first opportunity. As it turned out, Ted and AJ both stayed with me until we closed down the operation years later.

Next Airplane Up

Whenever we'd put a new aircraft on the line with older aircraft, everybody wanted to fly the newest ones. The new airplanes ran up an excessive amount of hours and the older ones wouldn't get flown. This forced me to implement a policy of strict rotation on the aircraft.

In other words, each outgoing pilot worked their way down the row of clipboards, known as first-in, last-out (FILO). The luck of the draw allowed everyone to get to fly a brand new aircraft once in a while.

Because I would hear every reason in the world why a certain aircraft wasn't being flown, I implemented my own personal policy of pick-it and fly-it. In the evening when I was sick of complaints, bankers and paperwork, when the air was still and pleasant to fly without the afternoon thermals, I would pick an airplane at random and go flying. I'd write up a squawk on any and every possible defect to be worked off on the next 100-hour inspection. This resulted in all of the aircraft being maintained in top condition. Additionally, I had the planes washed often and kept clean.

After an instructor with a student had dinged a prop and another had busted a wheel fairing, I called all the instructors together and questioned them in detail as to the circumstances behind the periodic minor damage. There were various excuses, but they all centered on the fact that the airplanes were damaged trying to prevent a more serious accident.

Look, I explained, "I have never heard of anyone being injured or killed in an aircraft that was not damaged. Take care of the aircraft first and it will take care of you."

After each screw-up, a hot check, unfilled-out-paperwork or whatever, I would write up the do's and don'ts of the incident and place it in a notebook on the counter.

When you operate 24-7, not everyone gets the word. So the instructors were required to check the notebook for new entries. Ted nicknamed the book *The Marvin Says Book,* and everyone picked up on the term. The many entries were eventually typed up and in its completed form it became our operations manual.

Antique aircraft fly-in at Denton Airport sponsored by Aerosmith the Piper distributor; new Cardinal aircraft; my Cessna 182 demonstrator at GenAero in San Antonio; dinner at the Hemisfair space needle. Mid-Cities fuel ramp looking south towards old American Airlines repair center at GSW; Aero Commander is plane we had to go repossess.

Chapter Seventeen
AIRCRAFT DEALERSHIP

From time to time, I would stand at the window of my office looking out over the ramp full of aircraft and think back to when I would have enjoyed owning any one of those airplanes to fly. Now I was so busy running this place that I didn't have time to go fly for fun anymore.

Like the airline captain who owned a Pitts Special biplane. He departed in a Boeing 747 flight and after reaching cruising altitude of 33,000 he slid his seat back and looked out the cockpit window at the beautiful sunshiny day below. "You know," he remarked to his copilot, "If a guy didn't have to work for a living, this would be a great day to go flying."

Just Sign Your Name

What I remember most about the Cessna delivery center at Wichita was a large map on the wall in the back office with three concentric circles drawn around the delivery center airport. On each of the circles was a series of stickpins.

When someone would ask what the pins represented, the man at the delivery center would explain that the first circle was the range of a Cessna 150, the second circle was the range of a 172 Skyhawk and the third circle was the range of a 182 Skylane. Each of the stickpins represented an aircraft that had crashed where some delivery pilot had run out of gas.

The first time I sent my new chief pilot Ted up to the Cessna factory at Wichita for a last minute pick up on a new Cessna, I told him to just sign my name to the delivery receipt and leave with the aircraft.

Apparently, the clerk at the desk had a suspicion that Ted was not who he said he was. We were supposed to telex any pilot name change to the center ahead of time, but as I recall there was some problem about it being over the weekend.

Ted continued trying to convince the man he was Marvin Arnold and had forgotten his wallet with his ID. The delivery center clerk went into the backroom and unbeknownst to Ted, called me on the phone for verification.

"Oh yeah." I said, "That's my chief pilot. It's okay to release the plane to him."

The clerk returned to the counter pretending he was convinced Ted was who he claimed to be and pushed the clipboard in front of Ted for him to sign for the aircraft. Without thinking Ted signed his own name. He looked up with a funny grin on his face, scribbled out his name and signed mine. After Ted departed, the clerk was still laughing when he called me back to tell me what had happened.

GSW Flight Operations

By the end of the second year in business, I had managed to upgrade most of the fleet to new aircraft. Additionally, we added a Grumman American two-seater and a four-seater to our fleet of Cessna aircraft. Because we had the newest planes and ran the school professionally, we became the number one flight school in the DFW Metroplex, flying more hours than our next two competitors combined.

Jim Hardy, an airline captain and personal friend, offered to buy white American Airline uniform shirts with captain epaulettes for our flight instructors at his cost. All the instructors were in favor and before long everyone got into the swing and wore dark slacks with their shirts. I ran a tight operation and was even told once that all I needed to complete my uniform was a swagger stick.

The main runway at GSW was over a mile long and students complained about their instructors making them taxi to the end of the runway for takeoff. It was probably a justifiable complaint, but as I explained more than once, "There would be no way I could explain to the FAA why a student had an engine failure with a mile of runway behind them."

One thing we had to be extremely cautious about, especially with students, was to be careful of the heavy aircraft shooting practice approaches to GSW. During the entire time we operated the flight school, we never had a fatality or serious injury. We did experience two crashes, but both times the pilots walked away. Luck maybe, but I prefer to think it was good training.

Cessna 150 Crash

A private pilot, building his time for a commercial ticket, checked out a Cessna 150 and flew out to the designated practice area north of Grapevine Lake. Late that afternoon, the telephone rang and it was the student calling from a small country grocery store. He explained that he had crashed the Cessna 150 in an open field and except for a minor cut on his forehead he was not injured, but the plane was seriously damaged.

Howard and I jumped into a Skyhawk and headed north to try and spot the plane. Sure enough, in an open field sat the Cessna 150 on its back. After making a low pass over the pasture to check out the terrain, I circled and landed my Skyhawk beside the upside-down Cessna 150.

Howard's mechanic helper had left in his truck to pick up the pilot at the grocery store and they arrived shortly after we landed. The student pilot explained that the cut on his forehead happened when he released his seat belt and fell head first onto the overhead map light. While practicing pylon turns, the engine started to overheat and then quit. He tried several times to crank it with the starter to no avail and leveled out to land in the open grass area straight ahead. The wind was calm at the time and it was a good choice of fields.

Unfortunately, the student stalled the aircraft prior to touchdown 10-15 feet in the air. The plane slammed down hard on the main gear and the nose wheel busted off of the strut. A short distance later, the nose strut dug a furrow into the dirt for not more than fifty feet. All of this was obvious by looking at the marks in the soft dirt. The final act of the crippled bird was to slowly turn over, landing gently on its back. The prop was not bent because it wasn't turning.

When I opened the engine cowl door, the oil spout filler cap/ dipstick fell out onto the ground. The inside of the engine compartment was covered with oil. The answer to the engine failure was immediately obvious. When the pilot had checked the oil during preflight, he had not tightened the filler cap. All during his flight, the engine had been blowing oil out the filler spout until the engine overheated and seized.

The young pilot came in to my office the following day and said he wanted to quit flying after his experience the day before. After thinking for a few minutes, I explained to the young man he was liable for the $1,000 deductible on the aircraft because it was clearly his fault. However, if he could overcome his fear and finish his commercial license flight training, the company would absorb the loss. Otherwise, we expected him to pay the deductible. The decision was up to him.

The young man finished the course and obtained his commercial pilot's license. Thus, proving an old adage, "If you get thrown from a horse, get right back up on it and ride or you'll be scared to ride for the rest of your life."

Piper Arrow Auto Gear

We purchased an almost new Piper Arrow, the retractable gear version of the popular Cherokee. The Arrow had an automatic landing gear extension sensor that dropped the gear at low airspeeds and retarded power settings. The override lever had to be held in the up position when practicing stalls.

I took the Arrow on a short trip. Returning to GSW, I hadn't played off my altitude to enter the traffic pattern. I did a power-on wingover in order to make a rapid descent, the kind they always show in the movies where the WW II fighters peel off.

It may have been the G-force that caused the gear to start down, but not a good thing to have happen at high speed. I reached between the seat with my right hand to hold the gear override lever up and stop the gear from extending. Letting go of the control yoke, I retarded the throttle with my left. The plane did kind of a squirrelly recovery coming out of the dive and my passenger exclaimed, "I thought we were going to die!"

"Not really," I replied with a smile, "I've been a whole lot closer to dying than that. Several times before!"

Piper Arrow Out Of Gas

A construction equipment salesman and his friend rented the Piper Arrow to fly to Atlanta. I was informed that the pilot had landed the aircraft, out of gas, in a Georgia hay field. The landing gear was extended and it might have been a successful forced landing, except they ran into one of the bales of hay that were scattered about the farmer's field.

The damage to the aircraft was not extensive, so I had an aircraft maintenance facility in Atlanta pick up the Arrow and repair it. The pilot had over two hundred hours of flight time. When he came to my office to explain how the accident had occurred, I told him, "I'm glad both of you were uninjured. However, it was not an accident! It was a crash caused by your failure to calculate your required fuel properly," and then I asked, "How high were you when you ran out of gas?"

The pilot said, "About 8,000 feet AGL."

Then I asked, "What is the glide ratio of a Piper Arrow with the wheels retracted?"

Of course, he didn't know. So I explained, "The glide ratio on that plane is about 18 to 1. Better than some gliders. This means that for every one foot the aircraft descends, the aircraft moves forward 18 feet."

"Okay?" the pilot replied. He didn't understand.

So I took out a WAC chart of the area and asked him to point out exactly where he ran out of gas, which he did. Taking a pencil, I multiplied 8,000 times 18 and arrived at a figure, which I then divided by 6,000 to equal nautical miles.

"What this means is," I continued, "you could have glided 24 miles in any direction and landed at an airport." With a protractor, I drew a 48-mile circle around the point he had run out of gas. Within that circle were three major airports, six uncontrolled paved runways and a half dozen grass airfields.

"Why did you land in a hay field?" I asked and added, "You are going to be expected to pay the deductible on the insurance and I strongly suggest you get some additional dual instruction on flight planning and forced landings."

Aerobatic Training

The first year Cessna introduced the Cessna 150 Aerobat, we purchased one. The plane was a standard Cessna 150 with some doublers in the vertical stabilizer and beefed-up wing strut attachments. We were one of the first flight school or rental clubs to offer aerobatic training in the new Cessna Aerobat.

Parachutes were mandatory during aerobatic training. Several of my instructors were Viet Nam vets and proficient in aerobatic maneuvers. The standard school rule, however, was no aerobatics below 6,000 feet AGL.

Late one afternoon, this tall lanky instructor pilot and his student came in carrying their parachute backpacks. Both looked a little green around the gills, so immediately I inquired about their flight and if there was a problem. The instructor explained that they had been at the required altitude in the south practice area over by Grand Prairie when they got the Aerobat into a flat spin and couldn't get the nose down.

The instructor explained that after losing about 3,000 feet, he was strongly considering pulling the door release and bailing out, but he could hear my voice in the back of his head saying, "If you take care of the airplane, it will take care of you." With one last effort he added full power and full opposite controls and the little Aerobat pulled out of the flat spin.

Aviation & The Press

A local television newscaster showed up at the airport one day looking for a human-interest story on the safety of light airplane flying. A few days before, an airliner had collided with a single-engine Cessna just north of Fort Worth. The airliner cut the Cessna in half, but the airliner was able to return to Love Field for a safe landing.

This topic was and continues to be difficult to explain to the non-flying general public. The headlines usually read, "Light aircraft collides with airliner." The fact is that the larger, faster aircraft overtakes and collides with the smaller and slower aircraft.

So I attempted to educate the reporter. "Simple physics dictates that the slower object cannot overtake the faster object. The slower object can be in the path of the faster object and be overrun, but it cannot do the over running. The fastest combat fighter generally has the advantage as it can overtake and shoot down the slower fighter."

Most of my dissertation had gone completely over the newscaster's head so I explained further, "A light aircraft is more maneuverable than a large aircraft and if it had collided with the larger aircraft, it was because the pilot of the smaller aircraft did not see the large airliner coming at him like a freight train and failed to get out of its way."

I asked the newscaster, "Did you know that I can land a small Cessna in less space than it takes to stop a car going 60 mph?" This the reporter didn't believe, so I invited him to come and go flying with me. He was looking for a story anyway, so he agreed and his video cameraman sat in the back seat and shot between our shoulders as I turned final for runway one-seven. There was about a 20 mile an hour wind blowing straight down the runway. Slowly, I increased the angle of attack and lowered the Cessna Paralift flaps to their fully extended position.

Keeping just enough power on to hold the stall warning horn on without stalling, I sat the Skyhawk down on the runway overrun. The video cameraman was able to record the top edge of the number seven out his side window as we came to a stop and swung the nose around. The story may never have aired on TV, but the newscaster and his cameraman left with a whole different opinion of light aircraft and their capabilities.

Skylane Glide To Landing

A middle-aged doctor, a private pilot, had been looking at a Cessna 182 Skylane we had for sale. One of our instructors had already given him a demo ride, but the doctor continued to be undecided about the purchase. I inquired as to what were his apprehensions. He explained that he just wasn't certain if single-engine aircraft flying was safe.

"Come on, let's go flying in the Skylane," I said, "You sit there and watch and I'll show you how safe they are, instead of us talking about it."

After takeoff, I climbed to about 4,000 feet and pointed the Skylane southwest towards the Arlington Municipal Airport, which was about ten miles away from us by that time. First I explained to my passenger, "Don't be alarmed at what I am about to show you." I reached down, pulled the throttle back slowly, increased the prop pitch and turned off the mag switch. Of course, the prop stopped turning and I established a normal glide. It seemed to take a long time before we descended to approach pattern altitude at Arlington Airport.

Entering the base leg for the south runway, I explained to my passenger. "Okay, we lost our engine some miles back and now we were going to make a normal landing at a local airport." For safety, I restarted the engine and left it at idle with the carburetor heat on as we glided to a final approach for landing. Actually, I was a little high and had to add flaps to lose some altitude before touchdown. I let the doctor fly the Skylane back to GSW and he bought the plane.

Missing Airplanes

Addison Airport north of Dallas was notorious for pilots running drugs in rented and borrowed aircraft. So much so, that the DEA had a full-time unit assigned there to plant hidden transponders on suspected drug running aircraft. This enabled the plane to be tracked by radar into and out of Mexico. We never had much trouble with that sort of thing at GSW as we took a lot of care to know the people who we rented to and our GI Bill students weren't that type of clientele.

Arriving for work one morning, I was greeted by one of our instructors asking where was our new Cessna 210. Looking out the window, I explained I had no idea unless someone had it checked out. "By the way, whose white Cessna 402 is that parked on our ramp?" I inquired. No one knew. An hour or so later, an FBO from Lake Whitney called to tell us that our Cessna 210 was on his ramp. The passenger seats had been removed and there appeared to be traces of marijuana grass all over the carpet.

Mystery solved. I then proceeded to check out the registration in the Cessna 402 and found out that it belonged over at Redbird Airport. The Cessna 402 was in the same condition as our 210 and both aircraft had the right amount of flight time on them for a round trip across the border.

Reconstructing the events of the night before, it appeared that the Cessna 402 was stolen at Redbird in the early evening and probably dropped its load somewhere south of Dallas before landing at GSW. Remember, the tower shut down at 10 pm. The brigands then stole our Cessna 210 making one more run in the wee hours of the morning and abandoned the plane at the small Lake Whitney airport.

After the DEA completed their investigation, we traded aircraft. The missing seats were probably laying somewhere in an empty field in the state of Coahuila De Mexico. Our insurance paid for replacement seats and we used our Cessna dealer parts discount to offset the deductible.

Aircraft Parking Lot

Butler Aviation, at the north end of the airport, serviced the transit aircraft. They had a large hangar, but had only limited ramp parking. One aircraft that was parked at Butler for a while was a Douglas Dragon. A one-of-a-kind custom modified plane rumored to belong or have belonged to Howard Hughes. I seemed to always miss whoever was flying it. If Hughes was, I never saw him. The plane was painted dark blue with a gold and red Chinese dragon painted on the rear empennage and up the vertical stabilizer. The wing design, nacelles and landing gear were vintage DC-3. Douglas built the Dragons in limited quantity called the B-27 and a C-67 model without the bomb bay.

On the other hand, the ramp space down at our end of the field around the old terminal had acres of empty concrete and attracted a unique collection of large vintage aircraft.

An old Douglas DC-6 airliner with the name *Jefferson Airplane* painted on the side was parked in our back door, but was soon replaced by a Lockheed Constellation. Except for the two planes' arrival and final departure, neither plane ever flew. They belonged to a rock group that I believe may have started in Fort Worth. The guys in the rock band would come out occasionally and play in the old airliners like a bunch of kids. Later, the group changed its name to Jefferson Starship and bought a private jet from Web Thomas and hired a charter pilot.

A fellow by the name of Covol owned a B-25 that never flew either. Covol and I had worked together as contract engineers. Whenever I saw him, I always inquired what name he was using before I greeted him as he often used different names on resumes he sent out to match a specific contract job's requirements.

Covol had this fantasy of building a casino on the coast of Honduras with its own private landing strip. When he retired, he planned to fly the gambling clientele to his casino in the B-25, which he was converting to passenger use. On any nice weekend, he would be out there in the shade of the old terminal building with B-25 parts scattered all over the ramp.

We gave Confederate Air Force planes like the B-24 Diamond Lil' free parking when they came through transit. And then there was the preacher's sky blue Convair 240.

Flying Fortress

Piccadilly Lil' was one of the B-17 Flying Fortress used in the movie *War Lovers*, starring Steve McQueen. In route home from the filming, the B-17 blew an engine and asked permission to park it on our ramp. The Delta Airline captain ferrying the B-17 and a mechanic worked on the plane off and on for a couple of months borrowing our shop tools. I jokingly said to the ferry pilot, "When you get her flying you owe me a flight.

The afternoon they finished, the Captain came up to my office and asked, "You ready to go fly the B-17?" I climbed aboard and the Captain pointed for me to get in the left seat. I paused. "Fly her just like a DC-3," he said.

During engine crank and run-up you could feel the awesome power of those four large engines. In order to see over the nose, I had to literally stand on the rudder pedals and lean against the back of the seat. In position for takeoff, the Captain told me to give her full throttle for takeoff and that he would hold his hand below the throttles at the pull back point for climb out. With not very much of a load on the B-17, she lifted off effortlessly with a relatively short ground run.

At about 1,000 AGL, we passed over the North Lake Power Plant and I remember thinking, "Bombs away!" I wondered around north of Dallas at about 2,000 feet as the mech checked out some things and then we headed for Addison Airport where a local TV station was to do a story on Piccadilly Lil's return home.

The old Addison airstrip looked like a postage stamp for this aircraft. I looked at the Captain to make sure he wanted me to make the landing and he nodded for me to go ahead.

Using my standard DC-3 approach technique, I made a perfect, almost three-point, landing on my first try. When I pulled the power back, the old B-17 became a pussycat and I didn't even use half of the runway. An amazing old bird!

During the TV interview, I remember the Captain saying, "We just stopped by to fill up with oil and check the gas."

I kept a large framed photo of the B-17 on my office wall. After the umpteenth person asked if I had flown B-17s in WW II, and I replied I wasn't that old, I took the darn picture down.

Divert to GSW

Dallas Love Field very rarely had ground fog, but on a chilly fall morning, the entire Dallas and Fort Worth area was experiencing drizzling rain and spotted ground fog. I knew there wasn't going to be any civil aviation flying that morning, but I thought I'd go to the office and catch up on some paperwork.

I unlocked the door to my office, turned on the overhead fluorescent lights and didn't bother to open the drapes due to the fog and the early morning darkness. Sitting at my desk, I was trying to figure out where to start when I kept hearing this high-pitched humming noise.

What was that noise anyway? Sounded like a bunch of sick trolls all trying to sing in harmony. I opened the drapes and couldn't see anything so turned out the overhead lights and pressed my nose against the windowpane. There were a dozen or so airliners full of passengers parked all over the terminal ramp with their auxiliary engines running.

Dallas Love Field, as it turned out, was zero-zero and GSW was barely at minimums so all that morning, ATC had been diverting the Love Field airline traffic over to our facility instead of putting them in a holding pattern.

The fog soon lifted and like a herd of turtles all the airlines departed. Once again, quiet returned to our big little airport. GSW had not seen that many airliners since the heyday of the piston engine passenger planes.

Signs around Greater Southwest Airport of Flight Dynamics and Mid-Cities Aviation; two views of GSW terminal and aircraft parking ramps; one of many Cessna 150s purchased new and used to train many new pilots; AJ in front of her favorite Piper a Cherokee 180, but she soloed in a Cessna 150; Marvin's ramp transportation; one of the few airplane accidents FDC ever experienced, a Cessna 150 turnover during a forced landing; factory new Cessna 210 fully IFR equipped.

Chapter Eighteen
GREATER SOUTHWEST AIRPORT

Trying to run a flight school, air taxi service and be a landlord kept me hopping. "I didn't have time to sell a $100,000 airplane because I'm too busy filling the Coke machine," was becoming my motto. When you're the one who runs the place, you end up doing everything that nobody else will do.

Nevada Aircraft Auction

This was the era of high volume General Aviation aircraft sales. A group of promoters in Las Vegas started a monthly airplane auction. At first, they tried to attract the high rollers by throwing cocktail parties the night before, but it soon evolved into a dealer's aircraft auction. Our used aircraft sales were going good at GSW, so I attended several of the Las Vegas aircraft auctions, but the promoters finally closed it down a year or so later as interest fell off.

On one such trip, I departed in the company Cessna 310 with Ted, my chief pilot, and a prospective aircraft buyer. We got a late start that evening and by nightfall, we were headed into a snowstorm approaching Flagstaff, Arizona. The night was pitch black and we were cruising at about 12,000 feet. Ted wanted to fly through the snowstorm, but I said no way, there are big rocks in the clouds out in this territory. At Flagstaff, the airport was still VFR and I insisted that we circle and land.

The courtesy car carried us to the Holiday Inn, which was having its weekly buffet dinner, which included a bottomless wine carafe. Our passenger soon gave up and went to bed, but Ted and I continued to try to reach the bottom of the remaining wine carafes until late that evening.

The last thing I remember that night was my head hitting the pillow after I managed to get to my room. Long after sunup the following morning, the bright sunlight glaring through a crack in the drape finally woke me.

It was then that I heard a loud Texan voice on the balcony exclaim, "Oh, she-it."

Stumbling out onto the motel balcony, I found Ted standing there in his pajamas looking straight up at the 14,000-foot snow-capped mountain to the north of our motel.

Laughingly I said, "See, I told you there were rocks in those clouds last night."

We purchased several planes at the Las Vegas Air Auctions. One, a brown and tan Cessna 310 F-model, I resold for a profit before we got out of town and Ted flew the other one back.

Air Taxi Certification

Greater Southwest Airport, the old Amon Carter Field, was located north of Six Flags Over Texas and in the center of a growing industrial park district in the Mid-Cities area of the DFW Metroplex. Commercial business was booming.

I formed Greater Southwest Aviation, Inc. (GSA), as a holding company for FDC and some other aviation assets. FDC was getting more and more requests for air taxi service, so it was time to get a couple of my instructors and myself certified under Federal Air Regulation Part 145.

When I took my air taxi check ride in our Cessna 310 with the FAA examiner, he asked me to climb to 6,000 feet AGL in the practice area. Then he said, "You have a fire in your right engine burning out of control, what are you going to do?"

Well, I really wasn't expecting that to be a question on the test. I thought the test would be on my flying skills like single engine-out procedures, things of that sort. Reasoning that if I really did have an engine on fire, I'd want to get the bird on the ground as quickly as possible, so I chopped the power, slowed the aircraft down, dropped the flaps and as soon as my airspeed slowed, lowered the gear.

We were coming out of the sky at about 2,500 feet a minute, which meant I was going to be on the ground in less than three minutes and I set up an approach to a large open cow pasture. The FAA examiner advised me to resume normal flight and return to Meacham Field. He certified me as an air taxi pilot, so I guess I had made the right decision.

Nearer My God To Thee

Airborne in a thunderstorm with objects floating around in the cockpit, good Christian or not, most pilots find themselves doing some serious praying. The saying goes "There are no atheists in a foxhole," and I can assure you there are very few atheists in an aircraft cockpit in a thunderstorm. When people ask me if I am religious, my standard answer is, "When you're a pilot, you're a little closer to God in more ways than one."

From time to time, we received calls to transport bodies and I never liked this type of flight. A few years back, I had gone with another pilot down to San Angelo to transport a stretcher patient with a serious head injury back to Dallas. Just after takeoff, the patient died. The wife and daughter were onboard and it was a really bad experience. I much preferred live healthy passengers after that on my air taxi runs.

One afternoon, we got a call to go pick up a body from out of town. Being the only pilot available, I scheduled a Cherokee Six we leased to make the charter run. As the afternoon wore on, a storm began rolling in with thunder and lightning crackling all around. Jerry, a Continental pilot I used for FAR Part 91 flights in the DC-3 and Convair 240, was hanging around. Jerry was what I call a people person, about as sanguine as you can get. He also loved flying and didn't care what in.

The weather got worse as the afternoon wore on and I told Jerry I was going to cancel the flight that night. He said, "I'll take the flight for you. I've carried a lot of those folks and I have never had a complaint out of one of them yet."

For what it's worth, when filing a flight plan, you do not report the body. If the pilot has no other passengers, the correct report is, "One soul on board."

Vice Presidential Candidate

The Convair 240 that parked at our ramp was owned by an evangelical church group. We inherited the Convair and Jerry with the purchase of Flight Dynamics. The church group contended they should get free parking, but did agree to lease us the aircraft from time to time, so I went along with the deal.

Jerry was type certified in the Convair, but the copilot only had to have a commercial and first or second class flight physical. Ted, one of the other instructors or myself would fly copilot with Jerry as needed.

Flying over to Addison Airport to pick up some passengers in the Convair, Jerry let me make the approch and landing. When I slowed the Convair on approch, the plane showed no indication of stalling, but set up an excessive sink rate in level flight. The controls had a stall-warning shaker that shook the yoke prior to a stall because of this characteristic.

Clark, the operator at Mangrum Field was type certified in the DC-3. He got a charter request from Sergeant Shriver, who was running for vice president of the United States at the time. We made a deal through Clark to provide two aircraft for Shriver to tour around North Texas and Southern Oklahoma.

Jerry and Ted flew the Convair 240 carrying Shriver and his entourage. Clark and myself, followed in the DC-3 with a rag-tag assortment of press people. It was a scene right out of the Bill Murray movie *Where the Buffalo Roam.*

Turned out to be a good thing Jerry was flying the Convair due to some of the short fields we went in like Childress. The DC-3 was okay, but tight for the Convair. We hopped around a half dozen small airports. Shriver would go into town, meet the locals, eat some bar-b-que and stump for a while. We'd wait at a local café and then back to the planes and off again.

The last stop on the tour was Altus Air Force Base where we waited in the pilot's ready room. An Air Force Captain came in and asked who was going to pay the landing fees for those two large aircraft sitting on his ramp. All three pilots looked straight at me and I quickly suggested that the Captain should see Shriver's press secretary.

What was going through all our minds was that this Air Force Captain was about to ask us for several hundred dollars in landing fees based on the weight of the two aircraft.

Jerry asked, "About how much will the landing fee be?" The rest of us hadn't even thought to ask.

The Air Force Captain was starting to get a little ticked-off at the runaround and replied tartly, "Twelve dollars!"

"Oh," replied Jerry, "Let me get this."

"No, let me get it," said Clark and all of us fumbled for our wallets, laughing.

After the tour was finished, we returned the group to Dallas Love Field where their large charter jet was waiting.

Preacher Man's Convair

The church group who owned the Convair 240 didn't feel like they were getting enough revenue from our occasional charter usage. They advised Jerry they were going to lease the aircraft full time to a guitar player named Buckwheat, which they did. The aircraft was taken down to the old Central Airlines hangar at the far south end of the field, which was now a paint shop. Both sides of the tail were custom painted with a large guitar and the giant letters "Buckwheat."

Ol' Buckwheat and his music group used the plane a couple of times and never paid anything on the lease. The church ended up with the aircraft back and had to pay to have the tail painted over. In the meantime, FDC started billing them $75 a month for ramp parking.

The small Saginaw Airport north of Fort Worth Meacham Field was rumored to occasionally been used for unloading bales of marijuana. The church group who owned the Convair leased the plane to some soldier-of-fortune pilot known to operate out of Saginaw and the plane ended up parked at Saginaw.

Jerry got a call asking him to go over to Saginaw and get the Convair. I flew him over in one of our planes. Jerry looked the airfield and the situation over. A large plane can be landed on a short airstrip that it often cannot be taken off from.

Jerry told the pilot who had landed the plane and who wanted it taken back to GSW that he would charge him $200 for flying it out, but first they would have to put a 55 gallon barrel in the far aft luggage compartment and fill it with water. Jerry knew his aircraft and knew doing this would bring the empty airliner back into CG. The pilot refused to comply with Jerry's request, so we left. Someone eventually returned the Convair to GSW because it showed back up on our ramp.

Two weeks later, the pilot who had used the Convair was found in the burned out wreckage of a Lodestar full of marijuana that crashed during an engine failure takeoff on a road in northern Mexico. After those two fiascos, the Convair 240 remained on our ramp and their parking fees were paid on time.

My Favorite Airplane

Warner-Lambert, an aircraft modification center based in St. Louis, custom modified a few lower-time ex-airline DC-3s with executive interiors. Many of the main line DC-3s exceeded the 60,000 hours TT for which the FAA required a main spar teardown and inspection. This was a very expensive repair and made the newer, lower-time Goony Birds much more desirable.

A Douglas DC-3 at Love Field, N37F, belonged to the vice president of Braniff Airline. The aircraft had the wildest interior with zebra skin seats, burnt orange carpeting and club seating with a mahogany inlaid map of the world card table. The DC-3 seated about eighteen passengers in living room comfort.

The Braniff VP had taken one of the lowest time airliners, about 25,000 hours TT, when Braniff stopped using them and had it modified at Warner-Lambert with the custom executive interior. Word on the street was that the DC-3 was not for sale, but if it did fly, it was not very often.

I contacted Web Thomas and asked him to see if the plane could be purchased and if so for how much. Web's wife had been a Braniff stewardess and later an executive secretary at the Braniff corporate offices. If anyone had an in, Web did. Web said the VP wouldn't sell the plane. I said ask him anyway. He did and the VP told Web to sell it to me for $25,000. He had gotten used to flying in jets and wasn't using the DC-3 anymore. Web couldn't believe the deal was made. "Simple," I told Web, "Three Seven Fox was meant to be my plane."

We operated the DC-3 under FAR Part 94. Very few DC-3s were ever operated under FAR Part 145 air taxi. The FAA, however, would have preferred that all aircraft over 12,500 pounds be operated under FAR Part 121 because this gave them more control.

The loophole was that the aircraft could not be leased with the flight crew. In other words, the user had to lease the aircraft and hire the flight crew separately. There was a standing order with most towers to notify the FAA Air Carrier division whenever our DC-3 or any non-121 large aircraft moved. The DEA also watched all transports closely.

Crows Hunt Ducks

There was one condition to the DC-3 purchase, actually more of a favor. Trammel Crow, whose construction company built every big project in Dallas, used the Three for an annual duck-hunting trip to Louisiana.

The pilot who flew Crow's jet was also a rated DC-3 pilot. Every year during duck hunting season, Crow's personal pilot would use the DC-3 to take Crow and his cronies over to some Podunk airport in Louisiana. Their company jet couldn't get in and out of the small airport's short runway.

We billed them handily for the trip every year and it helped with the expenses on the old DC-3. They even provided their own insurance and never complained as long as the aircraft was cleaned up and ready to go.

All Mechanics Are Not Equal

Howard was one of the best mechanics I ever knew, but he was a recovered alcoholic. Sure enough, one morning he didn't show up for work and I pretty well guessed what had happened. A couple days later, his wife called to let me know that Howard was in the hospital with bleeding ulcers. When I visited him in the hospital, I assured him if he would get back on the wagon his job would be waiting for him.

Good mechanics were hard to come by and I had hired one who claimed to be working on his A&P, but he wasn't worth a flip. The DC-3 had blown a fuel pump on the left engine and prior to leaving on a two-day trip in the Cessna 310, I told the mechanic to get the DC-3 running because we had a lease trip scheduled when I got back. When I returned, the DC-3 cowlings were strung out on the ground and the left engine still wouldn't fire. I should have fired the jerk then, but I didn't.

I called Big John in Paris, Texas, who had worked on my T-6 and knew radial engines. John was a former WW II Army Air Corps mechanic who worked for Brussard, the minister who collected WW II fighters and who had done the Garland air show for me a couple years before. Big John reminded me of John Wayne in looks and manner. He was the only man I ever knew who could hand prop a T-6 when it wouldn't start.

Howard was still convalescing at home and I needed the DC-3 up. When Big John arrived, I explained we had bought a new fuel pump and the problems we were having. I went back to my office and about a half hour had passed when I heard that distinctive sound of the old radial engine crank and fire. The connecting rods make this sort of clanking sound as the engine first starts to turn over. I went back out to the aircraft.

Big John, with a grin on his face said, "They had the fuel pump on back-ass-jack-wards, it was blowing instead of sucking."

One of those management lessons you learn the hard way when you run your own business is it's cheaper to pay a good mechanic twice the hourly rate of a cheap mechanic because the good mechanic gets the work done a whole lot faster. Luckily, Howard returned to work in a few weeks and stayed sober.

Air Taxi Flights

Returning from a long charter trip including several approaches at major airports and receiving excellent traffic handling, we were approaching GSW and I asked the tower for a straight-in approach. Either the tone of my voice was wrong or the tower operator was having a bad day, but I got a bunch of lip from the approach controller. Turning to Ted in the right seat, I remarked, "Oh, this must be GSW, we're home."

It was possible, however, that we had messed with them a little too much or they remembered my voice from when I used to fly Cessna 402 side number N04Q. Most pilots who flew the 402, couldn't resist the temptation to reply to instructions substituting "oh" for the zero and then four Q. Say it real fast, you'll catch on. This, of course, was always followed by a tort reply from the tower operator explaining that the correct side number on the aircraft was Zero Four Quebec.

Knowing how to talk to the ATC controllers and the tower operators could usually wangle a pilot a straight in approach for landing or at least a reasonably fast landing assignment. There was no place this was truer than at McCarran Field in Las Vegas and probably due to the numerous GA aircraft mixed in with the airline traffic. If you didn't follow their instructions and expedite, you were going to get what pilots referred to as a penalty approach, that being out to see the mountains and circle for a while until they could work you in.

The first time I flew into McCarran with Ted and he contacted approach control at Las Vegas, he didn't quite understand the controller's instructions. They vectored him about 20 miles out over the desert and then into a holding pattern before giving him landing clearance. Knowing that the controllers sometimes did this to newcomers, I just sat quietly and waited for him and approach control to work it out.

DC-3 Charters

Jerry, on the other hand, knew exactly how to talk the controllers into almost anything. On one of our DC-3 charter trips into Vegas, we arrived just after dark and I told Jerry I'd always wanted to fly low down the Vegas Strip at night. Jerry got on approach control and talked them into it. We flew at about 1,200 AGL in slow flight, like riding a magic carpet, down the neon boulevard. The casino hotel towers are now almost as high as the clearance we got that night.

Passenger behavior flying charter groups to Las Vegas in the DC-3 was predictable. Going out, everyone was drinking, joking, laughing and playing cards. Coming back, your passengers were quiet, hung over and otherwise not very talkative. That was particularly true, if they weren't coming home a winner.

On the DC-3 flights we often had private pilots, even some of our students on board. They were welcome to come up to the cockpit and visit or watch. Encouraged to do so by her pilot husband, one of the wives came forward. Obviously at a loss for what to say, she asked, "Is everything functioning properly?"

To kid her Jerry, picked up the PA mike and announced to the cabin, "Based on an inquiry from one of our passengers, there will be no functioning on this aircraft tonight."

While waiting on the return trip, I'd play the craps tables. I had perfected a system for taking the odds after reading a book on *How to Shoot Craps a*nd over several hours of play, if I paid attention and did the math I'd come out ahead.

An old oil field worker told me one time that a colored gentleman shooter, not exactly his words, would make you a lot of money at the craps table. He also contended that a lady in a red dress was good luck.

I was about to leave the Riviera one evening, but had $20 worth of chips in my pocket I needed to cash in. On my way over to the cashier's cage, I walked past a particular craps table. Fancy that, and in a casino no less. Walla! A large African American fellow was running the numbers and a little old lady in a red dress was making bets on the side.

What the heck, I'll just play out this twenty-bucks worth of chips. Stepping up to the craps table, I placed a $5 chip on the Come Line and the cocktail waitress asked what I would like a drink. Normally I did not drink when I was gambling or flying out the next day, but we had another day's layover. What the heck, "A bourbon and water, please" I replied.

One too many bourbon and waters and a couple hours later, my jacket pockets were full of $5 chips and I had a stack of $20 chips running up to my elbow when I finally decided I ought to quit while I was ahead. At the cashier's cage, I cashed in for a little over $1,200 and took a taxi back to my hotel. Twelve Franklins was not the most I ever won at the craps table, but it was the most I ever won starting with a single $5 chip.

DC-3 Glider

We had been leasing the DC-3 based on tachometer time, but all the other aircraft were rented based on an hour meter reading, so I had Howard install an hour meter in the DC-3. He wired it through the master switch and installed an oil pressure switch just like we had on all the other aircraft.

We had just taken off for Las Vegas one early evening. Jerry was captain and I was flying from the copilot's seat. Jerry was always screwing with something when he didn't have anything else to do. We were cruising at 10,000 feet somewhere west of Albuquerque when the subject of the new hour meter installation came up. Jerry insisted that it could be turned off and I explained that I didn't think so because of the way the mechanic had wired it the same as our other aircraft.

Jerry turned off the radio master switch and the hour meter kept running. He turned off the master switch. Lights went to standby power and the electric gyro started spinning down, but the hour meter kept running. Without thinking, he reached up and shut off the overhead all-kill button. At 10,000 feet on a cold black night and with only the props spinning down, a DC-3 really gets quiet when it becomes a glider.

It was the only time I ever recall just hearing the wind noise around the cockpit in a large aircraft. It seemed like about an hour, but was only about two seconds before Jerry turned the all-kill switch back on and added the usual explicative comment.

Several passengers who were pilots came forward to ask if something was wrong and Jerry explained that he had just forgot to switch fuel tanks, nothing was wrong. He sure didn't want to admit to some of the private pilots onboard what he had done.

Fun With The Gooney Bird

Most pilots, who flew the old DC-3, remember the plane with a certain affection. The truth is, they were slow, they were hot in the summer, cold in the winter and they couldn't get up high enough to get over very many thunderstorms. Still, there was something about the old Gooney Birds that pilots loved, myself being no exception. I think it was the feel of the plane.

An odd thing that I remember about the DC-3 was that the fuel switches on the floor were labeled Left Motor and Right Motor, probably because it was originally designed in the 1930s. All modern aircraft are labeled Engine not Motor.

In the Three, it was a lot easier to make a wheel landing and then coast out until the tail wheel came down than it was a full-stall three-point landing, but for short field landings, the full-stall was the best technique. The old saying that there were only two kinds of pilots, those who had ground looped and those who were going to, fully applied to the DC-3. An Air Force pilot with 6,000 hours in DC-3s told me that he thought he'd never ground loop one, but one day he did just that.

Avgas was 35 cents a gallon in those days, so I'd fly the Three for fun sometimes, but because I'd never gotten my type rating, I needed to take a rated pilot with me even though I owned the plane. By now, I had almost as many hours in the Three as a lot of the GA type rated pilots. Of course, nothing like the hours the old main line captains like Jerry had logged.

There was a fly-in at the small town of Denison up by the Red River, the town where President Eisenhower had lived as a boy. I loaded up the neighborhood kids and whoever else wanted to go in the 37F and we flew up to Denison to the fly-in. One of our flight school students who had recently gotten his type rating flew copilot, but basically I flew the hop.

When we taxied up, we were the largest aircraft on the ramp and the old DC-3 attracted a lot of attention. We let the airstair door down and allowed people to tour the plane with its bordello interior. 37F was the hit of the fly-in.

The following Monday when I arrived at the office, there was an FAA Air Carrier inspector waiting. He wanted to know where the DC-3 had gone, i.e.. we had been gone all day. I got a laugh out of it. Apparently we had never gotten high enough to be tracked on radar and ATC assumed the plane had made a low altitude run out of the country and back.

Tree Top Airways

In the early 1970s, Trans Texas Airways, a long time regional carrier in the Midwest, had bought into the Tropicana Casino in Las Vegas during its most profitable years. When the airline went bankrupt, it was put on the market and I looked into buying it. Actually, there wasn't any buying to the deal. It was only a matter of having a large enough credit line to assume the massive liabilities of the airline.

An idea, which I had conceived about three years earlier, was to develop an airline fleet of jumbo jets with sleeping quarters for the crews like a merchant ship. By using a 24/7 computer scheduling and command center, the fleet of aircraft would be able to rival the oceangoing shipping in the delivery of high-dollar, time-sensitive goods.

Federal Express came along years later with a small package variation on my idea. Air taxi services now pool their resources and using computer scheduling, to compete with the majors. Time, backing and interest ran out before I was ever able to develop the concept. When it comes to commercial and general aviation in the decades of the 60s and 70s, I been there, done that and got the T-shirt to prove it.

Main Concourse

The only American president I recall seeing in person was Richard Nixon. On a political trip to Fort Worth, Air Force One taxied up to the center concourse at GSW. Several others and myself had gathered to watch the President's arrival from the upstairs concourse windows. Nixon exited the front airstair of the Boeing 707 and paused to give his distinctive sideways overhand wave to the small crowd that had gathered.

The President's aircraft had parked on the center concourse. The same spot the Immigration Bureau used to load wetbacks onto a Convair 440 and return them to Old Mexico. I stopped once to watch them load and was visiting with one of the Border Patrol officers. He jokingly remarked, "Some of them will probably beat the airplane back."

As I watch them load I recalled the words to an old Woody Guthrie song, *They won't have a name when they ride that big plane, all they will be called is Deportee.*

Fuel Shortage

Most people associate the national fuel shortage or oil crisis with President Jimmy Carter, while in fact the first modern day fuel shortage the U.S. experienced was under President Nixon. Aviation gasoline jumped from thirty cents a gallon to fifty cents a gallon in a matter of a few weeks and became harder to get. The government was trying to keep the airlines flying, but cared less about General Aviation.

We didn't have our own fuel dump. The flight school and had been purchasing our gas from Butler Aviation who fueled our aircraft by truck. Butler Aviation had always been a pain in the backside. Careless line employees scratched the paint on the wings of the new planes and on one occasion, damaged a wing tip, but things got worse. Flights were delayed because we couldn't get a gas truck to come fuel our planes on a turnaround. Butler only wanted to come once a day to fuel all of our planes.

Via a clause in the original airport contract, Butler had been given the rights to all gas service on the terminal ramp. A small FBO on the field, Mid-Cities Aviation, was allowed to gas aircraft, but only on their own ramp.

While the free press is an essential factor to maintain a democracy, a wise man soon learns not to believe all they read in the newspaper or what's on television. A firsthand experience I had with this was when I went before the Fort Worth City Council to contest the monopoly on the fuel rights at GSW.

The Fort Worth Star Telegram reported the next day "Mr. Arnold had appeared before the City Council to protest the construction of the new DFW Airport and the closing of GSW Airport, the old Amon Carter Field."

251

Nothing in the City Council meeting was ever mentioned about the new DFW airport's construction, that I recall.

Rule 23 might work in this situation I thought and so I leased a fuel truck that was licensed on the street and began buying gas offsite a truckload at a time to fuel our own aircraft. This started an all out war between the Fort Worth Aviation Authority, Butler Aviation and FDC. I contended that Butler had failed to meet the terms of their contract by not servicing our planes properly.

Needless to say, I lost the battle and had to give up the fuel truck. However, I was determined not to lose the war and equally determined not to buy gas from Butler anymore, but if I didn't solve the fuel supply problem soon, it was going to have a serious effect on FDC financially.

Chapter Nineteen
REQUIEM TO GENERAL AVIATION

Twas the beginning of the end for the great era of General Aviation as 1980 approached. Soon only the well-to-do would be able to fly airplanes. Lawsuits eventually drove Cessna out of the light aircraft business.

All manufacturers have a responsibility to design the best product they can, but it seemed the person climbing into a plane also needed to assume some of the responsibility for flight safety. Every Tom, Dick and Harry sued Cessna and Piper for any and every crash regardless of the fault until it eventually became impossible to produce a light, single-engine aircraft at a reasonable price for private pilots.

Redbird Airport

The old Goble Aviation facility at Redbird Airport was now closed down and Mobil Oil Company had a fuel farm that went with the facility. We set up a meeting with the Dallas Director of Aviation whose office was at Love Field.

We only wanted to lease the Mobil fuel dump, but the director was trying to force us to lease all the vacant hangar space on Redbird Airport in order to get the fuel rights. The negotiations were going nowhere. Finally, I stood up, informed the director he was unreasonable and may have added something about his family heritage as I stormed out of his office.

As it turned out, Hughes Aircraft, d/b/a Summa Corporation eventually leased the empty hangars to store some of Hughes' old aircraft. They placed security guards around the facility, which effectively rendered about half of the airport a ghost town and the ramp space and the fuel dump were never used. The city got their money, but once again GA got the bureaucratic shaft.

Grand Prairie Airport

The City of Grand Prairie built a nice terminal building and quite a few T-hangars at their new municipal airport south of town. This had been done to justify closing the old National Guard Airport in the center of downtown, which was then sold off for an industrial park. The city had leased its airport to the operator of a small airport in South Fort Worth.

Pappy, the operator's nickname, wasn't old he just had that well-worn Willie Nelson appearance about him. He was kind of a cantankerous old fart, but I got him to agree to lease FDC the terminal building and the Enco gas facility. All he wanted was the rental income from the T-hangars. Great, because all I wanted was a dependable fuel supply at a wholesale price.

For the next several months, our instructors would go to Grand Prairie, have the students shoot a few touch and goes and then taxi up to the terminal where our attendant would fuel the aircraft. I gave the mechanic assistant that worked for Howard at GSW, the one I should have fired, the job as attendant to keep from laying him off and called him the airport manager.

Landing offsite sounds anomalous, but actually it worked out well. It allowed the instructor and the student to take a break and discuss the maneuvers they had been practicing. The students liked it because the short runway actually allowed them to spend a lot less time taxiing when practicing touch and go landings. They also received training at an uncontrolled airport as well as the controlled airport at GSW.

Two brothers had been giving clandestine flight instruction out of the Grand Prairie Airport. They wanted to lease the airport and were scheming behind the scenes to get us out. Looking back on the situation, it would have probably been best if I had shut them down when we first took the lease, but I didn't operate that way. For the most part, I've always advocated free enterprise.

The airport manager/gas-boy was also not providing good service and it wasn't long before private aircraft owners at the airport began to complain. All of this was mostly my fault because I had little or no interest in the operation and hadn't supervised the situation at all.

In less than a year, the Nixon fuel shortage began to subside and gas prices went back down a little. The Grand Prairie facility was now more of a headache than it was an asset. Pappy, I am sure, felt he could get more money for the lease out of the other group, so we mutually agreed to terminate our agreement.

I also terminated the worthless manager/employee that I should have fired a long time before that. The facility was an Enco gas station, an old name for the Standard Oil brand and they agree to put some pressure on Butler Aviation at GSW to service FDC better.

In order to obtain credit for our investment and cancel the Enco dealer agreement, it was necessary to inventory all the stock and supplies on site. Late on the afternoon we were to terminate the lease at Grand Prairie Airport, AJ flew over to the facility with me to shut it down. The new operator would take over the following day. AJ was one of those bookkeepers who never let a penny get by her that she didn't account for. When I signed all the paperwork and got ready to fly back to GSW, I couldn't find our trusty bookkeeper/secretary anywhere.

It was getting dark when I started looking around the airport for AJ in the office and out in the hangar, but couldn't find her. The wind was blowing hard when I walked outside and stood by the fuel truck. I could hear voices, but I couldn't figure out where they were coming from. Finally, I realized someone was on top of the truck. It was AJ in a tight skirt and high heels, clipboard and pen in hand, making the new gas boy re-check the gallons in the fuel truck with a dipstick.

"Get down off of there," I yelled up to her, "before you fall and break your fool neck. If they're going to cheat us, they're going to cheat us. Let's go, we're done here!"

Years later the small airport turned into a successful and I am sure profitable operation, but I'm glad I didn't spend twenty more years of my life fooling with the place.

Mid-Cities Aviation

A builder from Irving named Makus owned Mid-Cities Aviation and had constructed a very expensive all metal maintenance hangar when he put in a gas dump at the north end of GSW. A mechanic who worked on Makus' Cessna 401 had talked him into backing the Mid-Cities operation when Makus couldn't find a convenient place to keep his plane. Makus must have been an ol' country boy because every time he went to say FAA he'd always call it the FFA, like in Future Farmers of America.

Makus had indicated to me that he would be willing to sign over his lease if FDC would buy the hangar. He said with GSW closing in about a year, he'd take $20,000 for it. The hangar had cost three times that much to build it originally, so I financed it at the bank under our holding corporation GSA. The Mid-Cities Aviation sign on the side of the hangar was quickly repainted to read Flight Dynamics. We moved our offices out of the old terminal building and into the cramped quarters of the Morgan building at the Mid-Cities fuel facility.

One thing the old terminal had was plenty of office space and plenty of concrete ramp space. When we relocated our planes to the north ramp, we had to park the DC-3 tail up on the grass with the main gear on the concrete so as not to block the taxiway. Howard, our A&I mechanic, was pleased with his new maintenance hangar that even had a hoist for pulling engines.

Warner Aviation

Love Field in Dallas, lay to the east of GSW just over the Trinity River and was the only remaining major airport in the Metroplex close to the northern Mid-Cities area. Addison airport was to the far north of Dallas and Redbird was to the far south of Dallas. The new DFW International Airport, now under construction, would dominate all the airspace in that area and would necessitate the closing of GSW.

Time flew by as we continued to operate at the Mid-Cities facility, but the day was fast approaching when GSW Airport would close. I began to explore options and Love field seemed our best prospect to stay in business. Warner Aviation, a principal transit facility at Love, had several large hangars. They rented these hangars to high-dollar corporate aircraft.

One hangar had some really nice unused office space available in the front facing Lemmon Avenue. Corporate pilots liked an office to hang out, but no need for contact with the public. The whole front of the building, including a glass front lobby was available, but hangar space was at a premium. Our aircraft would have to be tied down outside. Not anything new for us. Warner would put our planes in a hangar when it stormed based on space available, but charged us by the night for this service. I rented one T-hangar for Howard to use as a shop.

Sabotaged Skyhawk

The afternoon that I flew over to Warner's facility on the north side of Love Field to finalize the ramp and office space lease, I had taken our newest Skyhawk. I left the new white and gold Cessna Skyhawk parked on the transit ramp for a short while. After the meeting, I departed Love Field. It was a beautiful fall day, a pretty afternoon for flying. As I made a tight turn out over the Trinity River, I remember thinking at the time, if one had an engine failure along here, the grassy area inside the river levy would make an excellent place for a forced landing. Looking back on the events to follow, I've often wondered why my mind drifted onto that subject that particular afternoon. Was it a premonition of some impending unknown?

The next day was Saturday, another pretty flying day and an active day for aircraft rentals at GSW. I had taken the day off. A young couple and their two friends had scheduled the Skyhawk for a weekend trip. This was the same Skyhawk I had flown to Love Field the day before. As luck would have it, the pilot was a very conscientious individual and prior to takeoff, he noticed that the temperature gauge was rising. He taxied back to the hangar. The instructor on duty grounded the plane and checked him out another aircraft.

On Monday, Howard ran the engine up and said that it appeared to be starting to seize up. There was nothing left to do but to tear the engine down to find the cause of the problem. Later that day, Howard came into my office with something on his finger that looked like oily sand. "What's that?" I asked.

Howard replied, "Carborundum. What we use in the spark plug sandblaster." What this meant was that someone had intentionally sabotaged the aircraft by pouring the compound into the crankcase. I reported the incident to the FBI as required by law, but they showed little or no interest in the problem.

Everyone makes enemies in business, your competition and dissatisfied customers, but one doesn't normally make the kind of enemies that would intentionally try to kill someone. The short flight from Love Field to GSW may have been just enough time not to damage the engine to the point of failure and the taxi-out time by the rental pilot was not enough time to finish locking up the engine. Fortunately, the combination of the two, in the sequence in which they occurred, prevented an airborne engine failure and a possible crash.

Who were the suspects? I decided to have an independent agency conduct a series of lie detector tests. We asked everyone who might possibly have had an opportunity or motive to do such a thing to take a lie detector test, which included a lawyer/pilot I had a run-in with one time. It became a joke because some of our competitors flew over in their airplanes and volunteered for the test, just to raze me about the incident. The only person who refused the lie detector test was the mechanic I had fired. Truth be known, it was only for him that we were using the others to try to get him to take the test.

However, one other odd thing had occurred a few weeks before the Skyhawk incident. A nondescript fellow had come into our office offering to sell us some type of damage insurance. It wasn't even very clear what he was selling and in retrospect it might have been the old protection racket, but if it was, I was not astute enough to catch on. If it was a protection racket scam, it seemed as though they would have returned to reap the benefits of their effort, but no such return occurred.

The best candidate for the sabotage remained the fired mechanic who coincidently was now employed at the Warner facility flight line where the Skyhawk had been parked. The carborundum was readily available in the maintenance shop and no one would have paid any attention to a line mechanic checking the oil on a transit aircraft.

Thus, the three components of motive, means and opportunity were there. The mystery was never resolved, although I did confront the fired mechanic some time later about the matter and accused him directly of having tried to kill someone. He only stared at me and never responded. Cessna covered our loss under their warranty policy even though we explained to them that the engine had been intentionally damaged. Maybe they were as thankful as we were that no one had gotten hurt.

Hangar For Sale

We moved the aircraft sales and charter operations to the Lemmon Avenue, Love Field facility even before we closed the flight school at GSW.

Planes are easy to relocate, but GSA still owned an airplane gas station, a Morgan building and a steel metal hangar. Some suggested the possibility of disassembling the hangar and moving it to a small airport. I looked at several sites including one near Lake Dallas.

One morning, a small rotund man came by our new offices. "You own that hangar out at the old GSW Airport?" he asked and added, "If so, we'd be interested in buying or leasing it. Oh, and the fuel dump too."

I didn't know who "we" were, but knew they weren't airplane people. The gentleman was a representative for the new regional bus line that would service DFW. They wanted the facility as a gas station and repair barn for the new DFW airport buses, Surtran, Dallas/Fort Worth's first attempt at a Metroplex transit system and the forerunner to DART. They offered $60,000 for the gas dump and hangar. I owed $20,000. Boy did they have a deal.

Wow! What this meant was I could stay in business at least another year. Like the farmer who won the lottery and said he figured he could now afford to farm for a few more years.

DC-3 And T-6 First To Go

There were enough parking spaces for our charter and flight school aircraft at Warner, but I had to reduce the number of fleet aircraft keeping only the newest and best airplanes. There was nowhere to park large aircraft like the DC-3, so I placed an ad in Trade-A-Plane.

A New Jersey aircraft broker called wanting the plane shown to his customer and prepaid the round trip. Jerry and I stopped in Dayton enroute and spent the night with Suzie's folks. Suzie's dad was a talker like Jerry. I went to bed and they stayed up half the night trying to out lie each other.

We left Dayton early. On arrival, we demonstrated the DC-3 to the dealer's customer taking him and his young son for a twenty-minute local flight. The broker used the demo to convince the man, who had always wanted a DC-3, to buy a newer model twin. I flew us home while Jerry slept.

One afternoon, two guys showed up, a large heavyset fellow and a short wiry little guy. They were looking for a cargo aircraft to haul electronics back and forth across the Mexican border as part of the border industrialization program. At least that was their story. They had been flying a Twin Beech, but were looking to purchase a DC-3.

Wanting to make the sale, I called Jerry and he came out to the airport to demo the aircraft. I explained that it was our policy to charge them rental, but it could be credited to the purchase price. The plane rented for $125 per hour with fuel and insurance. Jerry would go with them and they could fly the aircraft as much as they wanted. They flew about an hour with Jerry. On their return they said they liked the plane, paid for the flight in cash and left. I never expected to see the two guys again. Figured they just wanted to take a ride in a DC-3.

Two weeks later, they returned with a Safeway paper bag full of $5, $10 and $20 bills, totaling $25,000, the asking price for the DC-3. How was I going to account for depositing $25,000 in cash to our company bank account? The IRS would be on us in a New York minute, so I made up this cock-n-bull story that because we were a corporation we needed to have a cashier's check instead of cash for our records.

The two men left, but returned in a couple of hours with a single $25,000 cashier's check. How they got it I don't know and don't care to know. It was our policy to write a counter ticket on all transactions, even aircraft sales. It was our way of getting the information onto the books, so I wrote out a counter ticket and made a copy of the cashier's check before I deposited the check to the bank.

The two men and Jerry left in the DC-3 for El Paso. Jerry returned the next day by commercial air using his airline captain's pass. He told me that he had checked them out in the plane and that the big guy was a fairly good pilot. Of course, a pilot is supposed to have a type rating in a DC-3 to fly as pilot-in-command (PIC). Jerry didn't ask. He left the plane parked in El Paso and contended that they owned the plane now and it wasn't his or my concern who flew the plane.

Note that these were 1970 dollars. For example, the T-6 which I sold next brought $12,000 and in today's aircraft market a good T-6 would easily bring ten times that much.

SST Near Miss

Another classic example of the press screwing up an aviation story was the day the Super Sonic Transport (SST) arrived at the new DFW

Airport. At the time, Braniff Airline was a prospect for the purchase of the SST. Its arrival time had been announced on the radio and I wanted to see it land.

I departed Love Field and started a slow orbit northeast of DFW waiting for the Concorde to arrive. The new traffic pattern for DFW was the infamous upside down wedding cake. My plane was well clear and more than legal where I was orbiting.

I monitored approach control as the SST came in from the north and made a low pass in front of the DFW east terminal. Approach control advised the SST pilot of a small aircraft south of the airport. Not my location. The small aircraft, a Cherokee 140, had departed Grand Prairie Airport and was not a factor.

The SST made a low pass circled back and landed. The evening news and newspapers carried this story. *SST has to make go-around to avoid midair collision with light aircraft.*

The low pass to show off the SST to the crowd had been mistaken by the press for a forced go-around.

When I arrived home that evening, I was anxious to tell my wife about seeing the SST land. She met me at the door asking, "Did you hear the Concorde nearly had a mid-air collision with a light aircraft this afternoon?"

"Not true. I was there, I saw the whole thing!" but I was never able to convince her. She had heard it on the television and that made it a fact.

SMB Stage Line

A non-scheduled freight carrier airline on the west side of Love Field hired fairly low time, twin-engine rated pilots for cheap wages. It was a good way to build twin time and they had plenty of takers. The short-coupled fuselage Twin Beech aircraft they flew would ground loop easily. However, the worst aspect of the operation was that when fully loaded, the planes were in a maximum aft center of gravity (CG) condition and if stalled, would enter a spin at the slightest provocation.

Late one afternoon, several of us were standing out on the tarmac at Love Field visiting as a Twin Beech, model 18, belonging to SMB Stage Lines departed southeast out of Love Field struggling to make altitude. At about a thousand feet and a mile out, it rolled over, nosed down and crashed into a residential area. A puff of black smoke rose from the crash site. I jumped in my pickup and raced to the impact scene.

The Beech had gone nearly straight in landing in a small backyard. One wing had hit the back kitchen of a frame house. The tower must have called the fire department because they almost had the fire out when I arrived. There were not enough pieces left of the plane to fill the back of a pickup truck.

The woman in the house said that she had just walked out of the kitchen a few minutes before the plane hit. Results of the crash investigation disclosed that the Twin Beech had been loaded at full gross and had lost power on one engine.

Love Field Aircraft Sales

The Lemon Avenue facility on Love Field was a better location for sales and charter. Our new offices were first class and what we needed for better aircraft buyer contact. What we really needed next was a multi-engine dealership. The Beech distributor was owned out of Austin and they had a satellite facility at Addison Airport, north of Dallas.

The only twin-engine Cessna dealership in the area was Cooper Aviation, also at Addison. Ted Cooper was a nice guy and a true friend to General Aviation. He had been around a long time and even though they didn't sell the numbers of aircraft they could have for the area, Cessna was not going to abandon them as long as Ted Cooper was around.

Beech authorized us as a Pilot Center after we bought several single-engine Beechcraft. We had the single-engine Cessna franchise and a single-engine Grumman American franchise. However, never obtaining a principal multi-engine dealership was a missing essential to our continued success on Love Field.

The regulation against student pilots departing or landing solo at Love Field was a minor problem. I left the FAA and VA approved flight school at GSW until nearly the airport's last day of operation. We moved the flight school to Love Field and our instructors had to fly over to Addison or Redbird Airports to solo their student pilots. This wasn't a real serious problem because by now most of our VA eligible students were now working on commercial license, instrument and multi-engine ratings.

There was, however, an additional problem with the Love Field facility. We seemed to attract a lot more of promoter type high rollers. Those that pretend like they're going to buy an expensive airplane, get the dealer to fly them around for awhile and then never buy anything claiming that it was just a demo. We tried real hard to enforce the rule of renting the aircraft to them and then crediting it back to the purchase price.

What happened more than once was the pilot assigned to fly them was left standing on the ramp as they walked off without paying. The worst offenders were the Dallas white collar Mafia, those that owned restaurants and real estate. If we billed them, they would have some lawyer, who did their dirty work, threaten to tie us up in a lawsuit knowing it would cost us more in time and money to answer their frivolous lawsuits than it would be worth. We usually just wrote off the bill. It was the modern version of, *making you an offer you couldn't refuse.*

If we were brokering the airplane, we could usually get the owner to absorb the flight time and we would pay for the gas and the pilot's time. Spare Me The High Rollers.

Beginning Of The End

We had operated a little over a year at 8629 Lemon Avenue when my wife started sounding like the lyrics to the Reba McEntire song *Why Haven't I Heard From You.* We didn't have mobile phones, it the '70s. Well we did, but they weighed ten pounds. The business had been easy and fun to build and had grown exponentially. Now it was a struggle every month to meet the payroll and pay the bills. We had to make $20,000 a month before I made a dime. All of this was chipping away from my flying and spare time to enjoy what I did make.

FDC had a lot of assets, but cash flow had always been a problem. Like my ol' buddy JD said one time, "If they were selling box cars for a dime a dozen, all I could do is run up and down the track yelling, damn ain't they cheap!"

Those words were never truer than now. What was once fun had become a heavy responsibility. Once again, I stood at the window looking out thinking I could remember a day when I'd have been happy to own just one of those aircraft on the ramp and have the time to fly it for fun. It was time to re-think my choice of careers and I began to consider selling the business.

When the word hit the street that FDC was for sell, I started getting a few inquiries. The first to offer a buy out was some Texas oilman who bore a striking resemblance to Jimmy Dean, the sausage king. He began showing up every day and mostly wasted my time. After a week of this, I arrived at work one morning to find him sitting at my desk with his feet propped up. Someone had let him in my office because he had been going around telling everyone he was the new owner.

Something snapped inside me. I think it was his boots on my Amon Carter desk that had done it. I hadn't seen any money and I was getting tired of his bullshit. "Out," I said to him, "Get yourself up out of my chair, out of my office and don't come back until you can bring certified funds to purchase the place." Needless to say, I never saw the long tall phony again.

Goodbye To Old Friends

To the best of my knowledge, we never lost a student, instructor or rental pilot in an airplane crash. We did, however, sell a Piper Arrow to an airline pilot who flew it into the side of a mountain in Colorado returning from a ski trip. He was on instruments when it happened.

Although all airline pilots are proficient in instrument flying, it is much more difficult to fly instruments in a light plane without a flight director system than it is to fly a modern jet airliner on instruments.

Stan had sold an airplane to a wealthy doctor's son who showed an interest in purchasing FDC when he found out that the business was up for sale. His dad, who owned a prime medical clinic, co-signed for the purchase of the aircraft fleet and we negotiated a reasonable price for the corporation and good will.

It was time to start planning some options for those who had stayed with me over the years. Stan, my salesman, stayed with FDC, but eventually he opened his own aircraft brokerage over at Meacham Field.

AJ had an opportunity to take an executive secretary's job at Empire Central for about what she was making at FDC. As part of her severance pay, she was given clear title to her most recent company car. I lost contact with her, but understand she eventually remarried well.

Ted, my chief pilot, was picked up immediately by one of the corporations we shared the hangar with, as a copilot on their Gulf Stream II. Ted flies a company Lear 24 now and we still stay in touch.

Nevertheless, it was still a little difficult for all of us to break up the old team after being together for the better part of a decade. The buyout went smoothly and I walked away one afternoon and never looked back.

The last time I drove down Lemon Avenue, there was a Baron Thomas Aircraft Sales sign in my old office window. Baron, Web Thomas' son, had been a teenager when I first took over FDC.

The old GSW terminal building was to be torn down to make way for a planned industrial park. I always claimed I was going to hire on with the demolition crew and help. Of course, I never did. In fact, I was working out-of-state when it was finally torn down. That old terminal building would have made a great airline museum if someone could have gotten behind the project.

Parting With The Twin

The Cessna 310K was paid for and the new owners didn't particularly want it having recently purchased a relatively new twin from us. I decided to keep it. My wife, daughter and I made a few trips in the Cessna 310 and I really liked owning the ol' plane. However, without having the luxury of being able to charter or lease the 310, it was a little expensive maintaining, hangaring and providing insurance for the plane.

I advertised the 310 for sale and a buyer with an early model Aero Commander offered me the Commander and more than enough to boot. I made the trade. An Aero Commander twin was a good enough plane, but I never liked them as well as a 310 or Beech Model 55. Only flew the Commander once before I sold it.

Aero Commander Repo

A real estate promoter offered to buy the Commander for $10,000, but was supposedly waiting on a big deal to close. He put up a $3,000 deposit and a sixty-day promise-to-pay note. After two months were up, I went to his office, which I found closed. I tracked the guy down through a mutual friend who had been involved in one of the guy's shady deals in the past and was more then happy to rat on him. My ship was in New Orleans.

Picking up the phone on a whim, I inquired of the FBO at Lakefront if there was an Aero Commander by that N number parked there. The fellow on the phone told me he could see it through the window from where he was standing.

I called my old friend Jerry and asked him if he would like to take a run down to Lakefront and pick up a plane for me. Jerry could use his airline pass to fly down free on any major carrier. Jerry said he would and that he'd take along a multi-engine student that would like to log the flight time.

Discussing the possibility that the aircraft might be disabled in someway, I asked Jerry to be extra thorough in the preflight of the aircraft. When they arrived at Addison Airport with the Aero Commander, all had gone smoothly. They just went to the aircraft like they owned it, got in and flew back to Dallas. When I tied the plane down I disconnected one of the electrical system cannon plugs so it wouldn't start.

Some weeks later, I arrived at my new office at Sports Car Center to find the proverbial gentleman-in-a-suit was waiting for me. We had some parts stolen off a Porsche a few days before, but this fellow didn't look like a city police detective. Maybe an IRS agent, but no, there was a bulge in his jacket, must be FBI and I wondered what he wanted.

The Aero Commander had been reported stolen. There was no question as to the legality of our repossessing the aircraft. I had the signed letter of intent for payment and the FAA registration for the aircraft, which I showed the agent. After we visited briefly, the agent commented that about half of the stolen aircraft reports he followed up on were repossessions and he had already guessed that this was also the case.

A few weeks later, a man called and asked if I'd show him and his son the Aero Commander parked at Addison Airport with the for sale sign on it. I agreed, but put my .380 automatic in the holster and snapped it onto my belt under my jacket. A lot of air taxi and airline pilots like Steve were taking similar precautions since a recent rash of Cuban high-jackings.

The interested parties looked over the aircraft and then asked if they could fly it. I gave them the usual lame excuse about not being covered by insurance, but told them they were welcome to run up the engines or do whatever they needed to do to check it out on the ground.

I exited the aircraft and untied the wing chains, but left the tail chain on the aircraft while they ran up the engines. They were satisfied with the aircraft and the price. The man handed me a personal check, which I took to the bank and exchanged for a cashier's check. That afternoon I met them back at the plane, handed them a bill of sale and shook their hand. All of my suspicions were unfounded, but once burned, twice shy.

The Demise Of Braniff

About this time, one of Braniff airline vice presidents called and asked me to lunch at the Tahiti Room. He made a lot of overtones about my taking an active management part in the floundering Braniff Training Center they were starting. My reputation for excellence in training at FDC had preceded me.

Actually, I quickly figured out that all he was trying to do was pick my brains. Apparently, he had been given the job of setting up the new school and was in over his head. I wasn't about to give Braniff another free shot at me.

The first time was getting passed over for pilot's class. The second time was when I bought Braniff stock at $5 a share and they filed Chapter 11. My stock dropped to a nickel a share.

Bellanca Indian Jewelry Run

A long time aviation broker at the Plainview Airport had become the main Bellanca distributor for most of the U.S. He had accomplished this by staying with the brand, advertising in Trade-A-Plane and an aggressive marketing organization.

Having owned a Bellanca Viking and having been suitably impressed with the aircraft, I was interested when the Bellanca distributor in Plainview contacted me to go to work for him. Over the next few months, I demonstrated the Bellanca to some prospective buyers in Dallas.

When I went to Plainview on business in my Bellanca Viking demonstrator, I was already halfway to Albuquerque. I'd put the ol' Viking to good use. It was called the monthly Indian jewelry run, from the reservation direct to Dallas by air.

In the late '70s and early '80s, Indian jewelry became very popular. My brother had several good contacts with the traders that worked the Indian shops. I'd buy a couple hundred pounds at a time and double my money on arrival with dealers or take it to any flea market on weekends. Mark the price up eight times and make up a big sign that read *Indian Jewelry Half Price.*

One hot afternoon, leaving Albuquerque, the Bellanca was loaded with two passengers, full gas tanks and a couple hundred pounds of Indian jewelry. The Viking wasn't going to exactly leap into the air. It was sure nice to have that long former Sandia SAC Air Base runway for takeoff.

A Bonanza taxied into position in front of us and took off. In about three minutes, I was cleared for takeoff. Both planes were cleared for runway-heading departures west bound. By the time we passed over Tijeras Canyon, we were a thousand feet above and a mile ahead of the Bonanza. No one ever had to try to sell me on the merits of a Bellanca.

The Last Landing Of N37F

In the spring of 1989, years after selling FDC and getting out of the General Aviation business, I was at home in the backyard working on an old 1942 Lincoln Continental, which I had been restoring. A young gentleman in a three-piece suit walked up and asked if I had any knowledge of DC-3 aircraft N37F.

"Let me guess," I said, "FBI or IRS?" He showed me his identification. I missed it. He was a treasury agent. He began to ask questions about the DC-3. I told him, "I owned N37F, but I had sold it years ago."

The agent asked if I had any proof I had sold the DC-3 and I said, "Well maybe." I went to the garage to dig through several cardboard boxes of old tax records while the agent looked on. What I came up with was an FDC counter ticket with a copy of the cashier's check stapled to it.

The T-Man asked me if he could have the paper work. "No," I told him. "I don't know where this thing might be going, but you can sure make a copy of what you need."

The agent returned after making the copies and thanked me for my help. "Whoa," I said, "I've answered all of your questions and given you what you asked for, now tell me what's going on."

Holding back a smile, the agent explained, "Your old DC-3 was found wheels up on a cattle ranch near Truth Or Consequences, New Mexico. There were several bales of marijuana still onboard and the only paperwork in the aircraft was an old registration to Flight Dynamics Corporation."

Personal SNJ T-6; Warner-Lambert converted DC-3 N37F; photo "Three Threes"; Confederate Air Force Colonel, B-17 Piccadilly Lil used in movie War Lovers, got to fly her one time; Covol and his never-ending B-25 work project; photograph of B-17 which hung over my office desk; CAF colonel uniform; Convair with Buckwheat painted on tail; FDC aircraft sales offices at 8629 Lemmon Avenue on Love Field.

Chapter Twenty
ENGINEERS DO WHAT

During my second year of college at the University of Oklahoma, I took any part-time job I could get. I worked in a gas station, a men's clothing store and briefly as a car salesman. I dropped out of college for two semesters while in Ohio, but returned to enroll at Oklahoma City University that summer and took a job at Hayes Aircraft on the night shift.

As a self-taught photographer, I had learned to develop and print my own black and white photos, even winning a couple of amateur photo awards. Hayes needed a photo lab technician in their publication department and hired me. The lab burned photographic plates to print AF parts manuals using a large darkroom camera with a focal length of about twelve feet. One person outside the lab mounted the masters and the person inside the lab loaded the camera and developed the negatives.

They Went That-A-Way

A most interesting old fellow worked with me at the Hayes photo lab. He had served in the cavalry with General Pershing when the U.S. Army was chasing Pancho Villa all over northern Mexico. He'd tell us stories about how they would ride into town and ask the locals which way Pancho Villa had gone and then they would go the opposite direction because the villagers would always lie to protect 'ol Pancho.

According to the old timer, the Mexican-American War started when Pancho Villa rustled some cattle in south Texas and Pershing's cavalry chased him halfway to Mexico City. When the Mexican government heard that a large military force was moving towards the Capital, they assumed the United States had declared war on Mexico and the Army was on its way to attack them.

I Are An Engineer

Within a couple of months, the manager at the Hayes Aircraft facility on Tinker AFB asked if I could read blueprints and write technical reports. After all, I was an engineering student, of course I could. I was promoted to night supervisor and transferred to the Hayes Aircraft on-base operation.

In addition to technical publications, Hayes had a contract to remove corrosion from aging Air Force aircraft that were cycled through the air base for repair. The laborers, who wore heavy rubber suits and sprayed the aircraft with solvent, were referred to as corrosion engineers. It therefore, followed that my new title would be Technical Publication Engineer. Hey, someone actually called me an engineer for the first time. The week before I couldn't spell it, now I are one.

The project I worked on was called the Federal Item Identification Reduction Program. Its purpose was to find and eliminate duplicate part numbers in the Air Force material supply system. For example, a mechanic at Tooly AFB might order a fuel nozzle for an engine by part number and get an officer's club ashtray that had the same vendor part number.

Many parts had also been put into inventory with typographical errors. Sometimes the same part was in inventory under two or more part numbers. We spent hundreds of hours pulling drawings and looking up parts in the Illustrated Parts Breakdown (IPB) manuals. After a year or so, the Air Force came to realize what we already knew. It was a futile effort. We could reconcile about three parts an hour and it was estimated that the system errors were being created at a rate ten times that fast. The contract was cancelled and everyone working on the project was laid off.

During this time, I continued to attend regular day classes at Oklahoma City University and my wife worked as a secretary at the First Presbyterian Church in Midwest City.

Carl, a friend from college and I owned a Luscombe 8A/F high-wing monoplane together. We took turns working weekends at South Shields Airport fueling airplanes in order to pay our gas bill and the hangar rent.

Chance Vought

Founded by Chauncey Vought in the early days of aviation, Vought Aircraft had been a primary Navy aircraft supplier during WW II and Korea. Vought merged with Tempco, an aircraft parts sub-contractor who had built the little Swift aircraft. In the late 1950s a Dallas commercial electrical contractor, Jimmy Ling, gained controlling interest in the company. The reorganized corporation was called Ling-Tempco-Vought for a while, but soon shortened to LTV.

After four years of college and three years active duty in the military, I went to work as a design engineer for Chance Vought Corporation in the Human Factors Engineering Group, a pseudonym for Cockpit Design. Several other young engineers, some of whom I have remained friends with all these years, and myself all went to work there about the same time.

We all thought we were going to design the world's greatest aircraft only to find out that we were relegated to doing drawings of brackets for mounting hardware and writing technical specifications on various installations. Sometimes it took several hours for the hands of the clock to move between 4:15 and 4:30 quitting time.

The first aircraft I worked on at Chance Vought was the C-142 four-engine Vertical Take Off and Landing (VTOL) transport. There were only two C-142s ever built. The cargo plane had a tilt-wing with four turbo-prop engines. All four engines were tied together with a drive shaft running the length of the wing. The concept being that if one engine failed, the others would continue to power all four propellers equally. The aircraft could be flown with the wing in the standard fixed-wing position or it could lift off vertically with the wing rotated into the up position and then transition into wing level flight.

At best, the plane was unstable and underpowered. The prototype crashed south of Hensley Field near the shore of Mountain Creek Lake when something failed and the plane started to roll over on its side. The flight-test aircraft was equipped with ejection seats and the pilots both ejected.

Like many designs of that era, the C-142 lacked the control provided by the modern computerized fly-by-wire systems. The remaining C-142 went to an air museum. Northrop Aviation pioneered the building of flying wings in the late 1930's. The AAC withdrew funding for the design citing stability problems. Aero engineers are now able to design and build aircraft like the B-2 and V-22 due to computerized flight controls.

The Corsair II, basically a smaller F8U without a secondary after burner, was in design development, but not yet ready for production. So the second project I worked on was the French Crusader. LTV received and order for fifty F8Us from the French government. We assumed all the nomenclature on the aircraft would be changed to French, but when the French Air Force reps arrived, they told us it was easier to teach the pilots English technical terms than it was to ID an entire aircraft.

All the airframe drawings were done on white Mylar with dark green backing using a scribe. If mistakes were made, a kind of whiteout liquid was used to remove the scratch and a new line was scribed. This wasn't as bad as in the old days when they were scribed onto aluminum.

Some of the hardware we used dated back to the F4U Corsair. One time, I asked the blueprint crib for one of the old F4U Corsair drawings and they advised me that it would be a day or so before it could be retrieved from the archives. When I went to pick up the drawing, it was on a large piece of metal. I told them thanks anyway and I eventually found a drawing of the part I needed on microfilm.

Martin-Baker Seat

After both of these projects ended, I was assigned to work on an upgrade to the Martin-Baker ejection seat. The ejection seats currently being used were 100/100 seats. What this meant was that the aircraft must have at least 100 feet of altitude or 100 knots forward airspeed for the pilot to eject and the chute to deploy properly. The goal of the new project was to develop a seat with zero-zero capability.

In other words, if the aircraft was cranked up on the ground and burst into flames, the pilot could eject and be rocketed high enough into the air for the chute to deploy safely. Most of the testing had been completed at the Navy proving grounds and what remained to be done by the engineering group was to complete the drawings and specifications for the installation. I am sure my signature would still be on some of the old seat installation specifications.

The pilot had two options depending on how much time he had to eject. If there was a fire in the aft engine section, the pilot had several minutes to correct the problem, but if it was a fire in the compressor section, the pilot had less that sixty seconds to eject. The pilot could pull the lever between his legs or the face curtain handle located overhead. Sometimes, due to positive G-force, it was impossible for the pilot to reach the overhead handle.

The pilot had the option of manually releasing the canopy before ejecting, if there was time. Otherwise, a shotgun shell would blow the canopy a fraction of a second before the seat charge went off. If the canopy did not blow, the pilot had the option of ejecting through the canopy. The top lever had a face curtain and in this scenario, gave the pilot some protection over his face when ejected through the canopy. However, even with a crash helmet on and the seat hardware overhead, this was risky as it most always broke the pilot's legs.

The new zero-zero seat added a small rocket motor to the seat to boost the seat higher than the explosive charge could.

Part of my job was to read all the detailed reports of successful and unsuccessful pilot ejections that came in from the fleet, a large number of which occurred on carriers. We would then issue a service bulletin or warning to prevent subsequent failures of a similar kind, if appropriate.

Many of these reports were almost unbelievable. One such report described a Navy pilot who missed the tail-hook and upon applying full power, failed to get minimum airspeed for a go around. Just as his Crusader went over the side of the carrier, the pilot ejected. The carrier's crew immediately went into man overboard procedures. The crew could see the Crusader slowly sinking into the ocean as the carrier passed by, but no one could spot the pilot anywhere in the water. Then someone looked over the side of the ship and the pilot was dangling from his chute hung up on one of the ship's yardarms, the poles used for loading cargo onboard the ship.

The most fantastic report came in from a Marine Corps Major and read like the description of a Rube Goldberg invention. The pilot flamed out at high altitude somewhere out over the China Sea and could not get a restart. With no hope of returning to the carrier, he pulled the lower ejection seat lever and nothing happened. The problem was the firing pin cap for the canopy shell had not been screwed in all the way and had failed to make contact with the explosive shell. He could have elected to eject through the canopy, but opted not to. Next, the pilot manually released the canopy. If he had pulled the face curtain ejection lever at this time, his seat would have fired.

Convinced that nothing was going to operate, the Major unbuckled his harness, rolled his F8U over on its side and bailed out the old fashion way. The chute on the Martin-Baker ejection seats were packed extremely tight and designed for the weight of the seat to actually pull the ripcord, but the Major's seat was not attached. Falling at terminal velocity, he fed the chute out hand over hand. Finally, a few hundred feet above the water, he managed to get a squid, but the chute did not fully deploy before he hit the water. The squid broke his fall enough that he only sustained a fractured collarbone and bruises. Needless to say, that was one mad as hell Marine Corps pilot when he got back aboard ship and went looking for the seat-man.

Kennedy Assassinated

Most adults living at the time John F. Kennedy was assassinated recall where they were when they heard the news. I was sitting in a dentist's chair when Walter Cronkite broke into a regular daytime broadcast to announce the unconfirmed report President Kennedy had been shot. Several in the office commented that it must be a hoax, in other words disbelief.

Unfortunately, the rumor proved true and Kennedy died minutes later on the way to Parkland Hospital only a few miles from where I was at the time. Many Dallas people were amazed that martial law was not declared and that the area where the shooting took place was not cordoned off immediately. We do not apparently have that type of response capability then or now.

My friend Bobby and I were both NRA members and had fairly large gun collections. Both of us owned Italian Terni-Mannlicher rifles, the same exact model rifle that was used by the assassin. They could be bought mail order in good condition for $20. Bobby was an expert marksman and later tried several times to fire three rapid shots at a target about the same estimated distance with his rifle. He was not successful in consistently hitting the target, but the rifle he was using did not have a scope, as did the rifle used in the Kennedy shooting.

Rumors abounded among pilots and workers at Love Field that a pilot and a Bonanza with foreign registration was waiting at Southwest Airmotive and shortly after the assassination, a Cuban military officer boarded the plane and departed. The rumor probably had some basis in fact as it persisted for some time, but was never verified or publicly reported.

General Dynamics

Convair, short for Consolidated Vultee Aircraft, built planes during WW II, airliners and the B-36. Now affiliated with a submarine company back East, it was known as General Dynamics. The large factory was located across the airfield from Carswell AFB west of Tort Worth. In the mid-1960s, they finished building the B-58 Hustler. The B-58 was a minimum-crew, high-speed bomber designed to deliver a nuclear bomb carried in a pod under its belly. The B-58, like fighters of that era, required the crew to wear pressure suits and oxygen masks. Rumors were the B-58 was cancelled because SAC commander, General LeMay, disliked flying in a non-pressurized cabin, another urban legend I'm sure.

General Dynamics won the contract to build the new AF/Navy all-in-one F-111 fighter. All Navy fighter projects with Grumman were put on hold. The word fighter was a misconception from the beginning because the plane was more of a medium bomber. It outweighed a World War II B-17.

General Dynamics was hiring engineers at twenty percent over the market rate. Several of my buddies had already left Chance Vought and gone to General Dynamics in Fort Worth, so I joined their ranks. Roy, an AF bird Colonel now, had been one of the early project engineers on the F-111, but retired shortly before I went to work at General Dynamics.

I was assigned to the Environmental Design group. I knew nothing about the systems to be used on the F-111, but remember the engineer's credo, *Don't tell them you don't know what you are doing because by the time they figure that out, you will.*

The aircraft were to be assembled on the main floor called the mile-long assembly line. A half dozen F-111s were already in airframe jigs. The engineering design groups were located upstairs above the assembly line. The area was five acres in size filled with wall-to-wall desks and drafting tables lit by overhead fluorescent lighting. In those days, engineers wore the traditional uniform of dark slacks, white shirt and tie. Even wearing a colored dress shirt was considered in poor taste.

My first drafting board was located right at the top of one of the main stairwells coming up from the assembly area and I soon found out why no one else wanted it. Several times a day, a liaison engineer or lead man would hit the top of the stairwell with anger on his face and a death grip on a drawing that obviously didn't work. The first words out of his mouth upon approaching my desk would be, "Which one is this guy?" pointing their finger at the name on the inaccurate drawing.

Eventually, I began to handle these situations with a little humor. I would look up briefly from my work and point out over the several hundred desks on the floor and say, "He's the guy in the white shirt and tie just over there," and go back to my work. The shop guy with the problem would get a few steps away before realizing that he'd been had and generally would not return to ask for additional assistance.

Patent Rights

One of the projects entailed taking 2,000-degree bleed-air off the jet engine and rapidly decompressing it in order to provide air conditioning for the cockpit and avionics. Of course, it also involved routing a lot of ductwork and the installation of valves. The main decompression chamber off of the engine was located just below one of the main fuel lines. If the line were to leak and drip fuel onto the extremely hot chamber, it would probably ignite and explode.

They were not going to change the engine design so the problem was posed as to how to best insulate the chamber. After the theoretical engineers wrestled with the problem, I suggested there were only two materials commonly known that would stand up to those temperatures. They were silicone and asbestos.

The 3M vendor supplied me with some asbestos cloth and some spray-on liquid silicone. I laid out a pattern for an insulator blanket and took it to the upholstery shop. Luckily, I found an elderly lady who used to be a parachute rigger sitting at a sewing machine.

After getting permission from her lead man, I explained to her what I wanted. She proceeded to construct the blanket like she was following a Butterick dress pattern. With the blanket of asbestos completed, I sent it to the paint shop to have it spray-painted with the silicone. The blanket was baked, temperature tested and otherwise abused. It worked.

When signing a contract to go to work as an engineer with most firms, one signs away any claim to patent rights for work done on company time. A few months later, a full-page ad appeared in Aviation Week announcing the new 3M high-temperature insulating blanket material they had developed.

McNamara's Folly

Robert McNamara, Secretary of Defense under LBJ, was the one who had decided that the Air Force and the Navy would share the next generation of fighter aircraft jointly. This is the guy that gave Ford Motor Company the Falcon, in more ways than one.

The Falcon was to be the common man's car and boy was it ever common. The most ho-hum car ever built, with the possible exception of the Kaiser-Frazer's Henry J. This should have told us something about Mac's simplified designs concept.

The F-111 was grossly overweight and almost too heavy to land on a carrier. The Navy had requirements like tail-hooks for catching the arresting gear. The Air Force had requirements like large wheels for landing on unimproved airfield. The F-111 soon acquired the nickname McNamara's Folly.

Management began offering a bounty to employees who could suggest weight savings, in some cases as much as $50 an ounce. When we made a bracket to mount something, we drilled lightening holes in them to save weight.

It was, however, a no win deal to suggest a weight savings on one of your group's own installations as you would be told that it was part of your job. So the only guys who made out on the money thing were the stress group and the drawing checkers. Did I mention that design engineers hate drawing checkers?

Standard procedure for revising an engineering drawing was to issue an Engineering Change Order (ECO). The effectivity on each drawing was controlled by dash numbers and became a mystery unto its own. Our drawing effectivity system was complex.

The build of materials read like part -1 goes on AF1 and part -2 goes on NA1 and so on. In other words, each aircraft was being customized for its mission to the extent that we were really building two different models of the same aircraft design. There were days when all I did was write ECOs.

A Hundred F-111s

One Navy rep commented, "The F-111 is so heavy, it will go through a carrier deck instead of landing on it. The plane had been jammed down the Navy's throat politically and they were looking for an opportunity to cancel their part of the contract. At aircraft serial Number Five, the Navy finally managed to get out of the contract completely and re-entered into negotiation with Grumman Aircraft to build a new carrier-based fighter.

The order of the F-111s was finally reduced to only a hundred planes. Actually, the plane was a pretty good medium range bomber. With mid-air refueling, it could cover great distances to deliver its bomb load. The two-man crew cockpit could be severed from the aircraft in an emergency, which made high-speed ejection considerably safer.

During the bombing of Libya, the F-111s flew twelve hours to their targets. France and Spain would not approve the over-flight and the U.S. pilots had to take the Atlantic route around from England to complete their bombing runs. One aircraft was lost due to engine failure possibly damaged by Libyan anti-aircraft fire.

Technology had passed the F-111 by. It was too heavy and underpowered. While we were building the F-111, Northrop disclosed some of the new technologies they used on the A-11 Blackbird, the fastest airplane in the world. If some of the titanium technology used on the Blackbird had been applied to the F-111, it would have greatly improved the design.

Years later, my wife and I were at an air show and there was an F-111 on display. We went up under the aircraft and I was showing her the chamber and the insulator I had worked on when I realized that this was actually Air Force serial number one. It was the very prototype I had hand-fitted with the first high-temp cover. A young Air Force Captain stuck his head into the wheel-well where we were standing and said, "This is a classified aircraft. I'm sorry, but you'll have to leave."

My wife smiled politely at the Captain as we left.

Real Estate Business

While at General Dynamics, in order to make a few extra bucks, I started working weekends selling real estate. After a few months, I came home with my paycheck from General Dynamics and my real estate commission checks. I set my wife down at the kitchen table and showed her the checks for one month. My check for a month from General Dynamics was $650 and my real estate commission checks, working weekends, totaled $1500.

She looked at the checks then at me and said, "What you're telling me is that you are going to quit your job in Fort Worth." Thus ended my early years as a junior engineer.

Before long, I bought my first Lincoln Continental, a gunmetal blue sedan with suicide doors.

That winter, we took a vacation to Florida. Never before and never again have I felt as affluent as cruising down the Sunshine Parkway with the power seat rocked back in that Continental puffing on a fifty-cent cigar.

For the next few years, I built and sold houses in the Mid-Cities area of the Metroplex. The new DFW airport had been announced and investors were buying up every spare tract of land I could get my hands on to sell.

I got back to flying for pleasure again using a rented Bonanza or Skylane. For business, I'd occasionally use a plane to survey or show land for sale in the North Texas area and up at Medicine Park, Oklahoma. Our custom home building projects in the Stonegate Addition proved very successful for years, but in the late 1960s the real estate market cratered.

Artist's drawing the LTV C-142 VTOL cargo transport; Lockheed C-5A worked on in Marietta, GA; drawings of F-111 AF and Navy versions; 1963 Lincoln suicide door Continental and palm tree lined Florida Coast Boulevard; press releases and newspaper photos of C-142 and F-111.

Chapter Twenty-one
HAVE BRIEFCASE WILL TRAVEL

An expert is the guy who shows up with a resume' and a briefcase. An out-of-town expert is the same guy more than twenty-five miles from home. For the next several years, I worked as a hired gun, called job-shoppers in those days. The term did not imply shopping for a job, but its origin dated back to when jobs were sent out to a contract shop. Now days they are referred to as contract employees. Anyway, I had a briefcase, drafting tools and would travel.

Lockheed Aircraft at Marietta, Georgia was cranking up to produce the C-5A, the largest military jet transport ever built. Lockheed was hiring contract engineers for top dollar, so we left for Smyrna, Georgia, where I went to work once again in an Environmental Design Group.

Upon arrival at Lockheed, part of the indoctrination was to tour the full-scale static mockup. Looking out of the cockpit of the C-5A was like looking out of a third story window. Four greyhound buses, two abreast, could be parked inside the cargo bay of the large jet.

Lockheed was way behind on their engineering drawings. Some components were already being fabricated using preliminary drawings, but the contract called for pen and ink drawings on white Mylar. Every newly hired engineer spent their first two weeks trying to learn to draw in ink without it running under their ruler and smearing the drawing. Strips of masking tape under the T-square and triangles to hold them off the drawing surface were the secret.

Wong Way Mig-15

At Lockheed Marietta, I met a North Korean national named Wong. He was a graduate of MIT and worked in an unclassified position. He held the distinction of being the pilot who turned over the first MIG-15 to the U.S. Air Force. A lot of the engineers had very little to do with Wong, but I befriended him and to my benefit, he told me a lot of interesting stories.

He was born to an aristocratic family in North Korea and went to the Korean Naval Academy. When war in Korea was imminent, the Chinese demanded that Korean officers be trained by the Soviets. A government official assembled all academy cadets and officer candidates. He lined them up and had them count off by fours. Ones and twos were Army, threes were Navy and every fourth officer was assigned to the Air Force. Wong was a four.

After going through flight school, Wong was assigned to a squadron whose commanders were Russian officer pilots. His MIG squadron was based north of the Yalu River, the bases General MacArthur wanted to bomb, but was prevented from doing so for political reasons.

The U.S. Air Force dropped leaflets offering a large reward and political asylum to any North Korean pilot who would deliver a MIG to South Korea. The Russian officers had orders to shoot down any member of their squadron who made a break for the South during a mission. One afternoon, Wong found himself separated from his squadron and feeling no loyalty to the North Korean government, he turned south.

Two F-86D fighters quickly intercepted his aircraft. He slowed his aircraft and dropped the landing gear. These had been the instructions on the leaflet. He was escorted to a landing field in South Korea. The aircraft was turned over to the U.S. Air Force for study. To his credit, he refused the reward, but did accept a four-year scholarship to MIT and political asylum.

The First AWAC

While I was working at Lockheed Marietta, we rented a temporary apartment in the deep piney woods, but also purchased a small home in Winter Haven, Florida were we hoped to move eventually. I was commuting home on weekends.

The Lockheed Air Service Division at JFK International Airport on Long Island, New York obtained a contract to build the first Airborne Warning And Command (AWAC) aircraft. The earliest models used the C-121 Lockheed Constellation airframes. Later, they evolved into the now famous Boeing 707 AWAC version.

Lockheed Air Service desperately needed engineers with a secret clearance and offered to send me to Lockheed at JFK for more money. New

York was a *Great place to visit, but...* Available housing didn't exist and I was lucky to find a motel room at a weekly rate. My wife and daughter flew up when school let out. We visited Manhattan on weekends and enjoyed our brief stay, but we missed home. By home, I meant Texas not Florida.

The project was stalled and the lead engineer was over his head, so I gave my two-weeks notice to the job shop company. The shop asked if I would report to a job in Jersey the next day for more money than I was being paid at Lockheed.

When I first drove into New York and passed through a half a dozen toll roads and bridges, I recall thinking what if a person was broke, how would they ever get out of this place?

Speed Trap

Our minds were made up. We were going back to Texas, but we had to return to Florida first to sell the house. We headed back to Florida in the almost new Camaro Super Sport I purchased from a dealer in Fort Worth.

We stopped in Washington DC to visit Suzie's brother, a Naval officer who had been assigned to the Pentagon. Leaving DC, somewhere in Georgia, a patrol car pulled us over right out of a line of moving traffic. The constable told me I was speeding. Of course, mine was the only car with out-of-state plates. It was a speed trap, one of those old Southern traditions of deriving a little income from those passing through.

The constable ignored my argument that if I was speeding, then so was the entire line of traffic. He didn't say a word as he wrote out the ticket on what look more like a grocery store receipt pad. He handed it to me. The fine was $20.

I hadn't cashed my last paycheck and had been using a gas charge card. I fumbled through my pockets and my wife's purse, finally coming up with $17 and some change. I slammed the money down on the hood of my car so hard that some of the coins rolled off onto the ground. I told the constable that was all I had!

Without even cracking a smile, he took the ticket back from my hand, wet the tip of his pencil on his tongue, drew a line through the $20 and wrote $17. He handed the ticket back to me, picked up the $17 in bills, left the remaining change on the hood of the car, got in his car and drove off. True story!

VW Coast To Coast

As soon as we arrived back in Winter Haven, I put our small house with a screened in porch and orange trees growing in the yard up for sale. Kissing my wife good-bye, I jumped in the Camaro and headed for Dallas where I returned the Camaro and boarded the Braniff Red Eye Special to Los Angeles.

My brother moved to L.A. and had taken the red Volkswagon Beetle that I had co-signed for him. He had bought a Mercedes Roadster and no longer had any use for the VW.

After a couple days visit, I headed up the San Bernardino Mountains in the VW bound for Florida. The Pacific Ocean was in my rear view mirror. Seventy-two hours later, I would be almost to the Atlantic Ocean. No one has ever really had an adventure until they have driven a VW Beetle *from sea to shining sea.*

The hot afternoon sun beat down as I started across the Mojave Desert in the Beetle with no air conditioner. Whenever I could find a café or filling station, I'd stop and fill up a Dairy Queen cup I had with water. The cup fit neatly between the seat and the emergency brake handle. Dipping my handkerchief in the water, I would drape it across my head and in the few minutes it took to dry, it would temporarily cool my brain.

I had heard of mirages, but had never seen one. Cruising along across the sandy desert of Death Valley, I looked out across the wavy heat lines of the sand and saw a large lake. This was not good, I thought. As I got closer, a cabin cruiser came alongside me on the road. When my eyes finally focused, I realized there actually was a giant span of water out there and then I passed a sign that identified it as the Sultan Sea.

The old VW was doing about 80 mph with the accelerator on the floorboard. In my rear view mirror, I could see an old Chevy sedan coming up on me like I had that VW in reverse gear. When they went by me, it rocked my car and I noticed the car was loaded with what I assumed were Mexican nationals.

A short time later, I heard a siren. In my rear view mirror, I could see a highway patrol car gaining on me rapidly. Figuring that he was after me for running eighty, I slowed down to pull over. The patrol car went by me rocking my VW, as had the Chevy. It was then that I realized the patrolman was chasing the Chevy that had passed me earlier.

In Las Cruces, New Mexico that evening, I slept for about four hours in a K-Mart parking lot. The next day, crossing into Louisiana, I was passing through a small town and kept hearing a siren, but couldn't see a police car or ambulance anywhere. All I could see in my rear view mirror was a Cadillac sedan on my rear bumper. The driver was motioning me over.

A large gentleman in a gray Stetson got out of the car and I met him halfway. "Boy," he said, "don't you know a police car when you see one?" The gentleman who stopped me, it turned out, was the local sheriff.

Biting my tongue because I knew if I laughed out loud I was in trouble. "Nice car you got there," I said. I explained I was from Texas and not from California as the expired out-of-state plates on the VW clearly indicated.

I started to show him my ID, but he said he didn't need to see it, as he was a good judge of character. We visited for a while and then the Sheriff said he was late home for his supper. He told me to drive safely and have a good trip.

Later that night somewhere in Louisiana, I pulled into a roadside park. I was sound asleep when the beginning of the end of the world commenced. I finally fought myself awake and realized I had parked about ten feet away from a railroad track and a freight train was rolling past. That put enough adrenaline in my system to drive for the next dozen hours.

Early the following evening, I pulled up to my house in Winter Haven. Realizing I didn't have a door key, I rang the bell. When my wife came to the door, she looked at me and broke into tears. She hugged me and said I was quite a sight with those bloodshot eyes, wrinkled clothes and a 3-day beard.

Return To Texas

We sold the house in Winter Haven back to the builder we had bought it from. After renting a U-Haul, a tow bar for the VW, the California turnaround and paying off a bunch of bills, I was broke again.

With a ready-to-expire Enco credit card and no cash, we hit the road for Big D. Using the credit card at trucks stops I added a few dollars for cash to each fill-up. By eating five for a dollar McDonald's hamburgers and sleeping that night in the truck cab, we arrived in Dallas none the worse for wear. You can do things like that when you're young.

I stopped in Euless to check our old post office box. To my surprise, there was an income tax refund check for several hundred dollars in the box. We used the check to rent an apartment in Irving and I took a vow that very day that I would never be that broke again and I never have been.

It was now the height of the Cold War era. Space programs and government military contracts abounded and there was a great demand for engineers of any kind. Because I seemed never to be able to maintain a job more than a year or so without getting laid off, I became a permanent contract engineer.

The first job I was offered when I got back to Dallas was at Texas Instruments where I never figured out what the hell it was we were working on. One day, I just threw my badge on the desk and walked out.

Next, I went to work at Recognition Equipment Company in the Research and Development Department. They were designing the early prototype for what is now the post office optical reader system. The guy that founded the company had only one claim to fame, he had invented a remote control lawn mower. In my entire engineering career, never was I involved in building so many failed prototypes as I was at Recognition.

Beechcraft Wichita

We did leave Dallas one more time. I took a contract job at Beech Aircraft in Wichita. Beech was not used to running large engineering projects or prime government contracts like many of the larger aerospace companies. The cockpit design group was part of the electrical engineering group and both had a backlog of accumulated problems. The career employees were pensive about making decisions and stuck their head in the sand. Thus, they called in the out-of-town expert, me. I was assigned to review a series of electrical complaints with the Queenair and Kingair.

For example, the old style inverters used to generate three phase AC outputs from a DC power source were motor-driven field and armature type units. On the Kingair, the inverter was mounted in the wing near a fuel tank. A field report described an incident where there had been a fire from a small fuel leak in the wing. Suspicion was a spark from the inverter had ignited the fire. Fortunately, the plane was on the ground at the time and no one was injured, but there was extensive damage to the Kingair.

After reviewing the problem, I recommended that all Kingair be retrofitted with the new solid-state inverters now on the market. When Beech management estimated the cost of the retrofit, they squelched my recommendation. I sure hope they also burned my report because if there ever was a smoking gun, that was one.

On occasion, I would have a need to go to the corporate offices and would intentionally walk down the hall where Mrs. Olive Ann Beech's office was located. Her office was decorated in French provincial furniture and everything was done in pastel colors. Everyday, a vase of fresh flowers was placed on her desk whether she came into the office or not.

Walter Beech had been gone for several years when I worked there. The old timers in the factory told some funny stories about Mr. and Mrs. Beech. Seems ol' Walter had a weakness for pretty young girls and would hire them for a job, qualified or not. The details of which were hidden from Olive Ann, at least until she found out and fired the bimbo.

Gypsy Moths

While we were in Wichita, John Frankenheimer came to town to direct a movie starring Burt Lancaster called *The Gypsy Moths*. Burt went jogging on the school track behind our apartment every morning about 5:30am. The neighborhood ladies would get up early to go watch him. Not even Burt Lancaster could get my wife up at that hour of the morning.

On the weekend the filming was to wrap up, we went out to the little country airport where the movie was being shot to watch some of the aerial stunts. During the week, if anyone wanted to be a spectator in the air show scenes, they had to agree to wear the same clothes everyday, so we just watched.

It was the only time I had seen two aircraft with identical N numbers. The movie company had two DH Howards painted with identical red and white color schemes and the same side number, allowing then to film two scenes simultaneously.

289

Army U-21 WOG

The engineering group I was assigned to was also assigned responsibility for some problems with the military U-21 twin, designated the Ute. The Army and Air America were using these planes in Viet Nam. Air America was the front for a lot of clandestine operations in Southeast Asia at the time.

While they flew routine supply missions, they were also used extensively by the CIA and for transporting politicians around the country. The U-21 and U-22 were hybrids, part turbo prop Kingair and part non-pressurized Queenair.

The engines were rated for several hundred more hours than the service life they were getting out of them in the field. After talking to some of the Army pilots who leveled with me, I began to understand the problem and the supposed mystery became clear. There were air filters on the engines that were used to keep the dirt out of the intakes. These filters could be bypassed by use of an override switch for short field takeoffs, i.e., an unfiltered-air jet engine produced more power.

On the airfields in Viet Nam, snipers often shot at the aircraft. The pilots would bypass the filters with the override in order to get more power and a shorter takeoff run to get airborne and get the hell out a there. In fact, they left them in the unfiltered-air position most of the time. Wouldn't you? The result was a high intake of dirt and dust into the aircraft's turbo prop engines, especially during taxi.

In a conference between the Army reps and Beech, I proposed that we put a weight on gear (WOG) switch in line with the override switch. Thus, the filters would stay on during taxi and initial roll, but as soon as the gear strut expanded, the WOG switch would allow the bypass to operate and the aircraft could then develop maximum horsepower for liftoff and climb out.

Beech Flight Test

The new twin-engine Duke was undergoing final flight-testing at the time. The Duke was a pressurized, turbo-charged, reciprocating engine, light twin designed for speed. Tests were required to prove the Duke could make a short field landing loaded at full gross weight.

The top gun test pilot at Beech was known as a kind of hot rock and for showing off. I met him and I swear he swaggered when he walked. Anyway, he attempted to slow the Duke down and land it in shorter than required space. As he came over the fence, he was in a full stall and the tail hit first bending the rear fuselage. He and the copilot walked away, but I understand all of the sandbags onboard were DOA.

The new Model 36 was an extended cabin six-place version of the straight tail Bonanza and had recently been flight-tested and certified. The FAA had wanted the aircraft to demonstrate its ability to recover from a spin with the aircraft loaded at the full aft CG limit. On the first attempt, the aircraft never recovered from the spin and the test pilot bailed out.

Weber, who I had flown with several times, was the guy who had bailed out of the Model 36. He told me that he wrenched his back pretty bad when he hit the ground because he was looking up to see if the plane would recover from the spin by itself before it hit the ground, but it did not. From the Model 36 incident a long running joke developed.

After a pilot bailed out of a test aircraft, the pilot was called before a board of engineers to ascertain firsthand what had happened when the plane went out of control.

The first engineer asked what altitude had it occurred. The pilot indicated he didn't know for sure. The second engineer asked what the plane's airspeed was at the time. Again, the pilot didn't know that either. The third engineer, who had grown intolerant with the pilot's replies asked, "What were you doing at the time, looking at your watch?"

"Yes sir, I was. I figured some engineer would ask me what time it happened," the pilot replied.

Kansas Flying

During my first several months at Beech, I attracted some unwanted attention from engineering management. The department manager called me in and offered me a fulltime position at Beech. I turned the job down. We had bought a new home in Garland and didn't wish to relocate. This bounced me back under a group lead engineer who would have been under my supervision had I taken the offer. He made it crystal clear that he thought I was a prima donna and he'd welcome any opportunity to terminate me.

Knowing this, I had nothing to lose so whenever I could, I'd boogey out to the flight line, usually under the pretext of checking on something and jump in with one of the pilots going up to test-fly the new aircraft prior to delivery.

Flying with Weber one afternoon, I questioned him about aerobatics in a Model 35 like we were flying. He told me, "Any airplane is aerobatic if you keep the G-forces centered so that it won't overstress the airframe."

To prove his point, he put the Bonanza into a slow roll. This guy was so good, he could probably rolled the plane with a glass of water on the panel and not spill a drop.

Beech was producing the Model-99 stretched fuselage twin turbo-prop commuter for a growing market. I got a chance to fly the right seat in one with Weber. On the shakedown flight, we shot several instrument approaches over at Salina and then again at Olathe before returning to Beech in Wichita.

From 10,000 feet, Kansas always reminded me of one of my grandma's patchwork quilts. Except for where someone had planted and cared for them, there wasn't a tree on the horizon. I remember someone telling me one time the state tree of Kansas was a telephone pole.

On the east side of Wichita, there were three runways almost all in a line, Beech, Cessna and McConnell Air Force Base where Boeing was located. Needless to say, at times, the traffic got a little confusing. While I was in Wichita, there was a mid-air collision between an Air Force jet fighter and a Cessna. As I recall, the fighter was able to return to base, but the Cessna and its pilot were less fortunate.

It was fun working at the old Beech factory for the short time I did if for no other reason than the history and nostalgia that surrounded the place. I always thought it odd that three of the great pioneers of civil aviation, Walter Beech, Clyde Cessna and Lloyd Stearman all founded their aircraft companies on the plains of Kansas.

The Old Luscombe Plant

Upon returning to the Dallas area, I took a consulting job with Crescent Industries located in the old Luscombe aircraft facility in Garland. In fact, my first airplane might have been built there. Founder, Don Luscombe was a German national. When World War II broke out, the government confiscated his plant. After the war, Luscombe Aircraft was never really able to get back into postwar production and failed financially in 1949.

Crescent Corporation was building bomb casings and specialized armament for the Viet Nam War. Although I had been educated as an industrial engineer, this was the first and last time I ever worked in the discipline.

My prior engineering jobs had been in cockpit design and environmental systems. My experience in the Navy gave me a good foundation in electrical and electronic systems. Thus, as aircraft systems moved from mechanical to hydraulic and then to fly-by-wire systems, I learned avionics and computers the way the industry learned them, one failure at a time.

While in Wichita, I found out about volunteering to ferry aircraft from the Cessna plant into Dallas. I was able to build flying time and log a good number of hours ferrying aircraft. Beginning in the early '70s, I abandoned engineering completely in favor of fulltime flying. Over the next decade, I was airborne several times a week, in good weather and bad and it was then that I finally learned what flying was all about.

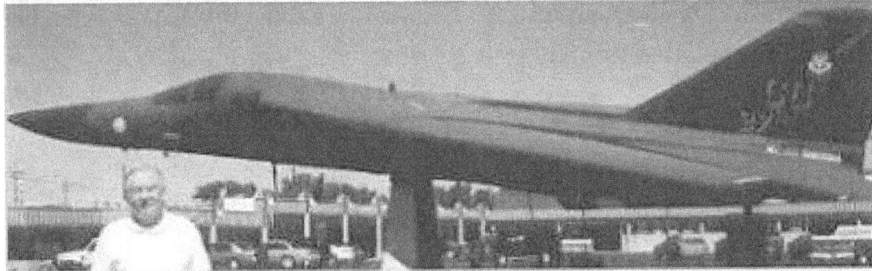

Laura hauling banana stocks on top of Camaro; California Volkswagon behind U-Haul headed back to Texas; two DH Howards with identical side numbers for filming of Gypsy Moths; brother Don enlisted in Navy and became a computer wizard for flight training; rare photo of Douglas C-67 Dragon version of C-47; retired F-111 at Cannon AFB; Bill Lear said, "When they want to advertise a car as modern, they photograph it in front of one of my twenty year old jets"; Suzie at Yankee AF with an F8U Crusader, she used to type the tech manuals for.

Chapter Twenty-two
AEROSPATIALE FACTORY

In the late 1960s, the management of the aircraft division of LTV, formerly Chance Vought, decided they wanted to get into the helicopter manufacturing business. I was not part of the company at that time and after their experience with the C-142, I often wondered why? LTV formed an alliance with the helicopter division of the French company Aerospatiale who built choppers for the military and for export to third world countries.

King Hussein, the ruler of Jordan and the current monarch's father, purchased and personally flew an Alouette helicopter built by Aerospatiale. The aircraft division of Aerospatiale also designed and built the SST in collaboration with a British aerospace company. The Shah of Iran ordered two SSTs for a new worldwide airline he planned to expand. The Aerospatiale commercial jet division developed and presently markets the Airbus, which continues to successfully compete with Boeing for a share of the airline passenger jet market.

Alouette, Lama & Gazelle

LTV eventually divested itself of their helicopter interests. French management being somewhat socialistic in their approach to business simply continued to operate the company under the name Aerospatiale Helicopter Corporation (AHC), which allowed them to continue having an inroad into the U.S. market.

AHC sold a few Alouette and SA315 Lama helicopters in the US, but only had a small share of the market, which was largely monopolized by Textron's Bell division. The Lama was a lifting platform or utility type helicopter and the Alouette was an antiquated military model similar to an early Bell Huey.

In the 70s, Aerospatiale introduced a civilian version of a military attack chopper called the Gazelle. The small, four-place helicopter was what a Jaguar is to a Buick Riviera. The Gazelle used a unique turbine blade tail-rotor called a Fenestron completely enclosed in the tail assembly and a three-blade rotor for less of a whap-whap ride.

When I arrived at the facility in south Grand Prairie for a three-month contract assignment, Eddie, an electrical engineer (EE) and avionics lead had just completed the certification of the Gazelle for IFR flight, a milestone in helicopter evolution.

New Facility

The AHC facility at Grand Prairie was located at the back of a large LTV warehouse north of the Grand Prairie airport. There was no ramp for the helicopters so we used a portion of the chain-link, fenced-off south parking lot. In order to get the helicopters in and out of the warehouse being used for assembly and maintenance, they had to be lifted by a small elevator to the loading dock level and then into the warehouse.

Eddie had only a liaison type and a contract draftsman working for him in the avionics engineering group when I arrived. We had a two-room hut with two drafting tables and desk on the floor of the assembly line. Eddie's boss CJ was the Director of Engineering. CJ along with other upper management staff were located in another building complex across the way. AHC was a fast growing organization, but still small enough that most everyone knew one another.

The first time I met the president of the company, I was doing a layout at the drafting board and this older gentleman walked in our shack and struck up a conversation. We visited for a while and when he left. I remarked to Eddie, who was coming in as the gentleman left, "Nice guy. Who was he anyway?"

"The president of the company you mean?" Eddie replied, "Yeah, he's a great guy to work for."

Eddie had a desk over at corporate and worked between there and the assembly hangar. The avionics liaison guy stayed out on the floor most of the time running down missing parts and our trusty draftsman seldom showed up at work on time and when he did, he usually wasn't sober enough to draw a straight line.

There were plans underway by management to build a new facility just south of the present location on the west side of the Grand Prairie

Municipal Airport. The Bell Customer Training and Delivery Center was located on the west side of the Arlington Municipal Airport a few miles to the west.

One of the conditions of the lease agreement with the City of Grand Prairie would be that the large drainage ditch would remain between the new AHC facility and the airport's FBO. Thus, preventing any type of aircraft other than helicopters from utilizing the west side of the airport. Ironic indeed because only ten years prior to this time, I had held the lease on the fixed-wing FBO facility at that very airport.

Helicopters

A heavyset Italian fellow, a mechanic who often taught training classes, claimed that helicopters don't really fly, they just beat the air into submission.

A helicopter owes a lot of its stability to gyroscopic action, not unlike the same stability provided a moving motorcycle. Many early aviation pioneers attempted to build and fly a successful rotary-wing aircraft. Even Leonardo da Vinci made a drawing of an airscrew several hundred years before the concept was actually tried.

A Russian American by the name of Igor Sikorsky figured out that the input to the spinning rotor was 90-degrees out of phase unlike others who had tried and failed. With this knowledge, he built and flew the first controllable helicopter. This can be demonstrated by spinning a toy top on a table and touching the top with your finger. The result is that the top will move ninety degrees out of phase to the direction it is pushed.

After being around helicopters for a while, most rotary-wing aircraft can easily be identified by the approaching sound. A two-bladed or 2-per revolution (rev) rotor like on a Bell has a whapping sound. A 3-per rev, like on the Astar has a smoother sound and the 4-per rev like on the Puma has a steadier more powerful sound. By the time you get to the 5-per rev like on the small Hughes helicopters it starts to sound more like a giant hummingbird fluttering through the sky.

For me, a guy who never liked helicopters and never even wanted to transition to them when I was in the Guard, there was a certain irony that I was now helping to build and equip them. Don't get me wrong, I believe in a strong national defense, but I always had a twinge of guilt building

297

combat planes knowing the mass destruction of which they were capable. At least now I was part of building aircraft for peaceful development.

Each year AHC attended the annual Helicopter Association International (HAI) convention. The first HAI I attended was held in Atlanta. The demo helicopters were flown in and out of a parking lot behind the convention center, but we had to return them to the civil airport for fuel and overnight parking.

Our pilots would struggle to get our large helicopters onto a committed approach pattern for the parking lot, but those darn little Hughes helicopters would come darting in and out of the parking lot like hummingbirds, sitting down wherever they chose.

Commuting to the convention center each morning in the Atlanta traffic was certainly not a problem. I'd catch a right-seat ride with one of our pilots, tree topping all the way with the bumper-to-bumper traffic below.

Astar & Twinstar

France had perfected a design called the Starflex rotor-head. It was a state-of-the-art, three-blade rotor assembly made of extremely strong composite materials. For years, Bell had stuck to the two-blade rotor design pioneered by their founding design engineer. The Bell design had trouble with vibration and fatigue and on rare occasions, the Bell rotor would hit the locks and cause catastrophic rotor-head failure. However, in lawsuits by survivors, mostly military veterans' families, Bell claimed excessive abuse to the aircraft.

The vice-president of marketing, a fellow named LeFluer had been a helicopter pilot in Viet Nam. He came up with the idea of designing and marketing a reasonably priced six-place jet helicopter, basically a streamlined fiberglass shell around the already proven technology used on the French military choppers. This concept became a marriage of convenience between the American facility and the French manufacturing company.

AHC had just begun receiving the first shipments of the newly designed and developed Astars from Aerospatiale France when I arrived onsite. The Astars were shipped with the unpainted airframe complete. The Grand Prairie facility installed a Lycoming jet engine and then fitted the airframe with the options ordered by the customer such as avionics, custom interiors and air ambulance equipment.

Although the American facility considered itself a manufacturing plant, it was more of an elaborate modification and customizing center. With the introduction of the Astar, marketing received orders for 600 helicopters, which back-ordered the assembly line for three years. The bulk of the orders for new helicopters were destined for oil exploration operations, mainly offshore drilling companies.

The Astar sold in other parts of the world were completed in France and had the French made Ecureuil engine. The French name translated to *squirrel*, which did not have the same unique connotation in French as it does in English. Aside from the name, the little engine enjoyed a reputation of being reliable.

The early installations of the Lycoming engines experienced several incidents of engine failures resulting in forced auto rotations. This caused delays in the delivery of the Astar during the first two years, so a few of the early American Astars were delivered with the Aerial engine.

Whatever the reliability problem with the Lycoming engine was, it was eventually resolved and also became a dependable power plant. Engine failures prompted a demand for a twin-engine version of the Astar called the Twinstar and the twin-engine Astar was introduced a year later. The Twinstar failed to be delivered in as great a numbers as the Astar, most likely due to the increased cost of the twin-engine model.

Presidential Puma

The President of Mexico ordered three Puma helicopters to be custom fitted with executive interiors and the latest commercial avionics. One of the three Pumas we eventually delivered to the Mexican Presidential fleet would be loaned to the Pope when he visited and toured Mexico several years later.

The job I was hired for was to custom design the instrument panel and flight deck avionics on these three Puma helicopters. The Puma was AHC's top-of-the-line turbo jet helicopter based on one of the most successful French military designs. Its twin-engines developed 3,200 horsepower and the Puma was the absolute Cadillac limousine of private helicopters available.

Jim Creighton, a great pilot and fine fellow had been a corporate pilot for LTV before becoming Director of Flight Operations at AHC. We got along well and whenever possible, I would fly copilot on the Puma test flights. The first time Creighton let me fly the Puma I took the controls at cruise with a good forward air speed. The Puma handled much like any of the light, fixed-wing twins I had been used to flying.

As we returned to the landing pad and I began to slow the Puma down to approach the landing pad, it became less of an airplane and more of a flying gyroscope. I knew to add rudder for lateral directional control and how to lower the collective.

Instinctively, I eased back on the stick like I would in a fixed-wing aircraft landing, as we were about to touch down. I had also been holding a little collective so as to touch down easy. The Puma slowed to a zero forward airspeed and started backing up like an old cow pony after roping a calf.

Creighton looked at me and said, "You know there's a chain link fence back there don't you?" He pushed the stick slightly forward, dropped the rest of the collective and the large Puma settled gently onto the ramp.

Eventually, I overcame my apprehension of approaching a full stall and falling out of the sky like a rock after a few more flights.

After about three months of preliminary design and layouts for the President's Pumas, we were ready to present the final proposal to the Mexican Air Force. The proposal included color weather radar provided by RCA and a Sperry flight director system. The order was quickly approved and the go-ahead given.

The President's personal pilot and flight crew arrived at our facility for avionics and flight training for the first time. It was at this time that I first met *Cap-e-tan* Chicone.

In the classes I instructed, the chief disappointment to the Mexican pilots was that the actuators on the flight controls could not be coupled to the flight director. The helicopter had to be manually flown by the pilot observing the flight director.

The French contractor that built the autopilot actuators for the Puma had not provided for electronic inputs from flight directors. They were eventually forced by market demands to build such an actuator, which were eventually retrofitted onto these three Pumas, the Golden Nugget and other Pumas.

Puma Avionics

These Pumas would have the distinction of being the most elaborately equipped helicopters built to date. The VHF communication and navigation equipment was Collins Pro-Line. The avionics was rack-mounted with remote control heads like the latest airline aircraft.

I designed a custom audio switch box system and sought out an outfit in Coral Gables, Florida to custom build them. Cables Engineering traced its avionics history backed to building radio panels for the old Pan American Flying Clippers.

An Omega navigation system, built by Canadian Marconi, was installed. The seven powerful Omega stations positioned around the world transmitted on ultra-low frequencies (ULF), which followed the curvature of the earth. AHC had no equipment for skin-mapping to identify the best location for antennas. Previous trial and errors had determined the best location for VHF COM and NAV systems, but no one had any idea where to place the antenna for the Marconi system.

Early one morning, I was walking around the Puma trying to decide where to put the Omega antenna when my eyes fell on a removable panel just below the pilot's rudder pedals. If this location didn't work, it would not be an extensive repair to patch or replace this non-structural panel. Handing the small round flush mounted antenna to a sheet metal mechanic, I instructed him by pointing and said, "Mount it there."

After the Marconi Omega installation was complete, the Puma was towed out on the ramp and we fired up the ULF. Channeling through the station signals, we received every station in the world except the one in Tokyo while the helicopter was still parked. Once airborne, even the Tokyo station came in. The latitude and longitudinal positions were accurate to within a quarter mile. This doesn't compare with what modern satellite (GPS) systems can do, but was darn good for those days.

The avionics installation on the first Puma to be delivered to Mexico was completed and we began extensive testing of all the avionics and electrical systems on the aircraft. Unlike some of the smaller helicopters that used only 28-volt DC systems, the Puma had a lot of three-phase AC voltage that would bite. However, even the 28-volt systems had enough amperage to burn you real good when shorted out. I quickly got in the habit of not wearing jewelry around them.

With the Hobart ground Auxiliary Power Unit (APU) plugged into the Puma, we were running the avionics systems in the hangar. One of the electricians had just finished installing a circuit breaker in the overhead switch panel and dropped a lock-washer. What were the odds of it rolling into the electrical bay next to where I was working, but it did. It was like sitting next to five Roman candles going off.

The washer fell exactly across the contacts for the APU solenoid, the only circuit without a fusible link or breaker protection in the whole aircraft. That ol' Hobart APU just hunkered down and kept on supplying power.

The Hobart was parked about 12-feet away from the aircraft. Other workers in the hangar kidded me later about only touching the hangar deck one time between bailing out of the side door of the Puma and hitting the power-off button on the Hobart.

During the time the first Puma was under going flight-test, it was parked on the ramp outside the chain link fence. The aircraft were usually towed to the warehouse/hangar through the fence by a tug. The weather bureau called saying that a severe thunderstorm with a possible tornado was headed our way.

Creighton took off running for the Puma with me right behind him. He cranked the Puma and lifted it about 200-feet in the air and asked if I thought that new color radar we had installed could pick up the heavy cells. I was already turning the radar on when he asked. Creighton pointed the Puma's nose directly at the storm and held it in a hover against the wind. We painted the actual red cells in the center of the storm.

Creighton landed the Puma on the loading dock lift. The waiting line crew pushed the Puma into the hangar with us still in the cockpit as the first few hail pellets started to fall. I'm not sure I would've trusted jumping that fence into that narrow loading lift with any other pilot except Creighton.

First Puma Delivery

When we completed the first Mexican Presidential Puma, it was sent off to the paint shop with patches and primer all over. I hadn't given any thought as to how the Puma might be painted. When the Puma came back, the ugly duckling had become a swan.

The Puma was painted off-white with wide brown stripes trimmed in gold. Both sides of the Puma and the tail boom were painted with a giant multicolored serpent. From an earlier trip to Chichen Itza in the Yucatan, I immediately recognized it as Kululcan, the feathered serpent god of the Mayans.

Chicone was one of those flamboyant, jovial people. He would have been successful in any endeavor he undertook, in any language and any country. He and several other pilots returned to Grand Prairie to pick up the first Puma that was ready for delivery. Chicone had a roll of $100 bills that would choke a horse and a shopping list a foot long.

When the Puma was ready to depart for Mexico City, we could barely get the door closed as it was loaded with exercise bikes, microwave ovens and cases of all kinds of goodies from K-Mart and Wal-Mart. I think it's referred to as diplomatic privilege.

Helo Mexico City

After the three Pumas had been delivered to Mexico, there was a request to modify the VHF transceivers to accept .25 MHz frequencies. The Collins equipment that had been installed already accepted those frequencies and so all that was needed was a minor modification to the control heads. Additionally, one of the Loran systems needed to be replaced under warranty.

Instead of sending a technician, I elected to go to Mexico City accompanied by my wife. Deplaning at the Mexico City International Airport, we were walking toward customs when a Mexican Air Force Major introduced himself and asked for our luggage claim check, one of which was for the new Loran. He handed them to his driver and instructed him to pick up our bags as he escorted us around the long customs clearing line. Didn't even get a souvenir stamp on my passport.

My wife and I were dropped off at a luxury hotel in La Zona Rosa, which I think means Pinkies. The well-kept hotel still had cracks in the hallway walls from an earthquake that occurred only a few days before our arrival. I was told an officer would be assigned to escort me back and forth to the International Airport to the *Major de Presidente*, main hangar.

The Pumas were housed in one of two large executive hangars with several medium and large corporate jets belonging to various government agencies. Lieutenant Aguilar was assigned to accompany me throughout my stay. The first thing I did was take the control head panels out in order to modify the channel changer. When I asked for a soldering iron, the first one they brought me had a one-inch head that could have been used to solder sheet metal.

The control head modifications were accomplished in quick time and the Loran unit exchanged. The rest of my visit was mostly social calls with the unit commander and training for some of their mechanics. I found words like tape and screwdriver are the same in Spanish as English. Just pronounce them with an accent and/or add a long O on the end.

The next day, Chicone and I took one of the Pumas for a test flight. Chicone let me fly after we were airborne. As he was checking out all the frequencies he asked, "Anywhere you want to go?" I pointed to the smoking volcano to the south. Chicone laughed and waved his hand for me to go ahead on.

We circled the volcano and headed back to Mexico City. It was interesting seeing the large city from the air as it spreads across an entire valley. The air pollution was far worse than any I had ever seen in Los Angeles.

Legend has it that the founders were told by prophecy to settle in the place where they came upon an eagle sitting atop a cactus with a snake in its beak. This is the symbol seen on the Mexican flag and coins today. The place this occurred was on a dry lakebed in the giant valley of what is now Mexico City.

On the last evening we were in Mexico City, I asked Lieutenant Aguilar to escort my wife and I to dinner and requested that we go somewhere that tourists would not normally go. Aguilar replied that he knew a very nice restaurant in the city, but that I would not particularly care for the part of town where it was located.

We stopped by the military barracks where he checked out a sidearm and shoulder holster to wear under his jacket. We then went to pick up a young Air Force WAF, his date for the evening. The evening was uneventful and the nightclub style restaurant where we dined that evening was exceptional by any standard.

AA Boeing 707

The next morning, we were delivered to the airport terminal and were graciously thanked for our visit. My wife and I boarded the waiting American Airlines Boeing 707. There were only about a dozen people onboard. My wife was the only female on the flight. As the pilot cranked the engines, the pressurization system gave out this awful gasping noise and the pilot shut the engines back down. The Captain came into the cabin and announced there would be a slight delay while some repairs were made.

It was Sunday morning and there were no regular mechanics on duty. The two linemen who boarded the aircraft scratched their heads and said they would have to call another mechanic that was off duty. The Captain was a wiry old gentleman with a white moustache who reminded me of Sam Houston. He had probably been flying for American since the DC-3 days.

The Captain told the two linemen to get him a screwdriver. He knew what the problem was and he would fix it himself. The Captain explained to us that some seats would need to be removed and one of the floor-plates pulled up. As it turned out, there was not a man onboard that was not either an engineer or tech rep. In about five minutes, we had the carpet up and the floor-plate open.

The ol' Captain dropped down into the hole while the copilot cranked the engine. After a few minor adjustments, the pressurization gasped one last time and came on. The floor, carpet and seats were quickly replaced and our flight back to Dallas was uneventful.

Pictures in and around the development hangar at Aerospatiale and avionics flight-test offices; Dolphin instrument panel is a dummy mockup of new Dolphin to be shown at HAI. Aerospatiale Puma, one of three custom built for President of Mexico; instrument panel with first color weather radar ever to be installed in helicopter; insignia on side is of Kukulcan the serpent god.

Chapter Twenty-three
AVIONICS TO COMPUTERS

The AHC engineering department consisted of two sections under CJ, the Director of Engineering. The mechanical engineering group was supervised by a chief engineer, but closely overseen by CJ. My group, the avionics and electrical section was more autonomous. Eddie, the Chief of Avionics Engineering was working on the proposal for a new U.S. Coast Guard search and rescue helicopter based on the Dauphin model 365, designated the 366.

With little or no supervision, I started working on whatever custom commercial orders came through. When the Coast Guard awarded the contract to Aerospatiale, Eddie was transferred to the newly formed government division, which resulted in my being promoted to Chief of Avionics Engineering.

Aerospatiale France was ready to release the commercial version of the Dauphin 365. The plan was to introduce the Dauphin at the next HAI convention in St. Louis. France shipped us a mock-up fuselage, which the upholstery shop finished with a plush interior. Working with all of our vendors, I acquired the latest avionics control heads and displays available and had them mounted in the dummy instrument panel and console.

For the static display, we installed a cabin stereo system and played the theme music from the movie *Superman,* a popular movie at the time. The mock-up passed as a real cockpit, except to the most discerning eye. It was a big hit on the floor of the convention. A 36-inch framed photograph of the mockup cockpit, which was given to me by the Flitephon vendor, still hangs in my office to this day.

The avionics group had a much closer relationship with the aircraft assembly area and flight-test than did the mechanical group, which primarily designed interior and structural modifications. The plans for the new facility on the west side of Grand Prairie Municipal Airport were being finalized and I was able to get the avionics engineering offices built into the main hangar adjacent to flight-test. This was a real coup on my part, not having to be located in the new corporate office building on the other side of the assembly area.

Chief Avionics Engineer

With my promotion to replace Eddie, my duties quickly broadened to cover all of the commercial helicopter models. The Pumas would remain my personal favorite of the fleet and I did most of the design work on them. Not being real keen on the Astar and TwinStar line, I promoted one of my newly acquired avionics types to lead man over those two aircraft, only reviewing the planned installations prior to starting the projects and signing off on the drawings before being released.

Aerospatiale did not really have a good drawing release system, so I implemented a standard drawing sign-off and ECO procedure. Of even greater value for delivery and support was a system of configuration control drawings, which I implemented, a top drawing that referenced all of the sub-installations. A drawing package was compiled and shipped with each helicopter.

Relations between engineering and marketing were poor at best the first year I took over the department. Basically, the sales people and demo pilots didn't know what to tell the customers what options were available. So I assigned Bill, my best draftsmen, the task of making a series of simple three-dimensional drawings of various optional avionics packages.

Bill, a contract draftsman, had worked as a truck driver before learning mechanical drafting. He had a gift for being able to visualize how a thing would fit and then put it down on paper. A description of each of the installation packages was added and I assigned an option number to the drawings.

These info sheets, complete with a drawing of the option were copied and placed in a three-ring binder for the sales people to carry with them. For the first time, they were able to make an informed presentation to the customer on available avionics options. Needless to say, this made us real heroes over at marketing. Not only did our orders for custom avionics installations increase, but the profits also followed as everything we quoted had about a forty percent markup. The end result was that the avionics portion of the company was no longer overhead, but a self-supporting entity.

Building Capability

The next thing I set out to do was hire some really good employees to add to the department. The first two people I hired were a clerk by the name of Gail and a circuit designer by the name of Bruce.

It is difficult to recall Gail, one of the most organized employees I have ever had, without recounting the story of her purchasing a new Toyota. Several of the engineers were having fun kidding her about the headlights being slant-eyed and one of them told her that the shocks were made of bamboo. That noon, when we were all leaving for lunch, we caught Gail bending down looking under the front end of the car with skepticism.

What we really needed was a good circuit and theory man. Eddie, an EE met those requirements, but he was busier than a one-arm paperhanger with the Coast Guard installations.

Although trained as an industrial engineer, I had picked up electronics over the years both in the Navy and on various engineering jobs. However, I knew my shortcomings and heavy circuit design was certainly one of them. A HAM radio license had been no problem for me. I had passed and held KA5WKL for years. The second-class radiophone license was another story entirely. I flunked the written exam the first time.

At my request, employment put out a search for a designer and Bruce applied. Bruce had been managing a Cessna dealer's avionics shop in Texarkana. When he came to work for me, Bruce remarked several times that he thought he knew me from somewhere. Of course, he did because we had met briefly in the Navy and we had talked on the phone about some warranty claims when I worked for Cessna, but I held off telling him exactly where he remembered me from.

Several of us from the avionics group joined the Avionics Electronics Association (AEA). The second AEA convention that we all attended was held in San Francisco. Bruce had worked for me about a year by that time. On the first night of the convention, there was a cocktail party and reception at the host hotel on Embarcadero. Both Bruce and I had already had a couple of martinis when Bruce said, "I just can't get it out of my head that I know you from somewhere."

It was time to put an end to my little charade. "Bruce," I said, "You really don't remember me, do you? Think back to 1961 when we sent the NAS Dallas reserve VP squadron to the A-bomb tests in the Pacific." Bruce began to smile as I continued, "I was the aircrew training instructor that assigned the crews and when you were late the morning of departure, I was the guy who grabbed your bags and ran for the last P2V on the ramp with you and boosted your young ass onboard."

Bruce yelled out, "Yes! That's where I remember you from, why you sorry..." He laughed so hard he spilled his drink.

Fixed Vs Rotary Wing

The FBO at Conroe, Texas was doing additional modifications on some Astars for an offshore oil-drilling operator, a regular customer of theirs. Our mechanical group was assisting on the project, but none of their designers held a pilot's license.

On occasion, the company would rent a Piper Cherokee Six and I would fly some of the group down to Conroe for the day. Conroe Airport sat right in the middle of the Piney Woods and was hard to find. The best way to locate the airport was with an ADF as there was a low power marker located on the field.

The young low-time flight instructor who had to check me out in the Cherokee Six said, "I'm a little embarrassed to be checking you out," when he handed me back my pilot's license with all the ratings which he did not have.

Reflecting back on this, I can recall that during routine flight checks when asked to demonstrate a stall, it was always difficult to force myself to stall the aircraft when my subconscious was telling me not to let this happen. Those who learned to drive on a manual shift car can remember how at first they would jump the clutch and the old car would lurch forward. Then after having driven for years, shift smoothly without even thinking about the process. Man and machine become one after a period of time and thus the controls of the aircraft, like other devices, become an extension of our own bodies.

A jet helicopter rented for about $650 an hour at the time and the insurance for a low time student pilot cost… well, if you had to ask you couldn't afford it. So logging solo flight time and going for an FAA check ride were financially out of the question. Even though I was not jet helicopter rated, most of the pilots were pretty good about letting me fly. It was also nice to have one of the experienced Viet Nam veteran chopper pilots along with me anyway because I would have been hard put to make an autorotation under 1,000 feet AGL.

In an autorotation with a failed engine, the pilot allows the rotors to coast on descent and just before touchdown the pilot must add collective for lift. This is similar to an engine-out glide to landing in a fixed-wing aircraft, but requires practice as once up collective is applied, rotor speed decreases rapidly. Timing and coordination was the key.

There is always one large boisterous know-it-all pilot and ours was George, a real hot rock. He was always buzzing the hangar and things of that sort. George and Eddie were personal friends and in fact, they owned a sailboat together. Ol' George didn't like me and indicated it at every opportunity. I was in good company, as I don't think he liked anybody that showed a dislike for his flamboyant style of flying.

Without intending to, I had embarrassed him badly one afternoon. A new IFR Gazelle was ready for delivery and needed its final flight-test. These tests were flown over on the Meacham Field ILS. George was the pilot scheduled to make the test flight and as this was one of the last IFR Gazelles we would deliver, I asked to go along and observe.

Inbound on the approach, George was all over the sky trying to intercept the ILS and once even executed a missed approach. Heading back around for another approach, I suggested that he let me shoot the next one. I got lucky, it happens, and I nailed the approach all the way down.

What made matters worse was one of my junior engineers was riding in the back seat and witnessed the whole thing. I wouldn't have mentioned it, but my engineer blabbed the story all over. After that episode, hot rock George refused to fly any check-rides with me and I had to get one of the other pilots. George eventually killed himself. I was told his helicopter had gone into a lake up in the Seattle area, but it was never clear exactly what had happened.

News Helicopters

The Astar, although it had some early power plant problems was a fairly dependable aircraft. Most crashes were due to pilot error and not mechanical failure. The local Dallas radio and TV stations were all starting to want their own eye-in-the-sky reporters, more for prestigious reasons than public service.

Some of the radio stations used the cheaper non-turbine engine brand of helicopters. WFAA, the big-dog TV station in Dallas, had to have the best, its own brand new Astar.

My wife was friends with the wife of the EVP at the Dallas Morning News, which owned the TV station WFAA. However, I am sure this had nothing to do with their choice of buying an Aerospatiale instead of a Bell Helicopter.

One very early Sunday morning, my home phone rang and it was Herb, the VP of manufacturing at AHC. He explained that I needed to drive out to a location south of Cedar Hill where an Astar had just crashed. The FAA and NTB were already on site conducting an investigation of the crash, but had requested additional AHC factory representation.

When I arrived on scene, there were no parts big enough to identify as being a reasonable facsimile of a helicopter. The largest chunk of metal on the ground was the core of the jet engine. The crash debris was, however, contained in less than an acre of land. It was immediately apparent that the helicopter had gone almost straight into the ground.

The weather was overcast that morning. The pilot had likely been flying under a low ceiling and gotten into the clouds. Thankfully, the mortuary had already removed two bodies, that of the pilot and of a female accompanying him. It was not very pleasant picking through the wreckage and occasionally coming across things that I would rather not discuss.

The young pilot flying the WFAA chopper may have been instrument rated, but the apparent cause of the crash was the old suicide spiral. More than likely, the pilot had lost orientation and made a left turn straight into the ground. It doesn't take long traveling at a hundred miles an hour to cover the distance of a couple of hundred feet in elevation.

Buck Stops Here

An Americanized Frenchman by the name of Orsetti was our Executive VP at AHC. Because my group worked closely with the manufacturing floor, it was not unusual when the company bid a new contract to receive a call from Orsetti or even from the VP of Marketing under the pretext of it being a social call. What they really wanted to know was if I though we would be able to meet the proposed delivery schedule.

In a frame over my desk alongside some photos of various models of aircraft hung this saying "I'm an engineer. I don't blow the whistle and I don't drive the train, but let the darn thing jump the track and just see who they blame."

My boss CJ and I always had a good working relationship. He claimed he didn't worry too much about piling new stuff on my department because if we didn't know how to do it, by the time we finished the project, my avionics gang and I would have figured it out.

I was over at corporate one day in the men's restroom and one of CJ's mechanical engineers was obviously hacked off about something. He began unloading all his complaints about the engineering department and management on me. As luck would have it, I consoled the guy by halfway agreeing with some of his complaints, but added no criticism of my own.

Later that afternoon, there was a phone message that CJ wanted to see me in his office. When I arrived at his office, we discussed some of the various problems facing the department, but I remained confused as to exactly what the meeting was all about. As I got up to leave, I am certain that I must have had a puzzled look on my face.

CJ grinned and said, "You know when you're in the restroom it might be a good idea to watch what you're saying or at least consider who might be in one of the stalls." I was almost out the door before I caught on and started laughing.

HAI In Las Vegas

The year that the HAI convention was held in Las Vegas, I was assigned to the convention floor to assist marketing with avionics questions, but they had plenty of help and I wasn't doing a lot of good standing around. AHC, along with the other helicopter companies, were giving demo flights to potential buyers in a couple of our helicopters. I managed to slip away from the convention center and headed out to the airport.

The old Starship facility on McCarran Field, which I mentioned in an earlier chapter, had finally been converted to and FBO as I predicted. We were operating our helicopters from there. When I arrived at the airport and located our motor home, chaos reigned. People were just walking out to the next arriving helicopter and climbing onboard.

I took the waiting list from the hand of the inundated flight department secretary and sent her for cold drinks and ice. Next, I screened the waiting crowd and divided them into two groups, the potential buyers and those after a free joyride. It was easy. I just asked a couple of simple questions like, "What type of helicopter do you own now?" or "Which model have you been considering for purchase?"

I gave the legitimate prospects a priority number and asked them to wait in the air-conditioned terminal lobby and enjoy a soft drink or their beverage of choice. I asked the secretary to hold the prospects there and visit with them until I called on the walkie-talkie to send the next group to me at the motor home. I turned away the tire-kickers saying we were booked, gave newly arriving prospects a number and sent them to the lobby. I did recognize a couple of fleet owners and expedited them like high rollers. What the heck, we were in Las Vegas.

When we had a light passenger load and someone I knew was a buyer, I'd hop in the back seat and ride along giving them a sales pitch as we flew around Las Vegas, down the Strip and over Glitter Gulch. It was a heck of a lot of fun flying over Las Vegas at low altitude, especially at night.

That evening, after one heck of a busy flight ops day, I told the chief pilot I would be going back to the convention center the next day. "No way!" he replied, "You're coming back out here tomorrow and help us!"

Its Color Coded

French engineers are a breed all to their own. About the time we began working on an idea for a product improvement on one of the helicopters, miraculously all of a sudden, the French engineers would be working on the same problem and they would ask us to stop. It got so bad I started not releasing any drawings until we had them fully developed.

For example, a lot of the harnesses we installed for avionics equipment were very similar. A lot of wiring and a little bit more weight was being added to each aircraft due to all the multiple runs of common wires like grounds.

To solve this problem, I laid out some of the most common harness drawings and started marking them up to see how much wiring could be eliminated. By adding prefabricated harnesses that could be installed in the aircraft we could connect the avionics through a common junction box. This was not a new concept. Boeing had been doing it for years. On our drawings, we specified a Mil-Standard (MS) cannon connector.

Word came down form management that the lead avionics engineer, my counterpart from Aerospatiale France, would be arriving in a few days to show us their newly developed version of a common avionics connector for harness installations. Most of the French engineers who came to AHC spoke English of a sort, but communication more or less ended there. The standard answer to any problem posed to a French engineer was "No prob-liem!"

A couple of my engineers and I sat down with the French engineer when he arrived and he began to explain the connector design which they proposed to install in the Astar and Twinstar.

The MS connectors that we were proposing were keyed. In other words, they could only be connected one way. The first thing we noticed about the French connector was that it could be connected 180 degrees out. Bruce asked, "What if the mechanic plugs the connector in upside down? A hot wire could be connected to a ground wire and short out the system."

The Frenchman replied, "Ah, but it is color coded!"

My other engineer asked, "What would happen if a mechanic was working in the dark?"

Again the Frenchman replied, "Ah, but it is color coded." After a dozen similar questions, which all received the same reply, we thanked the gentleman for his time and took him to lunch. A little wine solves a lot of problems.

The standing joke for some time after that when something didn't work was to simply say, "Ah, but it was color coded."

Another example was when our avionics vendors introduced their new lines of digital displays referred to as *glass cockpits*. The flight director

HSI, DG and other readouts were integrated into (CRT). The Dauphin 365 commercial aircraft were being delivered with elaborate interiors to compete with the new Sikorsky executive helicopter line, the Dauphin's competition.

France contended that there wasn't room in the 365's panel to mount a CRT. Bill, my best mechanical draftsman, did some layouts showing how the system could be installed at a slight angle to the existing instrument panel. As soon as I told marketing we could do it, word came down for us to stop work and to send our layout drawings to France. Within a few weeks, the French released their version of the all glass cockpit for the Dauphin. "No prob-liem!"

Computers Have Arrived

My wife was on staff at the University of Dallas, so I took the opportunity to enroll, at no charge, in the MBA program. Attending UD night and weekend classes, I began to get the feeling that I should be teaching the classes instead of attending them. The one class I did enjoy was a computer management class. This class gave me access to the mainframe Hewlett-Packard at the university.

Bernie, a math professor at UD and friend, got me a cradle-type phone modem and a workstation terminal to use from home so I could sign onto the university's computer. This was in a time when my TI home computer used a cassette drive for data storage and my Apple computer at work used a 180k floppy.

After one year, I dropped out of the MBA program, mostly for lack of interest, but I had maintained a 4.0 grade average. Having never done that before, I thought I'd just quit while I was ahead. Besides, Peter's Principle had set in on my engineering career a long time ago.

Last Helicopter Show

The last HAI convention I attended before leaving AHC was held in Anaheim. On a free afternoon, my wife and I had gone over to Disneyland. We were walking down Main Street when I heard the distinctive pronunciation of my name, "*Mar-veen,*" being hollered from out of the crowd somewhere. I would have known that voice anywhere. Looking around, I spotted *Cap-e-tan* Chicone with his family and entourage up from Mexico City.

We visited about old times and he told me about the Puma that had crashed some months back. The Puma and another helicopter were taking off from a dusty baseball field crowded with spectators. The rotors kicked up so much dust that the visibility went to zero.

The two choppers clipped rotor blades. Both helicopters went down, but due to a rotor out-of-balance condition, the Puma went over on its side resulting in extensive damage to the Puma and several fatalities.

Time To Move On

A longtime engineering friend of mine named Jerome applied at AHC to go to work in the mechanical group after being laid off at Bell. He and I had started as junior engineers at Chance Vought together and had crossed paths several times over the last twenty years and I gave him the highest recommendation.

Jerome had studied to be a Catholic priest, but ended up getting married and having six kids. Why he ever wanted to be an aeronautical engineer (AE), I'll never know, but he was a good designer and above average in mathematics. He put all six of his kids through college working as an engineer.

New helicopter sales were starting to taper off by the mid to late '80s. I had been at AHC for the better part of a decade and began to think in terms of *been there, done that*. There was one opening for a project engineer at corporate, but it was going to involve a lot of traveling.

One of the delivery pilots held an AE degree and was a former Viet Nam chopper driver, he was also being considered for the position. Even though he did not have the years of experience I had, he was younger and more energetic. I was sure he was the best candidate and would do a better job. I withdrew my name. In my gut, I was starting to think about leaving AHC even though I was well on the path to becoming a VP. Corporate management just never had been a serious goal of mine.

It has always seemed retirement is wasted on the old, we should retire when we're 50 and then go back to work and work the rest of our lives. So I decided to do just that. I took a year off to restore an old 1942

Continental Coupe, which I had been trying to find time to work on for years.

When I did give my two weeks notice at AHC, I guess upper management was pretty well blind-sided. There really was no one to replace me. CJ asked if I'd stay an extra month while they reorganized the engineering department and I agreed. Three years later, AHC merged with BMG and/or some other helicopter company. I understand that many of the older AHC engineers and managers were offered employment buyouts.

Over the years, every so often, the phone would ring and it would be Bruce, Jerome or one of the other designers I worked with calling just to shoot the breeze. Sorry to say, I've now lost track of most of them.

Hand In Avionics

During the next couple of years, I kept my hand in aviation engineering by serving on the board of directors for Terra Avionics in Albuquerque. Terra's hottest selling item was a hand held aircraft transceiver. The company was in an excellent position to move into the King and Narco market, but the management was reluctant to move into the TSO certified market.

A Technical Standard Order (TSO) certified that an item had gone through FAA and FCC compliant testing for use on IFR aircraft. I obtained a TSO for Terra and did some design drawings for some low-end, non-TSO avionics for Terra. I also purchased some surplus audio switchboxes and marketed them.

Collins Radio had a low-end avionics line called Microline and most of the units were TSO. Collins decided to discontinue Microline and I negotiated with them to buy their patent rights and remaining inventory for only $160,000. At the same time, Mr. King, the founder of King Radio retired. The new acting president of King was a real jerk. He got wind of my offer to buy out Microline and offered Collins a merger. Of course, King's management trashed Microline immediately after getting control to squelch the competition with the low-end King radios.

Dal-Fort was the overhaul and modification center at Love Field that used to be part of Braniff Airlines before they went bankrupt. Dal-Fort, now on it's own, did a lot of work on old Boeing airliners for various non-scheduled air carriers. Mainly they did interiors. Some of the jobs required rewiring a lot of the old avionics harnesses and I worked there on contract a short time doing some re-wiring diagrams.

Those old jet airliners had been modified and re-modified several times. Anyone who has ever worked on a modified Boeing aircraft can appreciate what a nightmare it was trying to trace wiring through pressure bulkheads when the diagrams no longer agreed with what was in the aircraft. If there were an award for Rube Goldberg aircraft wiring, the winner would have to be one of those old modified Boeing airliners.

French SE Fixed-Wing

Aerospatiale France had a couple of reps at AHC who worked for the civil aviation single-engine, fixed-wing division. This division built and marketed a little four-place, low-wing GA aircraft. Their marketing approach was really poor. After I left AHC, I contacted the VP of Marketing at Beech.

Beech management indicated a real interest in marketing the Aerospatiale light single-engine aircraft in the US. In fact, they might even consider discontinuing their low-end Aero line, if something could be worked out. Production costs were making the line unprofitable, but they needed an alternative product to market through their Beech Pilot Center dealerships.

Two guys, representing themselves as upper management from Aerospatiale France, flew into DFW for a meeting. I refused to divulge my contact until we signed an agreement. The Frenchmen continued to pump me for information, but I declined to divulge anything until they gave me a letter of intent. Our meeting broke up, as did their marketing aspirations in this country. You can always tell a Frenchman, but you can't tell him much.

DynCorp Fort Worth

One very hot summer afternoon while I was out in my garage working on one of my old cars, the phone rang and it was Bruce. He had left AHC and was working for DynCorp on a night vision modification project on the C-141 Lockheed Starlifter and C-5A. Odd that I would revisit the C-5A I had worked on in Marietta after it had been in service for lo these many years.

Seemed that DynCorp in Fort Worth, the contractor on the project, was desperate for people who held recent secret clearances and I was one. The hourly rate they were offering for this short-term project was extremely attractive. I signed on to the project knowing that my wife and I were planning to move to the Texas Panhandle as soon as she completed the school year. Bruce had rounded up several of our old AHC group and we completed the major portion of the project in short order. In fact, we worked ourselves right out of a job. I spent the rest of my time with DynCorp supervising the Computer Aided Design (CAD) group and learned the discipline myself.

The manager was a former Navy supply officer whom everyone referred to as Captain Queeg behind his back. This was the last aircraft-engineering job I ever worked on.

While I was at DynCorp, a car dealer and old car buff friend of mine by the name of Blessie was involved with the Kruse collector car auctions in Dallas. He called and asked if I could write some computer software programs for the auction company and for his three used car dealerships. One day I was studying the software I had designed and realized that with minor variations the programs could be made generic. From that, I launched a business software company, which was a leader in its field for almost two decades.

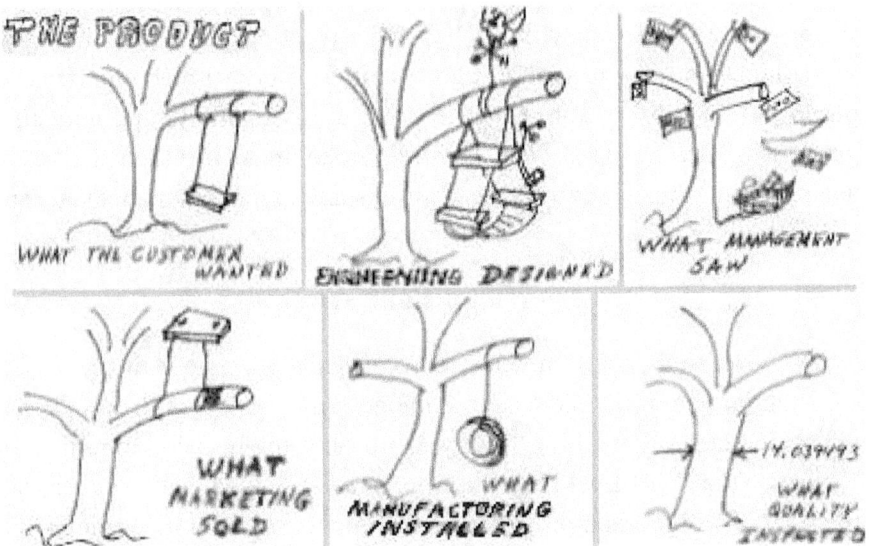

THE PRODUCT

WHAT THE CUSTOMER WANTED | ENGINEERING DESIGNED | WHAT MANAGEMENT SAW

WHAT MARKETING SOLD | WHAT MANUFACTURING INSTALLED | WHAT QUALITY INSPECTED

Chapter Twenty-four
AIRLINE TO AFRICA

A book of flying stories should include a chapter on our amazing world airline system. So this is about my airline flight to Africa. Visiting with our mission pastor on a Sunday morning, I commented, "Tim, I sure wish I was going with you and your group to Africa next week."

I guess it was just one of those things I was supposed to do because on Tuesday, the phone rang and it was Tim telling me he had made me a reservation to go on the trip. How was I to tell my wife of forty plus years, that I was off to Central Africa for three weeks to visit the David Gordon Medical Center at the Presbyterian Synod in Livingstonia, Malawi?

At Barnes & Nobles, I purchased a map of Africa and looked the place up in a travel guide. There were only two paragraphs on Livingstonia. The village sat atop a high plateau overlooking the eleventh largest lake in the world and described the place like something right out of the movie *Shangri-La*.

Carrying a small backpack with my camera, some personal items and one change of clothes, I donned a broad-brimmed, floppy safari hat I had been saving for just such an occasion and boarded a plane at Amarillo airport for the first leg of four flights to the interior of the Dark Continent. My American Airline flight to DFW joined me up with part of our group and we would meet up with the rest of the group in Detroit.

My journal began, "It is Sunday, the first of June about 4:30 in the afternoon. We are somewhere over Arkansas aboard Northwest Air Flight 696, high over a white cloud layer. There is rain forecast for the eastern United States, which may be a problem as we are tight on time to connect with our flight to London. Our Fokker-100 jet is a plane I've flown in several times and like. The air is rough now and a little hard to write." The trip was to be a milestone in my life experience and my journal ended up being sixty some pages when typed up.

Arriving at the Detroit airport, we had only twenty minutes before our London flight was to depart and of course, our connecting flight would leave from a terminal a mile away. I flagged down a golf cart for the less youthful of our group. We threw our hand luggage on and the younger ones took off running.

At the departure gate, I remembered I had left my favorite sweater behind. As I took my seat, I watched as a phantom hand with my sweater reached through the door and gave it to the steward, as he was about to shut the door. That ol' wash-n-wear knit sweater had taken many trips with me.

It was drizzling rain and almost dark as we taxied out in the large DC10. Passing behind rows of airliners parked at their gates, the fluorescent and neon lights from the terminal and the lights on the jets flickered by my two-story-high window seat.

The scene reminded me of something like *fly our friendly skies to paradise* right out of the movie *Blade Runner.* We were packed in like sardines. Northwest was not known for its roomy seating on international flights. My new seat partner, in a row of nine seats across with two aisles, was an attorney from Ohio who worked in Poland. A movie showing on the forward bulkhead was out of my view, but I wasn't interested.

Short Night

My journal continued. "It is the middle of the night Monday morning, June 2nd and we are flying somewhere over northeastern Canada. I can make out the outline of a large body of water by the sparse community lights along the shoreline. The pilot just announced we are cruising at 33,000 feet and will be arriving in London at 10:00am local time, that will be 4:00am in Texas."

An hour later, we were still over land. I could see the occasional cluster of community lights through a thin cloud layer. Odd, it had never occurred to me that when flying from Dallas to London, two-thirds of the flight was over land.

The North Star was a little ahead of our left wing, so we were still on a slight northerly heading as we passed over Newfoundland and out over the north Atlantic. I thought of Lindbergh in his small Ryan monoplane droning on into the night.

322

Checking our direction of flight by the stars reminded me of a joke between my daughter and I. On a trip to Ohio, Laura was driving as we headed east out of St. Louis. Passing through some construction, we were all visiting and missed seeing the detour sign or notice the setting sun had moved from our rear window to our left windows. Sixty miles up the Interstate to Chicago, we discovered our error so, *if the sun is setting in your left window, we must be headed for Chicago.*

Flying on into the night, only the dark blue-black of the Atlantic Ocean was below. The northern horizon was silhouetted by a bright glow. I wondered if this might be a light refraction from Polar ice caps or the sun's glow on the other side of the earth. Not the low and slow kind of flying I had done all of my life. This was the realm of high altitude flight.

Not having any success taking a nap, I remembered I had forgotten to say the short simple prayer I always uttered when I was piloting the plane and pushing the throttles forward for takeoff. I closed my eyes and softly said, "God grant us safe passage." My pocket watch was still on Texas time and it was past midnight in Amarillo. Suzie had probably just gone to bed.

In the Navy, on those twelve-hour patrol missions in the old P2Vs, I could sleep at my flight station and awake when called on the radio, but maybe I was a little younger then.

I found some big band music on the stereo and finally dozed off. Sometime later, I awoke with a crook in my neck and figured out what those C-shaped air pillows the experienced air travelers had around their neck were for.

From my window I could see the first light of morning on the horizon up ahead. The sky was turning from shades of deep blue to orange and magenta. Short night!

Atlantic In A Single Bound

Most of the morning, the Atlantic had been covered with a low cloud layer, but it began clearing and I could see the open sea. I looked for ships cruising on the ocean, but at 36,000 feet, a ship was just a speck. As the coast of Ireland came into view, I thought again of Lindbergh and how he must have felt at the sight of land.

The display screen on the bulkhead was showing we had traveled 3,470 miles. Looked like I would rack up some air miles on my Perks card. It doesn't take long to cross Ireland at 640 mph and we were soon on approach through scattered cloud layers into Gatwick airport south of London. On final, we came in low over several quaint little English villages with narrow roads that wound through well-kept, old two-story brick row houses.

Taxiing to the gate, I saw a Boeing 767 with green, yellow and black stripes, Zimbabwe national colors, parked on the ramp. I assumed it must be the plane that would take us to Harare.

London was about a thirty-minute trip by Express train ride from Gatwick and we arrived at Victoria Station in the heart of the city. We spent the day touring London atop a red, double-decker bus and had fish and chips in a local pub.

Ed and I returned to Gatwick early to check on our flight scheduled. We found no Air Zimbabwe ticket counter. We'd been kidding for days about the non-existence of Air Zimbabwe airline because when we called the 800 number, no one ever answered.

About an hour before departure time, a British Air ticket agent arrived with an Air Zimbabwe sign under her arm and placed it on the counter. After clearing customs, we waited in a high-priced shopping mall lobby to board our flight.

Amazing Machines

There were plenty of empty seats on the large plane and by raising the armrests between the seats, we were going to be able to stretch out and get a good night's sleep on this flight.

Shortly after sunset, in a light drizzling rain, our 767 taxied out, rolled down the runway and climbed out through the dark gathering rain clouds. I could see the lights on the coast of France as we crossed the English Channel.

My thoughts were of the WW II B-17 crews that crossed this channel on their missions of destruction against the Nazi empire and of the Luftwaffe and Third Reich's guided missiles that crossed back to rain down destruction on London. I am thankful that these magnificent large jets did not exist in those years.

There were ten attendants to serve a half-full airplane and it quickly became obvious that we were no longer in the hands of the Europeans. Even the airline captain, a tall clean-cut man, was black-African. There was reggae music on my stereo headset and the magazine print advertising was distinctly different.

They did not throw away the used soap bars, but placed them back in a paper cup. As I would soon learn, the people of Africa wasted very little. The less you have, the less you waste.

The night was dark. We were flying high above a heavy cloud cover obscuring any sight of the terrain below. We were served a dinner catered by British Air. By the middle of the night, most of our group was stretched out asleep. I often pasted the time trying to reason with God like Tevya in *Fiddler on the Roof.* But, I had bought one of those neck pillow thingies at Gatwick, propped myself up against the bulkhead and dozed off instead.

Flight To Africa

In the middle of the night, I came wide-awake, got out my journal and began to write. "It is 10:00pm Monday at home and Tuesday, June the 3rd 3:00am London time. I have just come to the sudden realization that I am suspended in an aluminum tube, 35,000 feet in the air somewhere over the continent of Africa!"

The time in Zimbabwe is plus seven hours from Texas, only one more than London as we were traveling mostly south and only a little east. Zaire, to the east of where we were headed, had just ended a bloody civil war and renamed the People's Republic of the Congo. Didn't we call it the Congo when I was a kid?

Soon after sunup, we would be landing in Harare, the capital city of Zimbabwe. I reasoned that we were now south of the equator. I had never been south of the equator before. I've always heard water goes down the drain counter-clockwise in the southern hemisphere, so I got up and went to the restroom.

Now this is funny. After washing my face, I filled the basin with water and pulled the stopper to watch the water go down the drain. When it went straight down the drain, I thought how stupid. All my years of working on aircraft and I forgot it was suction that drains the water in a plane and not gravity.

The only other person awake in the cabin with her light on was our Ph.D. nurse, Virginia. We discussed briefly the Larium tablets we were taking as a prophylactic against malaria. She was concerned about some rough air we had experienced awhile back. It woke her and several others up. She knew I was a pilot and asked if the rough air was anything to worry about. I told her unless things started floating around in the cabin with us, there was no need for concern and went on to explain we had probably passed over an arid part of Africa and the turbulence had been caused by warm air thermals rising up from the ground.

The sun was full up when we were served breakfast of ham and eggs about forty-five minutes out from landing. On the way back from the aft cabin, I stopped to visit with a white-African fellow returning from a business trip to London. Most of these folks spoke with a thick British accent even though born and raised in Africa. He smoked a cigarette as we talked. It was allowed on Air Zimbabwe, as tobacco was a main cash crop.

Looking out my window from time to time during the night, I hadn't seen one lighted city. In the morning light, I could see a few dirt roads, some small towns, a strip mine and cultivated areas. There was a light ground fog in the low-lying areas as our Boeing 767 approached Harare Airport and landed.

I got the feeling I had gone back in time. The aircraft parked on a large open ramp and we deplaned down an airstair rolled up to the door like Dallas Love Field in the 1950s. We hiked across the tarmac to the terminal building and a quick walk through customs consisted of little more than a stamp on my passport. Tomorrow we would depart for Lilongwe.

Remains Of Colonialism

That night, we stayed at the Bronte Hotel, a place right out of 1920 British colonialism. Sitting on the back porch of the Bronte, looking onto a well-kept garden that evening, I struck up a conversation with an interesting fellow. I assumed by his manner of dress he was a quintessential great-white-hunter. As it turned out, he was a retired Australian farmer who traveled the region with others on what he called a walkabout.

A walkabout into bush country for several days was more akin to a photo-backpacking trip. On this particular trip, the Aussie was after black rhino. He explained how his group of six walked with a guide in front and a native gun bearer in back in case of a wild animal attack. It was illegal to hunt the black rhino. They were extinct in most parts of Africa, killed off for their horns, a valuable bounty sold to the Japanese who made highly sought after potions from the horn. A few black rhino still thrived in a valley not far from Harare.

The Aussie told how the big cats in this part of Africa died off from a disease similar to one that kills the common house cat. The panthers that survived were now plentiful, but most were not large enough to attack a man. They did, however, come into towns to kill chickens and small dogs for food. My conversation with the Australian gentleman was rewarding and I listened with great interest to his experiences in Africa.

I shared the panther story with others in our group and whenever I would go for a walk and someone would ask where I was going, I would smile and reply, "I've got a poodle on a rope and I thought I'd go trolling for panthers."

"Wednesday, June 4th and we leave for Malawi today." My metabolic clock had already adjusted to the local time zone and I woke up minutes before my wakeup call.

We each must purchase a $20 exit stamp to leave. Free to come in, but costs to get out. On the ramp sat a vintage Boeing 707. We hiked across the tarmac and boarded the plane. I kidded Tim about how old the plane was and that they weren't even used in the U.S. any longer. I explained how hard a four-engine plane was to control with an engine failure and about my crashing the 707 flight simulator at the American Airline training center.

As we rolled down the runway for takeoff, the seat tray in front of Tim fell off on the floor. I laughed and pitched it over in the corner. Finally, Tim begged for mercy asking me not to explain any more about flying to him. It was a short, quiet, pleasant flight from Harare to Lilongwe.

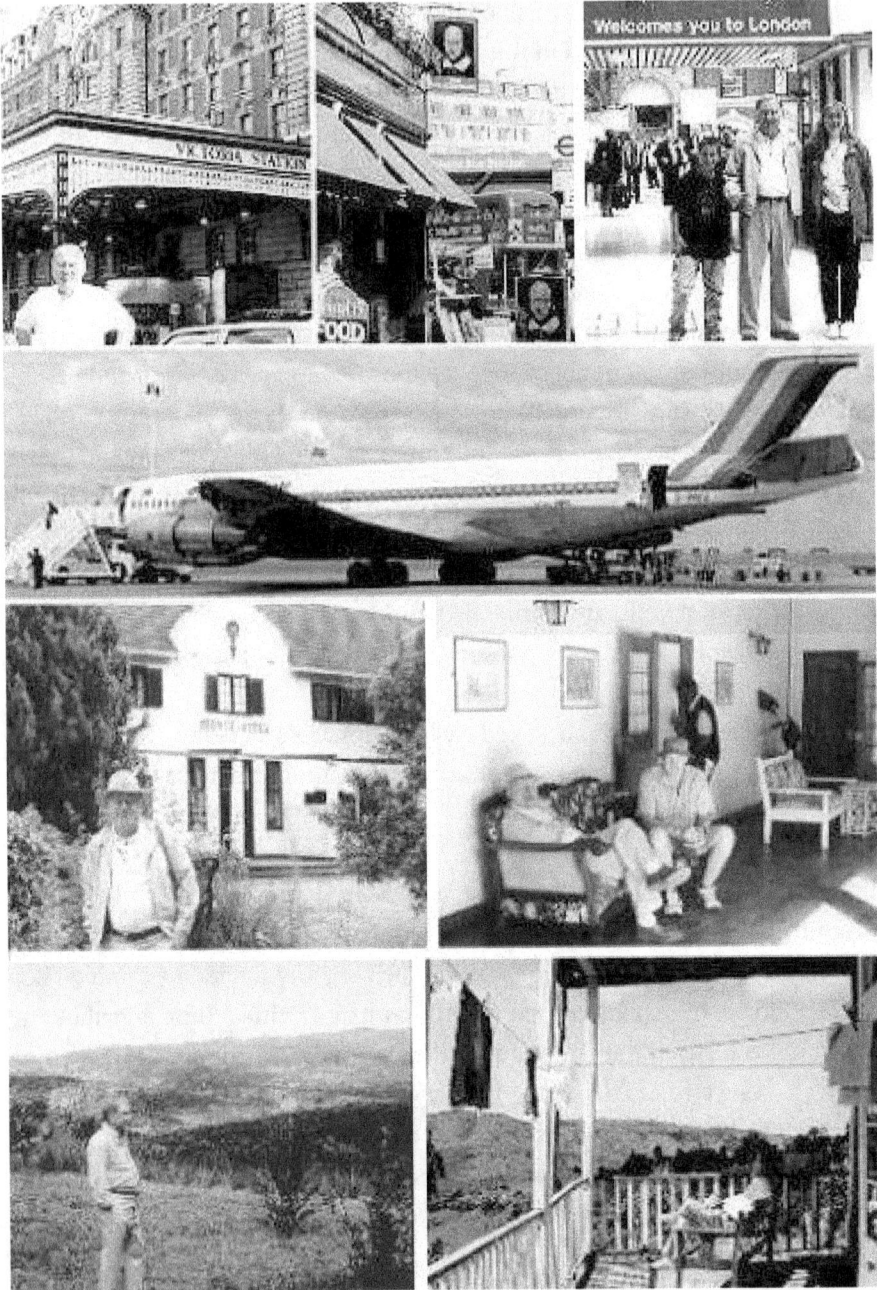

Arriving at Victoria Station in London; Air Zimbabwe airliner being loaded on ramp at African airport; Bronte Hotel; Great White hunter in Harrah off on a walkabout; Livingstonia in the mountains of Malawi.

The Real Africa

At the Lilongwe airport, we boarded a small Isuzu bus we chartered and headed north to Muzuzu, a village at the foothills of the dormant volcanic mountains along the Great African Riff.

It will suffice to say, my visit to Africa was one of the great experiences of my life. I wrote most of my journal by taper while in Livingstonia, as there was no electric lighting.

The humor of this may escape you, but whenever anyone asks me to describe what modern rural Africa was like, I reply, "Were you ever in Oklahoma in 1940?"

I will omit the details of our stay in Livingstonia and our work at the turn-of-the-century David Gordon Hospital save for this one brief anecdote.

While walking down a dirt road one afternoon, I met an elderly man and he stopped me to visit. He pointed to a distant hilltop. "See that high place. I was born there sixty years ago," and added he was a Christian.

"I'm a Christian too, an American. Pleased to meet you."

The old fellow smiled and said, "Oh yes, I know you white-man Christians. You are the ones who stand still when you sing."

Traveling to Africa was one of the great experiences of my life. The day we left, many of the villagers came to say goodbye and to say how sad they were we were leaving. At the time, we were only thinking about going home.

Returning to Lilongwe, we had dinner and spent the night at a Portuguese hostel. Early the following morning, I was awakened by what I thought was someone playing a loud radio, but it was a citywide loudspeaker system broadcasting Moslem morning prayers.

On Safari

We had about 36-hours before we were to fly out. After some repairs to our Japanese bus, Tim explained to the bus company manager we wanted our driver to take us over to neighboring Zambia to a wild life game park on the Zambezi River. A Dutchman who worked for KLM and his wife offered to pay their share to ride along. It was about a four-hour drive, but our driver had never been there before. Using a hand drawn map, some memorized instructions in kilometers and the bus's odometer, I eventually got us on the correct rutted and full-of-potholes road.

In mid-continent Africa, the nights are about as long as the days and it was soon very dark with no moon. I could see Saturn on the horizon, so we were headed generally in the right direction. We stopped once on the dark road for a wee-break and several teenage boys appeared out of nowhere. They asked for cigarettes. Out of luck as no one in our group smoked.

I gave the boys the last of some chocolates I had been saving and they assured us we were on the right road and indeed we were because we soon saw our first sign indicating the game park was up ahead. More and more animal's eyes glowed in the bush from our headlights as we passed by.

We arrived to a cold dinner served in a large wood-beamed, thatched-roof hut complete with a bar. The hut was open on one side where a bonfire was burning in a pit that overlooked the riverbank. Most of our group went to bed down in the bamboo huts provided. Ed and I got a couple of beers and went to sit by the fire. Cries of strange animals came from somewhere in the distance and occasionally my eyes focused on one of the hippos grazing on the dry riverbed below in the dark.

The night sky was clear and the stars shone brightly in the cool evening air. We were both too tired to talk, so we just sat there enjoying the fire as it slowly faded to glowing gold embers. I stared out across the darkened floodplain and said to Ed, "You know, it don't get any better than this." Ed grunted in agreement. Sleep came easily that night.

At sunup, two large, open-top Toyota Land Rovers and guides were waiting to take us to the wildlife park. There was some hot tea, but no breakfast till we would return three hours later. Our guide said to call him John, as we wouldn't be able to pronounce his real name. He headed down the dirt road to the Luangwa Game Park where we came upon a modern concrete bridge that crossed the Zambezi River into the park. It was not even the rainy season and the river was still a quarter mile across.

Stopping on the bridge, we watched as hippo floated in the river. At a distance, they appeared to be large rock outcrops on the river. Below the bridge was a crocodile whose head alone was at least four feet in length.

Winding in and out of high grass and wooded areas, we saw herds of impala and stopped to admire a forty-foot in diameter baobab tree. We saw lots of gazelle, warthogs, waterbucks, monkeys and tropical birds. We came upon a large open area that I realized was a well-maintained dirt airstrip. John told me that it was for charter planes to land, but was seldom used.

I didn't want to go home with a lot of nondescript pictures of animals in the bush, so I'd step out of the Land Rover occasionally and ask the Dutchman to take my picture with some animal in the background.

Returning to the camp for brunch, we asked the camp cook to bake a birthday cake for Bree who turn seventeen that day. I can only wonder what the icing was made of, but it was sweet.

There were a large group of baboons foraging in the dry riverbed below our camp. I took my camera and walked towards them. Most ran, but one large male stood his ground. One look at those K9 teeth and I said to heck with the photos and retreated.

Lion Is Still King

Late that afternoon, we boarded the Land Rovers again and were off to find cats. Panthers and smaller cats did not come out until night, but maybe we would come upon a lion. John drove through a thicket and past some elephants foraging. Elephants do not walk around things, they move forward pushing them over. A giraffe, three stories tall, was feeding on treetops nearby.

We came upon another Land Rover. The two guides spoke briefly in a soft voice in their native language, Tambuka. John turned to us and explained the other guide told him that there was a pair of lions a half-mile up the road, to keep our voices low and please remain seated.

I'd been told that a cat sees the Land Rover as a single large animal like an elephant and will not attack it, but if a person steps out of the vehicle, the lion sees them as a smaller animal and possibly something good to eat. Apparently, this is true, but I still failed to see what kept the cat from jumping right in the middle of the vehicle.

When we saw the first lion, a large older male with a full-grown mane, he was perched on a large rock across a small meadow. There was a herd of water buffalo near a bend in a stream and I assumed the lion had been watching them.

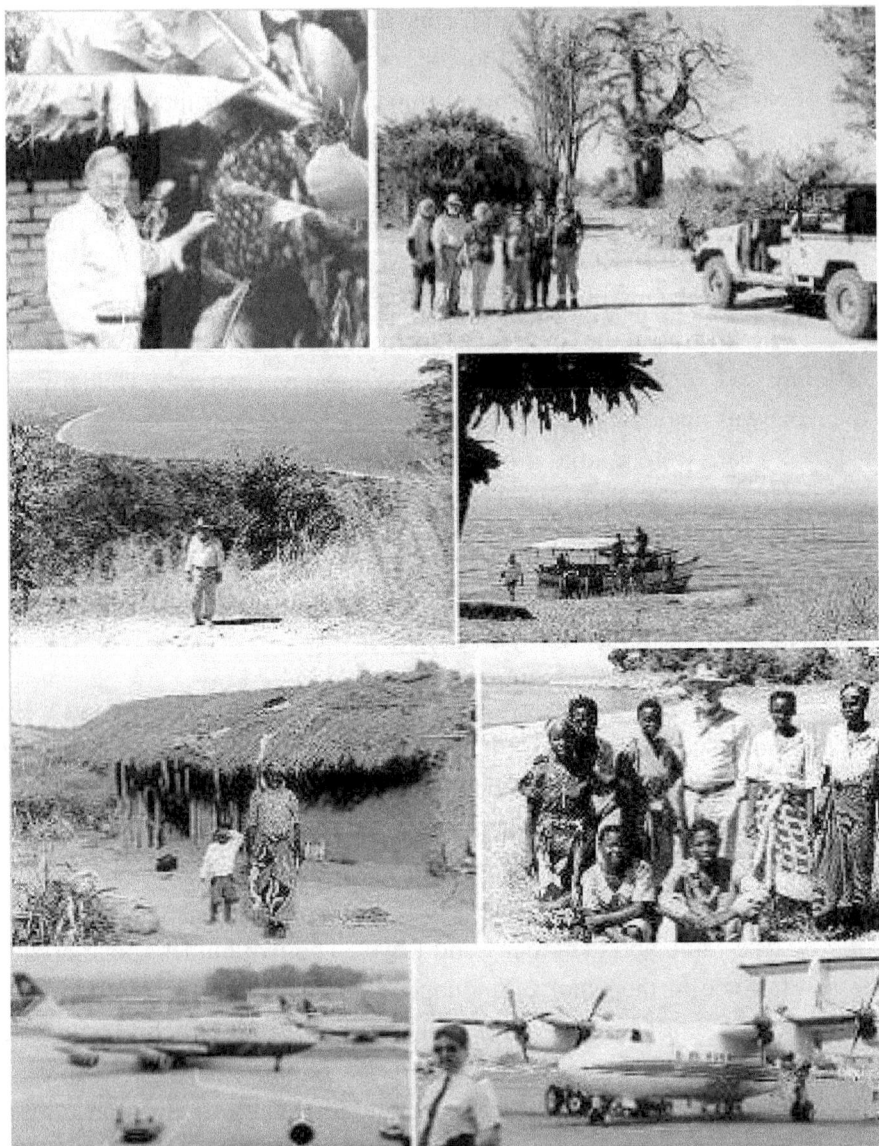

Bananas growing wild; group in Land rover at Luangwa Game Park, note giant baobab tree in background; Lake Malawi, which borders Tanzania and visiting the local people; British Air on ramp at Gatwick; Kenya Air on ramp at Nairobi on second visit to Africa.

There was also a group of about thirty warthogs foraging in a nearby ravine. Out of sight of the warthogs was a second lion. I thought it was a female, but John said that it was a younger male that had not yet grown a full-mane. This would be a rare delight to get to see, not only one, but two lions on the hunt.

The young lion crossed about ten yards in front of our vehicle and slowly wandered into the high grass on the other side of the road. The older lion moved in the open area in sight of the warthog herd to get their attention. He was only the decoy. Suddenly, out of the tall grass about fifty yards ahead, the young lion emerged in a full charge.

The young lion topped the crest of the ravine and charged down into the middle of the herd. Thirty warthogs went thirty-two different directions. The young lion put on his brakes in a cloud of dust and came up empty handed. He looked around kind of dumbfounded that he had actually missed his prey. We all cheered quietly for the lion's misfortune.

The old lion, about ten yards to our left, sauntered slowly towards the humiliated young lion and I put words into the mouths of the lions. The older lion saying, "You dumb kid. I thought I taught you better than that," and the young lion replying, "Aw, I didn't want warthog for dinner tonight anyway. We'll just wait and have water buffalo later."

Both lions crossed the road directly in front of our vehicle. The older proud lion never turned his head to give us a glance. John told me a mature lion would not look directly at you. It was said that he is too proud to do so.

As the young lion passed within a stone's throw, he looked directly at me as I snapped a photo. The setting sun over my shoulder reflected in his yellow-gold eyes and they glowed like gemstones. They were certainly the piercing eyes of a killer. It was an eerie feeling that sent a chill up my spine.

In the last line of *Ghost in the Darkness,* the narrator says, "And even today in a museum, the lion will strike fear in your heart." I'm not likely to forget it and I've decided I don't care for things higher on the food chain than I am.

John asked, "Would you like to take a break here?"

I think he was joking, but I replied, "No, I would like to put a mile or two between us and those two cats first, please!"

The sun was setting by the time we stopped beside a river with crocodiles on the far bank. We were having biscuits and squash blossom juice for a snack. The Dutchman asked, "Marvin, all day long you have been jumping out of the Land Rover and asking me to take your picture. How come when we were watching the lions you didn't jump out and ask me to take your picture?"

Everyone laughed as I replied, "Guess I just forgot." Now why would I tell you a lion's tale in the middle of an airline story? Well because that's the whole point. Due to the wonder of the modern jet airliner, this entire adventure took place only about 18-hour from my own front doorstep.

Time To Head Home

We loaded into our small bus before sunrise and made it back onto the main road at the little town of Chapata. Clearing border customs on the Zambia side and then again on the Malawi side, we re-entered Malawi and headed for the Lilongwe airport.

At the airport, I explained to the company manager I had purchased diesel fuel and had to pay duty on the bus at the boarder crossing as the driver had been given no money, probably for good reason. The manager deducted the amount from the price.

I handed the bus driver some clothes I had changed out of and a sack full of insect repellent, antiseptics and toothpaste. I had left everything else in Livingstonia.

The Lilongwe Airport had a nice restaurant on the balcony overlooking the aircraft ramp and the best thing about my lunch was the freshly brewed Malawi coffee. I had not had any luck finding roasted coffee up in the mountains where it was grown.

Our DC-10 arrived an hour late. Crossing the ramp to board the plane, I stopped to talk to the Captain, a white fellow, about to begin his walk-around. I introduced myself and walked with him. He had a distinct British accent and I asked him if he was English. He was not. He was born in South Africa to English missionary parents, but lived in Zimbabwe all of his adult life. He was a reserve pilot in what there was of a Malawi air force and had flown DC-3s in his younger days. We had something in common and joked about the Boeing 707 they were still flying.

He liked the DC-10s Air Zimbabwe was operating. They had bought two and both were fairly new. He explained that running late was not a problem. "The flight to London is also running behind schedule. Besides, they need all the paying passengers they can get. If they know we're enroute, they'll wait."

I smiled and said, "Hakuna Matata." A Swahili phrase, *not to worry*, made popular in the Disney movie *The Lion King*.

He laughed and replied, "You got it!"

After we were airborne and the standard welcome over the PA, the Captain added, "We'd also like to welcome the gentleman from Texas and his group onboard with us this evening."

When we arrived at the Harare Airport terminal, a tense atmosphere permeated the place. Each member of our group was physically searched in a private room, separate searches for male and female. The reason for all this security became apparent just prior to our boarding the plane for London.

Flight Back To London

It was dark when they finally called for us to board the London flight. As we walked out onto the tarmac, a security guard stopped us as several limousines and motorcycles pulled up followed by a pickup load of soldiers carrying AK47s. The soldiers jumped out and surrounded one of the limousines. The president of Zimbabwe was flying in the first class section of our flight to London. There were a bunch of foreign government types on the flight. Then I remembered reading about an international animal conservation conference held in Harare.

We had lost our white-African airline captain. Our new crew was the one who had flown us from London. The DC-10 climbed into the darkness and we leveled out at cruising altitude was we were served dinner. The president of Zimbabwe was addressed as Comrade President. He was welcomed aboard over the PA first by the head stewardess and then again from the cockpit crew.

I was seated next to the Minister of Conservation for Nicaragua. I asked him what they were doing about slowing up the cutting of the rain forests and he went on about how poor his park rangers were and how he couldn't afford shoes for them or gasoline for their vehicles. Of course, it was the fault of the Americans who didn't send more money.

I intended to get some sleep, but the minister continued to visit with the person seated ahead of us. I suggested that he might want to swap seats with his assistant who did not speak English. They agreed. I took a sleeping pill, inflated my neck pillow, put on my blindfold mask and I don't remember a thing until we were on final approach at Gatwick.

On arrival, I headed directly to McDonald's, which I never go to at home. I ordered a Big Mac, french-fries and a Coke. A young man with a Cockney accent said, "Sorry, sir, we are still serving from our breakfast menu."

I settled for a sausage dog on a bun and a Coke from the deli, purchased a bottle of Chanel No.5 at the duty free shop and returned to our departure gate. I called Suzie on the payphone to tell her I'd be home in 8-10 hours.

Home From The Sky

As the coast of Ireland disappeared under the right wing, my thoughts drifted back to Africa and to Livingstonia. When we left, our hosts all said that they were sad we were leaving. I did not feel sad at the time, as I was ready to be headed home.

Suddenly, my eyes begin to water and I realized that I was feeling some form of delayed sadness about leaving Africa. I scribbled these final words in my journal.

"There is a place in Africa were I know the footpaths through the high grass and strange trees. Where the waterfall is higher, the valley deeper, the mountain higher and the lakes more beautiful than any I have ever seen before.

There is a place in Africa where I have walked the clay dirt roads and been greeted by hello, how are you, I am fine too. I look at them, how little they have, failing to understand why they are not unhappy.

There is a place in Africa where there are some people who can call me by my given name because forever so brief a time, I lived among them. We shared our lives, our hopes, our dreams and our God together."

After lunch I went to the restroom and shaved my neck, but left my three-week-old mostly gray beard intact. We would now experience a thirty-hour day to make up for the eighteen-hour day we spent going over.

Deplaning in Amarillo, Suzie came to hug my neck. I had forgotten to put the blue mark on my forehead like I had intended for her and Laura. A blue mark like the witchdoctor had placed on the forehead of Sean Connery's girlfriend in the movie *Medicine Man*.

Charles, a preacher from Kenya, gave me the three-way African handshake I had now learned first hand. I got a couple of souvenirs out of Tim's shipping container and went to the car with Suzie, Laura and my two grandkids. We stopped at IHOP where I ordered a hamburger and an omelet. Something with seasonings sure tasted good again.

My body clock was still on Malawi time so in the middle of the night, I was up wondering around the house turning things on and off to see them work. Well what the heck, since I was up anyway, I'd pull up Microsoft Flight Simulator and try one more time to nail that Boeing 737 approch into old Hong Kong airport.

SECOND TRIP TO AFRICA

The year after I had flown to Malawi, I flew to Kenya on British Air. After a short time in Nairobi, just another large dirty city, I flew via Kenya Air in a small four-engine Fokker turbo-prop along the Tanzanian border down to Mombasa. Seeing Mt. Kilimanjaro off in the distance was a memorable experience.

With a missionary guide named Gary, I visited the small Christian groups working among the Moslem majority population in the countryside south of the city along the Indian Ocean coast.

The only cash crop I saw were the cashew nuts, which grew wild high up in the jungle trees. The beginnings of a European tourist trade had started to develop until the year before when the Kenyan army very heavy-handedly put down a rebellion in the area and the tourist trade was still staying away.

Returning to Nairobi, my British Air flight departed at midnight from the Nairobi International Airport, but I had a plan for the day. The driver and van I had prearranged were waiting for me at the small commuter airport when I arrived.

Foot Of The Ngong Hills

Most tourists chose to visit the animal farms and, if *Out Of Africa* fans like myself, to visit Karen Blitzen's home. However, I asked the middle-aged driver if he thought he could find Denys Fitch Hatton's gravesite. He told me it had been many years since he had been there and it was on private property, but he thought he could find it. It was a bit of a drive. We stopped once and I purchased two Cokes and we shared my last can of Vienna sausages and crackers. That was our lunch.

At the foot of the Ngong Hills, we traveled up a muddy road through small subsistence farms. The driver stopped at one gate and waited. He said someone would come. A short time later, an old man approached. My driver got out and asked me to wait.

While I did not speak Swahili, it was easy to understand the owner was saying he was not going to allow us to cross his land and equally understandable that my driver was only trying to determine the price. He returned to the van to tell me it would take a certain amount in shillings and assumed I would not pay that much and would want him to continue negotiating.

I handed the driver the amount, about ten dollars U.S. to give to the man. I would never pass this way again and would have willingly paid twice the amount. We were then allowed to cross through two gates and park outside a small fenced in garden area. I entered the garden alone.

A monolith stone, about eight feet high, stood in the center of the garden. The garden was well kept with a variety of flowers growing round about. The view from the top of the slow rolling hillside was not the vast open plain depicted in Sydney Pollack's movie where the lions lay on Fitch Hatton's grave. It was overgrown now with trees and checkered fields of corn.

Standing at the foot of the grave outlined in small stones, I read the inscription on the small brass plate mounted on the stone monolith, *"HE PRAYETH WELL THAT LOVETH WELL BOTH MAN AND BIRD AND BEAST. R.I.P. DENYS GEORGE FINCH HATTON 1887 – 1931"*

I Wonder As I Wander

On various occasions throughout my life I have had thoughts and discussions on the subject of reincarnation. I always joked about why it was that everyone always believed they had been someone famous in a previous life instead of someone ordinary.

For whatever reason, I seemed to identify with the white-Africans who lived out their lives in British East Central Africa. Possibly, the reason I had sought out this place. Fitch Hatton was a free spirit and an early aviator. He died in 1931 in a biplane crash. Returning from Mombasa in his biplane, it was believed he had flown into a severe thunderstorm.

I was born in 1936 and I always felt that I knew how to fly even before I ever actually tried. Also, as I had discovered during my trip to Africa the year before, I had an uncanny familiarity with the old British Colonial Africa. Was it possible for one to return and stand on one's own grave from a previous life? Was I standing on my own grave?

I stood there quietly for a bit, said a short prayer, took one final look off into the distant hills and went to find my driver. As we still had some daylight left, I asked him to drive me to Karen Blitzen's old home. To my surprise, it was about twenty miles away. Indeed, a sizable plantation in its day.

The house, now a small museum, had closed for the day, but I walked around the grounds briefly and returned to the van. My driver dropped me at the International Airport after a harrowing cross-town drive in heavy traffic with little or no right-a-way control, but we made it.

I changed planes in London and again at DFW. I suspect I will never again venture to the Dark Continent. At least not in this lifetime. If you want to see the real Africa, you better hurry it's disappearing fast.

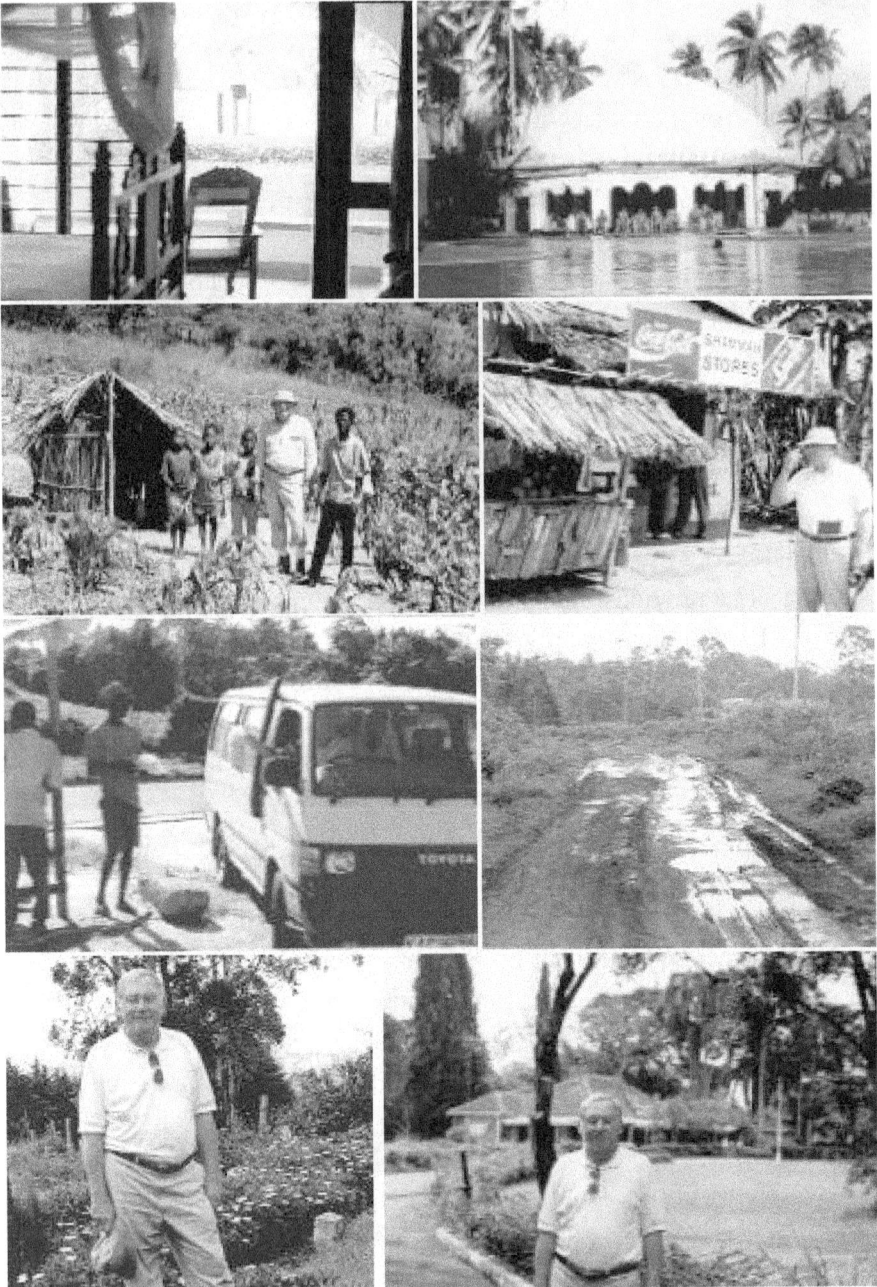

Southern Palms beach resort on the Indian Ocean south of Mombasa; daily ventures into the Moslem controlled interior, cornfields with youngster guarding and small villages; back in Nairobi, chips from a street vendor, muddy road up the Ngong Hills; respects at Denys Fitch Hattton's grave and Out of Africa author, Karen Blitzen's plantation home.

Chapter Twenty-five
THE EPILOG

At least once in every lifetime you're entitled to go do whatever it is you want, within moral and ethical limits. Such were the years after I divested Flight Dynamics. I had a little money put away so I did just that. This is the short version of how I left and came full circle back to aero engineering.

For a period of time, I entered into a loose business partnership at Sports Car Center, a used car dealership located on Lemmon Avenue down the street from Love Field. Lemmon Avenue was the premier strip for new and used car dealers in Dallas.

Possibly an appropriate name for a street lined with car dealers, but oddly enough, the street was actually named Lemmon Avenue many years before the first car dealership showed up.

Sports Car Center

A Brit by the name of Morris designed and built the MG roadster, which stands for Morris Garage. Our mechanic, who used to repair our cars, always claimed that ol' man Morris never dreamed in his wildest imagination that some Texan would be driving his roadsters around in 110-degree heat with an air conditioner hung on the little four-cylinder engine.

I split my time between entertainment promoting and selling worthless Jaguars and assorted roadsters to a wealthy Highland Park and North Dallas clientele. We sold a lot of those looks-neat and goes-fast, but mostly worthless and hard to maintain sports cars to the wives, daughters and girlfriends.

Their lawyer, CPA and doctor husbands bought the cars for them I guess to keep them happy. They drove them a couple of times, bragged at cocktail parties that they owned one and never drove the cramped, uncomfortable little beasts after the new wore off. Yesterday's hot iron soon became garage queens.

We'd often buy them back after the ashtrays were full. Guest held a couple of European style tuxedo auto auctions at the then prestigious Camelot Hotel to resell some of the really choice collector cars and high dollar antique racecars.

Music & Movies

About this time in my non-career, I was making a real effort to promote a couple of screenplays and movie treatments I had written. This led to my walking into the Peggy Taylor Talent Agency. Peggy said she didn't have a clue as to how to sell a movie script, but why didn't I hang around and see what I could learn when a movie company was filming in town.

Peggy would send me out on casting cattle calls with the rest of the movie star want-a-bees on tryouts for commercials and movies filmed in Dallas. My going would add to the numbers and give her better actors a shot at a part. More often than not, ironically, I'd get a callback because I'd do walk-ons and the pros all wanted dialog parts.

My best commercial credit was for Southwest Airlines playing the part of a cowboy. The theme of the commercial was *Spreading Love All Over Texas,* advertising flights out of Love Field. A little old lady and I stole the scene and the ad ran off and on for a couple of years.

My short-lived and never aspired-to-acting career led to a filmography of six less than memorable walk-ons including *Semi-Tough, Logan's Run, North Dallas Forty, The Graduates a*nd *The Lee Harvey Oswald Story* two versions.

I taught night classes at Video Tech and directed a few commercials. During this time, I also served on the City of Irving's Cable Board, for which the Mayor awarded all of us a nice wood and brass engraved wall plaque. I also worked a little with Perry Tong at Silver Bullet Productions in Fort Worth. Perry shot B-movies in 16mm and put them on 35mm to rent to drive-ins, but I never sold a screenplay.

Bronco Auditorium

Peggy gave me an office and asked me to see if I could help any of the mass of musical talent that showed up wanting bookings and this lead to my managing a rock group and a country band. By chance, I heard that Lamar Hunt was trying to revive the old Bronco Auditorium in Oak Cliff he had owned for years.

So I made an appointment with Hunt to pitch my idea for booking concerts into the auditorium. Hunt, who also owned the Kansas City Chiefs, turned out to be a rather quiet, unassuming fellow. He mostly listened and then told me to go ahead and try out my idea. I booked everyone from Moe Bandy and Kitty Wells to a Mexican band to play on Cinco de Mayo into the Bronco.

One reason Bronco was less than successful, it was located in a dry precinct and no alcoholic beverages could be sold on the premises. I imported Near Beer from a brewery in Arkansas and was able to pick up a few hundred extra bucks at each concert by operating the concession stand.

My sister-in-law, Nancy, worked the concession stand by herself for me on Cinco de Mayo one night when my help didn't show up. An old Mexican gentleman staggered up to the counter and said, "I drank six of these beers and I'm not feeling anything yet." Nancy didn't have the heart to tell the fellow that there was less than one percent alcohol in a can of Near Beer. Nancy still sends me a Cinco de Mayo card every year in remembrance of the night she worked her tail off at Bronco.

On Saturday nights when a big name performer was not booked into the auditorium, I promoted it as the Bronco Jamboree. I used local entertainers to makeup a C&W house band. They started calling themselves the Bronco Band. Taking turns as the lead singer, the band did the warm-up acts and worked for the exposure. Several went on to reasonably successful careers.

One of the male leads was a VW service mechanic on his regular day job, but he could sing *Jingle Bells* and make it sound like a country song. A tall fellow by the name of Ken played piano in the band. He was more of a Van Cliburn than a C&W star, but he'd put on a ten gallon Stetson and get a real kick out of the gig. Ken could play anything and follow anybody.

Bronco Auditorium; control room and radio broadcast booth; Nancy where she cornered the market on Near Beer; Robert "Rebel" Raines, motorcycle jump artist; Country & Western music promoter photos with Buck Owens, Mo Bandy and Dolly Parton. Mark II & Suzie's Continentals; '32 Lincoln Phaeton; couple of Harley Davidson FLH.

I haven't a musical bone in my body, but I often had to MC the show so I'd play with the band too. I'd stand out there and strum a C-cord on my Bona Venture guitar and mouth the words. I used to tell people, "I'm a professional singer. I've been offered money several times to stop."

Saturday night's work wasn't over till we struck our set and set up the stage for Sunday morning church services. A tall, gray-haired evangelist rented the auditorium for church services. The stage was set with a giant dove of peace on a red and gold velvet backdrop. The evangelist preached and his orchestra played praise music. It was not unusual to see diamond rings and hundred dollar bills thrown on the stage.

The auditorium seated about 3,000. I was never able to fill the place except for Cinco de Mayo, but the church services were standing room only. The evangelist hated Rock-n-Roll. I saw him one Saturday night in the balcony and spoke to him. He told me he was praying for the failure of the rock group on stage. As I recall, I don't think that particular group needed his help.

Country Magazine

There was a freebee music events magazine in Dallas called *Buddy,* named after Buddy Holly. The monthly magazine mostly catered to rock music fans and survived financially on paid advertising. There wasn't a good venue for promoting C&W entertainers in the area, so I started a similar publication and called it *Country* magazine. The record companies and saloons also needed a place to advertise and beginning with the first issue, *Country* magazine made a profit and caught on fast.

National Geographic magazine published an article on Willie Nelson that included a color photo of Willie doing a show in Dallas. On stage, he is wearing a red *Country* magazine T-shirt. Working with the local C&W radio stations, I was given free press passes to all the best concerts. My wife and I personally met Dolly Parton, Crystal Gale and William Shatner. I also worked with Buck Owens and Lorne Green. All were great folks.

After publishing *Country* for about a year, a photographer, who worked part time for me and who hung out down at Whiskey River with the Willie Nelson and David Alan Cole crowd, offered to buy the magazine. I agreed, mainly because with the exception of a few other colossal-failure concert promoters in Dallas, I was the sorriest promoter to come down the pike. I tried my best to revive Bronco to its glory days, but it was not to be!

The *Country* magazine photographer's brother worked Saturdays at the Bronco Auditorium helping me with the sound and lighting. After our last scheduled performance, we were tearing down to set up for the church services the next morning and we started talking about what we did for a regular day jobs. I told him I was a design engineer by trade and didn't exactly know how in the hell I had gotten into this business.

"Surprise," he said, "I'm a rep for a job shop engineering company." One thing led to another and he explained that he needed someone to fill a job at the Aerospatiale Helicopter Corporation located in Grand Prairie.

I told him, "No sweat, I could handle it," and that's how it happened that I went to work at Aerospatiale to do a three-month contract job and ended up working there for almost a decade, finally retiring as Chief of Avionics Engineering.

Rebel Raines

A young motorcyclist by the name of Raines used to help me out at the Bronco Auditorium. He ran errands for me, like hauling pickup loads of Near Beer in from Arkansas. Raines had perfected the skill of motorcycle ramp jumping and had aspirations of becoming as famous as Evil Knievel.

When he performed his jumps, he wore a bright red outfit decorated with the Dixie battle flag and called himself Rebel Raines. Reb came to me one day and asked if I would be his agent and try to get him booked into auto races and county fairs. Not wanting to be part of getting a nice kid hurt, I agreed on the condition that we do it scientifically.

Bernie, a math professor friend of mine on staff at the University of Dallas agreed to do the trajectory calculations. Bernie had worked for the Defense Department doing artillery and missile trajectory calculations. Reb was comfortable with a jump speed of 55 miles per hour and wanted to be able to clear the width of ten stock cars parked tightly side by side. Using the motorcycle and Reb's weight, Bernie gave us the exact angle at which the ramp had to be set.

Reb's first public jump was during intermission at a stock car racetrack in McKinney. As I lined up the ten stock cars to be jumped, I progressively lined up each car six-inches back. The drivers laughed when they caught on to what I was doing, but from the grandstand, the slight stagger wasn't discernable. Reb had come down short on one practice jump, so I was buying us touchdown room to land in front of the tenth car, instead of on top of it. Reb made it with two car widths to spare.

After a year or so, I lost track of Reb, but as far as I know, he never had an unsuccessful jump. As a footnote, the one idea I never got to try out was to use a Ryan Retro Rocket pack to assist the motorcycle. I still believe Knievel could have made the Grand Canyon jump using this concept. Reb contacted Caesar's Palace to promote the idea, but after Knievel had taken the bad spill jumping the entrance fountain, they said no.

Spruce Goose

During the late 1980s and early 1990s, I assembled a vintage collection of Lincoln motorcars that included two Continental coupes, a '41 and a '42, two '39 Zephyrs, a coupe and a sedan, a '48 Lincoln sedan that I drove daily, a white '56 Continental Mark II and my wife drove an '84 Continental.

In planning for retirement and leaving Aerospatiale, I sold off my collection. The '39 Lincoln 3-window coupe, used in a Paul Newman and Joanne Woodward film, was sold to a collector in Palm Beach. When I finished restoring the '42 coupe gunmetal gray Continental, Edsel's favorite color for a car, I sold it to a collector in Houston. The white Mark II also went. A few years later, I received a letter from the fellow in Denver who bought the Mark II. He said he still had it and loved the old car.

Since my youth I had followed the exploits of aviator Howard Hughes and his maiden flight in the Hercules flying boat, referred to as the *Spruce Goose* by everyone except Hughes. I had a few dealings with Summa Corporation, which he owned, but never met the man. I remember the day I was sitting in my office and my secretary came in and said, "It was on the news that Howard Hughes had died aboard his personal jet enroute to Houston."

Someone from Disney, the new owners of the Queen Mary and the Hercules, called saying they were looking for a '39 Lincoln to exhibit for a 1939 theme Expo. The Zephyr sedan was shipped to Long Beach and put on display beside the Spruce Goose. We traveled to California to see the exhibit and to tour the Queen Mary, but the biggest thrill of all was when I walked into the domed hangar and saw the Spruce Goose for the first time.

Howard Hughes giant HK-1 flying boat affectionately the Spruce Goose; photos in center are of H-1 when it was stored in Long Beach hangar. 1939 Lincoln Zephyr Sedan that went to Queen Mary '39 exhibit.

Going Once Going Twice

During the time I was collecting and restoring old cars, I also promoted and held several antique & collector car auctions in Dallas, Amarillo and Las Vegas, but abandoned the car auction business when the computer software company I started took off.

The last year we held a Las Vegas Collector Car Auction, we all stayed at the new high-rise Harrah's Casino Hotel. A friend, J. Woolley, my brother and I were standing looking out the 25th floor window. I remarked, "This is about the altitude ol' Jerry and I flew down Las Vegas Boulevard in my old DC-3 years ago."

Woolley, a retired minister, was a real old car aficionado. He had gone with the '39 Zephyr business coupe to Kansas City when it was featured in the movie *Mr. and Mrs. Bridge* and had a great time hanging with Newman and Woodward. J.W. moved on a few years ago, but I'll bet if heaven has any old V12 engines laying around, he's tinkering with one them right now.

I finally sold my Harley-Davidson FLH Dresser. Never was much of a long-distance biker, bandanna and all of that. I always wore a helmet. Maybe it reminded me of my youth or maybe flying. Its been said that aviators enjoy riding motorcycles because of the bike's ability to bank in a turn.

Airline Travel

My long distance travel is now relegated to riding in the backend of some luxury airliner. When I board an early morning flight and feel like I really didn't get enough sleep the night before, I think am I ever glad I don't have to drive this big beast for the next several hours. I can just sit back and relax.

I buckle myself into the standard issue airline seat, built for a guy about twenty pounds lighter than me and watch out the small oval window. I still like to see where I'm going. I watch as we taxi for the next fifteen minutes. In my head, I hear every radio call, "Cleared to cross three-five; taxi into position and hold; cleared for takeoff..."

After two trips to the African continent, I finally talked my wife into taking some long distance airline flights. The next spring, we flew to

London on one of the new Boeing 777s and recently we flew to Paris and back via Houston.

We now travel in business class and leave the flying to the guys up front. My wife is a good trans-oceanic passenger as long as I make sure she has taken along plenty of books to read. I still look out the window and listen to the stereo.

There is one thing that does worry me a little. When did they let all these young kids start flying these big jets?

Pearl Harbor To Tokyo

For some reason, Suzie and I had never visited the Hawaiian Islands, so we took an American Airlines Boeing 767 flight to Honolulu. We didn't really go to see the island beaches, but mainly to see Pearl Harbor and visit the USS Arizona.

We were not disappointed. The giant battleship USS Missouri BB63 is now retired and moored at Ford Island. It was on this ship's deck that General MacArthur accepted the signing of the Japanese surrender. It is fitting that it now rests in the bay near the USS Arizona and nuclear subs quietly pass by on their way out to sea.

A visit to the Arizona Memorial cannot be described in words, so I will not try. In my humble opinion there are three places and events that defined what America became. There were and are Valley Forge, Gettysburg and Pearl Harbor.

After a few days on Waikiki, we flew Northwest Airlines on to Tokyo. Our plan was to retrace the path of the attack on Pearl. We toured the Imperial Palace gardens and Asikusa, then on to Kamakura in Yokohama to complete our quest for what we had jokingly labeled as our search for the *Giant Buddha*. From the train, Mt Fuji loomed in the distance and reminded me of the Japanese signal to commence the attack on Pearl Harbor. The message received by Nagumo's Force was *Niitakayama nobore*, Climb Mt Niitaka. Japan is a beautiful country. I am pleased they are now able to live in peace.

In the early morning hours, we crossed the coast of California south of Los Angeles at 40,000 feet enroute to Dallas. Most onboard were asleep, but for an old pilot who had seen much of the world from 10,000 feet, the view of the lights of L.A. off our right wing was an awesome sight.

We returned to our home in Amarillo on September 10ᵗʰ 2001. What an eerie next few days it was with no sound of jet engines or contrails high overhead. Will this country never learn to be prepared?

Davis-Monthan Airbase

For many years of my flying career, I'd heard of a non-descript location somewhere in Arizona where old airplanes go to die. A few years ago, searching for display aircraft for a museum and/or even a restorable war bird, I actually discovered there was such a place where six-thousand plus aircraft were stored on hundreds of acres in the desert near Tucson. Through a contact at the Government Services Agency I was able to arrange a private tour of the facility for my wife and I.

It is impossible to explain exactly what is located at the site. I am certain the average non-aviation oriented visitor would sum the place up by saying it was simply acres and acres of worn out old military planes. To the flyer, the experience is a combination of gleeful excitement and deep felt sorrow. Some will be resurrected and fly again and some will have spare parts removed and reused, but sadly, most will meet the fate of the beer can maker's guillotine.

West of Tucson is a similar site for retired commercial aircraft. Operated by Evergreen, it is not open to the public.

Amarillo Sky

The collection of short stories herein, were written and then rewritten from our home in Amarillo, Texas where we retired after living in Dallas for thirty some years.

Without exception, the most beautiful sunsets in the world occur on the high plains of West Texas. In the blue sky high overhead, seemingly lined up along I40, are the contrails of the jet airliners. Our house is directly under the flight path of the Life Star helicopter's route to the regional hospital. The old Astar they operated for years, I am sure had my signatures on the engineering and avionics drawings from Aerospatiale.

The Rick Husband Amarillo International Airport, which was a B-52 base at one time, has a 13,500 ft runway and is an approved alternate for the Space Shuttle. The airport doesn't, however, have a lot of air traffic and so various AF planes use it to practice ILS approaches. On any given day, there might be a Texan trainer from Enid AFB, a KC-135, a B-1 and on occasion even a B-2 in the pattern.

Bell Helicopter Division of Textron continues to expand the facility at RHAIA and more and more tilt-rotor Ospreys designed for Special Forces operations are being test flown in the skies around Amarillo. Even our old C-142 four-engine cargo VTOL, a similar design concept to the Osprey, might have been successful back in 1963 were it not for it's underpowered engines and if it had the V-22's state-of-the-art computerized flight controls.

Amarillo By Morning

Headed home to Amarillo from Florida a few years ago, after returning once to Tampa for an in-flight emergency, we flew into the mother of all thunderstorms. In the middle of the night we landed in San Antonio for fuel. Most stayed aboard, we got off!

Our luggage stayed on the plane scheduled to depart in the wee hours of the morning. We spent that night in a motel with only what we had with us. By the way, it was our 43rd wedding anniversary. Thus, *up from San Antone and all that I got is just what I got on*, became a real life experience.

The next week Suzie flew to Belize with our church group. I departed the next morning with another driver and two teenage boys to deliver a medical trailer to a mission hospital. We spent the night in San Antonio and five more nights on the road in Mexico on our way to Belize.

Once again, Suzie and I flew home to Amarillo with a camera, a small bag of souvenir seashells and what we had on! We had given our extra clothes to people we met in Belize who seemed to need them a whole lot more than we did.

For a couple of Texas Caribbean tramps headed home, the song *Amarillo By Morning* took on even more meaning. I jotted down this variation on the words based on the George Strait song written by Terry Stafford and Paul Fraser:

Amarillo by morning, up from San Antone, everything that I've got, is what I've got on. When the sun is high in the Texas sky, I'll be setin' in my easy chair. Amarillo by morning, Amarillo I'll be there.

Our flight turned back over Tampa Bay. Broke and busted in Dallas yesterday. Lost my luggage and no place to stay, somewhere along the way. But I'll be feelin' great when that plane pulls out of the gate.

Maybe we'll make it this time. Amarillo by morning, Amarillo's on my mind. High up over San Antone, the clothes I've got, is what I've got on. Gave them away and didn't look back. Photos and shells in this here sack, if the Lord comes lookin' for me, tell Him Amarillo's where I'll be.

Keep On Flyin

My total PIC time is probably somewhere around 6,000 hours. When we flew at FDC or GSA, we filled out a counter ticket, even if it was a maintenance test flight. Eight years of my flight receipts were clipped in a manila folder that I had good intentions of transferring to my logbook someday.

When we trashed all the FDC tax records after storing them the required time, I realized later that my flight records were destroyed along with them. After leaving the Dallas area, I let my biennial check expire. Later, when I went for my check ride, the only logbook I had showed 4,200 hours TT and dated back to 1970, so I just started logging my time again from that point.

A while back, I joined the Buffalo Flying Club as I no longer owned a plane and there was nothing suitable to rent in the area. The club's two planes, a Cessna 182 Skylane with a STOL kit and a V-35 Bonanza were based at the Tradewind Airport.

The Confederate Air Force is now called the Commemorative Air Force, but I still remain a member. My membership number is 1148. Pretty low considering they are currently issuing membership numbers above 38,000.

Cessna T-37 Tweet and C-47 in salvage yard; Davis-Monthan AFB storage facility in Arizona desert near Tucson: TS11 Iskra, Polish trainer converted to private use; Buffalo Flying Club Bonanza flown by author.

I have only one last lament at this writing and it is that in all my years of hacking around aviation, I never got to fly a really high performance jet fighter. Oh, I've steered the occasional Ruskie jet trainer and exec jet around the sky, but I had hoped to finished this collection of stories with part of a chapter on going straight up in an F-16D or maybe about my ride with one of the Blue Angels. Alas, it was not to be.

So Write About What You Know

My fascination with the Lincoln automobile began decades ago with that baby blue cabriolet the Air Corps Captain next door to us had owned. A side benefit to having restored old Lincolns for years was an accumulation of old Lincoln literature and memorabilia. I used this material in a book I wrote, *Lincoln Continental, Classic Motorcars*, ISBN 0-87833-691-5. William Clay Ford graciously wrote the Preface for the book. It was published by Taylor Fine Books in 1989 and has become the definitive book on the history of the Lincoln and Continental.

Much of my spare time is now spent at the computer. When I am not working on a software design, I continue my writing and recently completed an action adventure novel *Flight of the Setting Sun*, which I am hoping will be made into a film. We'll need to restore an old China Clipper to shoot the story, as it is a 1930s fictional tale of a Pan Am pilot and adventurer.

Steinbeck, Kipling, Runyon and Gann were my favorite writers. Ernest K. Gann wrote *Fate Is The Hunter* and *The High And The Mighty* among others. As a teenager interested in learning to fly, I read his early articles in *Flying* magazine with great interest.

Flying Stories is not the kind of book ol' Ernie would have written, maybe as magazine articles. Gann wrote less and less as time passed and went back to flying as a bush pilot up north somewhere. Odd that I was thinking about Ernie Gann one day, wondering whatever happened to him and days later read in the newspaper that he had passed away on that very day.

In the end, there really is a theme to all these unrelated stories. It is the unequivocal and indivisible relationships between ambition, education, experience and technology. In simpler terms, the forces, both internal and external, which cause each of us to become who and what we are. A philosopher would put it this way. *We are the sum of all our yesterdays and the hope of all our tomorrows.*

Huffman Prairie

When asked to speak at a pilot's luncheon honoring the Wright Brother's 100th Anniversary of Powered Flight, my talk went something like this...

"I've always considered it a privilege to be introduced as a pilot. It implies a certain kinship, a shared experience with a special group of men and women. Or as Pilot Officer John Magee put it, *to slip the surly bonds of earth... on silvered wings... where never lark or even eagle flew.*

I want to tell you of a place. It was not the wind swept dunes of Kill Devil Hill or of Kitty Hawk, North Carolina. It was not yet December the 17th, 1903. It was a place in the countryside outside of Dayton, not far from the small Ohio town of Osborne.

Two young men, bicycle makers, were holding onto a large object with two ropes against the wind. The object looked something like a cross between a large box kite and an early biplane. They called it a glider and they were using it to test out various airfoils.

They built a rather unsuccessful manned glider and tried to fly it on a hillside near Huffman Prairie. Orville commented one time he thought *man would fly someday, but probably not in his lifetime.* Wilbur died fairly young, but he and Orville both lived to see man fly. Orville died in 1948. Aviation was only 45-years old and we were already approaching the sound barrier.

In the 1920s, the Army Signal Corps engineering branch moved from Dayton to a small valley just over the hill from Huffman Prairie airfield. Appropriately named Wright Field, it became Air Research and Development Command headquarters.

If you go out old Route 4 there is a wooded area behind Wright Field. At the top of the hill is a stone monument standing twenty or so feet in the air. On it is a large tarnished bronze plaque, a tribute to the Wright Brothers.

About fifty-yards behind the Wright Memorial is a lookout point that overlooks Huffman Dam. Behind it lies the now tree covered Miami River bottom of Huffman Prairie.

If you stand on that hillside and squint just right and gaze out over Huffman Prairie, you will be able to see the first U.S. Army Air training field where the likes of Hap Arnold, commander of the Air Forces in WW II, first learned to fly in a rickety old biplane. Or maybe catch a glimpse of Flight Lieutenant Brown, who was credited with shooting down the Red Baron in the First World War. He learned to fly there too.

Twelve miles over the treetops is the airport at Vandalia where the first test pilot school was located and the likes of Chuck Yeager and many others with the *Right Stuff* graduated.

To your right, you might see a C5A coming in for a landing at Patterson Field. It was the first runway that was built to hold a fully loaded operational B-36. The concrete on the runway was laid six-feet deep.

To your far right at Wood City was where a German engineer arrived with his family. He brought with him a dream to build a 3-stage rocket. He claimed *it would fly to the moon,* and it did.

The Wright Brothers Memorial is not a cemetery. No one is buried there, but it is nevertheless hallowed ground. It honors a birthplace. Within a fifteen-mile radius of this hallowed ground, the entire American civil and military aviation industry began, one hundred years ago."

Searching The Heavens

My wife and I have traveled to Florida to witness two space shots. The first shot we attended was Apollo 17, the only night moon shot. We parked our car at the edge of the bay along with hundreds of others. Facing the gantry, we sat and waited well into middle of the night for the launch.

When the Apollo finally commenced liftoff, it was as though the gantry had been set on fire and like a phoenix rising out of the flames, the Apollo slowly lifted off. There was a pounding on our chests and the sky lit up so bright you could have read a newspaper by the light. We watched in awe as it climbed faster and faster and faded into the night sky.

A few years later at sunup, we watched from across the bay as the third space shuttle was launched into orbit. The space shuttle's rocket, with its solid fuel boosters, took off like a tin can that some kid had put a firecracker under. It was out of sight in no time compared to the old Saturn rocket.

I continue my long time interest in the cosmos. We visited the large array radio telescope site at Socorro, New Mexico where my cousin Dan's son is an astrophysicist. We have also sought out Arecibo in the mountains of Puerto Rico.

These radio telescopes constantly scan the sky for any type of light wave signal, not static or white noise as it is called. Recently, Congress suspended funding for the Search for the Extra Terrestrial Intelligence (SETI) project. Private groups are continuing the quest for signals from the Very Large Array (VLA) sites at Socorro, Arecibo and Green Bank in West Virginia.

Several years ago, a blip from one sector of the galaxy appeared to be an identifiable signal. After searching the same section of the sky many times over, scientists working on the project have never been able to observe the signal again. Like thousands of other volunteers, I run the SETI data analysis programs on my computer.

ETI What Are The Odds

It would be nice to find intelligence here on the planet Earth first. Aside from that, our sun is only one star in a vast group of stars called a galaxy, our local neighborhood in the universe of stars. The probability of other planets orbiting at least some of those distant suns is mathematically very good. It is also very likely that when conditions are right, life similar to man could evolve on these distant planets.

The joker in the deck is timing! For example, if an advanced alien life form had phoned us as recently as a hundred years ago, we weren't home or at least we weren't able to answer the phone at the time. We think we know how long time is, we just haven't figured out how wide it is yet.

I'm still putting the finishing touches on my science fiction novel, *Starchild,* which I started many years ago. The fictional story is largely based on Albert Einstein's famous equation of *Energy equals Mass times the Constant Squared*. The constant, as far as is presently known, is the speed-of-light.

Thus, in theory, time slows at near light-speeds. So if one traveled to a distant world, when they returned the time period in which they had left would be ancient history. Einstein's equation is more or less a scientific way of stating *you can't go home again.*

Bottom line, we are presently wasting our time attempting space travel via chemical fuels, atomic or ion propulsion. There is a relationship between magnetic and gravity fields. It is very likely these forces can be dialed-up similar to tuning in a radio station. When we discover how to harness these forces, real space exploration can begin.

If we wish to speculate that UFOs are real, then we must be willing to accept one of the following three scenarios.

First, that the visitors are space travelers from a nearby solar system and are technologically advanced enough to be able to travel at close to the speed-of-light or have achieved some method of hyper-light space travel whereby speed is unaffected by mass. The latter being most popular with current science fiction writers that have their spacecrafts equipped with warp-drives or take space shortcuts through wormholes.

Secondly, the aliens may not be space travelers at all, but have somehow mastered time travel. A variation on this is the parallel universe theory where the aliens come from another plane of existence via a dimension unknown to us.

The recent raise in popularity of String Theory and now the M-Theory propose the possibility of eleven dimensions and an infinite number of universes.

Carl Sagan always used the word Cosmos to describe where we exist in deference to the word universe, which he felt implied all. Even Einstein suggested the possibility of at least a fourth dimension.

Lastly, we must consider the possibility that aliens are not aliens at all. That they did and do now exist undetected among us. We'll call this the *Big Foot Theory*. Certainly it would be easier for an advanced culture to stealth itself than for a primitive creature. UFO sightings go back to Bible times. Even Christopher Columbus's log records the sighting of strange lights on the horizon as his ships approached the new world.

The infamous Roswell Incident, which occurred on July 2nd 1947, continues in UFO folklore. There are still credible witnesses alive at this writing. Recently, a two-hour film of an alien autopsy surfaced. The most significant question presently being asked by amateur investigators is what happened to the debris from the Roswell crash.

Possibly a coincidence, but it was only a few years after the Roswell Incident that we developed the transistor, the microprocessor and made other quantum leaps in scientific advancement. Could there have been a trade? Could there have been some deal made? Remember our good old democratic American motto, *when in doubt, go with the conspiracy theory.*

Visit to London Stonehenge and Scotland; Hemi-Fair New Orleans, space shuttle Enterprise; Socorro radio observatory in New Mexico; UFO Museum in Roswell; telescope used to discover Pluto at Lowell Observatory, Flagstaff; visit to largest radio antennae at Arecibo, Porto Rico.

Exactly How Big

How big is space? That's an easy one. It's a really big place. The answer to the question of, "How big should we build a space ship?" Well now, that takes a little more explaining. The size of the Saturn rocket was determined as follows.

The contractor who built the main body of the Saturn rocket had to ship the finished product via rail. On the rail line was a tunnel that the assembly had to be able to pass through. A rocket body too large would not be able to go through the tunnel's diameter.

The railroads were built along old trails the width of which had been roughly determined by the wagon ruts in the road. The width of a wagon's axle had been determined centuries ago by the Roman roads.

The Roman road widths had been determined by the width of the two horses that pulled the chariots. Thus, the size of the most modern piece of equipment in modern times was determined over two thousand years ago by the width of two horse's asses.

The Pilot Who Shot Down King Kong

The stories in this book are based mostly on my own life experiences, but not this one.

There was one flyer that lived a life more full of adventure than any novel or movie ever written. Such a man was Merian Cooper, born in Jacksonville, Florida in 1893. He was a movie actor, director, screenwriter and producer. His most famous work was the 1933 film *King Kong.*

Cooper entered the U.S. Naval Academy in 1915, but left before finishing his senior year. In 1916, he joined the Georgia National Guard and went off to chase Pancho Villa all over half of Mexico. Cooper became a bomber pilot in the First World War. He was shot down and captured by the Germans, sitting out the remainder of the war in a German POW camp.

During Poland's fight for independence from late 1919 until the Treaty of Riga in 1921, Cooper and his friend Cedric Fauntleroy flew as volunteer members of the Kosciuszko Squadron, an American air group with the Polish air force fighting the Soviets. In July of 1920, his plane was again shot down and he spent nine months in a Soviet prisoner camp. Before the war was over, he escaped to Latvia and was given the Virtuti

Militari, the highest Polish military decoration for valor. General Józef Pilsudski personally presented him with the medal.

Early in his film career, Cooper was hugely innovative and soon became the number two man at RKO Studios. He continued his innovation with breakthroughs like color and wide screen.

Cooper had a bizarre dream about a giant ape destroying New York City. When he woke, he made notes about the dream and this was the basis for his classic 1933 movie *King Kong*. The film, which Cooper co-wrote, co-directed and produced, was a breakthrough in motion picture technical innovation.

Director Schoedsack donated $100 to the Officers' Mess at Floyd Bennett Field to secure the Naval pilots and their aircraft for the most famous scene in the movie. He also gave each of the pilots $10 under the table.

To show their appreciation, the Navy flyers did something special. As Schoedsack prepared to shoot the approaching planes, he realized they were linked together by lines decorated by colorful flags. Needless to say the scene had to be re-shot.

The planes used to topple King Kong from the top of the Empire State Building were basic Navy training models, Curtiss O2C-2 from Navy NY. Interlaced scenes were shot using the real planes, miniature biplanes and a full-scale mock-up.

The movie, made in time-lapse photography with an 11-inch animatronic, rabbit fur covered ape, took much longer to make than anticipated. Cooper, referring to the budget over-run of the production, jokingly remarked, "I'd like to shoot that ape myself." And ironically, he did.

Cooper and Schoedsack played the part of pilots flying one of the planes attacking King Kong. In a close-up, featuring a Vickers-style gun on a swivel mount, the pilot-actors made the final strafing run and Cooper personally fired the fatal shot that toppled King Kong from atop the Empire State Building.

Though too old to be drafted, Cooper volunteered to serve in WW II and was assigned to the Army Air Corps unit that took over General Chennault's Flying Tigers in Asia. Lieutenant Colonel Cooper became the executive officer of the squadron and flew on many missions. He was known for his hard work and relentless planning for minimum losses.

At war's end, he was promoted to Brigadier General and returned to RKO. Cooper was a pioneer in aviation, resourceful in the use of airplanes in movies. He served on the board of directors for TWA. Cooper's star on the Hollywood Walk of Fame is misspelled *Meriam C. Cooper.*

Cooper was John Ford's favorite producer with whom to work. Together they produced dozens of hit films like *The Quiet Man, She Wore a Yellow Ribbon* and *Rio Grande.*

Leave'em Laughin When You Go

The pilot, Andy, turned to his copilot and said, "Beautiful day for flying, don't you think, Buck?"

Buck adjusted the power settings on the throttle. "Yes, and this baby cruises real fine at thirty thousand feet. The view from up here is awesome."

Andy leaned over to check the engine instruments. "Isn't that oil pressure running a little high on the right engine?"

Buck looked intently at the gauges, "Yes and the RPM on the turbine is falling off too."

Andy saw the flashing red light on the instrument panel. "Damn it, there goes the right engine warning light."

Buck retarded the throttle on the right engine. "It's a fire in the compressor section."

Andy began an immediate descent. "Got to get the turbine speed down or it'll explode. Keep trying to shut her down."

Buck was worried now. "We're losing cabin pressure. Get this baby on the ground if you can, Andy!"

Andy fought to control the giant jet as it fishtailed sideways from the loss of the right engine. "I can't worry about that now! Hit the emergency oxygen mask release in the cabin. The worst that'll happen is some of them will pass out."

Buck adjusted his seat forward to help Andy. "You know we're doing about 4,000 feet a minute descent now, don't you?"

Andy shook his head, yes. "There's an airfield just on the other side of that large forest area ahead. I'm going to try and make a landing there."

Buck exclaims, "Those trees are coming up fast, we're not going to make it!"

Just then, the cabin door opened and a young man in blue overalls said, "You two guys will have to get out of the flight simulator now. We've got some maintenance work to do."

There We Were At Ten-Thousand Feet

There is this oft-told story of a salty old RAF pilot who was asked to give a talk at a ladies social club. The club president introduced the elderly gentleman as a local hero.

The Flying Officer began with one of his favorite war stories. "There I was at ten thousand feet. There were fokkers to the left of me and fokkers to the right of me. Where in hell did all them fokkers come from, I sez to meself?"

At that point the club president sprang to her feet to say, "I need to explain that our guest is referring to the German airplanes made by the Fokker Aircraft Company."

"Yes mum," replied the old pilot. "Those Jerrys had Fokkers too, but on this day them fokkers was a flyin' Messerschmitts." He began again, "There I was at ten thousand feet..."

If We Just Had Jets

Jim Hardy flew B-17s in WW II and when he started with the airline, they were flying the DC-3. Jim was an American Airlines captain and friend of mine from Flight Dynamics days. He came into my office one afternoon laughing about having just flown in from Arkansas and told me this story.

"In the old days, on summer afternoon flights crossing thunderstorm alley, we'd cruise at 12,000. Couldn't go any higher to get over the storm and we'd say, if we just had pressurization, we wouldn't have to go through these thunder bumpers. A few years later, American purchased DC-6 and DC-7 aircraft with full pressurization. Now we could climb above 20,000, but we'd look up ahead and see a line of thunderstorms at 30,000. We'd say, if we just had jet engines, we could climb over those storms and not have to go through them."

The trip Jim had just returned from was a 727 flight. He smiled and said, "We were at 32,000 feet and could not get over the top of this large thunderstorm and had to go through it. You know, if we just had rockets..."

Now Boarding At Parking Lot Three

The modern jet airplane has made it possible for us to travel the world like Superman, who could leap small buildings in a single bound. Now, even the most ordinary among us can leap whole continents. Most passengers board a modern jet airliner and watch the movie or read a magazine.

The marvel of traveling halfway around the world in less than a day is lost on most of us, but again so is the beauty of this planet we daily ignore as we soar high above.

Instead of thinking in terms of building giant six hundred plus passenger airliners and city size terminals, the aviation industry should be thinking about carrying passengers in smaller more economical VTOL aircraft that fly direct between local airports on GPS highways in the sky.

With advanced computer programs, the airline HUB system would soon be as out-of-date as a railway passenger station. Transports the size of a jumbo jet can and should be able to takeoff and land in little more than their own parking space.

The ultimate answer to air traffic control is fully automated aircraft. The Air Force is doing this now with their new Global Hawk.

The airliner of the future, it is said, will only have a pilot and a dog in the cockpit. The pilot will be there to monitor the electronics and the dog will be there to bite the pilot if he touches anything.

CAF Tora Tora Tora mock Pearl Harbor attack air show at Midland, Texas; Veterans Day at Albuquerque, Don and I with B-17 Flying Fortress Sentimental Journey, one of only a few still flying; Bobby and me in front of P-51 Gunfighter, Grandson Andy with B-24 Diamond 'Lil, his mother remembers this one as a young girl; flying in TS11 Polish Iskra jet trainer; Suzie and the CAF Air Show flight line static displays.

APPENDIX
Abbreviations and Acronyms

	Chapter	
AAC	1	Army Air Corps
AD & AT	13	Aviation mechanic & electronic Technician
ADF	8	Automatic Direction Finder
ADIZ	9	Air Defense Identification Zone
AE	12	Aviation Electrician
AE	23	Aeronautical Engineer
AEA	23	Avionics Electrical Association
A&E	12	Aircraft and Engine mechanic
AFB	2	Air Force Base
AHC	22	Aerospatiale Helicopter Corporation
AOC	12	Aviation Officer Candidate
AP	2	Air Police
APU	22	Auxiliary Power Unit
ARDC	2	Air Research and Development
ASW	11	Anti Submarine Warfare
ATC	13	Air Traffic Control
ATP	8	Airline Transport Pilot
AvCad	13	Aviation aircrew Candidate (enlisted)
AVG	1	American Volunteer Group
CAA	6	Civil Aeronautics Authority
CAD	22	Computer Aided Design
CAF	9	Confederate (Commemorative) Air Force
CAP	7	Civil Air Patrol
CAR	6	Civil Air Regulation
CAMCO	1	Central Aircraft Manufacturing Company
CBI	1	China–Burma–India Theater of War
CFC	16	Cessna Finance Corporation
CG	19	Center of Gravity
CIO	14	Chief Information Officer

Chapter

CNARESTRA	13	Chief Naval Air Reserve Training
CO	11	Commanding Officer
COM	13	Communication
CONELRAD	14	Controlled Electronic Radiation
CPO	14	Chief Petty Officer
CRT	23	Cathode Ray Tube monitor
DEFCON	14	Defense Condition
DFW	10	Dallas - Fort Worth
DG	8	Directional Gyro instrument
DME	8	Distance Measuring Equipment
ECM	13	Electronic Counter Measures
ECO	20	Engineering Change Order
EE	22	Electrical Engineer
EMF	14	Electro Magnetic Force
FAA	6	Federal Aviation Administration
FBO	6	Fixed Based Operator
FDC	16	Flight Dynamics Corporation
FDI	16	Flight Dynamics Incorporated
FILO	16	First In Last Out
G	15	Gravities as a unit of measurement
GCA	11	Ground Controlled Approach
GPS	22	Global Positioning System
GSA	18	Greater Southwest Aviation
GSW	16	Greater Southwest airport
HAI	22	Helicopter Association International
HF	13	High Frequency
ICS	12	Intercommunication System
IFR	6	Instrument Flight Rules
ILS	8	Instrument Landing System
IPB	20	Illustrated Parts Breakdown
IR	8	Instrument pilot Rating
JOD	14	Junior Officer of the Day
JP	12	Jet fuel
KP	11	Kitchen Police
MAD	12	Magnetic Anomaly Detection equipment

Chapter

Retracing flight of Pearl Harbor attack, Hawaii to Tokyo; USS Missouri; Tokyo bullet train; Kamakura and visit to the Giant Buddha.

Flight of the Setting Sun
by Marvin Arnold

For information about this book
Samco Publishing
www.storydomain.com

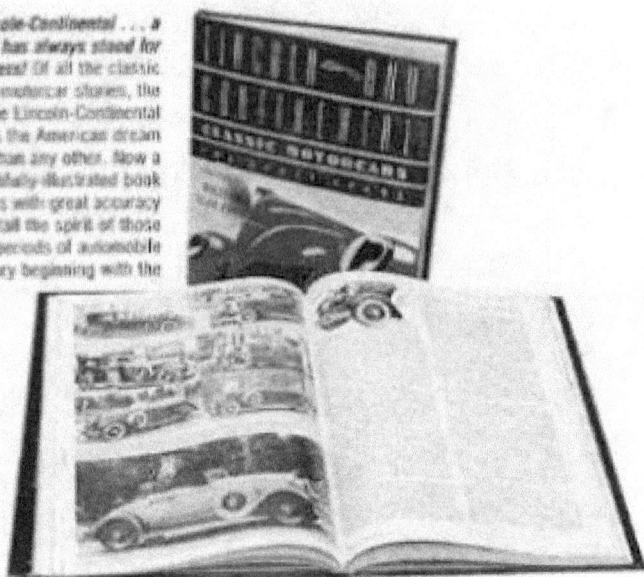

The Lincoln-Continental . . . a car that has always stood for greatness! Of all the classic American motorcar stories, the story of the Lincoln-Continental personifies the American dream better than any other. Now a beautifully-illustrated book captures with great accuracy and detail the spirit of those early periods of automobile history beginning with the

Lincoln and Continental
Classic Motorcars
by Marvin Arnold

For information about this book
Samco Publishing
www.storydomain.com

i

www.ingramcontent.com/pod-product-compliance
Lightning Source LLC
La Vergne TN
LVHW051449080426
835509LV00017B/1709